STORYTELLING IN SIBERIA

FOLKLORE STUDIES
IN A MULTICULTURAL
WORLD

The Folklore Studies in a Multicultural World series is a collaborative venture of the University of Illinois Press, the University Press of Mississippi, the University of Wisconsin Press, and the American Folklore Society, made possible by a generous grant from the Andrew W. Mellon Foundation. The series emphasizes the interdisciplinary and international nature of current folklore scholarship, documenting connections between communities and their cultural production. Series volumes highlight aspects of folklore studies such as world folk cultures, folk art and music, foodways, dance, African American and ethnic studies, gender and queer studies, and popular culture.

STORYTELLING IN SIBERIA

The Olonkho Epic in a Changing World

ROBIN P. HARRIS

Publication of this book was supported by grants from the Andrew W. Mellon Foundation and from the L. J. and Mary C. Skaggs Folklore Fund.

© 2017 by the Board of Trustees
of the University of Illinois
All rights reserved
C 1 2 3 4 5
♾ This book is printed on acid-free paper.
Printed and bound in Great Britain by
Marston Book Services Ltd, Oxfordshire

Library of Congress Control Number: 2017950623
ISBN 978-0-252-04128-0 (hardcover)
ISBN 978-0-252-09988-5 (e-book)

To my husband, Bill, whose enduring support and encouragement made this book possible, whose video skills masterfully captured the interviews during my fieldwork, and who changed my life forever by bringing me to Siberia.

Contents

List of Illustrations   ix

Notes on Transliteration from Russian and Sakha   xi

Acknowledgments   xiii

Introduction: Encountering Olonkho   1

1   Epic Traditions, Performers, and Audiences   11

2   Effects of Change during the Soviet Era   33

3   Esteem for a Masterpiece: The Quest
for Recognition   64

4   Examining the Role of UNESCO and Intangible
Cultural Heritage   89

5   Elements of Resilience: Stable and Malleable   108

6   Epic Revitalization: Negotiating Identities
and Other Challenges   135

7   Ensuring Sustainability through Transmission
and Innovation   156

Glossary of Russian and Sakha Words   163

Notes   165

Works Cited   203

Index   225

Illustrations

1.1. Pyotr Reshetnikov, master olonkhosut   12

1.2. Afanasii Solovëv, master olonkhosut   12

1.3. Introductory recitative from *Ėr Sogotokh*   25

1.4. Key to symbols in notated examples   26

1.5. *Kylyhakh* notated: "Song of the Spirit-Mistress of the Valley" (*Ėr Sogotokh*)   28

1.6. *Dėgėrėn* style: "Song of the Demonesses" (*Ėr Sogotokh*)   31

2.1. Map of the Republic of Sakha (Yakutia) in the Russian Federation   35

2.2. *Balaghan* in an outdoor museum near Cherkëkh, Yakutia   36

2.3. Pyotr Tikhonov, olonkhosut, in performance   43

2.4. Eduard Alekseyev and Anna Larionova with the author   51

2.5. A manuscript of an olonkho by Roman Alekseyev   54

2.6. Portrait of Roman Alekseyev in Borogontsy, Yakutia   55

2.7. Semyon Chernogradskii at the 3rd Ysyakh of Olonkho in Borogontsy   58

2.8. Nikolai Alekseyev, olonkhosut, in Mytakh, Yakutia   60

3.1. Valerii Kononov, Maria Kononova, and Bill Harris with the author   85

4.1. Sergei Vasiliev with the author   101

5.1. Graded Genre Health Assessment (GGHA)   112

5.2. Diagnostic chart for the GGHA   113

5.3. GGHA for solo performance of olonkho   114

5.4. GGHA for theatrical performance of olonkho   115

5.5. *Stable* and *malleable* for master olonkhosut performances   120

5.6. Musical materials   121

5.7. Heroic plots   122

5.8. Poetic form and oral-verbal arts   122

5.9. Performance contexts   123

5.10. Audience verbal responses   124

5.11. Compensation   124

5.12. *Stable* and *malleable* in olonkho theatrical productions   126

5.13. Script   127

5.14. Musical materials and physical movement   127

5.15. Ethno-ballet based on the olonkho *Kullustai Bėrgėn*   128

5.16. Story themes   128

5.17. Performance times and lengths   129

5.18. Funding sources   129

5.19. Expression of Sakha identity   130

6.1. Olonkhosut Yuri Borisov   154

6.2. The Association of Young Olonkhosuts   155

Notes on Transliteration
from Russian and Sakha

In quoted text, transliterations from Sakha and Russian remain as spelled in the source. In other cases, I use the Library of Congress system for transliteration, with a few minor adaptations for clarity and ease of reading for non-Russian speakers:

* Representations of the Russian letters transliterated as *iu*, *ia*, and *ts*, as well as the Sakha *ng*, do not include ligatures.
* The soft-sign diacritic [ь] is also omitted, and the letter [й] (so-called soft *i*), which appears frequently at the end of Russian words, is omitted after *y* and otherwise changed to *i*.

With those caveats, the romanization of transcribed words follows the chart below. Additional exceptions include words with strong precedence in print for another spelling, such as *toyuk* rather than *toiuk*, *Yakutsk* rather than *Iakutsk*, and *Nurgun* rather than *Niurgun* in *Nurgun Botur*; and names for which people indicated a preferred spelling—for example, some people prefer to include the *Y* with the *e* at the beginning of their name (e.g., Yefimovich rather than Efimovich) and also between two *e* vowels within a name (e.g., Alekseyev, Andreyevna).

А а	a	И и	i	Т т	t	Э э	è
Б б	b	К к	k	У у	u	Ю ю	iu
В в	v	Л л	l	Ф ф	f	Я я	ia
Г г	g	М м	m	Х х	kh	Ҕ ҕ	gh
Д д	d	Н н	n	Ц ц	ts	Ҥ ҥ	ng
Е е	e	О о	o	Ч ч	ch	Ө ө	ò
Ё ё	ë	П п	p	Ш ш	sh	һ һ	h
Ж ж	zh	Р р	r	Щ щ	shch	Ү ү	ü
З з	z	С с	s	Ы ы	y		

xii   NOTES ON TRANSLITERATION

The Library of Congress website provides standard romanization charts for various languages at http://www.loc.gov/catdir/cpso/roman.html. For Russian, see http://www.loc.gov/catdir/cpso/romanization/russian.pdf; for Yakut (Sakha), consult http://www.loc.gov/catdir/cpso/romanization/nonslav.pdf.

Acknowledgments

A myriad of relationships, both professional and personal, undergird and energize a project such as this book. It is therefore with immense gratitude that I acknowledge the crucial role of my colleagues, graduate students, and valued friends connected to GIAL's Applied Anthropology Department and its Center for Excellence in World Arts: Wendy Atkins, Kevin Calcote, Cory Cummins, Brad Keating, Michelle Petersen, Laura Roberts, Mary Saurman, Julie Taylor, Doug Tiffin, Pete Unseth, Steve Walter, and the rest of the faculty and staff—thank you for your encouragement and support, and for giving me the freedom in my schedule to complete this book. A special thanks to the graduate students who helped with transcribing my extensive reading notes (Julie Johnson, Rabea Saad, and Sarah York), and to Kerry Payton, who duplicated in Finale the incredibly complicated olonkho transcriptions of N. N. Nikolaeva. I am grateful as well for the time invested by my teaching colleague Neil Coulter, who read the entire manuscript and provided valuable input. Two Dallas-based colleagues played particularly significant roles in the creation of this book: Brian Schrag's example of integrated faith, purposeful creativity, and rigorous scholarship in ethnoarts inspires me in my academic work, and Katie Hoogerheide's numerous hours of attention to my prose greatly refined both my ideas and their written expression.

I owe an enormous debt of gratitude to my family, whose unflagging support made the many years of research and writing for this project possible. I am particularly grateful for the encouragement of my husband, Bill, to whom this work is dedicated; my intrepid offspring, James and Katherine, who spent their childhood in Russia; and my parents, Bob and Joyce Persón, who instilled in me the love for music, cross-cultural work, and lifelong learning that set me on this road.

If it were not for the Andrew W. Mellon Foundation grant and the "Folklore Studies in a Multicultural World" program, this book would never have come to fruition. I'm deeply grateful for the attentive support and reliable advice of my

xiv ACKNOWLEDGMENTS

editor, Laurie Matheson, throughout the process, and to Dorothy Noyes, who gave invaluable feedback on some early drafts. I'm also profoundly grateful to Ted Levin, whose careful reading and suggestions improved the book in significant ways. In addition, his engagement with and advocacy for scholars and musicians in the Russian Federation and across Central Asia provide a model to which I aspire.

In addition to the invaluable support and guidance of the faculty at the University of Georgia Athens during my dissertation work, I'm particularly grateful to my committee members David Haas and Elena Krasnostchekova for their insistence that this research be published, and to my dissertation advisor, Jean Kidula, whose unerring critical insight, personal example of outstanding scholarship, and steady support during my studies and beyond have given me the courage to persevere and aim high. I also appreciate the financial support received from the University of Georgia through the Dean's Award and a travel grant from the UGA Research Foundation, which ameliorated the high cost of fieldwork in Siberia.

I share the credit for this work with many Sakha collaborators, hosts, respondents, and colleagues: Irina Aksyonova, Anna Andreyeva, Maria Borisova and her son Mikhail, Vladimir Burnashev and his wife Tatiana, Olga Charina, Ekaterina Chekhorduna, Semyon Chernogradskii, Stas Efimov, Sargylana Elyasina, Dora Gerasimova, Vasilii Illarionov, Vasilii Ivanov, Dmiitri Krivoshapkin, Elena Kugdanova-Egorova, Anastasia Luginova, Boris Mikhailov, Svetlana Mukhoplëva, Alina Nakhodkina, Nadezhda Orosina, Olga Osipova, Elena Protodiakonova, Ekaterina Romanova, Spiridon Shishigin, Tatiana Semënova, Gavriil Shelkovnikov, Liubov Shelkovnikova, Elizaveta Sidorova, Vera Solovyeva, Maria Stepanova, Valentina Struchkova, Aleksandra Tatarinova, Pyotr Tikhonov, Sergei Vasiliev, Dekabrina Vinokurova, Agafia Zakharova, and Yury Zhegusov. Their hospitality, encouragement, openness, willingness to recount memories and opinions, and generous sharing of resources and research summaries have supported this research at every step. This project stands on their shoulders. In that regard, I would especially like to thank the Kononov family, Valerii and Maria, who rendered invaluable logistical help and insight during my fieldwork trips to villages around Yakutia, and olonkhosuts Pyotr Reshetnikov and Nikolai Alekseyev, who not only recounted their stories and performed for me, but also hosted me during my stay in their respective villages.

My collaborators in Yakutsk include Sue Hauge, a dear friend who has lived in Yakutia for two decades already, longer than any other American I know. She hosted me multiple times and obtained a number of key resources that have significantly impacted this research. Other non-Sakha friends in Yakutsk, Valentin and Lyuba Nikonenko and Michal and Agnieszka Domagala, also rendered warm hospitality and encouragement. To my Russian language teachers Vera Shelyakina and Liudmila Patrakova, you made this research possible—thank you for your investment in me.

In addition, I owe an enormous debt to Anna Larionova, a Sakha scholar and friend who facilitated and hosted highly productive trips to Yakutia during the winters of 2011 and 2015. The connections she provided to the dedicated scholars at the Institute of Humanitarian Research (IGI) and other institutions proved absolutely crucial to this research.

To Alexander Zhirkov, Speaker of the Yakutian Parliament, and his associate, Nurguyana Illarionova, a deep bow of thanks for your encouragement of this project and for giving me the opportunity to participate in conferences and on editing boards, to observe a great diversity of outstanding performances, and to enjoy warm Sakha hospitality at a variety of key events.

And finally, to my primary Russian-Sakha mentor and dear friend, Eduard Alekseyev, and his wonderful wife, Zoya, I owe an inestimable debt for wise advice, practical help, warm hospitality, inspiration, and encouragement. You are a gift to us all.

STORYTELLING IN SIBERIA

INTRODUCTION

Encountering Olonkho

> When I was a little boy, I used to sit "under the mouth" of the teller
> throughout the night, listening to his tales . . .
> —Aleksei Kulakovskii, in Emelianov, *Kulakovskii*

I sit, enthralled, as the rapid-fire poetic language of the epic narrative flows around me. Outside, the warm breezes fitfully attempt to keep the mosquitoes at bay. Inside, the smooth wood surfaces and the steeply sloping sides of the traditionally styled Sakha dwelling generate a strong echo from the voice of the storyteller. Pyotr Egorovich Reshetnikov, master performer of *olonkho*, the epic song-story tradition of his people, sits a few meters in front of me, his folded hands resting on his crossed knees as he begins to narrate the tale he has created.[1]

Though I have been connected to Yakutia for fifteen years, I have not met a master *olonkhosut* (performer of olonkho) prior to this summer day in 2009.[2] As I listen, I can't shake the thought that many Sakha people say this eighty-year-old gentleman is the last living master of the tradition. Deeply moved, I ponder the privilege I have to be "sitting under the mouth" (*syngaakh annygar* in Sakha, also rendered: "to listen or look intently, to try to absorb everything and every single word").[3] With the undulating soundscape resonating around me, I wonder: *How many years before this experience will no longer be available to Sakha people?*

We sit in a conical wooden museum several stories high in Reshetnikov's home village of Cherkëkh. Sakha material culture surrounds him—a large *charon* (a wooden goblet for drinking *kumys*, fermented mare's milk), a portrait of Platon Oyunsky (a Sakha intellectual, writer, and olonkhosut) as a young man, and, lying on a nearby table, books and recordings of olonkho. After several minutes of swift, declamatory narrative, Reshetnikov's intonation descends. He takes a deep breath and switches into song. Periodically, he raises his right hand to the side of his face in the classic olonkhosut pose, something I've previously seen only in drawings. These sung parts reflect the direct speech in the tale—each character with its own melodic peculiarities and intonation—and so the expressive and

2 INTRODUCTION

character-reflecting songs interspersed throughout this narrative contrast with the homogeneous flow of the tongue-twisting poetry. Time stands still. I am grateful that the video recording of this performance will serve in a small way to capture this moment for future generations, but most of all, I am grateful that, at least for now, it is still possible, with great effort, to "sit under the mouth" of a master olonkhosut.

Before the performance, I had encouraged him to sing as long as he wished, but perhaps now he doubts my sincerity or feels tired from his recent illness. He stops before an hour has passed, remarking that he has concluded the first section of his olonkho and is done for the day. He has arranged for me to hear and record one of his young students, and I am amazed by her ability. My traveling companions and I spend the rest of the morning exploring the large outdoor museum grounds with its many buildings. Finally, after a delicious lunch at the Reshetnikovs' home, I have the opportunity to ask the elderly olonkhosut a few of my many questions: How did he become an olonkhosut? How would he describe the performance tradition of olonkho? What was it like for olonkhosuts during the Soviet period? Did the situation change after the end of the Soviet Union? How has the genre of olonkho changed over the years? What influenced those changes? What is the likely prognosis for the future of olonkho? What might be essential factors in its revitalization? Does he think revitalization is even possible? He is glad to answer my questions with honesty, his advanced age serving to make him impervious to political correctness. Reshetnikov's mesmerizing personal narrative and profound insights into olonkho underscore the intense testing of the genre's resilience over the last century, and his reflections become one of the primary strands woven through the following account.

Early connections to cold places

My heart connection to Siberia stretches back to my youth, when I devoured books about people imprisoned in Siberia's frozen gulags for their religious or political beliefs. Growing up in Alaska, I was fascinated with stories of that "other cold place." They fed my imagination as I looked out my window at the similar landscape and wondered just how different Siberian life might be. It never crossed my mind that I would someday live for almost a decade near the very prisons where some of my childhood heroes suffered.

In 1995, my husband's work as a consultant on cross-cultural issues for a faith-based Russian organization landed us in Yakutsk, the capital city of Yakutia.[4] With my Alaskan roots and preference for colder climates, I was anxious about raising two young children in Siberia, but at least I was not afraid of the cold. To my delight, I quickly found that my proclivity for language learning brought me joy.

I poured time and energy into learning the language and culture, serving endless cups of tea at the kitchen table, the hub of friendship and hospitality in Russia, and navigating the significant challenges of raising and educating two children in a different cultural and linguistic environment.

The coldest inhabited city on earth

Located in northeastern Siberia in the Russian Federation, the Republic of Sakha (Yakutia) is home to the largest indigenous group in Siberia.[5] Although they claim "Sakha" as their official self-designation, most Sakha continue to use the term "Yakut" in casual conversation to refer to both the people and their language.[6] We lived in Yakutsk, the largest city in the republic, with demographics largely dominated by two groups—Russians and Sakha.[7]

As I adapted to life in "the coldest city on earth,"[8] I enjoyed building close relationships with both Russian and Sakha people, especially musicians. Our family's new friends became a support system, surrounding us with warmth and acceptance (even in the face of our inevitable cultural gaffes) while also "raising us" well—gently correcting our blunders as we grew in cultural competence over a decade. I enjoyed exploring the remarkable creativity of Sakha expressive culture, occasionally participating in *ohuokhai* (call-and-response round dances) and taking lessons on the *khomus* (jaw harp). Although I'd been trained as a classical musician, the pull toward both anthropology and a deeper study of Sakha music landed me in a discipline that fit both goals perfectly—ethnomusicology.[9]

Our decade in the Russian North, along with my research on Sakha music, gave me a firsthand look at the dynamics of the Sakha cultural revival in its broader post-Soviet context. In particular, the epic storytelling and song tradition of olonkho held my attention, and after we returned to the United States, I began to delve deeply into documenting its decline and revitalization (Harris 2012a).[10] After 2005, I noticed an explosion of interest in olonkho revitalization. In contrast to the virtual absence of olonkho when we arrived in Yakutia during the mid-1990s, the genre now occupied a conspicuous place at the forefront of Sakha consciousness. During my visits, I observed that olonkho had risen to a prominent place in national discourse, and I found the shift intriguing—what had caused this abrupt change in attitude? When I discovered its inclusion in UNESCO's Masterpiece proclamation (UNESCO 2006), I was captivated.[11] What factors contributed to olonkho's almost complete extinction? What lay behind its sudden rise to prominence? In what ways is the genre changing, adapting to audiences of the twenty-first century?[12] What might be the keys to effective revitalization for olonkho, giving it a chance for sustainability as a performed artistic genre?[13] These became the central questions of my research.

4   INTRODUCTION

Emerging themes

The years in Yakutia, while not quite qualifying as a *longue durée* study (Lee 2012), provided a rich web of relationships with people who had lived through decades of Soviet history. Recognizing that the subject of olonkho revitalization had the potential to become a productive topic of inquiry for at least a medium-term longitudinal study of multiple decades, my aim became to present—and hopefully begin to untangle—the complex narrative strands as related by my collaborators (Bruner 1986). I wanted to trace the process of change, not just for the genre of olonkho, but also within the broader Yakutian context.[14] Most specifically, I wanted to pursue a better understanding of the people who were re-creating and reexperiencing this artistic legacy in the present (Rice 1987, 474).

Kay Shelemay (2013) describes a "multi-temporal ethnographic study" as one in which multiple internal timelines are embedded: institutional (political/economic), individual (biographical), and musical (performance). Although generally organized as a diachronic study, this book includes all three of these internal timelines, providing a multitemporal perspective on the ways olonkho has been affected by—and in turn has strongly affected—the sociocultural contexts in which it was rooted.

In the process of organizing this research, several overlapping themes emerged that are relevant to the range of internal timelines woven throughout the narrative of this book. Three of the key terms are based on unusual semantic domains: (1) Center (Russian *tsentr*), (2) nation (Russian *natsiia*, adj. *natsionalny*, "national"), and (3) epic *sreda*.

The first concept, *Center*, denotes Moscow's power and political control relative to the geographically far-flung regions of the country. Center-periphery issues commonly appear in Sakha books and conversations, highlighting a marginalizing power dynamic against which the Sakha negotiate a space for self-expression and self-autonomy (Bahry 2005, 127).

Likewise, when used by the Sakha in the context of discussing Yakutia or Sakha people, a second concept, *nation*, refers to distinctly Sakha conceptions of community, as opposed to the geopolitically defined state of what is currently known as the Russian Federation.[15] Even more broadly, ethnic groups throughout the region of Siberia use *nation* or *national* to refer to anything perceived as belonging to them or reflecting some feature of their cultural identity.[16] If *nation-ness* is related to "an imagined political community" (Anderson 2006, 6), then certainly the Sakha people form a nation.[17] While translating the narratives of my collaborators, I have faithfully reflected their use of the concept *nation*. To bring clarity to my own prose, I will use the adjectives *Russian*, *Soviet*, or *state* (depending on the historical context) for descriptive terms related to the larger geopolitical entity of which Yakutia is a part, and *Sakha* to refer to distinctly Sakha cultural elements.

Finally, the Russian word *sreda* encompasses not only the physical surroundings and visible environment of a place and time, but also the broad social environment, including the attitudes and perceptions of people in relation to the object being discussed.[18] Sakha scholars and performers often speak nostalgically about the current lack of an epic *sreda*, lamenting the absence of musical understanding, linguistic comprehension, or artistic appreciation for olonkho. Since the meaning of the term is too broad for any one translated word—with the possible exception of another foreign word, *milieu*—I will use *sreda*, in hopes that the reader will become comfortable with this useful Russian term. Its rich semantic field encompasses not only appreciative attitudes based on musical, artistic, and linguistic understandings, but also a constantly changing mélange of performance preferences, practices, and venues, all affected by an ongoing series of both grassroots and "top-down" interventions.[19]

Applied ethnomusicology and multidisciplinary approaches

This volume, which joins a growing number of case studies that address the revitalization of epic narrative poetry and song genres, specifically focuses attention on Siberia, a broad area of the world that is woefully underrepresented in ethnomusicological works.[20] Primarily a "subject-centered ethnography" (Rice 2003, 152), this account turns its gaze not only to the genre of olonkho, but also to the stories of Sakha people who as agents of cultural revitalization negotiate the place of olonkho in contemporary Yakutia and beyond.

This work represents the multidisciplinarity required by a complex topic such as olonkho, including methods and theoretical approaches from ethnomusicology and its closely related disciplines of anthropology, musicology, and performance and folklore studies. Other disciplines, such as sociolinguistics, comparative literature, and oral traditions, also contribute to the multidisciplinary approaches of this volume.[21]

This work finds its methodological home and desired outcomes anchored in the field of *applied ethnomusicology*, which combines ethnomusicological field research with community work and advocacy, "applying knowledge about music in the public interest in order to assist people and communities to reach their goals . . . [aiding them] in their efforts to document, interpret, and promote their music" (Fenn and Titon 2003, 126).[22] In the process of documenting revitalization in Yakutia, I have become a small part of the revitalization process itself (Shelemay 2008, 141). Ongoing relationships of reciprocity afford me a means of "giving back . . . to colleagues, friends, and teachers" (Titon 2015b, 157); they consider

6   INTRODUCTION

my writing and speaking on the topic of olonkho beneficial to the olonkho re-vitalization movement.[23] These relationships of reciprocity (Summit 2015, 202) have greatly enriched my life and continue to supply stimulus for research and action.

Schrag's statement of vision in the landmark volume *The Oxford Handbook of Applied Ethnomusicology* resonates with my own motivations for applied work: "I believe that ethnomusicologists can help minority communities navigate these tides [of change]. We can . . . be present when influential people make decisions affecting minoritized artistic traditions. We can exert considerable winsome in-fluence in local, regional, and international arenas when we combine a vision of artistically thriving humanity, commitment to artists on the margins of global communities, personal stories of friends in these margins, and rigorous scholarship contributing to a growing body of data" (2015b, 341).[24] That vision for human thriving, seen in the context of my relationships rooted in Yakutia, spurs me on in the conviction that this story of olonkho, while providing a valuable case study from within a minority context, will also yield encouragement and insights into other contexts of revitalization.

After outlining the historical processes leading up to the present, I will be-gin to reflect on how olonkho, as recounted by master performers, slowly lost its resilience. We will then explore ways in which that resilience might still be strengthened toward a goal of sustainability—"a music culture's capacity to maintain and develop its music now and in the foreseeable future" (Titon 2015b, 157).[25] Themes emerging from the narratives throughout this study of olonkho include cultural change, post- and neocolonialism, festivalization, globalization, heritage and heritagization, nostalgia, performance and performativity, Soviet and post-Soviet studies, and the negotiation of national, ethnic, ideological, and religious identities.

The process of research and reporting

A written narrative about a genre as multifaceted as olonkho needs audiovisual resources to help readers see and hear its performance practices and acquaint themselves with at least some of the characters in the story. Fortunately, the deft video skills and intrepid fortitude of my husband, William Harris, have greatly aided the documentation of key people and narratives. He recorded much of my olonkho-related fieldwork in Yakutia, providing me with priceless footage of in-terviews and performances. Our recorded interviews include a wide spectrum of Sakha people: musicians, poets, ethnomusicologists and other scholars, religious leaders of diverse persuasions, olonkho audience members, relatives of deceased olonkhosuts, and living olonkhosuts of varying levels of performance ability. Most notably, we captured my interactions with elderly tradition bearers, some of whom are now gone. In order for readers to access the original language, emotion, and vocal inflections in the voices of Sakha respondents, a website containing video and audio clips of my interviews complements this book (http://www.press.uillinois.edu/books/harris/storytelling/).[26]

Since my Sakha language abilities are limited to musical terminology and some commonly used words, I conducted my research for this book largely in Russian. When I offered my respondents the choice of using my Sakha translator or speaking in Russian, they invariably chose Russian rather than endure the vagaries of a translator.[27] While I regret that this Russification of the linguistic landscape in Yakutia has had a negative effect on the use of Sakha and other minority languages, my situation underscores Ted Levin's observation that "the ubiquity of Russian as a language of scholarship in the former U.S.S.R. has made it an indispensable tool for musical ethnography" (2006, xxi).[28]

My olonkho research has involved observing and participating in a variety of events, such as olonkho festivals in Borogontsy, Berdigestyakh, and Churapcha; the Ysyakh summer festivals near Yakutsk; international conferences in Yakutsk and St. Petersburg (Harris 2015) featuring a broad range of cultural themes, including olonkho; and staying in the homes of two olonkhosuts for two to three days at a time.[29] Field-based research has been augmented by email, Skype, and personal contact with Sakha scholars, which has included collaborating with them on presentations about olonkho at Harvard University's Loeb Music Library.[30] In addition to featuring conversations with Sakha collaborators, this study draws from an unusual wealth of Russian-language scholarship, including the work of ethnomusicologists and academics from a broad range of other culture-related disciplines.[31]

This book foregrounds the voices of respondents, presenting first-person narratives that recount perceptions and interpretations of historical events related to olonkho performance, thus privileging the discourse of the community in the text.[32] Self-representation not only supports human rights (Smith 2012, 151) but also helps to correct the inadequacies of written histories. For example, interviews that record candid views of Soviet history may provide access to otherwise unavailable stories, because of the ideological limitations imposed upon writings of the Soviet period (Ignatieva et al. 2013; Tichotsky 2000, 1). In a roughly diachronic approach, older historical narratives generally appear earlier in this volume, followed by reflections on how the olonkho tradition is being revived, as well as the ways in which groups of Sakha people are "reencountering and recreating" olonkho in the post-Soviet period (Rice 1987, 474).[33]

The Sakha voices in this book occasionally disagree with one another, reflecting a spectrum of views on widely contested olonkho-related issues in Yakutia. For

8   INTRODUCTION

some aspects of this narrative, however, Sakha voices speak in unanimity, and in the case of Sakha ethnomusicologists and folklorists, with highly warranted authority.[34]

Olonkho's path from the past into the future

Given the relative rarity of case studies documenting the heritagization of intangible culture (Bendix 2009, 259), this work begins to fill that gap both by examining the paths olonkho has taken toward diminished resilience and by looking ahead to its future potential, focusing on the Sakha as they engage in the process of olonkho revitalization for a broad variety of meaningful outcomes. This introductory chapter has included some of my personal narrative to help the reader better understand my initial encounter with olonkho and to acquaint the reader with Yakutia and its people. In addition, I have presented some key themes, terminology, and applied ethnomusicology approaches that undergird this work.

Chapter 1 lays the foundation for the rest of the book, supplying descriptions of key olonkho performance features and definitions for terms related to epics in general and olonkho in particular. In addition to discussing interactions between the verbal and musical aspects of olonkho, I explore the role of oral formulaic theory in understanding the emergent character of olonkho told by master olonkhosuts.

The historical section begins in chapter 2 with a description of olonkho performance practice during the years immediately before and throughout the Soviet era. My survey of the effects of change during these years illustrates the pendulum swings that render studies of Soviet history remarkably complex. The accounts in this chapter particularly emphasize the role of orality in the lives of the early olonkhosuts and also indicate the extent to which olonkho embodies the worldviews and values of many Sakha.

Continuing the historical narrative, chapter 3 describes the post-Soviet saga of the people who led Yakutia in a quest to bring olonkho back from being "forgotten." Beginning with the stirrings of cultural revitalization after the fall of the Soviet Union in 1991, the Sakha's story continues in a heart-stopping narrative of their race for the prize—UNESCO's recognition of olonkho as a Masterpiece of the Oral and Intangible Heritage of Humanity in 2005.[35] I also describe the current state of olonkho revitalization and propose some ideas regarding how to further revitalize this tradition.

Due to the remarkable consistency of Sakha voices pointing toward the pivotal role of UNESCO and the Intangible Cultural Heritage program in the revitalization of olonkho, chapter 4 focuses exclusively on these institutional structures. Topics include an exploration of the Masterpiece proclamation, clarification of the term "safeguarding," and a comparison between UNESCO's desired outcomes and Yakutia's Action Plan for revitalization.

Chapter 5 draws on the implications of the preceding historical narratives and the institutional influences of UNESCO to consider issues of continuity and change in revitalization. Building on well-researched parallels in language and music revitalization, I demonstrate two keys in providing resilience for an epic tradition—effective transmission and appropriate levels of innovation. In turn, the concept of innovation requires engagement with the stable and malleable elements in olonkho, in hopes that ways can be found to allow the tradition to maintain connections with historical practice while still remaining dynamic enough to adapt to changing contexts.

The role of negotiated identity in olonkho revitalization is explored in chapter 6, along with related issues of postcolonial and neocolonial relations with the Center. I examine two other Asian epic traditions undergoing revitalization, the Kyrgyz *Manas* trilogy and Korean *p'ansori*, then outline some conclusions regarding the challenges of revitalizing living epic traditions.

Finally, chapter 7 reflects on the nature of revitalization, seeking to differentiate between "foam" and more effective contributions to the process. I propose three possible paths for olonkho's future and offer some recommendations for ways to support tradition bearers by creating better contexts for transmission and by encouraging innovation. Despite the trend of pendulum swings in Soviet and post-Soviet realities, I hope that Sakha people will respond wisely and strategically to the challenges of their ever-shifting context, and that their efforts to revitalize olonkho will see success.

CHAPTER 1

Epic Traditions, Performers, and Audiences

> [The epic singer is] . . . not a mere carrier of the tradition but a
> creative artist making the tradition.
> —Albert Lord, *The Singer of Tales*

An oral epic tradition composed of alternating sections of narrative poetry and song, olonkho demonstrates many of the characteristics common to other epic narrative traditions that recount at length the adventures of legendary, historical, or mythical heroes surmounting the challenges facing them or their people.[1] The oldest known epic poem, the Babylonian *Epic of Gilgamesh*, dates back to 1700 BCE (Abusch 2001, 614). Homer's *Iliad* and *Odyssey* continue this tradition in a poetic recounting of the events surrounding the Trojan War.[2] Today, epic poetry can be found in many countries, including India, Kazakhstan, Kyrgyzstan, Mongolia, and Tibet, as well as in the regions of Southeast and Central Asia, the continent of Africa, and various parts of the Russian Federation and Eurasia.[3]

The Sakha epic tradition of olonkho features the longest and most complex epic tales of all the Siberian indigenous groups, combining drama, lyric song, and poetic narrative in telling the stories of the great heroes of the past.[4] For centuries, specialists known as olonkhosuts have performed this unaccompanied solo genre. Each epic may include tens of thousands of lines of text performed in an improvisatory style based on formulaic and thematic elements. With ancient historical roots and a strong connection to the culture of the Sakha, olonkho themes center on the exploits of Sakha heroes and heroines in battles of good versus evil in the spiritual and physical world around them.[5]

Before the Soviet period, peripatetic singers entertained large numbers of Sakha families during the long, dark winters of the Siberian North. Their listeners sat "under the mouth," intently absorbing the riveting narratives of olonkho.[6] During the twentieth century, the number of olonkhosuts greatly declined in Yakutia, as master performers passed away without training others to take their place. In 2011, only two olonkhosuts recognized for their improvisational abilities remained—Pyotr Reshetnikov (fig. 1.1) and Afanasii Solovëv (fig. 1.2). By the beginning of 2013, these two were gone as well.

Fig. 1.1. Pyotr Reshetnikov, master olonkhosut (June 16, 2009). All photographs taken by William Harris, unless otherwise noted. Used by permission.

Fig. 1.2. Afanasii Solovëv, master olonkhosut (June 20, 2010)

Defining "epic"

The term "olonkho" refers to both the broad genre of olonkho epic style and the individual stories that make up the genre (Larionova 2004, 43). As seen from the description above, olonkho tales feature both structural traits and contextual features common to other epics, including "poetic language, narrative style, heroic content, great length, and multigeneric qualities. The contextual traits include legendary belief structure, multifunctionality, and cultural, traditional transmission" (Johnson 1992, 6–7). In addition, olonkho tales contain themes common to epics, such as some form of miraculous conception and birth augmented by special heroic gifts and abilities, and "Herculean deeds, extraterrestrial journeys, fierce individual battles with heroes, divinities, animals, dragons, and monsters; possession of extraordinary magical devices; tests of strength and intelligence; games" (Biebuyck 1976, 25–26).

Situating olonkho among the other epics of the world necessitates clarifying the relation of the various stories of an epic with each other and with the collection as a whole. For example, literature about epics does not always provide precise terminology regarding the differences between an epic *cycle*, an epic *tradition*, and an epic *tale*. More often than not, these categories receive separate treatment (cf. Bynum 1980, 330; Nas 2002, 140; Park 2003, 14–15) rather than comparison, contrast, or exact definition.

In this book, I use these three terms in the following manner: (1) "epic cycle" describes traditions like the Kyrgyz *Manas* and *Sunjata* from Mali, in which a series of stories relate to one cultural hero and his descendants; (2) "epic tradition" describes a style of storytelling that includes multiple tales not necessarily related to one central hero, such as the Korean p'ansori and the Sakha olonkho; and (3) "epic tale" refers to the various performances, literary variants, or constituent parts of these cycles and traditions—for example, each part of the *Manas* trilogy, each of the five p'ansori narratives, or each of the various literary versions of *Sunjata*. As applied to olonkho, "epic tale" refers to an individual story, while "epic tradition" refers to the collection of these tales.

Another term, "epos," reflects a close link through its dictionary definitions: (1) "an epic"; (2) "epic poetry"; (3) "a group of poems, transmitted orally, concerned with parts of a common epic theme"; (4) "a series of events suitable for treatment in epic poetry."[7] While both "epos" and "epic" stem from Greek roots, *epos* and *epikós*, respectively, the term "epic" may appear as either a noun or an adjective, while "epos" always functions as a noun. Within those grammatical constraints, both terms occur here interchangeably as a matter more of writing style than of definition.

Olonkho is not an epic cycle like *Manas* or *Sunjata*, in which all the episodes revolve around one main hero and his descendants. Instead, the tales in the olonkho

14   CHAPTER 1

tradition function independently of one another, although some characters appear in more than one tale (Larionova 2004, 42). Each olonkho story is named after the main protagonist. Most tales feature a male warrior hero, called a *bogatyr*, such as *Nurgun Botur the Swift*, *Muldju Bëghë the Invincible*, or *The Longsuffering Èr Sogotokh*.[8] Other tales showcase a female protagonist, such as *Kyys Dèbiliiè* or *Tuiaaryma Kuo* (Danilova 2014).[9] Most of these olonkho stories share a similar compositional structure, including the following elements:

1. Exposition: a portrait of the *bogatyr*, including a lengthy description of the hero's riches, weapons, and homeland, complete with a holy tree.
2. Call: the motivation for the hero's expedition and exploits.
3. Development of Action: the hindrances overcome during the expedition.
4. Culmination: the *bogatyr*'s battle with enemies, eventual victory, and single-handed combat in his pursuit of a bride.
5. Further Development of Action: the return path of the *bogatyr*, the overcoming of difficulties on his way home, and the punishing of his vanquished enemies and those related to them.
6. Conclusion: the arrival of the *bogatyr* at his homeland. The concluding lines convey that the hero lives happily and richly ever after with his wife, relatives, and children, thereby multiplying and proliferating the line of the Sakha nation.[10]

Historicity

As I began the study of olonkho, I wondered about the level of historical accuracy in these oral tales. In discussing this question with Sakha specialists, I found a broad range of opinions. Some olonkhos reference early ancestral figures of the Sakha people. On the other hand, most scholars do not consider the historicity of olonkho to be the primary value of the genre for Sakha people. According to Sakha intellectual Dmitrii Sivtsev, "The historicity that exists in the 'Manas' or 'David of Sassoun' [Armenian epic] is not present in the Yakut olonkho. . . . The historical character of olonkho is expressed in its general reflection of the culture, values, past history, geographical environment, and spiritual and material culture of the ethnic Sakha" (2003, 17).[11]

By featuring broadly "historical characters" rather than presenting only protagonists with specific historicity, olonkho reinforces Sakha identity, thereby serving a key function that focuses not on loss, but on the genre's current relevance and potential integration into contemporary practice (Levine 2014). Naturally, other ways of recounting history, such as history textbooks, also reflect the worldviews and values of the writers. The intertwining of narrative with metanarrative, while

Olonkho as embodiment of worldview and values

The concept of worldview extends far beyond mere religious *beliefs* and runs even deeper than *values*, both of which can change over time.[12] Scholars have described worldview as "an intellectual conception of the universe from the perspective of a human knower" (Naugle 2002, 59) and "a mental map of what is understood to be real" (Bunkowske 2002). Anthropologist Paul Hiebert uses the metaphor of an iceberg to compare worldview with beliefs and behaviors. Pointing out that only a small proportion of the ice in an iceberg appears above the surface of the ocean, as compared with the mass beneath, he contrasts the more visible aspects of beliefs and behaviors with the larger, unseen worldview that supports and connects those beliefs and behaviors. As part of that foundation, Hiebert asserts, "Worldviews are the most fundamental and encompassing views of reality shared by a people in a culture" (2008, 84). In that vein, he suggests three types of presuppositions that contribute to how humans assess reality: cognitive, affective, and evaluative (15). The tradition of olonkho exemplifies all three categories: a cognitive affirmation of the spiritual nature of reality, an affective embodiment of Sakha traditional musical and poetic aesthetic values, and the evaluative nature of a metanarrative in which good must always triumph over evil.

Reflecting on his own convictions as a master olonkhosut, Reshetnikov described elements of worldview, beliefs, and values as essential characteristics of olonkho: "Olonkho includes all the traditions, beliefs, and customs of the Yakut people, everything, their life. In the person of the *bogatyr* they create their heroes. Olonkho is long. It recounts not only the battle between two worlds, the middle world and the lower world, but it also includes the life of the upper world, the heavenly kingdom, where our Creators live, those who help those living on the Earth, on our planet, so they could vanquish the unclean powers of the lower world and the devil.

"The life of the Yakut people used to depend on nature. All of it! If it was a good year for the harvest, the lives of the people got better. If there was a good hunt, or good fishing, their lives also got better and they became richer. So they worship before the High God of the heavenly kingdom, Ürüng Aiyy Toion, who created the earth and all of them, the human race. Olonkho starts with this—the creation of the middle earth, the human race, and how their lives developed.

"In short, an olonkhosut tells about the efforts of the Yakut people toward a better life. So Yakut people are victorious over the hindrances of the lower world and invisible powers and spirits, and continue on to the most wonderful and rich

16   CHAPTER 1

life. So olonkho has a very deep purpose, not just for Yakut people, but as the dream and the strivings of all people on Earth."[13]

A strong connection between contemporary Sakha and the worldview and values of olonkho seems to operate as a significant factor in the desire to revitalize the genre. For example, on November 26, 2015, following the official holiday known as the Day of Olonkho, the head of the republic affirmed olonkho as one of the priorities of the cultural politics of the region: "a unifying philosophy of life, the eternal battle of good and evil." He went on to say that the epic "teaches each one of us to endure trials, overcome barriers, follow the law of conscience and righteousness, to emerge as victors from any kind of difficult situation . . . [and functions as] a compass in this modern world, in today's complex political situations."[14]

Olonkho integrates a spiritual-physical worldview affirming the existence of demons, good spirits, a High God, and upper, middle, and lower levels of a created cosmos. The inclusion of characters who operate within their *dramatis personae* as shamans and shamanesses leads some Sakha to assert a strong, even indivisible tie between olonkho and shamanic systems of belief.

While olonkho certainly reflects a vision of reality in which the spiritual and material worlds seamlessly intertwine, the question of whether it reflects a direct connection to shamanist religiosity remains a contentious topic in Yakutia.[15] This discussion is becoming increasingly polarized through the continuing influence of Soviet methodologies for co-opting the arts to create and reflect socially acceptable identities.

Just as a socially enforced materialist-atheist philosophy dominated the Soviet era, an increasingly prevalent current in Sakha discourse reifies a shamanistic Sakha identity.[16] Within this discourse, multiple streams of belief provide various perspectives in active competition with one another (Balzer 2010, xiv).[17] While socioreligious politics purport the widely accepted assumption that being Sakha includes embracing traditional religion, this ethnoreligious oversimplification marginalizes those who maintain a more nuanced, layered approach to their Sakha identity (Slobin 1996, 8).[18]

The notion that "Sakha-ness" equals a belief in traditional religion resembles what Solomon calls "self-conscious practices of strategic essentialism" (2014, 144). While this approach affords advantages for those influential voices managing the discourses of identity, many among my Sakha friends say that this rhetoric creates difficulties for those who overtly self-identify as both Sakha and Christian.[19] Expressions of Sakha Christian faith, when stated openly with conviction, are "usually rebuffed and sometimes ridiculed" (Balzer 2005, 64). Eleanor Peers, a social anthropologist studying religious revivalism in relation to the Ysyakh summer festival, speaks of a "sanctification of ethnic identity" (2013, 109), noting

EPIC TRADITIONS, PERFORMERS, AND AUDIENCES   17

the irony of how this mindset appears to be rooted in the legacy of modernism from the Soviet period. With regard to the festivalization of Ysyakh as well as previous forms of "Sovietized Sakha cultural production" (108), Peers remarks, "The Sakha case is particularly interesting because it shows the transformation of historical materialist Marxist-Leninist approaches to understanding ethnicity into contemporary forms of Sakha nationalism and religiosity" (94).[20]

The increasing promotion by official Sakha political voices of the link between shamanic spirituality and Sakha cultural identity comes with parallel assertions of the connection between shamanistic belief systems and olonkho.[21] On the other hand, a broad review of the literature on olonkho, as well as the responses I received in interviews, shows widely varying opinions at the grassroots level regarding the question of whether olonkho connects to uniquely shamanist beliefs or merely presents a broadly spiritual view of reality.[22]

Opinions especially differ sharply among Sakha self-identifying as either Russian Orthodox, Catholic, or Protestant Christians. A few reject olonkho as pagan and therefore completely unsuitable for expressing a Christian worldview. Others propose that the picture of spiritual realities presented in olonkho, while not perfectly representing their own beliefs, offers enough overlap to resist a wholesale identification of the genre with shamanistic beliefs. Proponents of this approach feel that the underlying worldview of olonkho allows room for a wide range of religious beliefs. As a result, they suggest that the genre should belong to all Sakha people, not only to the dominant voices supporting the revival of various streams of shamanism in Yakutia.

For example, respected Sakha literary giant Dmitrii Sivtsev (Suorun Omolloon), who affirmed his Christian faith late in life, was passionate about the role of olonkho for all Sakha people and argued against viewing the genre as inextricably tied to shamanistic beliefs:

> The myths of olonkho do not have anything in common with the religious shamanistic mythology of the Yakuts. The people themselves attest to this, as do the olonkhosuts, and even the ministers of the cult themselves, the shamans, don't accept the myths of the olonkho . . . which are artistic compilations and inspired, ingenious symbols. It is my conviction that all this, these broad poetic constructions of threatening powers of verse and society, battling, on one hand between themselves and on the other, battling against man, created in the image of God . . . [a hero] who is always victorious, always conquering them on behalf of the good of mankind.[23] (2003, 18)

Although Sivtsev endured criticism, including accusations by fellow Sakha scholars that he had "rejected it all and hurt us all" (Balzer 2005, 17), historical records from more than a century ago support his assertions. In the late nineteenth century, Seroshevskii wrote that the *abaasy* (evil spirits) in olonkho should not

18   CHAPTER 1

be confused with the shamanic *abaasy*; he supported his claims with information from a personal conversation in 1890 with a shaman from the Namskii district (1993, 590–591). Furthermore, he felt that the most powerful idea in olonkho centered not so much on the gods, or even on fate, as on the power of the living, active human will (592).

As with all archetypal tales, the themes of olonkho resonate with a broad spectrum of belief systems. Yakutian-born ethnomusicologist Eduard Alekseyev submits that olonkho tales can express various systems of belief, including Christianity: "The very idea of creation in both olonkho and the Bible, an understanding of how the world was created, and how it developed—these are close, archetypal ideas. We see similar ideas in many religious books, inspired books. For that reason, it seems to me that when we see living offshoots that combine religion and olonkho, we will discover a type of living hybrid, if you can call it that.

"In any case, I imagine that it is quite possible that through the means of olonkho, one might be able to convey some of the concepts and ideas that lie at the heart of religious books. Not the details—this is a crucial point—but the most important things, such as faith in one's belief system and one's worldview."[24]

In short, a definitive assessment of the connection between the worldview of olonkho and Sakha shamanic beliefs remains elusive; however, conflating the two systems oversimplifies the issue. At this point, Sakha people generally agree only that olonkho reflects, at minimum, and in a broad and prototypical way, their best ideals, their traditional way of life, and a Sakha worldview from centuries past.

Features of olonkho performance

During pre-Soviet centuries, olonkho flourished as an unaccompanied solo epic genre in which both dramatic narrative poetry and song alternated throughout the extensive, multiple-evening performance of the work (Okladnikov 1970, 263). Although often referred to as *teatr odnogo cheloveka* (one-person theater), the performances do not feature blocking or props. The olonkhosut generally sits with crossed legs on a low stool, and either rests both hands on the top knee or holds one hand cupped to the side of the face. A Sakha style of narrative poetry, often referred to by the Sakha as *rechitativ* (recitative), delineates the "telling" sections, while sung material conveys the characters' direct speech (Larionova 2010).[25] A gifted olonkhosut maintains a balance between the alternating textures of song and recitative as the story unfolds during the performance.[26]

Distinct leitmotifs, vocal registers, and intonations signify the sung speech of each of the characters in the olonkho, including the voices of animals such as the *bogatyr*'s horse. Moving beyond prosaic narration, the recitative sections also contain musical elements such as central tones and other melodic ambitus-related factors—rising and falling contours, organization in phrases, and rhythmic and temporal characteristics. Highly complex formal elements of Sakha poetry mark those texts considered most aesthetically pleasing, incorporating literary devices such as parallel grammatical constructions, symbolism, descriptive imagery, epithets, metaphor, simile, and hyperbole (Larionova 2000, 39; Nakhodkina 2014, 275).

Epic performers

The focal point of creativity in the olonkho performance tradition is the olonkhosut, the musical recounter of olonkho tales. For the listener, the olonkhosut seems to have an almost magical ability to recount at length the narrative-song tales of his or her repertoire. The German scholar of Turkic epics Karl Reichl proposes two categories of oral epic performers: *reproductive*, those who perform memorized sections, and *creative*, those who are able to improvise within the structure of the genre. He adds a crucial caveat to this bifurcation, noting that "while some singers can be clearly classified as either 'creative' or 'reproductive,' others can be less easily put in one or the other category" (1992, 82). I propose that the difficulty in placing olonkhosuts in one or the other of these groups can be solved by visualizing the two kinds of performers as poles of a continuum. This continuum stretches from a Sakha child who memorizes a short ten-minute fragment of olonkho, for example, to an eighty-year-old master olonkhosut like Reshetnikov, who can recite an entire olonkho in an improvisatory manner over a period of several days.

This view of seeing performers on a continuum arose from conversations with olonkhosuts, who sometimes describe their performance practice as having begun toward the reproductive end of the continuum. Then, as their fluency in the art of oral formulaic expression increased, their performance practice also gradually moved in the direction of the creative master performer. Despite the reality of the middle ground, the two extremes of the continuum represent significant realities for researchers, and Sakha scholars tend to refer to olonkhosuts as either olonkho performers, denoting those who present memorized versions without improvisation, or master olonkhosuts, for those who are proficient at improvising within the aesthetic boundaries of the genre. Scholars not specifying a level of performance skill generally use the simple title "olonkhosut." I also adhere to these conventions, while recognizing that the permeable boundaries of these groupings reflect a more nuanced reality than two disparate categories.

Both men and women sing olonkho, but although the olonkho researchers with whom I talked reported no cultural taboos against women becoming olonkhosuts, I noted fewer women performers than men. This tendency may reflect the historical reality that women generally have not earned their living by performing, as male olonkhosuts did.[27] While they were not forbidden to become master olonkhosuts,

20   CHAPTER 1

no financial or societal structures provided the necessary support for them to travel and perform extensively, thereby earning a living.

In reality, the primary qualifications for olonkho performance appear to revolve around talent rather than gender. That talent, widely described by Sakha people as a phenomenal gift of verbal and melodic expression, also includes the ability to perform *iz sebia* (literally "from oneself," that is, in an improvisatory manner) rather than just reciting a memorized version.[28] When these abilities become visible in a person who has also had long-term exposure to the live performances of others, then that person, male or female, may develop the necessary capacity for becoming a master olonkhosut. In fact, in 2005 the Sakha government recognized two people, one man and one woman, as master olonkhosuts. Although the woman, Daria Tomskaia, was a member of a smaller indigenous group in Yakutia, the Evenki, she spoke Sakha and performed in Sakha.[29]

Oral formulaic theory and improvisation in olonkho

The significant difference between a master olonkhosut, who improvises, and an olonkho performer, who produces a memorized concert, lies in the oral nature of the tradition. The master olonkhosut's abilities represent a special kind of improvisation codified in literature on epics in terms of *oral formulaic theory*. First postulated by Milman Parry, this theoretical framework continued to gain traction after Parry's death through the work of his collaborator and student Albert Lord. In 1960, Lord published the seminal work in the field of epic studies, *The Singer of Tales*, now considered a classic text for understanding oral and written epics (2000, xix).[30] This work documents how Parry and Lord studied the oral tradition of epic poetry in Yugoslavia, seeking to understand how the singers of that tradition were able to "compose, learn, and transmit their epics" (xxxv).[31]

Lord's groundbreaking work formulated definitions of several key concepts now considered foundational in epic studies. For example, he defines "oral epic song" as "narrative poetry composed in a manner evolved over many generations by singers of tales who did not know how to write; it consists of the building of metrical lines and half lines by means of formulas and formulaic expressions and of the building of songs by the use of themes" (2000, 4). Lord's emphasis on the oral nature of epics proved essential for the future of epic studies by uncovering the connection between orality and the formulaic aspect of epic expression. His definition of "formula"—"a group of words which is regularly employed under the same metrical conditions to express a given essential idea" (4)—helped epic scholars understand a key feature of how a "Singer of Tales" could improvise such long stories.

Lord describes the creation of epics as a flexible system relying less on memorized text than on the linguistic "grooves" that manifest themselves as patterns of melody, meter, syntax, parallelism, and word order. He compares the process for learning the language of formula with that for learning a normal spoken language—as one becomes skilled in syntax and word forms, one grows in the ability to express thoughts. His analogies for how singers absorb their craft also employ linguistic metaphors. He asserts that the patterns of oral poetry come from its "grammar," superimposed onto the particular grammar of the spoken language used for the narrative: "The speaker of this language, once he has mastered it, does not move any more mechanically within it than we do in ordinary speech. . . . He does not 'memorize' formulas, any more than we as children 'memorize' language. He learns them by hearing them in other singers' songs, and by habitual usage they become part of his singing as well" (2000, 36).

Using these formulas obviates the need for mechanically memorizing tales word for word. As a result, no two performances of an epic are ever the same, even from the same singer. Lord summarizes this unique characteristic of oral epics: "The picture that emerges is not really one of conflict between preserver of tradition and creative artist; it is rather one of the preservation of tradition by the constant re-creation of it" (2000, 29; Bakan 2012, 29). This concept of "constant re-creation" proves essential to understanding the art of the master olonkhosut.

The linguistic parallels continue. Lord observes that epic singers share many common formulas in their performing vocabularies, just as a community shares a common corpus of words and phrases within any given spoken language (2000, 49). Singers may vary the length of the formulas and clump them together into clusters of words, phrases, melodies, meters, and parallelisms. Recurring clusters of formulas and lines reveal a tradition's oral roots, as the performer uses these formulas comfortably, almost like an automatic reflex (58).

Another significant concept in understanding the performance of epics, the notion of *theme* refers to various events, descriptive passages, or ideas that are commonly grouped together (2000, 4, 68). The singer employs these themes to anchor the ever-unfolding text in the re-creation process of a particular perfor- mance. Lord writes that "the theme is in reality protean; in the singer's mind it has many shapes, all the forms in which he has ever sung it, although his latest rendering of it will naturally be freshest in his mind. It is not a static entity, but a living, changing, adaptable artistic creation" (94). Despite this malleability, certain themes commonly occur together within epic stories. Observing epic singers' instinctive grouping of themes, Lord remarks, "We are apparently dealing here with a strong force that keeps certain themes together. It is deeply imbedded in the tradition" (98).

Parry and Lord hypothesized underlying similarities in epic poems around the world. Their research compared Yugoslavian epic poems of the early twentieth century with Homer's epic poetry from the eighth century BCE, a comparison that crossed significant cultural and historical boundaries. The vast body of subsequent

22   CHAPTER 1

research undertaken by others in epic studies has since validated many of Parry and Lord's claims.[32]

In examining Lord's book, the ethnomusicologist will regret the absence of musical analysis related to the Yugoslav epics. Lord's approach was largely text-oriented, possibly a reflection of his connection to the discipline of comparative literature.[33] Thankfully, a few recordings accompany the second edition of the volume, and Lord provides some melodic transcriptions that offer at least minimal descriptions. He also gave the term "epic singer" new depth, observing that "singing, performing, composing are facets of the same act" and that the epic singer is "not a mere carrier of the tradition but a creative artist making the tradition" (2000, 13). Parry's descriptions of oral formulas and themes in the epic tradition of the southern Yugoslavs help clarify the role of improvisation in the olonkhosut's art. Lord's discoveries allow us to see how olonkho follows the formulaic and thematic grooves of epic singers in other places and other times, albeit with improvised melodic, poetic, dramatic, and narrative materials distinctive to the Sakha culture.[34]

Emergent character of olonkho

Building on its oral and formulaic features, olonkho also demonstrates an emergent quality. The interaction between the olonkhosut and the audience amplifies the improvisatory element, producing a performance that "emerges" in the moment (Bauman 1975, 302–306). In each re-creation, the olonkhosut reacts to the surrounding context, adapting the performance to the audience's response, the length of time allowed for the performance, his or her personal level of energy, and other similar factors. The master olonkhosut responds to nonverbal cues from the audience, especially signs of attentiveness, but also to their verbal responses, such as short cries of approbation and amazement when the olonkhosut draws a long breath.[35] According to Bauman, "the emergent quality of performance resides in the interplay between communicative resources, individual competence, and the goals of the participants, within the context of particular situations" (302). Bauman traces the concepts behind "emergence" back to Lord's *Singer of Tales*, calling this influential volume "one of the first works to conceptualize oral literature in terms of emergent structures" (302). Viewing Lord's descriptions of oral epic performances through the lens of emergence, he observes that "the flexibility of the form allows the singer to adapt his performance to the situation and the audience, making it longer and more elaborate, or shorter and less adorned, as audience response, his own mood, and time constraints may dictate" (303).

Reshetnikov's description of his first two olonkhos provides a practical example of these performer-audience dynamics: "My first olonkho was criticized for hav-

EPIC TRADITIONS, PERFORMERS, AND AUDIENCES   23

ing a *bogatyr* who was too much of a humanitarian Yakut warrior—he allowed his evil spirit opponent to live.[36] They told me that these kinds of olonkhos don't exist. So then I created a second olonkho with a very angry, harsh, fierce man. This time I didn't leave anyone alive among his enemies. All of his enemies were destroyed! That is the way the second olonkho was created. This long olonkho is about ten hours each time I sing it, if I extend it out, of course. The length and performance of olonkho depends on the abilities of the olonkhosut himself. As he performs, he extends the olonkho, adding new subject matter."[37]

As we will see, olonkho audiences in Yakutia today remain far more passive during performances than their counterparts did a century ago, presumably due to a decreased understanding of the genre as a whole and a weaker comprehension of the archaic Sakha language used. Consequently, the emergent nature of traditional performances surfaces as a conspicuous feature both in my analysis of current trends and in my resulting prognosis for the revitalization of olonkho.

Interactions between verbal and musical aspects of olonkho

In describing the intricate interactions between various verbal and musical facets of olonkho, I have relied on Sakha music scholar Anna Larionova (2000, 2004) and on her mentor Eduard Alekseyev.[38] One of my primary collaborators in this research, Alekseyev contributed perspectives from decades of experience as a researcher of Sakha music and other related Central Asian traditions.[39] His creative insights and grounded musicological understanding of Sakha music have influenced the writings of Sakha and Russian musicologists for decades.[40]

In his introduction to a musicological analysis of the olonkho *The Mighty Èr Sogotokh*, Alekseyev underscores the special connections between the genre's musical and verbal aspects: "Olonkho is predominantly noteworthy as an inimitable and organic artistic conjoining of grand poetic speech and expressive, diverse song styles. It is truly unique as a musical-poetic phenomenon, possessing its own two-in-one (melodic-poetic) language, a highly developed and complex (yet streamlined and economic) system of verbal and musical expressivity, special poetic devices, and melodic improvisation, all connected tightly and flexibly interacting one with another" (1996, 44).[41] This interactivity renders olonkho performance a complex artistic form. Olonkhosuts must operate at a high level of melodic and poetic fluency while also flexibly interacting with their vision of the plot line, the audience's level of responsiveness, and the time frame of the performance arena.

Noting the sonic nature of both the musical and verbal portions of olonkho, Alekseyev emphasizes the importance of timbre, a high aesthetic value in Sakha

24   CHAPTER 1

music. He asserts that the essential aptitudes related to singing olonkho are the capacity to improvise freely, the ability to sing "melodic pictures" expressively, and "a special prowess in regard to the timbral characteristics of vocal re-embodiment" (1996, 45).[42] In light of the importance of the interactivity between the narrative and the musical aspects of olonkho, I will examine the narrative mode in more detail, providing a description of how recitative resembles, but also differs from, the musical mode.

The narrative mode

Narrative sections of olonkho are marked by crisp articulation, deep breath control, and a fast tempo that generally runs around four hundred syllables per minute but may range up to five hundred.[43] Careful pitch calibrations allow for a rough notation of contours: "In spite of the storytelling style of enunciation, in recitative it is fairly easy to hear a specific pitch, which allows an approximate notation of its fundamental contours. The pitches of the recitative are built on two foundational tones. . . . The distinctive characteristic of the lower tone is that it is rather consistently pulled toward the upper tone, as a glissando rolling into the upper tone" (Alekseyev 1996, 46).[44]

The notation for the introductory narrative of *The Mighty Ėr Sogotokh* (fig. 1.3) clearly demonstrates the tonal tendencies described by Alekseyev.[45] Note the presence of the two tonal anchor points, with the pitch often starting at the upper level, dropping to the lower one, and then climbing back up. This phenomenon changes toward the end, where the pitches typically move downward, finalized by a descending glissando. The recitative of master olonkhosut Pyotr Reshetnikov also manifests these contour characteristics.[46] The intonation of his narrative employs a sparse tonal inventory and a recitation style with generally flat contours, imbuing the narrative with a transcendent, timeless quality (Banti and Giannattasio 2006, 296).[47] The falling intonation at the end of each section provides emphasis and prepares the audience for an imminent pause, during which the olonkhosut will replenish his breath and listeners may express encouraging exclamations (Alekseyev 1996, 47).

Another essential characteristic of Sakha poetry, making its oral re-creation in the moment of performance an accomplishment of astonishing complexity, is the presence of both horizontal and vertical parallelisms for sounds and syllables.[48] Points of alliteration at the beginnings of lines and repetitions of sounds in succeeding lines undergird the poetic form. Whole words and other forms of parallelism may also repeat in subsequent lines.

The same Sakha-language recitative from *Ėr Sogotokh* (fig. 1.3) exhibits these poetic devices. Note the parallel use of the word "caxa" (*Sakha*) in the first four lines and "илигинэ" (*iliginė*) in four out of the first five lines. The layout of the transcription highlights the rhythmic and poetic parallelism.

Fig. 1.3. Introductory recitative from *Ėr Sogotokh*. Notated example is from Alekseyev (1996, 59). Original notation: N. N. Nikolaeva. See http://www.eduard.alekseyev.org/work20.html. Used by permission. Re-rendered transcription in Finale by Kerry Payton. (See http://www.press.uillinois.edu/books/harris/storytelling/ for recording.)

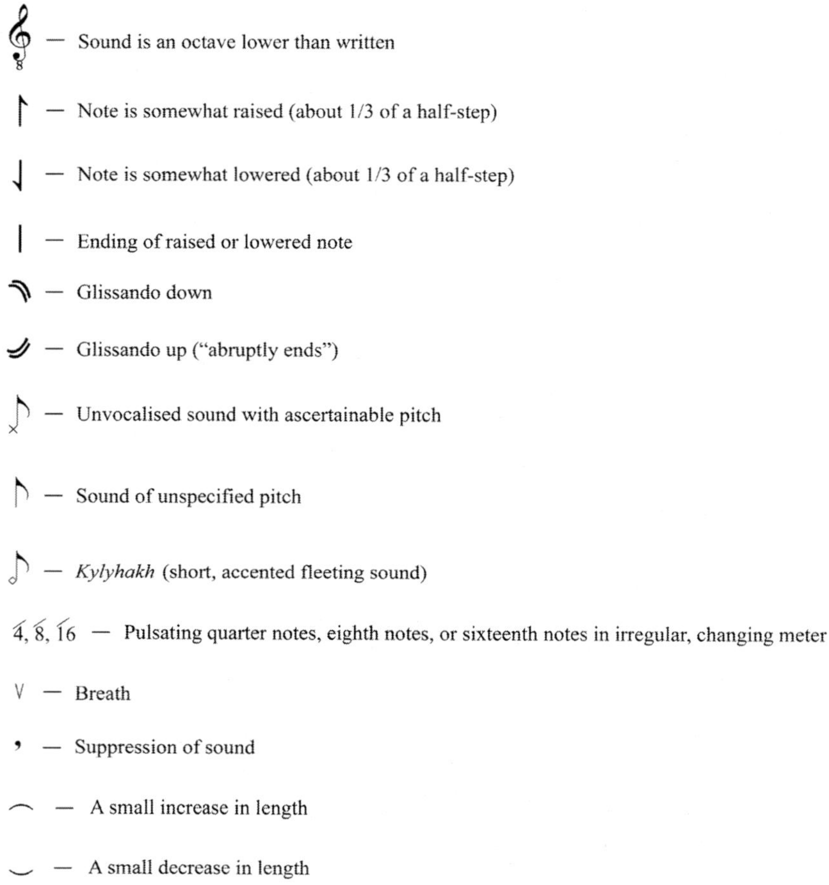

26   CHAPTER 1

♪ — Sound is an octave lower than written

↑ — Note is somewhat raised (about 1/3 of a half-step)

↓ — Note is somewhat lowered (about 1/3 of a half-step)

| — Ending of raised or lowered note

↷ — Glissando down

⤴ — Glissando up ("abruptly ends")

♪ — Unvocalised sound with ascertainable pitch

♩ — Sound of unspecified pitch

♪ — *Kylyhakh* (short, accented fleeting sound)

4̆, 8̆, 1̆6̆ — Pulsating quarter notes, eighth notes, or sixteenth notes in irregular, changing meter

V — Breath

' — Suppression of sound

⌒ — A small increase in length

‿ — A small decrease in length

Fig. 1.4. Key to symbols in notated examples (Alekseyev 1996, 58). Re-rendered in Finale by Kerry Payton.

Music-related materials and characteristics of olonkho

The character-specific motifs, formulas, intonation, timbre, and styles of singing connect the verbal and poetic content of the text tightly to the musical fabric of olonkho. Sonically, the genre fits well with other types of Turkic-rooted musics, especially in their strong aesthetic focus on timbre. Sakha ethnomusicologists draw parallels between the sonic materials of ornamented Sakha song and the bifurcated sound produced by the throat-singing techniques of Tuvans and Mongolians (Larionova 2010).

Valentina Suzukei, a Tuvan ethnomusicologist, describes the timbre of many Central Asian string instruments and the primary aesthetic of throat singing and

EPIC TRADITIONS, PERFORMERS, AND AUDIENCES   27

jaw harp playing as "sonic texture" (Levin 2006, 72). Traditional Sakha vocal and instrumental musical expressions reflect this predilection for timbre-rich sonic textures.[49] According to Levin and Suzukei, although some ethnographers claim that "timbre-centered sound-making . . . represents a protomusical form that antedates the rise of melody (or more generally, fixed pitch-height) as a musical organizing principle," there is "no hard empirical evidence [that] supports such a claim" (58). The continued persistence into this globalized age of complex, timbre-focused sound systems in Mongolia, Tuva, Yakutia, and other Eurasian contexts reveals this aesthetic to be an uncommon but viable parameter in the wide diversity of world sound systems.[50]

In general, each Sakha song genre relates to one of two broad song styles, *dègèrèn* or *dièrètii*. Olonkho actually employs both styles, but with a far greater use of *dièrètii*, a manner of singing marked by the extensive use of *kylyhakh*, a unique Sakha style of ornamentation.[51] Larionova describes *kylyhakh* as "a system of guttural overtones; a complex conglomerate of ornaments. It can be expressed in a variety of ways—vibrato, grace notes, glissandi, fleeting tones, and flageolets" (2010). Effectively employing visual metaphors to impart a sense of the ornamentation's essential characteristics, Alekseyev provides this excellent description in his musicological introduction to *The Mighty Èr Sogotokh*: "*kylyhakhi* are short, accented flageolets, and merit special mention, as they are characteristic of Yakut epic singing. *Kylyhakhi* are distinctive in their high, clear timbre, like a sharp twinkle that shimmers, as if from far away, like a spark, layered onto the sound of the fundamental melody, frequently giving the illusion of a bifurcation of the singing voice. Decorating and embroidering the sound, it imparts to Yakut song an inimitable texture" (1996, 56).[52]

Like other timbres, *kylyhakh* remains notoriously difficult to define without resorting to metaphors or vocabulary drawn from non-aural avenues of human sensory perception. Despite this descriptive limitation, notations of this feature afford a fascinating view of the pitch relationships between the melodic and ornamental structures of both *dègèrèn* and *dièrètii*. See, for example, the representation of the *dièrètii* style in "Song of the Spirit-Mistress of the Valley" (fig. 1.5), which depicts *kylyhakh* with smaller note heads than that of the primary pitches.[53] The following sections explore these two traditional Sakha song styles in relation to their performance features, sounds, possible notation practices, and characteristic usage in olonkho.

Unmetered song style *(*dièrètii*)*

Typically abundant with *kylyhakh*, songs in the *dièrètii* style are through-composed, with significant structural and rhythmic freedom. This improvisational style also features typical Sakha modal elements such as whole tone scales and

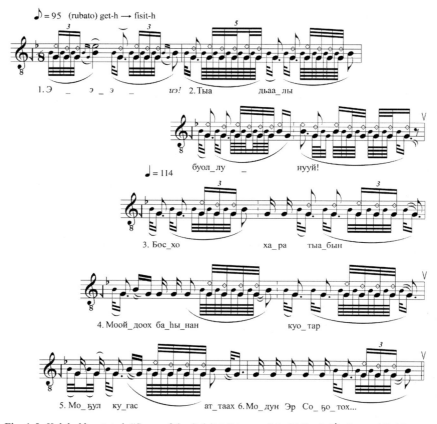

Fig. 1.5. *Kylyhakh* notated: "Song of the Spirit-Mistress of the Valley" (*Ėr Sogotokh*). Notated example is from Alekseyev (1996, 68). Original notation: N. N. Nikolaeva. See http://www.eduard.alekseyev.org/work20.html. Used by permission. Re-rendered transcription in Finale by Kerry Payton. (See http://www.press.uillinois.edu/books/harris/storytelling/ for recording.)

the "unfolding mode" of Sakha traditional song (Alekseyev 1969, 117; Grigorian 1957; Larionova 2004, 5).[54] In terms of affect, Sakha ethnomusicologists describe the drawn-out, flowing *diėrėtii* style as heroic, majestic, solemn, and exalted.

Toyuk (exalted or praise songs), the most characteristic genre within the broader category of *diėrėtii* song style, communicates the direct speech of the good characters in olonkho. These protagonists can be either good spirits (*aiyy*) from the

Upper World or humans (Alekseyev 1996, 48). The vocal expression of the heroic characters, sung in the style of *dièrètii*, "helps the listener to understand his inner life, revealing his solemn and noble character" (Larionova 2010).

Far from monolithic in expression, *dièrètii* comes from two geographically centered performance schools: the central region near the Lena River, and the Viliui River basin. The Viliui River style tends toward a distinctness of rhythmic pronunciation and a general lack of long, sung-out words, setting forth the contents of the song as if giving a pronouncement. In contrast, the Lena River style features profuse *kylyhakh* ornamentation and drawn-out words. The typical singer from the Lena River area, in a considerably slower manner than the Viliui performer, "wrings it all out," elongating and ornamenting each syllable of the text (Alekseyev 1969, 117–118).[55]

Larionova describes the intricate, logocentric interaction between the verbal and musical content of *dièrètii* as "a special technique, a manner of vocalizing poetic improvisation" (2004, 12).[56] Alekseyev characterizes this dynamic as "syllabic-based," with each syllable in the text elaborated upon using a limited number of variations of a "tonal-rhythmic micro formula" (1989a).[57] These micro formulas result in a remarkably homogeneous song texture, rendering any text singable.[58] As Alekseyev notes, "this produces a general impression of transcendent, elevated, and majestic epic speech"—"an inimitable 'singing recitation' style."[59] Although a comparison of the *dièrètii* song style with the cantillation of other musical traditions is beyond the scope of this work, it would likely produce some interesting parallels with Alekseyev's concept of the tonal-rhythmic micro formula. For example, I am intrigued by the similarities I have observed between *dièrètii* and accounts of the "flowing rhythm" of Jewish *nusah*, as described by Frigyesi (1993), or of the "prosodic rhythm" of Jewish sacred music in the Persian-speaking world, as analyzed by Rapport (2016).

Melodic-rhythmic song style *(*dègèrèn*)*

The other major singing style, *dègèrèn*, features less ornamentation and more precise rhythm, although the metrical organization of *dègèrèn* songs in olonkho often proves complex (see fig. 1.6). Operating within these intricacies, the normal speech rhythm of the improvised text remains subordinate to the rhythm of the *dègèrèn* song formulas (Larionova 2010). In her book devoted to this song style, Larionova writes: "*Dègèrèn* song is . . . based on a strictly organized metrical rhythm with a developed, clear-cut, well-defined, structurally looping, individualized melos" (2000, 37).[60] The texts used in the *dègèrèn* style follow the normal tendencies of Sakha poetry, including abundant alliteration. As seen in our previous discussion of the narrative mode, this alliteration includes both

30   CHAPTER 1

vowel and consonant agreement, sometimes at the beginnings of the lines, but also within the lines themselves.

In olonkho, this song style occasionally expresses the direct speech of protagonists, but more frequently expresses the direct speech of the comic trickster-slave figures and the female demons and shamans (Alekseyev 1996, 53; Larionova 2004, 54). For example, the *dègèrèn* style conveys the song of the demonesses in *Èr Sogotokh* (Fig. 1.6).

Regarding pitch, "the tunes in *dègèrèn* style are differentiated by their larger intervallic content and wider tessitura, visibly transcending the comparatively modest pitch norms of the *toyuks*" (Alekseyev 1996, 54).[61] Since the majority of everyday and lyrical songs employ this melodic style, *dègèrèn* impacts a wide range of Sakha genres: *ohuokhai*, love songs, songs about nature, lullabies, play songs, work songs, *tüösüü yryata* (love songs in which a man or a woman addresses a beloved), *tangalai yryata* (palatal songs), *khabargha yryata* (throat songs), comic songs, and sung *chabyrgakhtar* (tongue-twisters).[62] In the twentieth century, a distinctive national choral style grew out of the *dègèrèn* style, as did streams of modern Sakha popular song.

Kylyhakh is more commonly identified with the *dièrètii* style of song but appears to a lesser extent in *dègèrèn* (see fig. 1.6), further evidence of this ornamentation's importance to much of Sakha music. Alekseyev describes the use of this embellishment within the *dègèrèn* style: "Pronounced and multi-pitched *kylyhakhi* appear like separate ornamented accents on particular beats in the motifs and formulas of *dègèrèn*. At other times they blend expressively with the vocal vibrato. [. . . *Kylyhakh* is] integral to the national singing culture of the Yakuts, and for the art of the Yakut olonkhosuts, is an idiosyncratic method of sound production" (1996, 56).[63]

A multigeneric genre

In summary, olonkho incorporates both styles of Sakha traditional song and draws on elements from artistic domains such as narrative, poetry, drama, and improvisatory performance (Sivtsev 2003, 17), making the genre truly "multigeneric."[64] Is olonkho predominantly a song? A poem? A story?[65] In my interviews with Sakha respondents, I noted that some used the term "sing" when referring to olonkho, while others used the term "tell." As Alekseyev notes, olonkho presents a profoundly interactive fusion: "In many languages and, what is particularly important, among bearers of traditional cultures, there are expressions that unmistakably point to the organic link existing between melody and speech: Russian *bylinas* [tales] are not sung but are recounted. Yakut epic singers have an expression, *ètèn yllyyr* [to sing, uttering the words].[66] . . . [Each] culture develops its own sound world, where a spoken word and a sung word are united into a timbral-rhythmic-

EPIC TRADITIONS, PERFORMERS, AND AUDIENCES   31

Fig. 1.6. *Dëgërën* style: "Song of the Demonesses" (*Ėr Sogotokh*). Notated example is from Alekseyev (1996, 69). Original notation: N. N. Nikolaeva. See http://www.eduard.alekseyev.org/work20.html. Used by permission. Re-rendered transcription in Finale by Kerry Payton. (See http://www.press.uillinois.edu/books/harris/storytelling/ for recording.)

intonational complex that is extremely hard to define in words, but which is empirically well detected" (1989b).

Adequately descriptive terms for the multigeneric olonkho would necessarily consist of too many parts to make them useful. Writers on the subject of olonkho must resort to shortened descriptors, thereby protecting readers from unwieldy

32   CHAPTER 1

portrayals such as *an oral, improvised, emergent, song-poem-narrative-dramatic tradition with two traditional song styles and abundant ornamentation, presented by one person who fills a wide variety of roles over many hours of performance.* In reality, olonkho's complexity may be one of the biggest factors contributing to its decline—this kind of one-person theater is not easily mastered.

Having outlined the relevant components of olonkho performance, I turn now to the primary task of this research: examining changes in the performance and reception of olonkho over time. The historical approach of the next chapters brings to light the degree to which change has already happened, but also probes the trends of current changes, all in the quest to understand the process and effects of change within the tradition of olonkho performance practice.

CHAPTER 2

EFFECTS OF CHANGE DURING THE SOVIET ERA

> When side by side for a long time
> An old and strong people lives with a small one
> The younger people is treated unfairly
> In secret and patently, but always in everything.
> —Aleksei Kulakovskii, "Snovidenie shamana," trans. Anatoly Khazanov

The watershed historical event for cultural revitalization in Yakutia occurred with the dissolution of the Soviet Union in the early 1990s.[1] The surge in freedom of expression for minority peoples during that period of Russian history laid the groundwork for widespread cultural renewal among the Sakha. This new vitality, in turn, contributed to the political and cultural environment necessary for supporting olonkho revitalization.[2]

The resulting effort to rescue olonkho from extinction came in the form of a successful bid for the genre to be recognized by UNESCO as a "Masterpiece of the Oral and Intangible Heritage of Humanity." To highlight the significance of this Masterpiece award for olonkho revitalization, I will begin by exploring the political, social, cultural, religious, and musical influences of the various periods of Soviet history. I rely primarily on the words, opinions, and memories of my Sakha respondents. Their stories and research particularly emphasize the internal timelines—the institutional, individual, and performance-related factors that they feel most significantly impacted the decline and revitalization of olonkho performance. I found their personal accounts gripping in their intensity, innovative in their insights, delightfully human in their transparency, and at times widely divergent in the views they expressed, reminding us that a multiplicity of perspectives often brings a broader, more nuanced understanding of historical events.

This revisiting of history will show how the past effectively grounds the Sakha vision for the future, thereby providing a foundation for olonkho revitalization efforts. Symbolically reimagining years to come as a continuation of years gone by, the Sakha can maintain a layered metanarrative that offers a voice of hope in a time of economic, political, and global turmoil.[3]

34   CHAPTER 2

The early olonkhosuts

Centuries before the advent of Soviet power in Yakutia, olonkhosuts passed along their tales and their craft orally from one generation to the next. Reflecting their earlier history in southern Siberia, many of the olonkho stories tell of the time before the Sakha lived in the North. As the group slowly migrated north during the early centuries of the second millennium CE, the oral transmission of olonkho gave olonkhosuts a way to incorporate key historical events into their epic stories.

From Central Asia, the Sakha people first migrated toward the Lake Baikal region, then continued on to the shores of the middle Lena River in the thirteenth and fourteenth centuries, finally displacing and assimilating smaller minority groups as they moved farther north to the Arctic Ocean (Cruikshank and Argounova 2000, 101; Khazanov 1993, 176; Okladnikov 1970, 298–299). By the middle of the seventeenth century, Russian Cossacks and settlers had arrived in the area, establishing a tsarist presence in eastern Siberia (Cruikshank and Argounova 2000). The resilience of orally transmitted olonkho afforded continuity and even the further development of this epic genre throughout all these changes in location and population (Okladnikov 1970, 263–264; Sivtsev 2003, 21).

Olonkho in pre-Soviet times

Largely because of the vast distances in the Siberian North, the performance practice of olonkho remained largely undocumented in pre-Soviet times. Russia's rail lines reached only the southern parts of Yakutia until the Amur-Yakutsk line was finished in 2014.[4] Even today, roads remain scarce, and some routes become available only in the winter, when the rivers freeze and their snow and ice can be bladed into a relatively passable condition for cars.

In the pre-Soviet years, before motorized forms of travel, olonkhosuts traveled on the backs of horses or cattle (Tokarev and Gurvich 1964, 259). Boris Mikhailov, artistic manager of Archy Diėtė (the House of Purification), a center for Sakha traditional religion and cultural expression in the city of Yakutsk, bemoans the paucity of knowledge about olonkho and olonkhosuts during the pre-Soviet period. As we conversed in his office at Archy Diėtė, he mused, "We don't know things like, for example, at the end of the nineteenth century and the beginning of the twentieth century, a true olonkhosut, over the period of one year; how much could he recount? Where did he recount, and what were his audiences like? On average, how many times a year would he recount olonkho? This has not been studied yet. Also, the geography of where they were located, what was the size of their territory? Because Yakutia is very large."[5]

Almost the size of India, Yakutia's 1.1 million square miles cover one fifth of Russia's territory, forming the largest subnational entity in the world.[6] Figure 2.1

EFFECTS OF CHANGE DURING THE SOVIET ERA 35

Fig. 2.1. Map of the Republic of Sakha (Yakutia) in the Russian Federation

shows the republic's size and location relative to the other regional boundaries within the Russian Federation.

During the pre-Soviet years, most Sakha people lived during the winter not in towns but in small settlements comprised of one to three log yurts, known as *balaghans* (Tokarev and Gurvich 1964, 261–262). Located on the edge of an *alaas* (grassy meadow), these clusters of dwellings nestled in the forest at a significant distance from the next such community. Olonkhosuts worked then as traveling bards, performing in the intimate spaces of these traditional Sakha family houses, where extended families and close friends would gather around the fireplace to listen (see fig. 2.2).

We may never know for sure how many olonkhosuts lived during the pre-revolutionary period, but researchers in Yakutia note that they were present throughout the republic, with concentrations in a few regions.[7] Zakharova and Protodiakonova report on one of these pockets, found within the Tatta district: "according to the research data, the 'Tatta School' of olonkhosuts was being formed by the second half of the eighteenth century. Each county had a handful of olonkhosuts.[8] According to the archival and written sources available to us today, there have been more than seven hundred olonkhosuts (in the seventeenth to twenty-first centuries), including both past and present, testifying to a true flowering of this oral tradition in the past" (2010, 22).[9]

One of the aforementioned Tatta olonkhosuts, Pyotr Reshetnikov, was born in 1929. Expecting that a living olonkhosut could provide valuable perspective on the lives of past olonkhosuts, I interviewed Reshetnikov in 2009 at his home in

Fig. 2.2. *Balaghan* in an outdoor museum near Cherkëkh, Yakutia (June 16, 2009)

Cherkëkh, in the Tatta district. He offered me insight into the life and performance practice of olonkhosuts from pre-Soviet to modern times.[10] When asked about olonkhosuts at the end of the nineteenth century, he replied, "You have correctly noted that our very best olonkhosuts, great olonkhosuts, appeared—were born and lived here and created their olonkhos—in fact at the end of the nineteenth century and the beginning of the twentieth century. There were hundreds of them in various districts—they could be found in all of the districts. The peak of olonkho development was in fact in the nineteenth century and into the beginning of the twentieth century, before the appearance of Soviet power.

"One can say that olonkho is a great oral work, the creation of individuals—the olonkhosuts. They create a long story, with songs and heroes. The length of an olonkho, they say now, went for three whole days among the very best olonkhosuts. We have a tradition among the Yakuts for listening to olonkho. We don't listen day and night without stopping, but usually after work has finished, you sit down and listen to olonkho, after the midday meal, for example, and listen into the deep night, and it continues sometimes even until the morning. And so if it's three evenings and three nights, you could say that's three whole days."[11]

The intimate space for olonkho performance during the pre-Soviet years influenced the genre's conceptualization as an extended event, not to be consumed in one sitting. A performance for a small circle of family and friends, olonkho provided an adventure, a "virtual" family vacation into a legendary world. When I inquired about the nineteenth- and early twentieth-century attitudes toward the olonkhosuts themselves, Reshetnikov relayed this picture: "During those days, of course, there was no television, radio, things like that, publications—books, journals—so the Yakut people were entertained only by these olonkhos. Because an olonkhosut was highly prized, as a creator of beliefs and traditions of his people. At that time there was truly a community of listeners for olonkho. If the olonkhosut traveled from one family (or *balaghan*, as the Yakuts say) to another, all the people who lived in that *balaghan*—relatives—would gather to listen to the olonkhosut, as we were discussing, for the whole night. It was like a celebration, the appearance of an olonkhosut. Really great olonkhosuts were rare during that time as well. Lesser olonkhosuts of course lived during that time—now they are all being counted—so during that time you could say there were hundreds of olonkhosuts. They lived, created, and recounted their olonkhos. So for this reason, from that time to our generation, olonkhosuts and their creations were highly valued."[12]

Boris Mikhailov, an active proponent in Yakutia for olonkho revitalization, recounted the story of an unusual context for performance—a gold rush in the late nineteenth century at Bodaibo, located west of Yakutia's present-day boundaries. According to Mikhailov, olonkhosuts at Bodaibo joined the migrants in the gold fields, interacting with each other and even influencing one another's singing styles and storylines: "During the time of the gold rush in Bodaibo, which is now in the Irkutsk region, but used to be part of Yakutia, people rubbed shoulders with olonkhosuts then, because it was a time when everyone was working toward getting money by mining for gold. At that time, people came in from all the regions—the Viliuisk group of districts—came together, and from the central group of districts, and we all know now that at this place, in particular, people knew one another well and could hear the olonkhosuts from these regions. At this time there were these connections between these groups of districts. [. . .][13] Many olonkhosuts could exchange plots. [. . .] After all, the olonkhosut could catch it on the first hearing, and upon returning to his own region he would recount a plot taken from the Viliuisk region. [. . .] This mining for gold even happened before the revolution. We have a lot of material that describes these memories about Bodaibo where the various olonkhosuts were able to gather together."[14]

These olonkhosuts, probably for the first time in their lives, were performing for broader audiences than a small family context. This new space for olonkho performance not only allowed olonkhosuts to exchange their musical and verbal materials with one another but also supplied them with discriminating audiences, thereby encouraging the honing of their art.[15]

One olonkhosut's astonishing experiences have particularly captivated Mikhailov's attention. Innokentii Ivanovich Burnashev (Tong Suorun) started to perform as an olonkhosut during the pre-revolutionary, pre-Soviet period.[16] During the civil war immediately following the Communist Revolution, when

38   CHAPTER 2

he found himself on the wrong side of the winners, Burnashev's profession as an olonkhosut even led to his life being spared. Mikhailov told me about his own volume describing the story of this colorful individual: "In the book it explains how he became a professional [olonkhosut]. He traveled around a lot to different families that invited him. Of course, most of them were rich families. And of course, they could reward him. Because of this, he was able to be involved exclusively in the performance of olonkho and feed himself that way, and his family too. They gave him a lot. He died in 1946, and was about seventy years old at the time. So his best years of storytelling were at the end of the nineteenth century and the beginning of the twentieth.

"During the time of the civil war, he was sentenced twice to be shot, each time put up against the wall, waiting for the shot that would end his life. He was saved by olonkho, because the people, regardless of whether he was a bandit or Red Guard, understood that an olonkhosut was a unique kind of person. Because he carried within himself folk wisdom (the 'folk word' they call it), they knew it was shameful to kill someone like that, someone that held so much folk wisdom in him. So his storytelling art saved him from the threat of death."[17]

These personal, moving stories about outstanding olonkhosuts describe what may have been the apogee of the genre, a time when audiences eagerly awaited the arrival of the olonkhosuts and highly valued their performances. Valerii Kononov, a retired Sakha man who joined our field research team and drove us many miles over rough Yakutian roads, explained to me his understanding of olonkho performance practice during these peak, pre-revolutionary years. When I asked him for his personal opinion about the tradition, he replied, "I would say that olonkho is really our 'folk achievement.' . . . It used to be performed even when we didn't have concerts, or dramatic theater, cultural enlightenment work—we didn't have those things in the old times, so the people only listened to olonkho. When the olonkhosut came to visit, it was for sure the happiest moment of people's lives. And they would send messages around to people, 'Come on over tonight! The olonkhosut will begin to sing!' And the people of the *alaas* would gather in the *balaghan* and listen to olonkho from evening until morning. They would forget during those hours how difficult it was to live, and so on.

"It used to be that it was truly difficult to live in Yakutia. To live with that kind of cold—to fight that kind of freezing weather, and on top of that to take care of their herds—it was really difficult. So the people, when the olonkhosut would come, when he would sing, to perform, the people would forget themselves. The people would accept, spiritually, whatever was sung in that olonkho. The contents of the olonkho were mostly about our heroes. The people would listen from evening until morning, and they would forget all about sleep. They would even forget about their difficult life. In the morning they would all leave for their

EFFECTS OF CHANGE DURING THE SOVIET ERA 39

homes, to do their work. They would agree on a time to get back together again. When an olonkhosut came, the shortest time he would sing was three days. That was the shortest. He'd sing up until one week—seven days. It depended on the olonkhosut himself, how much he knew, what his level of ability was. The higher his ability, the more olonkhos he would know."[18] Representative of common understandings among Sakha people regarding olonkho performance practices during the pre-Soviet period, Kononov's description most likely represents a close approximation of historical reality for those years.

Olonkho in the Soviet period

In October 1917, with the tsar's family under house arrest, Lenin and the Bolsheviks seized power from the Provisional government (Service 2009, 59–62), sowing the seeds of the Soviet governmental apparatus in Russia. The effects of the 1917 October Revolution took time to reach Yakutia, and the bitter, drawn-out civil wars that followed the revolution in this far-flung province delayed the consolidation of Soviet power in Yakutia by several years compared to many other parts of Russia. The proclamation of the Yakut ASSR (Autonomous Soviet Socialist Republic) eventually occurred on April 27, 1922, with the ratification of the constitution of the USSR (the Soviet Union) following just seven months later, on December 31 (132–133).

One of the most significant changes for olonkho during this time period involved the transition from orality to literacy within the Sakha culture. Scholars of epic traditions have posited that the infringement of written literacy on an oral tradition moves audiences toward seeking entertainment and information from books rather than from the "living songs of men" (Lord 2000, 20). Alekseyev noted how societal preferences moved away from strictly oral performances to mediated and written versions of olonkho: "There used to be an environment during those times when everyone believed in [olonkho], and listened to it. That was replaced by everything that we have now—radio, television, and concerts, as well as the written form of olonkho. When everything [about olonkho] was well-known and published and people were just repeating what was already in print, it destroyed the world that existed in the olonkho."[19]

Naturally, these concepts of "literacy" and "orality" do not function as impermeable categories but stretch along a continuum, possibly even a multidimensional grid, reflecting the complexity of their interaction.[20] Over time, printed pages slowly replace oral traditions, thereby strongly affecting their transmission, performance practice, and often their viability.[21]

At the Institute of Humanitarian Research and Problems of the Minority Peoples of the North (IGI), Yuri Zhegusov and Dekabrina Vinokurova outlined for me

40   CHAPTER 2

some of their research on olonkho's history and reception.[22] Zhegusov reported that the lack of literacy before the formation of the Soviet Union provided a more conducive *sreda* (milieu) for an oral epic tradition like olonkho than does today's high literacy rate. When asked to elaborate, he said, "Between two and five percent of the [Sakha] people could read before the revolution. People interacted with one another orally. Olonkhosuts went from community to community and were in great demand. They didn't have books."

Later he said, "The language of that time was richer than it is now. Now there's so much Russian language influence. It was much different then. People spoke with imagery, and to listen to an olonkho took not only strength and energy on the part of the olonkhosut, but strength and energy on the part of the listeners. The listeners were ready to do this, to delve deep into that world. Now, people speculate things like, 'Soviet power came and ruined it all,' but the deal is that during the Soviet years, olonkho was put into written form."[23]

Sitting beside him, Vinokurova immediately added: "You know, philosophers say that the change to written format is the 'straight path to being forgotten!'"[24] These scholars' concern over the loss of traditional oral methods indicates that the issues surrounding olonkho's decline are more complex than the factor of Soviet repression alone.[25]

The Soviet policies on minority language and culture did at times favor the use of the Sakha language, but this support, dependent on the whims of changing power figures, never proved stable enough for long-term gains. The Russian Revolution of 1917 produced a multifaceted and somewhat contradictory effect on Sakha language use in Yakutia. Early Soviet policies supported the use of minority languages, encouraging their use in the public school system and other aspects of both public and private life, thereby resulting in increased Sakha language use. At the same time, prevailing attitudes minimized the value of orality and verbal arts, effecting a decreased use of the language over the long term. In 1938 the pendulum swung further, moving in the direction of universalizing the Russian language. Overtly touted as a means to unify all the Russian peoples in preparation for war with Germany, the drive toward Russification, and toward Russian literacy in particular, continued unabated after World War II (Balzer 2006, 582; Schiffman 2002). Some Sakha scholars think that this campaign negatively affected competency in the oral-verbal arts. Even Soviet-era anthropologists wrote that the Soviet ideal of full literacy would have a detrimental effect on the epic *sreda* necessary for olonkho to thrive. In his classic tome *Yakutia before Its Incorporation into the Russian State*, Okladnikov asserts: "writing and literacy [are] factors that could have had a corrupting influence on epic creativity, acted on it, changed its content, and wholly displaced epic works by more . . . literary models" (1970, 263–264).[26]

EFFECTS OF CHANGE DURING THE SOVIET ERA   41

Olonkho from the Revolution to World War II

Under Lenin, the earliest years of the Soviet period saw ideological support for the indigenous and national entities within the country's borders (Service 2009, 113–114). For example, in the 1920s, universities in Moscow and Leningrad produced the first professionally trained Russian ethnographers (Knight 2004). In her article on the Sakha round dance (*ohuokhai*), Susan Crate notes that from 1923 to 1928 the government supported a policy of "*korenizatsiia* (nativization), which was designed to support ethnic diversity and diminish Russian elements, as well as other policies that promoted local language, education, and culture. . . . Every republic passed *korenizatsiia* decrees, some specific to the ethnicity involved. In Sakha (Iakutia) the decree took the form of *Iakutizatsiia*" (2006, 168).

Within just a few years, these early Soviet policies supporting the diversity of Russian culture changed drastically. By 1928, Stalin had inaugurated the country's Great Transformation, an initiative aimed at wiping out all "backwardness" while attempting to "leap over centuries and catch up with Russia's perennial nemesis, the West" (Crate 2006, 168). This effort focused especially on the amalgamation into one Soviet people of the diverse cultures within the expansive USSR. Interestingly, during this same time period, folklorists and ethnographers at the Institute of Languages and Cultures intensified their scientific expeditions around Yakutia. As they collected folklore and other ethnographic material in the mid-1930s, they laid a foundation for the extensive ethnic research the state would request during the 1940s (Ignatieva et al. 2013, 13).

Soviet policy makers were suspicious of any artistic expressions not supportive of the atheistic views of the party. By embracing the spiritual dimension of reality inherent to a Sakha worldview, olonkho clearly clashed with this ideology (Leete 2005, 233; Peers 2013, 103). As a result, this tradition endured marginalization for most of the central Soviet government's years in power, even when other Sakha expressions of the arts received at least nominal support. One scholar of Soviet history wryly observes, "Communism, as a secular religion, was much more jealous than any sacred one" (Khazanov 1993, 185).[27]

Ignatieva and her colleagues have published some fascinating archival documents from this period. For example, they point to a 1939 article, "A Few Words on Olonkho," in which historian G. V. Popov contends that a recently performed olonkho contained "elements of religious opiate and the imprint of bourgeois ideology." In his mind, these ideas had nothing to do with true folk creativity. He suggested that stripping these harmful and completely unnecessary elements from olonkho would render the genre fit for forming the proper mindset of the "new Soviet person," complete with suitably communist, atheistic ideals (Ignatieva et al. 2013, 20–23).

42   CHAPTER 2

By Slobin's reckoning, three pillars supported the Soviet system of keeping music and musicians under control: (1) a bureaucracy of rules "offering the carrot of patronage and brandishing the stick of censorship" (1996, 3); (2) standardized formats and venues, including festivals, competitions, Houses of Culture, and music schools; and (3) official repertories (2–3). The festivalization of culture, used to control and limit cultural expression, also served to disseminate Soviet-approved ideologies such as modernism and atheism (Peers 2013).[28] Even today, although cultural politics now lean in favor of olonkho, the festivalization of culture continues as one of various remaining vestiges of the former Soviet top-down system.[29]

When asked his opinion of how Soviet atheistic policies affected olonkho, master olonkhosut Pyotr Reshetnikov responded with a potent warning regarding the dangers of ideological repression: "After Soviet power was put in place, olonkho was not congruent with the politics of the party and the Soviet government. If you study the history of politics, you yourself know that they opposed any kind of faith of the people: Russian Orthodox, Christian, or Yakut beliefs—these were all marginalized. Evil spirits, good spirits, devils, and shamans were opposed or denied. For this reason, the politics of Soviet power did not recognize all of this, but rather considered it to be charlatanism or something of the sort, not part of the creativity of the people. And so olonkho was marginalized and eventually almost completely forgotten.

"They even criticized olonkhosuts when they performed for the people. They even criticized our great Oyunsky! He was himself an olonkhosut, and he was the first to write out a really long Yakut olonkho—*Nurgun Botur the Swift*—which was considered a work of unique quality among olonkhosuts, and even among other kinds of writers. Even *this* person was criticized! But he endured all that and put olonkho onto a high plane. He led the Humanitarian Institute of Languages and Literature and was able to preserve olonkho, so we are grateful to Oyunsky—Platon Alekseyevich Sleptsov. That's the way it was at the beginning of the twentieth century—people started to forget olonkho, and after that, olonkhosuts completely disappeared."[30]

Additional accounts also convey the marginalization of olonkhosuts. With well-deserved pride, beloved olonkho performer Pyotr Tikhonov (fig. 2.3) told me about one of his predecessors: "My great-great-grandfather was an olonkhosut—on my mother's side. He used to gather olonkhosuts together. He was already an old person, and during the years of Soviet power he experienced repression for this [connection to olonkho]. . . . He is remembered, not as a person who was repressed, but because he was noticed by Tong Suorun—Burnashev; you've probably heard of him, the most famous olonkhosut in the Megino-Khangalaskii district—who got an interview with him . . . and he said that there were two epics he learned . . . from my great-great-grandfather. They were fair-minded in those days, and Tong Suorun said that he didn't create them himself. He later created some of his own works, but his foundation was my great-great-grandfather."

When I asked when the grandfather lived, Tikhonov replied, "He lived in ancient times, my great-great-grandfather did.[31] Probably in the thirties they took him away."

Surprised, I responded, "Took him away?"

"Yes, he was repressed."

Hoping for clarification, I continued, "They exiled him?"

Tikhonov responded quietly, "Yes, and he died there."[32]

Similar descriptions of marginalization and repression, while absent from Soviet-era historical literature, surfaced frequently in my conversations with respondents about their ancestors. Family members who had experienced such pressures found it difficult to work past their fear and perform with more freedom even during times when the oppression eased.

During the Soviet years, fear often inhibited people from naming the composers of ubiquitously sung Sakha songs. Instead, communities passed such songs off as anonymously composed "folk songs."[33] While these songs differed from those of olonkho in many ways, both types of music reminded people of the common heritage they shared. Their music united them with those who had gone before, connecting them with an expanded Sakha community extending over years of history and miles of geography.[34]

In the 1920s, the Sakha political club Sakha Kėskil played a large role in efforts to publish olonkhos (Larionova 2004, 43).[35] Soviet leaders considered such

Fig. 2.3. Pyotr Tikhonov, olonkhosut, in performance (June 20, 2009)

44   CHAPTER 2

olonkho supporters "backward" in orientation and suspected them of political motivations toward nationalism. As a result, olonkho enthusiasts began to feel pressure from Soviet power structures, and olonkho performance practice waned considerably.

Not only olonkhosuts and religious figures suffered under the Soviets; great writers and thinkers of all kinds were targeted. Since the works of indigenous authors had the potential to ignite "nationalist" sentiment, they came under special scrutiny. Beginning in the 1930s and continuing into the 1940s, Stalin's purges devastated the intelligentsia of Yakutia, incarcerating Sakha writers and scholars, along with millions of others, in gulags across Siberia (Cruikshank and Argounova 2000, 102; Knight 2004). Boris Mikhailov, drawing from his scholarly work on olonkho's history, described how these purges affected olonkhosuts and the writers who rendered olonkhos in literary forms. In particular, he focused on Platon Oyunsky—a member of the Sakha intelligentsia, a gifted poet, olonkhosut, and epic scholar, and the compiler of the written version of the well-loved olonkho *Nurgun Botur*:[36] "In the twentieth century, olonkho began to slowly but surely disappear during the Soviet period. During this period, people appeared who openly battled shamanism and the performing art of olonkho, believing that it was all part of 'the past' and that it didn't provide any benefit for modern humanity of that time. So they [olonkhosuts and shamans] were persecuted and sent to the camps. We have a lot of material demonstrating that olonkhosuts felt persecution.

"Platon Alekseyevich Oyunsky became a victim of this during the Soviet period. He himself built a kind of 'Soviet' life; he rebirthed Yakutia and helped it to achieve autonomy. He suffered for that in the camps. They arrested him, and he died in the camps. We don't know if he was killed by them, or if he just died—we don't even know where he was buried. He was an opponent of those who opposed the folk epos. He was listened to by a lot of people. Our people supported his opinions, believing that the things which were the creation of the people should not disappear into the past."[37]

Cruikshank and Argounova write about the close ties between this period's great Sakha writers and the olonkhosuts who influenced their lives. In exploring the interactions between memory and indigenous identity in the Tatta district, they report that Sakha people came to associate the histories of their great writers with the olonkhos they had transcribed and the olonkhosuts who had performed the tales. Although these Sakha writers were repressed and persecuted for crimes of "bourgeois nationalism," their service to olonkho later rendered them literary giants in Yakutia (2000, 109).

Sakha writers also suffered repression for their dedication to using their language. Since olonkho taps into the vast reservoir of archaic, poetically expressive Sakha speech, olonkhosuts shared the writers' passion to preserve this treasure trove of linguistic richness.[38] One of the most famous Sakha writers, Aleksei Kulakovskii, wrote a letter to Eduard Pekarskii describing olonkho's profound effect on him before he had gained proficiency in the Sakha language: "When I was a little boy, I used to sit 'under the mouth' of the teller [olonkhosut] throughout the night listening to his tales . . . this passion of mine very soon pushed me to learn my native language. Gradually, I started to understand the past, everyday life, and mainly the language" (Cruikshank and Argounova 2000, 109).[39]

Although he called Sakha his "native language," suggesting some level of proficiency, Kulakovskii's fascination with "sitting under the mouth" resulted in a desire to pursue a deeper mastery of the language. Much of the power of his and other Sakha writers' works lay in their skillful use of Sakha. This high level of competence, combined with an ardent love for the language, bound authors and olonkhosuts together in the minds of Sakha people.

During the early decades of the twentieth century, traditional solo olonkho performance practice expanded, producing a related form—collective performance (Tomskaia 2006, 103). These unstaged joint performances resembled readers' theater, with narrative and songs distributed among multiple performers. Agafia Zakharova, who at the time of our interview was the head of the Folklore Department at the Institute of Humanitarian Research (IGI), described some insights from their research on this development within olonkho: "Collective performance began in 1906, I think. Talented olonkhosuts gathered here in Yakutsk and did the first collective performance in the Clerks' Club. There was a famous olonkhosut—Pyotr Ammosovich Okhlopkov (Naara Suokh)—who came in from the Ust-Aldanskii district—it was easier for him that way—and they did a dramatized section from his olonkho. In that show, a lot of famous olonkhosuts participated. They divided the olonkho up by personages. It was quite interesting for people because they had great voices. . . . It was one of the first collective settings of its kind, but it is continuing to this day in folk theater and in kindergartens."[40]

By connecting those early collective performances to the current situation, Zakharova observed how even an old, established genre like olonkho can flex under stress. Group performances provided an ideal new setting for celebrating the "great voices"—the promise of multiple talented performers drew larger crowds, while the context offered olonkhosuts some relief from the difficult demands of traditional solo olonkho.

Performers started to specialize either as singers or as narrators; it took a rather remarkable performer to master both skills: "Of course, the most widely practiced performance was solo performance—song and recitative. But there came a time when there weren't any of the really great performers left—those who had both of those gifts in one person. Then 'pair singing' appeared, when one olonkhosut is a good storyteller, for example, but he's weak in singing[, . . . so] you begin

46   CHAPTER 2

to see 'separate' performers—good at singing, or good at recounting. In these cases, they perform in pairs. This began to happen in the first half of the twentieth century."[41] At least two factors drove the innovation: a lack of gifted olonkhosuts competent in all aspects of olonkho performance, and the performers' desire to keep the olonkho tradition alive. Rather than remain bound by centuries of tradition, the olonkho community flexed for purposes of survival. In the same way that deep roots and flexible branches allow a tall tree to weather a storm, the genre of olonkho proved able to bend with the winds of change without abandoning the foundation of centuries of epic creativity.

Soviet-era anthropological literature also describes the collective performance phenomenon, noting that even the advent of this more easily performed version did not halt the decline in the number of olonkhosuts and their performances: "Sometimes the poems would be declaimed by several storytellers together, who to some extent or other dramatized the story, dividing the main roles among themselves; one sang the role of the hero, another, the role of his adversary, while the third undertook the narrative part of the poem. The knowledge and narration of these poems was fast declining by the beginning of the 20th century, and there were fewer and fewer good storytellers of this kind; the collective singing of poems almost died out completely" (Tokarev and Gurvich 1964, 282).

The appearance of collective performance early in the twentieth century eventually led to the proliferation and development of another olonkho form, the fully staged theatrical setting. One of the early examples, *Tuiaaryma Kuo*, appeared in 1938, just one year after the creation of the first republic-wide House of Folk Culture (Ignatieva et al. 2013, 20). Other theatrical performances followed, but this form did not gain real popularity during the Soviet years. Ultimately, both theatrical settings and collective performances would resurface with the revitalization of olonkho after the end of the Soviet Union. Today these two forms exist alongside solo performances of the genre.

Olonkho during the 1940s and 1950s

The decline in olonkhosut numbers became a sharp concern for olonkho scholars in the 1940s. Statistics for olonkhosuts before the twentieth century had indicated there were hundreds of them, with "handfuls" in each *nasleg* (county), but by the 1940s the numbers had dropped to the lowest levels ever reported.[42] According to Zakharova, "In 1941, during the Great Patriotic War, there was a large expedition in which they counted approximately eighty olonkhosuts throughout Yakutia. They documented over three hundred olonkho plots that were known by olonkhosuts."[43] Folklorists and ethnomusicologists continued to document what remained, and olonkho gained intermittent support from the state during World War II.

EFFECTS OF CHANGE DURING THE SOVIET ERA   47

This "support" took several forms, all of which seemed calculated to benefit the state. For example, an initiative for creating a consolidated, synoptic olonkho text resulted in an olonkho performance competition calling for submissions from all over Yakutia. Of course, submissions had to include communist slogans in order for the credentials of those participating in the competition to be established as ideologically Soviet (Ignatieva et al. 2013, 26–29). In the end, the project folded—given such variety in the texts, a consolidated text stripped of any "religious opiate" and "bourgeois ideology" proved an impossible task. The collection of texts, on the other hand, inspired a period of productivity for folklorists, providing momentum that continued right through the war.

Boris Mikhailov, musing on this swing of the pendulum in the direction of support for olonkho, noted the less than sterling motivations for the changes in the Soviets' attitude toward the genre. As he poured me a cup of milky Sakha tea, he regaled me with a gripping account of the surprising twists and turns of olonkho politics during World War II: "Then all of a sudden the Great Patriotic War came in 1941, and at that time there was a revitalization of olonkho. The olonkhosuts were held up like a banner, because the plots of olonkho are basically about good and evil, and this idea was used in the battle against fascism to facilitate a rebirth among the people through olonkho.

"They even built a tank (Number 34) and named it '*Nurgun Botur*'! They gathered money from people living in Yakutia and gave it for the building of a tank. They built this tank somewhere in a war factory, named it '*Nurgun Botur the Swift*,' and sent it to serve in the war. That was the kind of rebirth it went through then. . . . Then they began to consider olonkhosuts to be 'writers.' They accepted a list of olonkhosuts into the USSR's Union of Soviet Writers, and all in one day, these olonkhosuts became 'writers.'[44] This was a Soviet idea—to give them recognition and consider them as being on the same level as writers so that they could create and write. So there was revitalization at that time."[45]

Romanova and Ignatieva (2012, 47–48) document the Soviet co-opting of Sakha cultural expressions during the mid-1940s, including this 1946 telegram to the party's district committees:

Last year individual collective farms opened Ysyakh by performing old anachronistic ceremonies comma various kinds of rituals of religious nature stop Such occurrences must not be permitted in upcoming Ysyakhs stop Ysyakhs must be organized as holiday of Soviet peasantry . . . stop We recommend Ysyakhs be opened with brief meeting comma speech by chairman of Soviet or collective farm stop At meeting organize report of production figures by collective farms comma readiness for hay harvest comma acceptance of written commitment to Comrade Stalin stop After meeting proceed to kumis drinking comma mass events stop Ysyakh sites need to be set up

48   CHAPTER 2

> for holiday colon posters slogans photo exhibits comma urging to work productively comma increase productivity of animal husbandry comma set about hay harvest in organized manner comma ensure tending of crops and so on stop Post boards with collective farms' work statistics in prominent place also board of top workers stop Submit results of Ysyakhs to oblast [regional] Communist Party by July first stop (Natsional'nyi arkhiv 5, 7)

Mikhailov also recounts a swing of the pendulum in the direction of disapproval: "But then 'those days' returned, and there were articles written against many famous writers, including our local ones, which said, 'We raise our fists and our swords against olonkho.'"[46] The state's effort to engage olonkhosuts and other Sakha leaders, including them in structures of prestige such as the Union of Writers, helped the Soviets gain the people's support during the war while still keeping the population under government control. In actual fact, Sakha writers censored their own work, fearing the repercussions of creating texts that did not adhere to state ideology.

The pendulum did not stop swinging. Anna Kulikova, writing on the ethno-cultural and ethnoreligious processes in Yakutia, summarizes the ideology of assimilation prevalent after the war: "The Soviet leadership affirmed an ideology of integration of all peoples of the USSR into a socialistic culture as well as integration into a 'new historical community' of Soviet peoples.[47] This was achieved by means of a liquidation of national regions, reorganization and transformation of national minorities into the language of Soviet republics, and also the closure of national schools" (Kulikova 2009, 98).[48] These persistent ideological pendulum swings, shifting from support of national language and culture to repression and back again, had a disastrous effect on many aspects of artistic and personal expression in Yakutia, including the performance practice of olonkho. The absence of stability fostered a culture of paranoia. Writers, performers, and other artists, expecting the worst, generally preferred to keep a low profile, even during apparently safe times. Ultimately, the state's pressure on national minority languages and other expressions of ethnic identity, combined with other globalizing factors, almost completely eliminated the traditional performance practice of olonkho.

The stories of two women born around the time of World War II inform this picture of a genre on the brink of disappearance. Maria Kononova and Ekaterina Chekhorduna both tell of olonkhosuts in their families. Chekhorduna recalls vivid early childhood memories of performances, while Kononova does not, demonstrating two types of experience of those closest to olonkho at the time.

Kononova's account parallels the experience of many who grew up hearing only *about* olonkho, without the opportunity to hear live performances: "When I was born, olonkho had long since disappeared. I never saw living olonkhosuts, and I only heard about them from my parents. They told me that on my mother's side, my grandfather had been—I guess you could say—a great olonkhosut. They called him 'Yrya Semyon.' *Yrya* means 'song'—'Singing Semyon,' so you can see they saw olonkho as song.

"This old man, my grandfather, would sing for three days and three nights in a row; he would gather people together for a performance. All the time my relative Proskovia would remember and describe to me what a great olonkhosut he was, and how well he sang. Proskovia . . . lived for a very long time, so she was the one who told me about it. My mother died very early. So I never heard from her that my grandfather had been an olonkhosut. But in my family, none of us sing [olonkho] because everything was forbidden, everything was forgotten about olonkho."[49]

Chekhorduna was more fortunate—her own father was an olonkhosut, giving her the rare chance at this point in history to experience live olonkho performances. Vividly remembering her father's performances for the family circle, she poignantly drew me into the world of the sights and sounds of an olonkho performance as experienced by a small child during the 1950s: "During that time, my father's health was not so good, but he sang olonkho. As a result, my mama told me, he was asked to perform olonkho during the holiday times. During the regular workdays there wasn't any opportunity to do that, but during the holidays he was asked to perform during the evenings.

"In those days we didn't have any telephones, no radio, and no electricity during my childhood. All that appeared later, when I was in the third, fourth, and fifth grades. [. . .] This was during the 1950s. All there was for entertainment was the olonkhosut. So people would hear the rumor: 'Pyotr Afanasevich is going to sing this evening!' And the guests would begin to arrive.

"My father sits before the fireplace, usually facing the east, and all of us sit around him—some seeing him from the front, some from the side, some even from the back. He crosses his legs, tips his head back just a little, closes his eyes, and begins his recitation. At first, as if from a long ways away . . . [*she begins to recount an olonkho in a "recitation" tone of voice, imitating what she remembers*] this is how the olonkho starts.

"At first he starts slow, a little at a time, then the tempo picks up. Because of this, every kind of vision begins to appear before my eyes. I was, after all, very little at the time, five, or maybe four, even. My mother has her arms around me, and I sit and I listen. I don't understand it, but his voice—the timbre, the tempo, how he goes slower, then more quickly, then into his upper register, then, 'Ha ha ha ha ha!'—like that—the singing of the demons, then the [*eh-he, oh-ho*] singing of the *bogatyrs*, solid-like . . . then the song of the *udaghana* (female shaman) [*dje-bo-o-o*] . . . then the crying song of the girl . . . and more singing of the girl demons—this is the 'theater of one actor.'

50   CHAPTER 2

"It seems to me, in my memories, that he didn't gesticulate a lot—he just sits still, not moving, and only with his voice, his voice . . . that is what stays in my memory. Now you see olonkhosuts who perform with all these techniques—I don't enjoy that so much. Because my father would just sit, and although he'd do this [*turns her head*], he didn't do any other kinds of movements. It was all done with his voice."[50]

Pyotr Reshetnikov also recounted memories from the 1940s and 1950s. During one of our conversations, the master olonkhosut reflected on the Soviets' fleeting recognition of olonkho in the 1950s, when he was in his twenties: "One cannot say that olonkho was completely forgotten, because olonkho is the foundation of the literature of the Yakut people. Olonkho tells, in very artistic form and with deep meaning, the life and the struggle of the Yakut people, and not only of the Yakut people, but the people of the whole world. So for that reason, some parts of olonkho were recognized by the Soviet powers. For that reason, olonkho was set as a dramatic production in the theater. First, *Nurgun Botur* was set as a theatrical piece in 1957, in Moscow, of all places. . . . But in general, as a great work of art, olonkho was marginalized."[51]

For the Sakha, the occasional symbolic tokens of Soviet support for indigenous arts, at least in concertized versions, did not completely counterbalance their treatment as a marginalized minority. While an affirmation such as *Nurgun Botur*'s theatrical staging in Moscow gave olonkho more visibility, that visibility went to a form of olonkho fundamentally different from the solo version generally performed in Yakutia. Other genres experienced similar pressures—state sponsorship, directly linked to control, often resulted in the transformation of traditional solo forms into larger staged or concertized versions (Rice, Porter, and Goertzen 2000).

When I met with Eduard Alekseyev and Anna Larionova in 2010 (fig. 2.4), they discussed some of the implications of moving olonkho performances from intimate family spaces to public spaces such as the concert stages of large towns and cities. They felt that this shift in performance venue radically changed the reception of olonkho's improvisatory dimension. In fact, they assert that people forgot what defined the traditional, emergent art of olonkho and could no longer tell the difference between a memorized performance and the improvisatory art of a master olonkhosut. As Alekseyev noted, "It used to be, when there was just self-styled performance, the concert versions of olonkho, they thought that these were 'true performances'—short sections of olonkho, memorized and not created. They thought that was the real thing."

Larionova added, "When I was really little and lived in the village [at the end of the 1950s], I remember my father took me to hear performers. . . . When we moved to the city, I only heard it on the radio and on TV or onstage. And the stage performances were very short—just one song. By the seventies and eighties, people thought that this was the real olonkho."[52]

Fig. 2.4. Eduard Alekseyev and Anna Larionova with the author, near Boston (2010)

Although Soviet policy during the 1940s and 1950s supported some artistic activity, the Soviets' predilection for control allowed only concertized expressions. Performances of olonkho were drastically condensed into short sections of song for the concert stage, and the content had to be endorsed in advance. In this way indigenous arts, although ostensibly supported by the government, could no longer effectively transmit worldviews and values unapproved by the censors.[53] In addition, because olonkho concerts now featured primarily short songs, audiences were less aware of the differences between an olonkho tale and the shorter genres of the *diėrėtii* style, such as *toyuk* (exalted or praise songs) and *algys* (blessing songs).

The suppression of traditional uncondensed performances stemmed from the Soviets' fear of allowing the Sakha national identity to become too strong. As in earlier times of repression, activities or ideas that tapped into Sakha identity were interpreted as manifestations of "bourgeois nationalism" (Cruikshank and Argounova 2000, 102). These restrictions on "collective self-images" (Daughtry 2006, 243) arose from the Soviets' concern that a strong awareness of Sakha identity would threaten communist ideologies. If Sakha people were to tap into a sense of belonging that transcended the Soviet ideal of a "brotherhood of nations," the resulting community might create a competing set of heroes and other gods.[54]

Rather than attempt the nearly impossible feat of preventing people from creating at all, the Soviets chose the easier route of censoring tangible products like song lyrics, poetry, sermons, and books. Olonkhosuts faced the delicate challenge of navigating an oppressive system of censors while balancing two competing desires: a desire to tell the authentic olonkho stories, without a communist overlay, contrasted with a desire for state recognition of this genre that so powerfully expressed Sakha views and aspirations. Stripping their art of complex and socially embedded understandings of the world proved impractical, at best—epic traditions like olonkho employ a unique combination of "performance, poetics, politics, and power" (Buchanan 2014, 6), elements not easily untangled.

52   CHAPTER 2

Clever Sakha olonkhosuts responded by adapting their olonkhos and including communist themes. As a reward, they received permission to perform, sometimes even securing a prominent performance opportunity. Alekseyev recounted a humorous story of how Sakha olonkhosuts dealt with this reality: "In my book *Folklore in the Context of Modern Culture* there is a section of a chapter . . . [that] talks about the first wave of anything, how it is often not the real thing.[55] For example, at the end of the war, and even before then—the 1930s—there was a renewed interest in olonkho. It was connected to the 'personality cult'—the need for heroes, the bombastic, and so on.

"[For example], they decided to send an olonkhosut to Moscow during that time, and there were two candidates. Which do you think went? The good one or the worse one? It wasn't the best olonkhosut who went. He was too smart for that. He understood that it was dangerous. So he deliberately sang an olonkho in which there were ideologically dangerous words, words that would not pass the censors. [. . .] So of course, they set him aside. Of course, he was the 'real thing'—a true olonkhosut.

"So the fellow that went sang things like 'Glory to Great Lenin' and 'The Day of Great Victory,' things like that. The true olonkhosut ended up going as a singer of praise songs, but not as an olonkhosut, because he didn't have the 'right plots' to his olonkho. But the one that recounted the plots that resonated with that epoch, that one got to go. This is a rule that always seems to happen. Who gets recorded on recordings? The people who are the best? Or the ones who are right at hand? And who are easy to catch."[56]

The marginalization of olonkho during much of the Soviet period did not eliminate the desire for acknowledgment of the Sakha epic tradition as a masterpiece of oral poetic and musical art. That dream would be latent for decades, reemerging only after the dissolution of the Soviet Union, when a few Sakha scholars seized the opportunity to tap into UNESCO's Masterpiece program and gain olonkho a spot on the world stage. In the meantime, olonkho descended rapidly, from enjoying its brief spurt of state support during World War II to becoming virtually dormant for almost half a century.

Olonkho from the 1960s through the 1980s

The decline in Sakha cultural expressions continued throughout the 1960s and 1970s. Ethnomusicologist Margarita Mazo, who lived elsewhere in the Soviet Union, observed that the pressures of the Brezhnev years resulted in "no stagnation in the inner spiritual and artistic creativity during the 1960s and 1970s.[57] If anything, these aspects of societal life grew creatively intense under political pressure, presaging dramatic social changes" (1996, 272). Minority groups such as the Sakha, however, experienced exceptional challenges, struggling to

EFFECTS OF CHANGE DURING THE SOVIET ERA   53

keep even their language alive during those decades. Argounova reports that the state drastically curtailed the number of Sakha-language schools and preschool educational institutions while also requiring all Sakha schools, beginning in the seventh grade, to teach only in Russian (1992, 75).

Soviet ethnographers Tokarev and Gurvich, reflecting the official state position of support for cultural artistic expressions, wrote a state-approved, sanguine account of the state of olonkho performance in the early 1960s:

> Following the Socialist Revolution, profound changes occurred in the oral folklore of the Yakut people. Many genres of the traditional folklore, such as shaman spells and chants, fell into disuse, while others continued on in a completely different form (singing at the *ysyakh-kumys* festival.) The heroic tales—olonkho—have remained the favorite form of oral folklore; they are frequently sung on the radio and at club concerts, and are included in other performances. The talented narrators of these epics, or olonkhosuts, are very popular among Soviet audiences. Many of them are members of the Union of Soviet Writers. There are now more than 400 such storytellers on the registers. (1964, 302)

This Soviet-era portrayal gives a rosier overall impression than is warranted, especially in light of the fact that the state tolerated only those cultural expressions that were performed in controlled contexts and endorsed by the censors. In addition, descriptors such as "frequently sung" and "very popular," when compared with the personal testimonies of my respondents, appear hyperbolic.

By this point the state had realized the danger of marginalizing artistic expressions, especially of minority peoples. Recognizing the political importance of demonstrating controlled support for indigenous arts, the state showed approbation for the folklorized artistic expressions of its minorities while keeping religious expression, unacceptable worldviews, and competing forms of community from becoming officially recognized. It achieved these objectives, in part, by creating the Union of Soviet Writers, which limited artistic freedom and required participation in the "socialist construction" of the Soviet agenda (Eaton 2002). Another method of control relied on the "fear-driven self-censorship that made artists commit their work to oblivion before it was ever submitted to a censor or audience of any sort. The pervasiveness of self-censorship and the harnessing of art to state service makes it impossible to know all the treasures that were sacrificed by those who could say, with Mayakovsky, 'I have stepped on the throat of my own song'" (xxi–xxii).

All the same, a few living olonkhosuts continued to perform their improvisatory and masterful art during those days. Roman Petrovich Alekseyev (1900–1977) stands out because of his family's dedicated efforts to document and publish his work. In what the family described as a "heroic" task, his daughter, Akulina Romanovna Alekseyeva, coordinated the documentation of his orally performed olonkho texts. Simultaneously raising her own six children, working as a dorm mother in a boarding school housing one hundred more, and hosting dozens of visitors, she also managed to engage and organize the whole family, along with some of their guests, in transcribing the texts of her father's olonkhos and other songs (see fig. 2.5).[58] Their accomplishments include three volumes preserving Roman Alekseyev's remarkable 50,000-line *Ala Tuigun* epic, the story of three generations of *bogatyrs* (Illarionov 2013).

While in his hometown of Borogontsy in 2009, I met with three of Alekseyev's descendants. Our conversation underscored the importance of documenting olonkhos by masters like Alekseyev (fig. 2.5). The interview also provided insights into the experiences of olonkhosuts during the postwar years. Alekseyev's granddaughter Liubov Shelkovnikova reminisced about the attitudes toward olonkho during this time: "To say that no one did olonkho during the Soviet period would not be correct. Because we know that people came to visit our grandfather during that time; a few people every year, and they were interested in him. This means that those who were specially working in the area of folklore, they always were interested, and they always did all they could to make sure that the olonkho of the Yakut people, that in general the epos and the folklore of the Yakut people, would be preserved and would continue.

"The mass [staged] performances, like for Ysyakh and for large gatherings of people—of course there was nothing like that during that time. But all the same, those who valued olonkho, they always were involved in these things, always. So that is why it was preserved. And now, of course, it has become more for the masses, for all the people. That's the main difference."

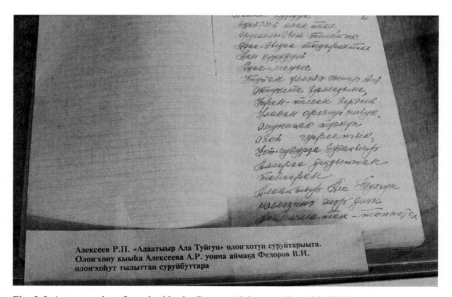

Fig. 2.5. A manuscript of an olonkho by Roman Alekseyev (June 20, 2009)

By commenting on the lack of mass staged performances in the past and the more recent changes toward olonkho performances for the masses, Shelkovnikova touches on two aspects of olonkho that hid the genre from the public eye in the decades before the collapse of the Soviet Union. First, during those years, olonkho only rarely appeared on public stages, and staged events would certainly not have occurred at large gatherings that celebrated Sakha identity, such as the Ysyakh summer festival. Second, the small band of remaining olonkhosuts could not cover much territory to provide home-based performances. As a result, they performed mostly in their own areas, and only the most intrepid researchers would brave the few badly maintained roads to travel to one of those locations in order to experience a performance in a traditional family context. These researchers' forays into the field, aptly termed *ekspeditsii* (expeditions) in Russian, constituted rustic adventures, to say the least—not the sort of journeys attempted by ordinary people.

Shelkovnikova's aunt Anna Andreyeva underscored the lack of opportunity for Sakha people to experience their indigenous arts during the years before the 1990s: "When we gained sovereignty, [we heard] all kinds of folk songs and the like, even the use of *khomus*, which wasn't [seen] during that time. . . ."[59] We

Fig. 2.6. Portrait of Roman Alekseyev in Borogontsy, Yakutia (June 20, 2009).

56   CHAPTER 2

didn't know anything during that time—how to sing, how to dance *ohuokhai*, we didn't even know how to say *chabyrgakh* [tongue-twisters]! Because they didn't teach us."[60] These kinds of conversations gave me a glimpse of the Sakha world before the freedoms of the 1990s, a world with few public expressions of Sakha music and arts. Only a few fortunate people like Roman Alekseyev's relatives and Ekaterina Chekhorduna retained treasured memories of family performances.

Gavriil Kolesov

In addition to the few masters like Roman Alekseyev who still performed for family gatherings in the 1960s and 1970s, another performer stands out as the iconic olonkhosut in the memories of many Sakha people. They heard this performer not in live performances but on the radio, something that was present in almost every Sakha home. The Soviets made sure that radio was accessible to all, although they maintained strict control of broadcast content. During my field interviews with Sakha people from all walks of life and levels of understanding of olonkho, they immediately mentioned Gavriil Kolesov whenever I asked where they had heard about the tradition.

Gavriil Kolesov (1932–1997) gained recognition as the featured performer on the recording of the best-known olonkho of the twentieth century, *Nurgun Botur the Swift*.[61] His recorded performance stretched to more than twenty-eight hours, including close to nineteen hours of singing and about nine hours of recitative-like narration (Larionova 2004, 54). In the late 1990s, when I first commenced my study of Sakha music, a pensioner in our church gave me the full set—a one-inch stack of vinyl records—telling me solemnly, "If you want to understand Sakha music, you need to listen to these."[62] I treasured his gift, and his comment helped me understand how reverently people viewed this recording.[63]

Sakha recollections of hearing Kolesov's performance reach back to the late 1960s, testifying to the power of one recording in influencing a whole generation of listeners. Olonkho researcher Dekabrina Vinokurova sat down with me one afternoon in December 2011 and recalled memories of her own youth: "Olonkho was really played a lot on the radio. They played Kolesov constantly. I still listen to radio today. It is my habit to do this; I can't live without the radio. I remember as a child that olonkho was heard a lot on the radio. My grandmother listened to it. And when we traveled to the Gorny district, the older generation said that they heard it a lot on the radio, through those records that were played. So don't ever say that it wasn't heard during the Soviet years, because it really was. It's a different issue, of course, when you talk about the higher level of government, but through mass media [at the republic level] it was played. . . . This was during the seventies and the sixties. Especially during the seventies it was really spreading, because the vinyl records were just beginning to really be used during those years."[64]

EFFECTS OF CHANGE DURING THE SOVIET ERA   57

Vinokurova's memories underscore Kolesov's crucial role in maintaining appreciative olonkho audiences through the mediated means of a recording. Even without access to the set of vinyl records, Sakha people could listen to Kolesov's performance via the radio. In cities and towns, families did not even need to buy a radio, since the homes built by the communist government all included radios installed in the kitchen walls. The state likely found Kolesov's recorded performance to be a convenient way to satisfy people's hunger for Sakha traditional music through a predictable, controllable, mediated form with fixed content. Live olonkho performances, with dynamic content emerging in the moment of performance, remained extremely rare during those decades.

Over the years leading up to the 1990s, a broad range of Sakha people enjoyed the Kolesov recordings, from scholars like Vinokurova to various kinds of musicians and even budding olonkho performers whose own careers would bloom in the decades following the 1990s. Although Elena Kugdanova-Egorova hardly considers herself a fan of olonkho in general, this professional musician and teacher has positive memories about Kolesov during these years: "I like the olonkho performances of Gavriil Kolesov. He himself is a *samarodok* [literally "gold nugget," but in this context refers to the self-taught nature of his talent].[65] He laid the foundation. I like his kind of performance."[66] When asked why she appreciated his style in particular, she responded, "Because it is 'classical' olonkho. [. . .] First, it is accessible, right? And second, in the way it is done correctly. You can learn a lot from him about how to do it right. I am hooked on his manner. Also, I knew him personally. He was simply a good teacher."[67] For Kugdanova-Egorova, the personal connection to Kolesov gave her a more positive view of olonkho, even if the genre never became one of her favorites.

I discovered yet another fan of Gavriil Kolesov in Maria Stepanova, an elderly Sakha woman who served as one of my hosts and tour guides at the 2010 summer Ysyakh of Olonkho festival in Berdigestyakh. When I asked her if she had heard olonkho in her childhood, she could not recall ever hearing a live performance during those years. On the other hand, she eagerly told me how Gavriil Kolesov had played a part in fostering her enthusiasm for olonkho. For Stepanova, just as for many others, the Kolesov recordings led to a lifetime of olonkho appreciation, thereby moderating the decline of the epic *sreda* in Yakutia.

Sakha musician Irina Aksyonova sometimes sings traditional genres such as *toyuk* and *ohuokhai* at church and family gatherings. She recounted the following memories of her parents' recordings of Kolesov: "We heard it on a record. In my time, there were already no olonkhosuts in our village. So I heard it on a record, Gavriil Kolesov's performance. . . . Everyone bought those records. My people didn't have any relationship with the arts whatsoever, other than Grandpa, who was an amateur. But we always bought records."[68]

Sakha people's memories of Kolesov and his recordings should be understood in the context of a severe attenuation in opportunities for hearing traditional music of any kind, especially olonkho. Dora Gerasimova and Maria Kononova, two of my traveling companions during field research in 2010, reminisced about the level of Russian language domination in the areas of language and music. For example, during the 1960s and 1970s, the state broadcast only fifteen minutes of content per day in the Sakha language. In schools, Sakha language and literature studies were offered only as special subjects, while Pioneer songs and dances displaced Sakha song genres like *toyuk*, *ohuokhai*, and olonkho.[69]

The Kolesov recordings played an essential role in the career of a popular olonkho performer in Yakutia today, Pyotr Tikhonov: "My favorite guru was Gavriil Gavriilovich Kolesov. It was through his work that I heard about this song called the epos of olonkho. Despite the prohibitions, despite the lack of attention, we always had these kinds of people. I was nineteen years old when I first heard his song. . . . I listened to it and learned the words by heart. At that time, there was no special program for this. There was no attention for this kind of thing."[70] Although Tikhonov says he performs from memory, and does not create his own olonkhos, many people seem to find his performances very engaging—he often travels as an olonkhosut, visiting towns and villages around Yakutia to teach children olonkho and to perform at competitions and various other events.

I interacted via email and Skype with another performer of olonkho, Semyon Chernogradskii, after my students and I had studied a video recording of his role as olonkhosut in a theatrical presentation of *Müljü Böghö* (see fig. 2.7).[71] Chernogradskii's story about becoming an olonkho performer weaves together many of

Fig. 2.7. Semyon Chernogradskii at the 3rd Ysyakh of Olonkho in Borogontsy (2009). Photo by Maria Vasilyeva (www.ysia.ru). Used by permission.

EFFECTS OF CHANGE DURING THE SOVIET ERA   59

the themes of this research: written versions of olonkho stories, Kolesov's voice on the *Nurgun Botur* records, and practicing in secret until encouraging friends discovered his talent. Born in 1948, he recalls his encounters with olonkho as a young boy: "My childhood was spent in a yurt with a dirt floor three kilometers from the village. . . . I used to walk to school on foot. . . . On the side of the road two kilometers from the school, I noticed a piece of book protruding from the snow. It was a book of olonkho, *Büdürüybėt [Sure-Footed] Müljü Böghö*, by Dmitrii Govorov—written in the old-style Sakha script, which used Latin letters rather than Cyrillic.[72]

"The next year, when I was in fourth grade . . . Marta Borisova, a middle-aged woman who was literate and knew the Latin alphabet, helped us take turns reading olonkho by candlelight. So it was in 1959 that I encountered the original olonkho, *Müljü Böghö*, for the first time. After ten years, the record set of the olonkho *Nurgun Botur* became available for purchase, performed by the honored artist of Yakutia Gavriil Kolesov. When my parents were not at home, I sang all the songs of this olonkho. I believe I was successfully imitating the characters, but no one knew about it.

"Fifty years later, in 2009, the Third Republic-wide Ysyakh of Olonkho was hosted by Borogontsy, the administrative center of the Ust-Aldanskii district. There were no old performers of olonkho left, so the artistic advisor of the Ust-Aldanskii House of Culture, Elizaveta Danilova, organized a three-stage competition for olonkho performers.[73] She was very insistent that I participate in this competition, for which I am deeply grateful. At the competition, I came out the winner, and was entrusted with executing the role of narrator/singer for this olonkho that was to be performed at the national [republic-wide] level. Together with theater artists and the Yakutsk State Circus, we performed at the opening ceremony.

"After the performance, the highly respected professor and olonkho scholar Vasilii Vasilievich Illarionov shook my hand and congratulated me, inspiring me to continue performing and competing successfully as an olonkhosut. It was symbolic that this olonkho, *Müljü Böghö*, was chosen by the organizers. I was sixty years old and I was born in 1948, one hundred years after the birth of this olonkho's author, Dmitrii Govorov."[74]

Chernogradskii's narrative and other stories recounted to me by respondents indicate that the accessibility of Kolesov's recording of *Nurgun Botur* somewhat ameliorated olonkho's continued decline during the 1960s, 1970s, and 1980s. Apart from a few relatives of olonkhosuts who could participate in traditional family performances, most people heard olonkho only through radio and the Kolesov records. These mediated means kept the memory of olonkho alive, if only tenuously.

Olonkhosuts at the end of the Soviet period

By the end of the Soviet period, the olonkho tradition had almost completely vanished. Dekabrina Vinokurova contributes crucial information regarding general levels of knowledge about olonkho in the last decades before the fall of the Soviet Union: "When I was preparing the documents for UNESCO, I was using a questionnaire in the Gorny district, and talking with some young people. They were very interested in why we were 'all of a sudden' talking about olonkho. I asked them if they remembered any olonkhosut who would travel around the villages and perform (I have this in my questionnaire). And I was talking to the policemen at the police station, and they said, 'Oi, we had someone like that here! When we went fishing and hunting, he always went with us. It was kind of like he was always underfoot.' I asked them if they could even remember his last name, and they said, 'Ah, *nyet*! He was an old man.' They said he would sing and sing, and then they would share [the catch] with him, and in that way he would provide for himself. This was during the seventies and eighties. . . . There were these lone performers who continued to spread olonkho during those days. It wasn't completely as if it died out all at once; there were these occasional appearances like this. . . . but the *sreda*, the community of listeners, really did disappear completely."[75]

These kinds of memories bring to light the small number of olonkhosuts who still performed into the 1980s despite the virtual lack of an epic *sreda* or formal performance opportunities. One of those few remaining olonkhosuts, Semyon Gregorevich Alekseyev, used the Sakha pseudonym "Uustarabys."[76] His grandson Nikolai Alekseyev (seen in fig. 2.8) hosted our research team during the 2010

Fig. 2.8. Nikolai Alekseyev, olonkhosut, in Mytakh, Yakutia (June 20, 2010)

olonkho festival in the town of Berdigestyakh, in the Gorny district. Uustarabys had raised Nikolai and passed along to him the art of olonkho. Eager to hear about the transmission process between grandfather and grandson, I asked Nikolai about his experiences living with the famous olonkhosut.

He recalled his early memories: "Well, my grandfather worked as a carpenter, and built homes, worked. He hunted and fished, using nets under the ice in winter. When people would gather there, he would start to sing the songs of olonkho, and when I was little, I asked him, 'How do you know this long story by heart?' He told me, 'You just have to know the names of the *bogatyrs*. The rest goes by itself!' were his words. And at the end of the eighties, some scholars came and began to teach about olonkho, what it is, and how many there are. . . . I asked my grandfather how he learned the olonkhos. He listened to it from his childhood. And he parodied it, as a joke or whatever, and then when he was in his older years, he himself started to perform."

Not sure exactly what he meant by "older," I probed: "Older years?"

"Sixty years old or something like that. I don't know exactly. When I was in the fifth or sixth grade, somewhere in the seventies or maybe 1980, he already sang olonkho. He had a big *mungkha* [fishing net] for under-ice fishing, for big *karasei* [fish]. And he also sang then, people say. I never went with him to fish under the ice. Others went, my brothers went fishing with him, but I was the youngest, so they left me behind. They said, 'You'll freeze!'"

When I asked him how he began to sing olonkho, Alekseyev replied, "As a joke, I parodied him. When I was growing up—at school, you know—at after-school concerts, I participated, and I sang olonkho. But only new ones."

"New plots?"

"Yes, new ones," he said. "I would take them from songs, then other things, as a joke. It's okay to try, right? Jokingly—it was simply a joke!" He suddenly launched into an impromptu olonkho tale, parodying the story of *Nurgun Botur* with anachronisms like pistols and motorcycles.

Intrigued by the creativity and playfulness of his tale, I remarked, "This is very interesting! It's especially interesting that parody is important, that it plays a big role in this for you." When I concluded that "the person parodies, then becomes more experienced," Alekseyev affirmed my observation.

"My grandfather also parodied," he noted. "He parodied all kinds of people. He would even parody how they spoke. So probably from my earliest years, I learned this from him. So I saw it, and parodied it. When my parents got drunk and spoke badly, I parodied it; my father, my grandfather, my mother, my brothers. Then even others—from concerts and on TV, I would parody famous people in our village. I'd even parody my friends. How do they say it? I mocked them. Like that."[77]

As we continued our conversation, Alekseyev professed a recent change of heart, saying that he no longer mocks people, but his storytelling style remains

62   CHAPTER 2

rooted in this playful, improvisatory approach. Over many years of interactions with Sakha friends, I have often observed them use humor for purposes of nuancing commentary on social behavior or addressing and perhaps even solving disagreements. In this light, the ability to recount an olonkho tale in a joking manner seems like a rare gift, an unusual form of emergent, creative, and improvisatory performance that taps deeply into a broader cultural value. Researchers rarely discuss this performance style, although Ekaterina Chekhorduna, both in conversation with me and in her subsequent book (2014), mentioned olonkhosuts who habitually employed this approach.[78]

Pyotr Reshetnikov began to improvise in the olonkho style during the late 1980s. Although he had heard many olonkho performances as a child, prior to retirement he had never tried his hand at singing olonkho himself. In an amusing story, Reshetnikov recounted the attitudes toward olonkho during the 1980s. Despite the genre's marginalization, its status as a Sakha art gave him adequate opportunity to learn that he had the gift.

"It was kind of by happenstance," he began. "In my early years I only sang *toyuk*; I didn't do olonkho at all. Around here they usually have festivals of amateur music-making between the counties. And one time, when I was already retired and elderly, I was invited by the cultural workers to come to the House of Culture. They said, 'Pyotr Egorovich, you sing *toyuk* really well. Maybe you can recount an olonkho. We are including a passage from an olonkho in the concert program.'

"But I told them, 'Olonkho is long; it is impossible to use it in a concert.' They said, 'Without some olonkho, we'll get points deducted.'" Reshetnikov laughs, "So that is how they let me onstage for the first time! So I thought and thought, and then began to recount my first olonkho. But within five or six or ten minutes, they came up to me and said, 'Pyotr Egorovich, we wanted it fast! Old man, you are wasting a bunch of our concert time!' And they chased me from the stage! It was then that I first had the thought, 'I guess I really do have the ability to recount an olonkho improvisationally.'"[79]

Another key milestone for olonkho in the 1980s came with the initiation of a gargantuan collaborative work, a multivolume series titled Monuments of Folklore of the Peoples of Siberia and the Far East. Two volumes, published in the 1990s with accompanying recordings of example songs and full textual translations into Russian, featured the topic of olonkho.[80] These volumes also included notational, historical, and musicological commentary, providing a rich resource in folklore studies for future generations of students, teachers, performers, and olonkho lovers.[81]

Anna Larionova commented on the importance of the Monuments series in preparing the way for the UNESCO Masterpiece application: "Olonkho began to be forgotten. . . . If it had not been for UNESCO, who knows what would have happened to olonkho. Of course, in my opinion, there was a wave of interest in folklore when they started to work on the Monuments series. Folklorists began to travel to the regions and show interest in the carriers of these traditions, and that in turn created a wave of reaction in people, and it began to live again. This was in the eighties—from 1984 to 1986. So, slowly but surely, interest began to rise."[82] This work done by scholars at research institutions in preparation for the publication of the Monuments series provided a solid foundation for the later submission of the UNESCO Masterpiece application.

As the period of Soviet power drew to a close, Sakha cultural revitalization commenced in earnest. At the end of the 1980s and the beginning of the 1990s, Yakutia gained a new name—the Republic of Sakha—and hopes for a change in the relationship between the Sakha Republic and the Center grew stronger. Unfortunately, the damage from the more than five decades of marginalization of olonkho, its singers, its worldview, and its values would take time to reverse. From 1994 to 2004, when I spent large amounts of time in Yakutia as a careful observer of music and culture, I never had the opportunity to "sit under the mouth." Instead, I would experience olonkho in live performance only after the genre was awarded Masterpiece status by UNESCO in 2005.

As I began to uncover the gripping story of how Yakutia leveraged UNESCO's Masterpiece awards to bring international recognition not only to olonkho but to the Sakha people as well, I began to appreciate more deeply their passion for revitalizing the genre. The story that follows demonstrates tenacity and adroit maneuvers within an energetic collective enterprise that competed successfully against other regions of the Russian Federation for the coveted prize: inscription on UNESCO's list of "Masterpieces of the Oral and Intangible Heritage of Humanity."

CHAPTER 3

ESTEEM FOR A MASTERPIECE

The Quest for Recognition

> Change is intrinsic to culture, and measures intended to preserve,
> conserve, safeguard, and sustain particular cultural practices are
> caught between freezing the practice and addressing the inherently
> processual nature of culture.
> —Barbara Kirshenblatt-Gimblett, "Intangible Heritage as Metacultural
>   Production"

When the Soviet Union dissolved, the political climate for supporting olonkho revitalization saw a season of thriving and growth. At the same time, Yakutia's demographics began to change. As Russians fled the North for warmer climes in western Russia, the overall number of people in the republic declined, but the percentage of Sakha people in Yakutia increased. Census results show that the Russian population in Yakutia dropped from 50 percent in 1989 to less than 38 percent in 2010.[1] During the same period, the Sakha population rose from 33 percent to almost 50 percent. These statistics clearly show that the percentages of Sakha and Russian people in Yakutia exchanged places in only two decades. The next largest non-Sakha group, Ukrainians, also mirrored this outward migration trend, dropping from 7 percent to just over 2 percent between 1989 and 2010.

Now a minority in the Sakha Republic, those who self-identify as ethnically Russian feel the impact of their decreased numbers. In December 2011, a Russian friend complained bitterly to me about the demands she faced at work from the Sakha majority. She felt pressure to celebrate Sakha ethnic holidays with coworkers on weekends and to wear Sakha jewelry "for solidarity's sake"—demands she was stubbornly resisting.[2]

The stirrings of cultural revitalization

Despite the economic difficulties during perestroika and the post-Soviet years of the 1990s, the rebirth of the Sakha language and Sakha cultural expressions gathered momentum. I asked Maria Kononova, a key Sakha collaborator during

ESTEEM FOR A MASTERPIECE   65

my fieldwork in the summers of 2009 and 2010, about her memories of olonkho during those transitional years. She reminisced, "After 1985, perestroika started in Russia. And little by little, things that had been forgotten were restored. . . . In the beginning of the rebirth period, in cultural events, they began with short olonkhos. But now olonkho has its own strength and its own propagation. You could say that people even come from faraway countries to study our olonkho!" Looking pointedly at me, she laughed, then affirmed, "To study it and look at it and put it in the realm of science, this is a very praiseworthy thing."[3]

Olonkho promoter and researcher Boris Mikhailov remembers the joy he felt in the newfound freedom for cultural renewal in Yakutia during Yeltsin's rule: "Thanks to Boris Nikolaevich Yeltsin, who gave us freedom, this kind of revitalization happened. What did he say? 'Take as much water as your bridge can handle.' It was that kind of time; there really was revitalization then! They were such happy days because we knew we were revitalizing our language and culture."[4] At the same time, Mikhailov has watched with disappointment as the more recent trends in Yakutia once again swing away from self-determination: "From 2000 on, they have been slowly but surely taking things back. . . . They have been decreasing the hours that get taught in schools on national cultural topics, and so forth. We've been fighting that, and they so far have let us continue. . . . Of course, these policies come from the top, from the Center of Russia."[5]

Mikhailov echoes the opinions of many in Yakutia who resist encroaching control from the Center. The legislative process offers one of the most effective recourses available to Sakha people. Although Moscow may overturn laws perceived as conflicting with the interests or laws of the state, the Yakutian legislature continues to develop legislation aimed at protecting Sakha culture. Research into modern cultural and ethnoreligious processes in Yakutia shows that in the two decades following the end of the Soviet Union, the legislature passed more than thirty regulations aimed at protecting human rights and the traditional culture, religion, and customs of the republic's peoples (Kulikova 2009, 144–145).

The cultural revitalization movement that swept Yakutia in the 1990s has continued to gather strength to the present time. To demonstrate the various threads of how such a movement impacted a moribund genre like olonkho and catapulted it into the spotlight of an international arena like the UNESCO Masterpiece awards, this chapter recounts the story through the eyes of a few key participants in the drama.

UNESCO's Intangible Cultural Heritage program and the Masterpiece award

The General Conference of UNESCO met in Paris in the fall of 2003 and codified the text of the document titled "Convention for the Safeguarding of the Intan-

66   CHAPTER 3

gible Cultural Heritage" (UNESCO 2003). The convention entered into force in 2006 for the states that ratified the resolution.[6] While 163 nations have ratified, accepted, or approved the convention, Russia is not among them.[7] This lack of participation means the Russian Federation has not obligated itself to protect or promote Intangible Cultural Heritage (ICH) in its territory. In turn, the Russian Federation also does not receive funding for any ICH listings, including olonkho.

While some have framed the question of protecting ICH as a human rights issue (Aikawa-Faure 2009, 26; Barthel-Boucher 2013, 27–52; Errington 2003, 728; Titon and Pettan 2015a, 58), the Russian Federation seems to ignore the welfare of its threatened genres. Olonkho enthusiasts chafe at the observation that the energy behind revitalization has come only from the regional level, proceeding almost entirely from governmental and educational institutions in the Republic of Sakha.[8] With state support unlikely to be forthcoming, olonkho scholars and enthusiasts have simply forged ahead, not waiting for the Center's support before pursuing the path they believe is necessary to achieve olonkho revitalization.

From "forgotten" to Masterpiece

The story of how the Sakha epos shifted from "forgotten" to "Masterpiece of the Oral and Intangible Heritage of Humanity" reminds me of an olonkho tale, complete with heroines and heroes, good and evil powers, comic characters, enemies, and warriors. Affording insight into the inner workings of the ICH Section of UNESCO at the time, this saga begins with an application in late 2003 and culminates in 2005 with the Masterpiece proclamation.

Elizaveta Sidorova, cochair of the National Committee of Yakutia for UNESCO, served as one of the primary figures behind the initial ICH application. Sitting in December 2011 with colleagues Elena Protodiakonova and Anastasia Luginova in a modest temporary office for the "House of Olonkho" in Yakutsk, she described the turning point for olonkho.

"It was a very, very complex and difficult task, and we had to do it quickly," she began. "At the end of November 2003, I went to Paris on a business trip, and there I found out, before the pronouncement of the Convention for the Safeguarding of the Intangible Cultural Heritage, that they were having three competitions between countries and these cultural objects, in 2001, 2003, and in 2005. . . . So I obtained a meeting with the UNESCO sector, in Paris.

"In the sector for Intangible Cultural Heritage, Dr. Rieks Smeets—a Dutch gentleman who is now retired—and I sat and talked about the convention and the competitions, and he asked me if we in Yakutia could participate. . . . At that time, the idea of epos didn't even enter my head. I thought right away about the Yakut festival Ysyakh, and he asked if it was a governmental celebration, and I said that it was. He told me that it would not make it through the competition, and I asked why. He said that the convention would only support those elements that were disappearing, in order to help them, to protect them. This was one of the main criteria.

"So I suggested the possibility of choosing 'shamanism' [for our entry], and he said that probably it could work, although there is shamanism among *all* peoples. . . . At that time, I had no idea of what epos even was. To me, *toyuk* and epos were the same thing! . . . In fact, it was like that for everyone! When people would mention 'epos' to me, I would think that they meant *toyuk*, that kind of singing.

"But when I mentioned about epos to him, he thought, then said, 'Yes, the Yakut epos could make it through the competition.' It turns out that he himself was a scholar of epics! He said that he knew about all the epics of Siberia and the Far East. He had even studied the Mongolian epics, so he knew about the Turkic epics. And we got all inspired, and he told me, 'Fill out the application!'"[9]

Sidorova's transparency in admitting she did not know the difference between the *toyuk* singing style and the epic genre of olonkho, and her suspicion that many others shared this rather vague conception of olonkho, suggest that even the two volumes devoted to olonkho in the Monuments series had not widely influenced the culture.[10] Fortunately, this lack of knowledge about olonkho in the mainstream consciousness of Sakha people was about to change. This amazing Sakha woman, with her combination of collaborative leadership skills, love for Sakha culture, and sheer determination, would pull together several streams of resources, including an entire scholarly community, thereby catalyzing a revitalization movement for olonkho.

Sidorova continued her story: "[Smeets] gave me all the regulations for the competition. . . . It was a lot of work to prepare these documents, and the time available was very short, very compacted. . . . So we took the English version home, translated it into Russian, and then I appealed to Vasilii Nikolaevich Ivanov at the Institute of Humanitarian Research and told him about the competition, and said, 'We should participate in the competition!' He said, 'Yes, of course, I suppose we could do that.'"[11]

The Department of Olonkho at the Institute of Humanitarian Research (IGI) included a collective of scholars, most of whom had played significant parts in writing the volumes in the Monuments series. During the winter of 2004, the department gained a new director, Agafia Zakharova, to lead the UNESCO research project for olonkho. Sidorova described Zakharova as a dynamic, strategic person who could get the work done quickly. With Zakharova's appointment, the collaborative power of Sakha academia was quickly set in motion.

"After that we worked fearfully hard," Sidorova reminisced. "The demands of the application were *horrific*! By the end of May we had a pile of paper—eight

68   CHAPTER 3

hundred pages. In five months they wrote eight hundred pages! And so with all of those pages under my arms, I went to Moscow. I had to get a special recommendation letter from the Russian House of Folk Creativity. I had to get the official approval of the Russian minister of culture and the minister of foreign affairs so that the candidature could be representative of Russia, because they would only accept *one* candidate from Russia."[12]

As Sidorova's story unfolded, the ferocity of the competition became apparent. According to Sidorova, the Russian Federation had also nominated a genre, the Tatar *sobontoi*, with the proposal supported at the federal level and the organizing committee led by none other than the president of the Russian Federation, Vladimir Putin. The power differential between the characters in this story highlights the skill and determination displayed by Sidorova and her collaborators in their negotiation with the Center. Courageous and determined, these women not only proved themselves resolute, wringing the needed permissions from the powerful Center, but they also showed themselves remarkably willing to sacrifice their future for what they valued.

Sidorova continued, shaking her head and laughing. "I arrived in Moscow, and didn't even know before I arrived that I was going to need all those signatures. Oi! I became so scared. It was such a shock for me! How in the world am I going to get the signature of the minister of culture? The minister of foreign affairs!? For two days, I didn't eat or sleep, I just chewed myself out so hard . . . what a *fool* I am! Not knowing all this stuff. What was I thinking? Why have I made all those people do all that work . . . day and night?

"And all of a sudden, almost like from above, I hear someone say—it was early morning, and I haven't slept at all; I'm thinking, *"My God, how am I going to return to Yakutsk? What am I going to tell people?"*—I hear, '*Call Mikhail Efimovich Nikolaev*—the first president of Yakutia.'

"And I ask, '*What in the world for?*'

"And I hear, '*There was an association of olonkho that he created in Yakutia. Let him gather those signatures for you.*' Like that! As if someone from on high was dictating to me!

". . . So I called Mikhail Efimovich [President Nikolaev] and said, 'I'd like to meet with you. It's very urgent.'

"He said, 'Okay, five o'clock, come to the Yakutian *pospredstvo*—the permanent place of residence for the Republic of Yakutia in Moscow.' So I went and told him about what we wanted to do.

"He said to me, 'Okay, let's just say olonkho becomes a [UNESCO] Masterpiece. Who is going to renew it? Who is going to work on it? It has completely disappeared!'

"I told him, 'Well, we have an Association of Olonkho in the republic. They will work on it.'

ESTEEM FOR A MASTERPIECE 69

"'What's this association? And who heads it up?' he said.

"I told him, '*You* are the president of the association! You created it . . . in 1999.' That stopped him short, and he started to pace back and forth. Then he asked, 'What do you need from me?' So I showed him all the work we had done, and I told him we needed these signatures. I told him I would prepare the letters for the minister of culture, to get the signature of Minister of Culture [Aleksandr] Sokolov. And I told him I'd prepare the letter for the minister of foreign affairs, too. And I told him to go to those ministers and get their signatures, and then I would take it all to Paris and get it registered, so that we could participate as the Russian candidate. Right away he grabbed the government telephone and called the minister of culture.

"[A few days later] . . . they said Sokolov, the minister of culture, would be there at six in the evening. They said to come with my diskette and the forms; they would get it all set up and Sokolov would sign it. I arrived at the ministry at five o'clock, and no one would let me in. They said no one had invited me! I didn't have a pass or anything. Somehow or other I slipped through, and made it to the reception room for the minister of culture. The secretaries were sitting there, one younger and one older, and I told them, 'I have come to see your minister. He is supposed to sign this paper.' They told me they did not know whether he was going to come or not.

"I said, 'Yes, I know he is. He's at the Legislature Building now, and at six he is coming here. While we are waiting for him to come, let's get this letter printed out on your letterhead so it will be ready when he comes.' In short, I started bossing them all around, and they were being very helpful.

"We got everything printed out, and this guy all of a sudden shows up. The new minister, by the way, was Aleksandr Sokolov, and the folks sitting there were attached to the old minister and were on their way out, because he had chosen new workers. So anyway, some guy comes into the office. He grabs the papers from me and says, 'What in the world is this? What's going on? Who gave you permission to do this?'

"So I said, 'And who exactly are *you* to tell *me* what to do?' [laughter] . . . He just about exploded with apoplexy.

"'I am the *only* official representative of the minister today!'

"And here I had asked him, 'Who do you think you are?' . . . and was bossing him around! Then I became afraid and said, 'Yes, yes, will you please . . . ?' So he read it and said, 'Oh all right, let's cut this and cut that,' and I'm thinking to myself, 'Shorten it in a thousand places, just let him sign it!'

"At six o'clock on the dot, Aleksandr Sokolov comes in, the tall, handsome minister fellow, takes it from me, and signs it. I took it to the bookkeeper to get it all approved. But I had to get the signature of the Department of Folklore first, but they had all been fired, and the new ones hadn't shown up yet! I *had* to have

70   CHAPTER 3

those signatures for the bookkeeper to sign off, and the bookkeeper had to sign off or the document was not valid. So I said to them, 'My Lord God, nobody is *there*! What am I supposed to do?'

"They say, 'Oh, all right.' And they approved it.

"After that, on Wednesday or Thursday, President Nikolaev went to Sergei Lavrov, the minister of foreign affairs. All I had left in the world was 50 rubles [$2], and I still had several days left! So in short, I arrive at the Ministry of Foreign Affairs with my diskette and my project for the minister to sign.

"The minister drives up in his car, and I give it to him. He comes in and I stand there near the ministry buildings. The rain is pouring, and the wind is cold—I was frozen. So I crossed the road and went into a cafeteria and got a cup of coffee for 50 rubles. It's a good thing that coffee was only 50 rubles then, and not the 250 it is now! I drank a cup of coffee on my last bit of money. . . . Anyway, after a couple of hours, the minister of culture comes out and throws the paper in my direction, all angry, and I jumped and grabbed it out of the air! Our 'golden paper'! And that is how we got the only spot representing Russia for the competition."[13]

Sidorova's story poured out, recounting the work during the intervening months until November 2005 and the announcement of the voting and competition results. She painted a picture of intrigue and maneuvering, but she also pointed out that Yakutia's application not only won the award, but also set a standard for excellence. Proudly, she recalled the events of the day that would go down in Yakutian history as the "Day of Olonkho."

"On the twenty-fifth of November, when they announced the winners, the [UNESCO] general director said in his concluding remarks that the very best packet of documentation was submitted for the Yakut olonkho, that it had been very scholarly, very grounded, the best packet of materials among them all! All the other countries should try to follow that model."[14]

Predictably, this triumph garnered a jubilant response back in Yakutia. Sidorova, with her team of scholars and olonkho enthusiasts, had achieved an international coup of sorts, and the Republic of Sakha erupted in celebration. She recalled with pleasure the reception they received upon their return to Yakutia: "When we arrived home, there was jubilation! Everyone rejoiced, and from that time, we have moved forward with enthusiasm in every form of olonkho. In the oral form, and in the theater, in teaching methods, ballet, opera, the Yakut circus even puts on olonkhos; they do a great job with the demons! The [Zverev] Dance Ensemble has done some performances too. So, we work! And it is extremely interesting."[15]

Most Sakha people cite UNESCO's Masterpiece proclamation as the primary impetus for olonkho revitalization. For example, Sergei Vasiliev, at North-Eastern Federal University (NEFU) in Yakutsk,[16] told me, "When the status of 'Masterpiece' was announced by UNESCO, there was a very emotional reaction of joy

ESTEEM FOR A MASTERPIECE   71

on the part of many people and an explosion of activity to begin putting the plan into place. Even Russian physics professors approached me with their sincere congratulations and delight at the pronouncement. It was especially appreciated by the 'carriers' [olonkhosuts], who felt affirmed and valued by this pronouncement."[17]

Sakha scholar Anna Larionova stated that the 2005 UNESCO Masterpiece proclamation "turned things around in the direction of support for olonkho."[18] In my conversations with Sakha people, more than just scholars pointed to the Masterpiece declaration as the turning point for olonkho revitalization—many ordinary Sakha citizens, both musicians and nonmusicians alike, expressed similar opinions.[19]

A billboard four stories high, placed on a building at the central bus stop in the capital city of Yakutsk, celebrated UNESCO's proclamation of olonkho as a "Masterpiece of the Oral and Intangible Heritage of Humanity." The Sakha Republic's president at the time, Viacheslav Shtyrov, issued a decree declaring an "Olonkho Decade 2006–2015" and called for legislation to support ten years of government-sponsored programs for the preservation, study, and promulgation of olonkho.[20] That legislation, drafted over the next year and signed into law in March 15, 2007, provided Yakutia with an "Action Plan" for safeguarding olonkho.

Olonkho reception at the time of the Masterpiece proclamation

Dekabrina Vinokurova and her colleagues at IGI have been researching olonkho and its reception since 2004. In 2007, near the beginning of the Decade of Olonkho, Vinokurova surveyed 505 people in Yakutsk and the town of Berdigestyakh to examine general levels of familiarity with the genre. In summarizing her research results, she reveals that there was a noticeable lack of appreciation for olonkho at the time of the Masterpiece declaration. Only 3 percent of the respondents identified themselves as admirers of olonkho, while 15 percent claimed complete disinterest in the genre. Among the Sakha respondents alone, 19 percent stated that they had never heard olonkho in any form. The other 80 percent had heard the genre at venues that included, among others, the national Sakha Ysyakh festivals (53 percent) or concerts (17 percent), in which olonkhosuts presented short memorized sections of olonkhos for exhibition purposes (Vinokurova 2007, 113).[21]

When asked about the prognosis for revitalizing olonkho, 43 percent of survey participants assumed that olonkho would disappear. Another 25 percent thought the genre might become at most a hobby for amateurs. Only 24 percent of respondents gave olonkho a prognosis of probable rebirth. The most common reasons chosen by participants to explain olonkho's demise included the small number of true olonkhosuts (32 percent), a declining interest in olonkho (28 percent), and a

72   CHAPTER 3

lack of focused, systematic work toward supporting olonkho (11 percent). Three percent listed other reasons, while 27 percent chose not to answer the question at all (Vinokurova 2007, 114).[22]

The current state of olonkho reception

When I spoke with them in 2011, Vinokurova, Zhegusov, Romanov, and their colleagues at IGI had just returned from another period of field research investigating the current level of knowledge of and attitudes toward olonkho. I was hoping to compare a preliminary overview of their findings with the conclusions I was formulating from my own fieldwork. Not yet published at the time, their results already revealed similarities with mine.[23] For example, I too had noticed an absence of appreciative audiences for traditional olonkho performance at the olonkho summer festivals of 2009 and 2010.[24] When I asked about this apathy, Vinokurova's response echoed the familiar refrain I had heard from many others, including the olonkhosuts themselves: "There weren't many listeners! . . . That *sreda* no longer exists."[25]

Naturally, specialists contribute to a *sreda* of appreciation for olonkho. In addition, at least a few Sakha without a background in olonkho performance also show genuine interest in the genre. For example, my friend Dora Gerasimova traveled with me during the summer of 2010. On our way back to the capital city from the Ysyakh summer festival, I asked her for her impressions of what she had seen and heard at the event, specifically inquiring if she had learned anything new about olonkho.

"I came to understand many things at that Ysyakh," she said. "We have not heard olonkho for two, or three, or even four generations. We grew up almost without olonkho. So I saw that olonkho is sung pretty much in the old way. That's what I observed and heard. It's almost the same as it was, especially in the texts, which were all similar. This very much surprised me—the main idea of olonkho: that there is a description of nature, then the description of the *bogatyr* who saves the girl, and that's it. I didn't see anything new in those olonkhos. I was disconcerted. I think maybe the interest in olonkho is being extinguished among the people because of this [lack of new material].

"It appears that the government is trying to revitalize our culture, but among the people, I have not seen much. . . . Because people are not used to listening, and they probably already know all the things that olonkho talks about; like a fairy tale that tells how the girl is rescued from the evil spirits by the *bogatyr*. I liked that they performed [*Jëbiriëljin Bërgën*], I liked it very much, the theatrical version that they did at the opening. That was new."[26]

From Gerasimova's vantage point, new stories reflecting the worldview, values, and modern life of Sakha people would provide greater interest for audiences: "Most people now say that olonkho is backward. It's kind of like no one is interested. . . . But it seems to me that we need to change the content of olonkho and bring in the new, and then maybe there will be a reawakening of interest, I think."[27]

When asked about her perception of the level of audience engagement with the traditional form of olonkho, which is performed solo, she answered, "There were virtually no listeners! There were performers, and your group, and me, and that's all. Even the children who came to perform from my district, the Megino-Khangalaskii district, they were telling their teacher that they didn't want to perform, and when she asked why, they said, 'There aren't any listeners; nobody needs this.' They [the children] kind of wanted to be involved in olonkho, but the fact that there weren't any listeners is, of course, very bad."[28] Clearly, Gerasimova not only identified with the misgivings of the young performers from her home area, but also felt pain in acknowledging the lack of active interest in the traditional solo olonkho performances.

Pyotr Reshetnikov also mused with regret about the lack of enthusiastic audiences for olonkho performance: "I have been to many festivals of olonkhosuts here in my own republic, the very best of the olonkhosuts. . . . If you look at those events, they give twenty minutes, or at maximum half an hour—that's all! So they are not recounting all over the place, not singing olonkho, so it is not developing. Olonkhosuts can't exist in those conditions! Like I said, there isn't a community of listeners. I will tell you about a funny episode that happened. Last year they invited me to the House of Culture of the republic, named after Kulakovskii, and videotaped me there. At first there were two listeners, and they were listening pretty well. Then later on, there was only one operator, and that one started to fall asleep! The cassette was for one hour. I'm recounting the olonkho, and thinking that the hour is up, and so I began to wake up the operator.

"If that is the kind of listeners we have, then olonkhosuts will not develop. We have a saying, '*If there are a lot of listeners, then the olonkhosuts will sing with feeling*.' But if the listener sleeps, the olonkhosut can't sing, of course."[29]

Interestingly, these observations about a lack of attentive audiences surfaced only in contexts of the traditional solo form of olonkho. Large Ysyakh summer festivals regularly feature grand-scale theatrical presentations of olonkho, with hundreds or even thousands of performers, dancers, props, animals, and all the main characters and staging requisite for the story.[30] These renditions, apparently quite popular and enjoyed by all ages, may provide a related form of olonkho that can endure regardless of the health of the traditional solo, improvised version.

74   CHAPTER 3

Key elements of change in olonkho performance

The accounts reported so far touch on the change in the performance practice of olonkho during the pre-Soviet and Soviet periods. The following sections expand on several key elements of this change: verbal responses of audiences, the transformation of olonkho from an oral-based to a literature-based art form, emerging forms related to olonkho, the importance of broad Sakha language fluency for olonkho reception, and the role of youth in olonkho performance.

Audience verbal responses

In traditional solo olonkho performance, pre-Soviet audiences showed their engagement with the story by interacting audibly with the olonkhosut (Okladnikov 1970, 266). Similar phenomena appear in other epic traditions, such as Korean p'ansori (Pihl 1993), the *Sunjata* of Mali (Johnson 1992), Japanese Kabuki theater, and the *Pabuji* epic of northern India (Jang 2001, 103n).[31]

Chekhorduna, in remembering her own childhood experiences listening to olonkho, described the driving force behind the audience's verbal responses. From her perspective, these exclamations usually came in the form of reactions to a specific character: "Sometimes they are responses of empathy, like for the plight of the girl who is in captivity among the demons; they empathize with her verbally. Or they are amazed at the feats of the heroes, or even the feats of the villains. The timbre of their responses is expressive, and reflects their emotional response."[32]

When asked why people no longer respond significantly during modern olonkho performances, she pointed to a general disengagement from the olonkhosut: "They don't get into the *temp*—they can't get into the rhythm of the olonkho. They just listen and try to understand what is being recounted. The listeners of an earlier time, the listeners during my mother's time, they could go right away into the rhythm of the olonkho. They would *live* with the characters of the stories for three days! Living only in the world of olonkho. They would go, with the olonkhosut on his horse, the horse of the *bogatyr*, to the upper world, the underworld, the middle world, they could go everywhere with him. Only *then* do you get that kind of reaction. If you don't have that, you won't get the reaction, and in fact, they can even fall asleep. They fall out of the rhythm! They get tired, after all.

"The *mir olonkho* [the world of olonkho]—that is the real olonkho. This is what we are trying to pass along to children. We should have been creating this kind of epic *sreda* of olonkho for children. [. . .] Olonkho is of course a heroic epos. It tells about light powers and dark powers—that's required. So it helps preschool children to develop wonderful aesthetics."[33]

As I confirmed with her later, Chekhorduna uses the term "aesthetics" here to refer not purely to artistic aesthetics, but more broadly to moral aesthetics—how

ESTEEM FOR A MASTERPIECE 75

to appreciate and serve as stewards of beauty. Considering worldview issues paramount for the proper raising of children, she channels her passion for olonkho into developing curriculum, thereby seeking to nurture in the younger generation an *obraz myshleniia* (way of thinking) that embodies Sakha moral and spiritual values.

As audiences changed and the attentive, appreciative epic *sreda* disappeared, the audience's traditional verbal responses also waned. Without this feedback, olonkhosuts struggled to find their groove, in the end often producing shorter performances. Over time, this trend created a cycle of less and less attention to solo olonkho.

Transformation from an oral-based to a literature-based art form

The movement from orality toward literacy during the Soviet period also appears to have affected olonkho.[34] Vinokurova considers literacy a primary factor in the demise of the improvisational art: "With the appearance of written language and literature, people began to collect olonkhos and turn them into literature, as well as studying and interpreting them. In time, they began increasingly to use pre-processed texts of olonkho. Little by little, professional artists and amateur performers learned to perform olonkho as a memorized work. In this way, there was a process in which the performance of olonkho and its actual creation (authorship) became divided. This led to a loss of the originally unified creator-performer aspect and variability of olonkho" (Vinokurova 2007, 109). Indeed, few olonkhosuts alive today demonstrate proficiency in improvisatory creation, and public figures in Yakutia, while often strong proponents of published texts for preservation purposes, have expressed their concern. In November 2011, the Speaker of the Yakutian Parliament, Alexander Zhirkov, observed that recordings and printed publications of olonkho cause performers to "follow each letter of the text."[35] He sees this trend leading to the loss of a distinctive of traditional olonkho performances—improvisation.

Beyond transcriptions of oral performances, the twenty-first century has seen the introduction of printed versions of new olonkhos published in literary form by the singers themselves. In 2008, a high school student, Aelita Egorova, wrote and illustrated a new olonkho tale, *Kü*rü*ng Küll*è*i*. A few years later, a talented young olonkho scholar and performer, Yuri Borisov, published an olonkho tale titled *Basyrgastaah aattaah Baabe Baatyr* (2014).

Borisov offers an unusual combination of gifts in olonkho creation, performance, and scholarship.[36] Winning several olonkho competitions in his youth, he eventually went on to study olonkho in graduate school and now works at the Olonkho Institute connected to NEFU. His book includes some innovations in the olonkho tradition, including shortened texts accessible to children, a glossary for defining archaic words, and colored illustrations rendered by a gifted artist,

76   CHAPTER 3

Kyma Zhirkova.[37] The resulting product helps younger audiences understand and appreciate olonkho, especially since Borisov himself loves to interact with children and tell them the story from the book. Regarding its short length, the author refers to a historical genre of short epics called *seen*— olonkhos that could be recounted in one evening before bedtime.[38]

In addition to contributing innovation to the olonkho tradition, Borisov's books create strong ties with older olonkho tales. In studying Borisov's work, olonkho scholar Galina Popova notes the presence of many elements of master olonkhosuts: epic themes, epic approaches to time, creativity, and "genetic heritage." In her opinion, he lacks only a more fully developed concept of the underworld and some time to grow in his abilities as a performer.[39]

Most people would not see a need to label Borisov's level of innovation as "derivative," but olonkho scholars face the difficult task of differentiating between "real olonkho" and liminal performances (Schrag 2015b, 329). Instead of contrasting "authentic" with "derivative," we might consider employing metaphors related to DNA, family traits, and ancestral family trees. Some instantiations of the genre may more closely resemble the original progenitor than others, but all will demonstrate familial relation through commonalities of features. In this way, shared "genetic traits" provide stability, while traits not widely shared impart opportunities for innovation and adaptations to change (Bohlman 1988, 26).

The epic *sreda* also resembles the environmental nurturing of a tree, which requires air, water, light, and soil in order to thrive. This metaphor extends to periods of dormancy and drought, in which the tree may miss some of these elements and even appear to be dead. A change in *sreda* may bring renewed life, although possibly with the loss of some former limbs and the growth of new limbs in places where none formerly existed. In light of this analogy, the next section surveys the emerging "descendants" of olonkho. Each new form presents a unique combination of resemblances to and differences from its progenitor—the improvised, solo form of olonkho.

Descendants of the family tree of olonkho

Although rarely performed in the Soviet period, olonkho-related forms such as theatrical performances appeared in the early twentieth century and continue through the present.[40] For example, the performance of Oyunsky's *Tuiaaryma Kuo* took place in 1938, while Mark Zhirkov and Genrikh Litinskii adapted the same artist's musical-drama olonkho *Nurgun Botur the Swift* for the operatic stage in 1947, with restagings of it in 1957 (Moscow) and 1977.[41] Early in the twenty-first century, folklore collectives gave staged performances new life (Biliukina 2006, 125). In addition, the 2007 legislation for revitalizing olonkho provided for the creation of the government-sponsored Theater of Olonkho, directed ever since by Andrei Borisov, the minister of culture at the time. Many Sakha see hope for olonkho's future in these popular staged versions.[42]

Yuri Zhegusov expressed concern that olonkho-related creations may lose the core of what makes olonkho feel authentic to Sakha people. His observations, described in a conversation that included his fellow researcher Dekabrina Vinokurova, demonstrated ambivalence especially toward new olonkho-related forms that lack significant common "genetic material" with the genre that inspired them.

"It became available in audio form—records—and was played on the radio," Zhegusov reported. "The next stage was in the visual arts; Timofei Stepanov put it into visual form. He was the first to incarnate olonkho into pictures so that people could not just hear it, but see it as well.[43] Then the next stage was needed, something that was audiovisual like animation or films. But this has not happened yet."

When I mentioned that someone had recently produced an animated film, he responded, "Well, they wanted to do an animated version, but it turned out to be a kind of Hollywood version. Not the real thing, more like an imitation of some kind."

Vinokurova quickly added, "Not truly 'national.' The people that did it didn't know the Sakha language. It's possible that they didn't even read olonkho, didn't even listen to it, maybe; this is the kind of people who made that film."

Zhegusov likewise expressed his distaste: "Yes, a lot of dilettantes have grabbed onto olonkho. Comics are the latest thing—have you seen those? Some kind of girl who doesn't even know the language or have an artistic education has made *Nurgun Botur* into some kind of a striptease." They both chuckle at the idea. "You look at it, and it's just not the real thing. I have talked to experts, and they say that many dilettantes have begun to create things."

Vinokurova added, "You should note this in your book, unfortunately."

"The person who did the film just wanted to make money," Zhegusov concluded.

"And after the [Masterpiece] proclamation, it became a fad," Vinokurova complained. "Anyone who is not too lazy latches onto it, and some projects are more successful, some are less successful. This is a natural process. There are always those who want to 'get in on the act,' as they say."[44]

Sakha scholars Romanova and Ignatieva write with derision regarding what they perceive as the commercializing of olonkho—the practice of labeling everything "olonkho" simply to increase sales:

An alarming trend of domination of neofolkloric theatricalization in the festival narrative is now being seen, where epic narrative is being transformed into the viewing of a "slide show." The attributes of olonkho, including the name of the epos genre

78   CHAPTER 3

itself, its characters, and plots, have begun to be used for commercial purposes (the "Olonkho" shopping center, "Olonkho" restaurant, "Olonkho" vodka, "Éllei" beer, etc.). In particular, we note the construction of the widely advertised Olonkholand as a center of the entertainment industry. All this is destroying the fabric of the national festival and, with time, transforming it into a surrogate product of "clip culture." (2012, 53)

At the same time, Zhegusov and Vinokurova themselves suggested the likely necessity of alternate forms in the future. According to Zhegusov, "Probably we just need to change to another means of transmission for the young generation. [. . .] I think maybe something like film. This is what people tell me: 'It would be so great to have an olonkho film in the style of *Lord of the Rings*.' They tell me that it would be so interesting if it had special effects and all that."

"After all," Vinokurova added, "the story itself is really a 'fantasy' story, so that's maybe why there seems to be a pull toward doing a film in the fantasy genre. . . . And by the way, children's reception of these kinds of presentations is really strong! It attracts their attention."

"If I'm understanding you correctly," I said, "you're saying that there is little hope that the live tradition will be passed along—the oral tradition."

"Yes, there's little chance [that oral tradition will be passed along]," Vinokurova replied, "because you yourself saw what happens at these performances for the olonkho festivals. I was also in Borogontsy myself, and was talking to people in a focus group that I had gathered, and they said that the olonkhosuts had left that festival completely offended, because there were so few listeners, and they were taken off to some kind of a not very great place for their performances, and there were the circus performances and all that.

"But this is a natural process, basically. It's a result of the mass orientation of the venues. This is not a 'mass' art, you will agree! And the further we get from the traditional venue, the more it becomes an elite art, for the specialists. So to make it a 'mass art,' you have to do it in a different way, new methods.

"I even had this put into our questionnaire, and people responded that you needed to change it. You have to change it! The traditional performances are only for the specialists—for the elite."[45]

Some distantly related "olonkho-themed artistic expressions" have also materialized during the post-Soviet period. For example, an increasing number of Sakha artisans have begun creating arts and crafts on olonkho themes. They may knit and crochet with horsehair or yarn; carve with wood, mammoth bone, or stone; make paper cuttings; or fashion rugs and hangings from yarn, leather, fur, and other materials. Each summer the Ysyakh festival features booths for exhibiting and selling these products to festivalgoers.

One of the craft exhibitors, Valentina Struchkova, creates large knitted wall hangings on olonkho-related themes. She chose olonkho as a theme even before the revitalization process started in earnest and considers her artistic work to be contributing to the movement. The spark for her creativity on the theme of olonkho came from an unusual experience with none other than Gavriil Kolesov himself.

"I was in the hospital for a long time," she recounts, "and over the years, as a result of nothing to do, I learned how to knit and crochet, and am now a specialist in it. After I went on disability, I began to create clothes and sweaters, but at exhibitions, people were not that interested in knitted things. So I searched for a theme, and found the theme of olonkho. I have been doing this now for ten years on the theme of olonkho. . . . Well, olonkho is very complex to read these days, but if a person can see it, if young people see it, then it is easier for them to receive it. So I thought about it and began to do works on the theme of olonkho. Then when I had done this for three years, it became a Masterpiece of UNESCO, and now I travel around to all the Ysyakhs on the theme of olonkho and set up these displays.

"In those years [before the Masterpiece declaration] it had been kind of forgotten. It used to be that there were no olonkhosuts as such, just concert numbers. *Toyuksuts* would sing them. One time a musician came to our town—the performer who did the *Nurgun Botur* records, Gavriil Kolesov—and he came for a concert. But in the hall there were only three or four people who came to listen! It was so disappointing to me! His face just fell, totally changed, and I felt so sorry for him. I thought to myself, 'If a person is willing to do this kind of thing, I want to help him in some way.' I felt I owed him this, so with my knitting I created this work. It's impossible to haul around large pictures of olonkho, but my works are transportable. So, through UNESCO, when olonkho was defended as a Masterpiece, they took it with them to Paris. And through my work, I got to be [vicariously] in New York.

". . . So I'm glad that I chose olonkho for my work. When children—you know they have competitions for children olonkhosuts sometimes—and they say that when they have these works nearby with these kinds of *bogatyrs* of olonkho, it helps them to better receive and experience the olonkhos, and they perform better; that's what the children say. So it appears that I chose my theme well. [. . .] In some way it has helped this masterpiece to be restored, I think."[46]

Her palpable satisfaction in contributing to the revitalization of olonkho suggests a connection between this widespread engagement in depicting olonkho themes through other, nonmusical artistic domains and the pride that many Sakha feel toward the genre. In the musical arena, contemporary music artists have also started referencing olonkho.

80   CHAPTER 3

When I toured the Yakutsk National Gymnasium, a grade school and high school that specializes in teaching national culture, the teenage student body president served as my guide. When he showed me the studio for their rock band, I asked him whether he felt that olonkho had influenced the rock scene to any extent. He suggested that the tradition had had little impact before 2007, but in the few years since then, olonkho's effect on rock music had grown steadily. He saw *etno* (ethno) themes, including some elements drawn from olonkho, increasingly appearing in the rock music performed at festivals and special events.[47]

In a study of the pop-rock scene in Yakutsk, Peers observes that *estrada* (pop) singers Vitalii Ochirov and Aleksandr Diachkovskii include traditional Sakha genres such as *algys* and olonkho in their repertoire. In addition, bands such as Cholbon and Ajar Khaan create fusions of acid rock and Sakha song elements, with Ajar Khaan incorporating "episodes from [olonkho] into a prog rock concert" (Peers 2015).

Sakha language vitality

The use of archaic language poses an enormous barrier to the revitalization of olonkho. As with many epic traditions around the world, antiquated linguistic features bring a sense of sophistication while at the same time hindering accessibility for modern audiences.[48] As far back as 1896, Seroshevskii noted that the language of olonkho contained archaisms that even the olonkhosuts themselves did not understand, yet stubbornly repeated (1993, 589). Vinokurova and Zhegusov underscored the difficulty of transmitting the olonkho tradition when the level of comprehension of Sakha language vocabulary had sunk so low, especially for descriptive imagery.

"They say that they don't understand the archaic language," Vinokurova observed, "especially the children with whom I talked. They say it is very difficult to understand—it is not very accessible.[49] I don't know if our linguists will be able to do something with these archaisms, if someone will take on this task."

Zhegusov added, "The most important thing in transmission is language. In order to listen well to olonkho, you need to really know the Yakut language very well. If you don't know Yakut well, it's useless to try and listen to it."

"Even Yakut people sometimes struggle with the archaisms in olonkho," Vinokurova noted.[50]

In pondering olonkho's future, Pyotr Reshetnikov emphasized that the improvisatory nature of traditional solo olonkho performance may have an essential role in preserving the Sakha language: "Just as was acknowledged by UNESCO, olonkho is the unique work of an individual person—the olonkhosut. The great Suoron Omolloon [Sivtsev] wrote and said that the olonkhosut is 'the one and only performer/actor of the grand theater of olonkho.' He performs all the roles of all the heroes, which can be more than thirty; around forty can happen in one olonkho. And the olonkhosut creates all the heroes with various words, motifs, *toyuk* songs, with different tones, and during the performance they create the words and plot of the olonkho, which is why it turns out so long. They don't learn them from memory! . . . When he tells an olonkho, the needed words come from within him, which is why he is called an *iye-olonkhosut* [master olonkhosut]—that's the kind of olonkhosut he is.

"So this is why I say that olonkho could only be developed further in the Republic of Yakutia—because our leadership, as well as our scholars, our linguists, are all turning their attention to the development of the Yakut language, because in Asia, the Yakut language is already considered an ancient language."

Clearly concerned about the potential loss of the language, Reshetnikov continued, "Some say that our Yakut language will be forgotten within fifty or sixty years as a language of the people. So there is a danger. In Yakutsk, our children are not speaking in Yakut, and olonkho is not understood at all! . . . This is not only in Yakutsk, but even in the districts we can see this kind of behavior. So now, through olonkho, they are turning their attention to the development of their mother tongue, the Yakut language, because as a people, we should preserve our own language, the Yakut language. So for that reason, there are good prospects for the development of olonkho."[51]

Reshetnikov's connection between language vitality and olonkho recurred in a number of my other resources. In 2010, Vera Solovyeva interviewed me for a video for the Sakha Diaspora website, which she manages with her husband, Zhargal. Although the interview focused on my study of olonkho revitalization, Solovyeva linked this topic to what she regarded as an alarming trend of waning interest by the federal government for Sakha and other minority groups' language development. She told me, "There's a danger that if there aren't teachers of the Sakha language, if the federal program won't support them, kids will just study the Russian language. So there's a danger that eventually the Sakha language will just disappear."[52]

In most people's minds, this concern about language revitalization appears connected to the topic of olonkho.[53] Pyotr Reshetnikov hopes that the threat of Sakha language decline will motivate the government to continue to support olonkho. People envision this process unfolding in a variety of ways. Some want to see olonkho's language modernized to reach broader audiences; others want to preserve the archaic language and provide education so that audiences can understand the older words better. Whether they believe that olonkho revitalization or Sakha language revitalization should happen first, many people anticipate a symbiotic relationship between language vitality and epos appreciation.

82   CHAPTER 3

Youth and olonkho

The involvement of youth in modern olonkho performance contexts provides significant hope for the future of the genre. The government program for revitalization trains young people to appreciate olonkho and encourages them to participate in competitions, performances, and research. Even during the Soviet years, scholars such as Pukhov recommended childhood as the best time for learning the art of olonkho: "Olonkho was learned from childhood. In the past, it was not rare to meet children five to seven years old who could not yet sing, but were completely familiar with the texts of enormously long olonkhos and who retold them to other children. Most of the outstanding olonkhosuts learned their skills at a young age" (1962, 8). He maintained that repeated exposure to the improvisational art of olonkho would increase the number of young olonkhosuts. In addition, sharing with other children and receiving opportunities to practice in front of relatives and neighbors not only improved the young olonkhosuts' skills but also positively affected the size of audiences.

Reshetnikov grew up hearing olonkho because of his father's habit of gathering olonkhosuts for performances: "In my youth, my father was a nobleman of the third Noshkhomskii district—which was called the Baturusskii district at the time—here in Cherkëkh. He loved to listen to olonkho. So he would gather together all the best olonkhosuts from nearby—the Churapchinskii and Tatinskii districts—and listen to them. So from our earliest childhood, we listened to olonkho. Olonkho is attractive to all listeners, including children. Although we were small children, all the same, it was very interesting to us to hear the best olonkhosuts."[54] Although he began to recount olonkho only later in life, he credited his performing ability to those early years of intense olonkho exposure.

Reshetnikov also described his work with children in the town where he lived, noting that his position as a government-recognized master olonkhosut involved making himself available to teach his art form to interested youth. Up until now, the dearth of master olonkhosuts has limited the availability of such instruction to just a few locations throughout the Sakha Republic. On the other hand, this model, if replicated in more places, would likely have a positive impact on the sustainability of olonkho traditional solo performance.

Reshetnikov particularly enjoyed his relationship with the preschool "Alënushka" in Cherkëkh: "This preschool is the only one that is training children in the spirit of olonkho, through an 'olonkho method.' Preschool teachers and children's workers come in from around the republic, from the districts, for seminars . . . and they often invite me to go and teach.

"I wrote three short half-hour olonkhos for children, and one hour-long olonkho. Two of these olonkhos . . . have been printed in books this year. They printed many copies, which are being used around the republic in preschools. Because recently there has been a lot of attention given to the training of children in their own mother tongue and in the traditions of their people. This is the kind of preschool in Cherkëkh. They came from the institute expressly for the purpose of attaching me to the preschool. And I often perform for them. Preschool children, although they are small, do a good job of performing the roles of heroes in olonkho."[55]

Regarding the practical benefits for children studying olonkho, Vinokurova reported from her research among schools and kindergartens that some parents have discovered intriguing positive side effects from their children's study of olonkho. "I have noted that among parents there has appeared a kind of pragmatic interest in olonkho. One time I was interviewing a parent and asked her why she was having her children study olonkho. . . . She told me that it develops their memory! In school they aren't having children memorize poems anymore, so how are we going to develop their memory? She said they need to memorize a very large body of texts, and that also, she found that they immediately improve their abilities in their schoolwork. They become very goal-oriented and learn how to value time. Not just chatting with friends, but they have to go here and there, and they begin to decide rationally how much time they can spend on something. In all of that, she was very content with the results.

"She said that one child had begun very strongly and then got interested in something else, but even then, the good things he had learned still stayed with him. And another child wants to continue learning olonkho into the future, for a longer period of time. She said she doesn't know how it will turn out, but she is convinced that in any case it will help them in their studies. . . . So, in short, there is a pragmatic side that exists. Parents have already seen this.

"In the Ust-Aldanskii district, a preschool teacher who has worked all her life in preschool training institutions . . . told me that young people in the villages . . . don't talk much with their children, and the children develop speech defects. . . . The children that are learning olonkho from her—she said they are very enthusiastic about this—learning how to breathe more correctly, and within just a couple of months they are freed of their speech defects. She said they don't even need a speech therapist! So that's the first thing; the second is that, naturally, their memory is developed. The children that have studied in her group are all getting As and Bs."[56]

Many of the people I interviewed considered the involvement of children the key to olonkho's future. Their vision focuses on effectively transmitting the appreciation for and the skills of the tradition to the next generation. In Zakharova's view, "Realistically, if children will start to sing olonkho from their youth, these children, with texts in their memory, turn out to be very thoughtful children. They

84   CHAPTER 3

are good students, they are polite, they are good children. They are not going to quit doing olonkho. Olonkho really helps them to get through life. There are a lot of children like this. They have dedicated their lives to olonkho, and in the future they can become researchers, performers."[57]

I noted that she predicated her generally positive prognosis for olonkho with the word "if." In addition, given that these children memorize olonkho texts, she did not address the question of revitalizing the traditional improvisatory quality. Instead, she simply suggested that children now working with olonkho will stay involved in ways that will support the performance tradition. For example, she expects to see an ongoing cadre of researchers studying olonkho, like the students currently under her tutelage at the institute where she works. Naturally, adults with this level of background in olonkho will also provide larger, more attentive audiences.

When asked about the loss of interested audiences, Zakharova pointed out, "Yes, it is because the epic *sreda* is already gone. We think that it has to be revitalized locally, not with a lot of people, but like it used to be, in families. To gather only those who love this kind of thing, and then it spreads in a more natural way. During the winter weekends, on Saturdays, we have begun to do this . . . in the families. So that it can be heard in the family circle. We are doing this in Yakutsk now, but hope to spread to the villages as well. We also want to teach classes to children here at the Olonkho Center, to have a studio. My students want this. There are a number of children in the city here who want to learn."

While serving as a driver for my fieldwork during the summers of 2009 and 2010, Valerii Kononov (fig. 3.1) commented that he found children's performances more interesting in some ways than those of adults, especially in terms of clarity. "The thing that makes me most happy is that children and young people perform it, not like in the past, when only old people performed it . . . the elderly, old folks. Now young people, with their young imaginations and voices—it's very clear to understand what they are saying, what they're singing about. Everything is clear."[58]

Kononov also remembered the performances of Kolesov with great fondness, mentioning Kolesov's relative youth at that time. When asked what he liked in Kolesov's performance, he responded, "The level of his performance was very high. He was an artist. So he performed really well. And when the folk singers performed—this is my own opinion—they were elderly—completely old. But Gavriil Kolesov was young, and when the young people perform, it's good. You can feel their energy—the creativity you can feel."[59]

In 2009, while introducing me to the website www.olonkho.info, Sergei Vasiliev showed me information about a yearly event for children in the Suntaar district.[60] He observed, "The town of Kiukei . . . started an olonkho club for kids in 1999, and it eventually became a summer camp for kids in 2005. . . . Time will pass, and some of these kids will become performers."[61] This website also notes that there is an olonkho-themed summer camp for children in the Khangalaskii district.[62]

Fig. 3.1. Valerii Kononov, Maria Kononova, and Bill Harris with the author (June 15, 2009)

Already available in the five years leading up to the Masterpiece proclamation, opportunities such as these camps and the yearly competitions and training offered by some preschools and grade schools encourage children who wish to learn more about olonkho.[63]

Sysoliatina (2006, 181–184) outlines the history of children's olonkho competition-festivals in Yakutia, noting that since the beginning of these festivals, children have been able to participate in one of three categories: solo performance, scientific research, and theatrical interpretation of the epic.

1998–1999: two festivals in which children from ten districts participated
2000—3rd Festival of Young Performers of Olonkho: 218 children from 13 districts, including the city of Yakutsk
2001—4th International Festival of Young Performers of Olonkho: 282 children and their trainers came from Kyrgyzstan, Buryatia, Tuva, and Altai, as well as 14 districts of Yakutia
2002—5th Festival: 78 people from 8 districts
2003—6th Festival: 131 participants from Yakutia and Tuva
2004—7th Festival: 57 children from 8 districts

An online source continued the report, showing the following numbers of participants in children's festivals for subsequent years:

2005—8th Festival: included 117 children and 37 teachers from 8 districts and Yakutsk
2006—9th Festival: included 145 children from 11 districts
2007—10th Festival: included 150 participants from 11 districts of the republic and the city of Yakutsk[64]

86   CHAPTER 3

The generation of children currently learning about olonkho tends to memorize texts rather than practice the improvisatory art of the epic tradition. This approach will necessarily result in a change to the performance of olonkho, producing a more static form. Despite Albert Lord's assertion that using fixed texts leads to the demise of the oral creative process and to "the rise of a generation of 'singers' who are reproducers rather than re-creators" (2000, 137), many Sakha seem to prefer to nurture a "close relative" of olonkho rather than not to have any "relatives" at all.

Respondents' prognoses for revitalizing olonkho

Sakha opinions are divided concerning the prognosis for olonkho revitalization. Some feel confident that such efforts will succeed; others seem certain that the artistic tradition will die. Their responses continue to feature major themes already explored in this chapter—audience appreciation, oral tradition, olonkho-related forms, language revitalization, and the engagement of youth in olonkho performance.

Spiridon Shishigin, a renowned *khomus* (jaw harp) performer, wants to see the genre revitalized in a way that will preserve the original solo character: "You need to revitalize it in its clean form, its traditional form. Like it used to be; one person performing the whole thing, and creating it right there, not performing from memory, but improvising . . . imagining. He closes his eyes, like this, and 'sees' it, and everything he sees in his imagination, he recounts. This is the kind of olonkhosuts that we need, who will perform true olonkho." Regarding the lack of audiences at traditional performances, he reflected on the successful revival of his own instrument in Yakutia: "There will be [listeners], probably, slowly but surely. Take *khomus*, for example. It is being played more and more!"[65]

Many other Sakha people feel that the traditional style of olonkho performance is gone forever. In 2015, respected scholar Anatolii Kudiarov remarked at a summer conference on epics of the world that "it's impossible to resurrect an art form that was a product of its time."[66] Likewise, Boris Mikhailov, although actively involved in olonkho revitalization, argues that the current renewal efforts, in contrast to the brief revival of olonkho that happened during the "Great Patriotic War," will bring a significant change in performance practice: "The storyteller's art had a period where it really flourished, a peak time. But I somehow feel that although there was a decrease, then a kind of revitalization that replaced it, the long-term revitalization will be in a little different format in the modern world. But the youth will remember that it is not the 'real olonkho.'"[67]

Dekabrina Vinokurova expressed similar sentiments when remarking on the responses she received during her fieldwork: "When I asked people about the further development of olonkho, they of course responded that it will be for

ESTEEM FOR A MASTERPIECE   87

shows—like concert performances. Not so much the development of language and images, plot lines, and the like, but more along the lines of performing what has already been written."[68]

An employee at the Berdigestyakh Museum related a viewpoint I often heard from respondents concerning the most important elements of preservation from the olonkho tradition: "The 'canon' should be observed, but at the same time, olonkho should be allowed to develop in its own way." As he pondered the possibility of changing certain aspects of olonkho in order to attract a new generation of listeners, he suggested, "This is absolutely needed, but with caution. You still need to hold to the canon. You can, of course, use some kinds of new means to update it, like to 'arrange' it, but it should be done with caution, in order to not lose the 'salt' of its central meaning or significance."

When asked to elaborate on what should remain unchanged, he identified the following core elements: "The canon—it's the oldest epos in the world, you understand. The plots: how it started, how our world came into being, the main *iziuminka* [flavor/zest], the dark powers and the light powers, good and evil, that good will always win—this is the most important—for good to always be victorious, and that the three worlds that we have, upper, middle, and lower, do not disappear. This is the thing—our world, our *worldview*, should not be violated and should not disappear. So if we are doing something new, and we throw out these things, then it is not olonkho anymore. [. . .] You have to be very careful, very careful that the most important part of the 'canon' remains, the worldview. You need for the new generation to understand, yes? But you need to somehow present it to them in a way that they can accept it, right? Use new technical means, like you can use television, cinematography, and so on, but only in a way that protects the canon, the plots, the worldview, and is understandable and accessible. [. . .] You need to attract their attention from the earliest years, so that they can accept it into their souls. This is my fondest wish—that little children can fall asleep to the sound of olonkho and wake up to the sound of olonkho. Then a new generation, without losing the canon, will be able to create their own olonkhos."

In reflecting on the prospect of the youth of the next generation creating their own olonkhos, with their own plots to reflect their own imaginings of the world, he mused, "In order to produce one's own olonkho, you will need *life experience*. You need to fathom—to penetrate the core, the essence of it. Do you understand? A boy, or a girl, fourteen years old or so, has only a worldview that is the purest childlike worldview. So they cannot understand the essence of it and might deviate or stray. They need to listen to it from their childhood and remember it and get some life experience."[69]

One teacher I met has taught folklore to children for the last ten years, focusing on olonkho performance. She brought a group of children to the Berdigestyakh

88   CHAPTER 3

summer festival in 2010 to perform their own olonkho and to learn more about the performing tradition. She explained her approach for training children to love olonkho: "Our method is simple. It is a project activity. The children choose their own role—either a *bogatyr* or some kind of a [shamanness] woman (*udaghan*, *analakhchytun*), some kind of character. So they choose their own hero to act out. They even draw and write about that character—its age, appearance, clothing, even the smell of their hero. So they themselves study their role, and I am just a helper, like a supervisor. So they themselves choose and fill out their role."

In sharing her opinion on the resurgence of interest in olonkho, she focused on the connection between the revitalization of the artistic tradition and the broader revival of the language and culture: "During the many years of Soviet power, the hours given to teaching the Yakut language [in the school] were very few. Lessons on folk traditions didn't exist at all—lessons in Yakut national culture. In recent years, they have started putting on large Ysyakhs. Ysyakh used to be like a [Soviet-style] 'meeting'—now it is done with all the traditional songs. So I think that our leadership thinks that we are on the verge of extinction. How many of us are there in this republic? Four hundred thousand in all. So we will disappear eventually if we lose our language, our folklore, our roots. So that is where the revitalization comes from. In this way we can be revitalized."[70]

In short, the prognoses I hear from Sakha people regarding the future of olonkho range from grim and dire to hopeful and even confident. Those involved in the revitalization process give the most positive projections, sharing their hopes for a sustainable future for olonkho, but those who are not involved are less likely to predict success in revitalization efforts. Across the board, responses generally follow one of two common threads. On the idealistic side, some people feel that olonkho "should" be revived in the traditional manner. Other people assume change and try to envisage the new forms or other potential modifications that might accompany the revival of the genre.

At the end of 2015, the first "Decade of Olonkho" drew to a close and the second decade began.[71] With the current crisis surrounding the Russian ruble, support levels for the second decade may not match those of the first, but some funding seems guaranteed by the announcement of the regions hosting an Ysyakh of Olonkho through 2021.[72]

How did the educational and administrative heads of Yakutia approach the revitalization efforts of the first decade? To what extent did they draw from UNESCO ideals, terminology, and goals in creating their plans? To what degree did they achieve their objectives? What lessons from the outcomes of the first Decade of Olonkho might guide future plans? The following chapter delves into the world of strategy behind olonkho revitalization efforts.

CHAPTER 4

EXAMINING THE ROLE OF UNESCO AND INTANGIBLE CULTURAL HERITAGE

A real tradition is not the relic of a past that is irretrievably gone;
it is a living force that animates and informs the present . . .
Far from implying the repetition of what has been,
tradition presupposes the reality of what endures.
It appears as an heirloom, a heritage that one receives
on condition of making it bear fruit
before passing it on to one's descendants.
—Igor Stravinsky, *Poetics of Music in Six Lessons*

UNESCO's proclamation in 2005 of the Sakha olonkho as a Masterpiece of the Oral and Intangible Heritage of Humanity gave the genre special visibility in Yakutia. This prominence launched revitalization programs that changed olonkho's trajectory in significant ways and led to the establishment of the government-sponsored "Decade of Olonkho." Although UNESCO's Intangible Cultural Heritage program has received criticism for some inadequacies (Grant 2014, 41; Labadi 2013, 151) and has not delivered the same positive results in every context, the Masterpiece proclamation for olonkho has had a profoundly energizing effect on the genre's revitalization.[1] In Yakutia, perceptions of UNESCO values, as gleaned from the terminology and especially the Russian translations of key terms used in the official documents, strongly shaped subsequent olonkho-related activity.

Key terms of the convention defined

The Convention for the Safeguarding of the Intangible Cultural Heritage carefully defines some key terms with the intention of providing clarity for desirable outcomes. The following sections elaborate on UNESCO's definitions of *intangible cultural heritage*, *masterpiece*, and *safeguarding*, then identify potential threats to safeguarding.

90   CHAPTER 4

Intangible Cultural Heritage

UNESCO defined the concept of *intangible cultural heritage* as early as 2001: "peoples' learned processes along with the knowledge, skills and creativity that inform and are developed by them, the products they create, and the resources, spaces and other aspects of social and natural context necessary to their sustainability; these processes provide living communities with a sense of continuity with previous generations and are important to cultural identity, as well as to the safeguarding of cultural diversity and creativity of humanity."[2] The ICH program supports the protection and production of cultural heritage, allowing cultures to "produce something new in the present that has recourse to the past" (Kirshenblatt-Gimblett 1995, 369–370). UNESCO has fostered programs for cultural heritage since 1972, beginning with the Convention Concerning the Protection of the World Cultural and Natural Heritage, which covered both the conservation of nature and the preservation of cultural properties.[3] The Sakha found the new ICH program interesting because UNESCO expanded the concept of cultural heritage to include intangible cultural expressions "such as oral traditions, performing arts, social practices, rituals, festive events, knowledge and practices concerning nature and the universe or the knowledge and skills to produce traditional crafts."[4] As noted in the wording of the final two phrases in this list, the expansion from safeguarding tangible, material objects to caring for intangible cultural elements emphasized the *transmission* of the expertise related to traditions more than the simple preservation of the concrete cultural manifestations themselves.[5] This core UNESCO goal of transmission has proven one of the most challenging aspects in revitalizing olonkho, and as a primary factor involved in sustainability, it figures prominently in discussions of the revitalization process.

Masterpiece

The ICH program has evolved over time, sometimes retreating from earlier established emphases. The Masterpiece program provides an example of a fairly short-lived initiative with tremendous impact in Yakutia. In this program, which was formulated in 1997 and implemented proclamations in 2001, 2003, and 2005, UNESCO focused on six crucial features for judging applications (UNESCO 2005). To compete for a Masterpiece award, cultural expressions of ICH must:

1. demonstrate their *outstanding value* as [a] masterpiece of the human creative genius;
2. give wide evidence of their *roots in the cultural tradition* or cultural history of the community concerned;
3. be a means of affirming the *cultural identity* of the cultural communities concerned;

4. provide proof of *excellence* in the application of the skill and technical qualities displayed;
5. affirm their value as unique testimony of *living cultural traditions*;
6. be *at risk* of degradation or of disappearing.[6]

In addition, each application dossier had to "provide proof of the full involvement and agreement of the communities concerned, and to include an action plan for the safeguarding or promotion of the cultural spaces or expressions, which should have been developed in close collaboration with the tradition bearers."[7] Olonkho would easily have met most of the requirements, although the fifth point, regarding status as a "living cultural tradition," provided a potential challenge. Apparently, the presence of one or two master performers sufficed.

When UNESCO discontinued the "Masterpiece" designation and moved toward safeguarding "representative" examples of ICH, the Masterpiece awards list was merged with the Representative List of the Intangible Cultural Heritage of Humanity.[8] Interestingly, I have never heard people in Yakutia mention this fundamental change in status for olonkho. Instead, they always refer to the genre as a Masterpiece.[9] Olonkho's designation as a Masterpiece connects deeply with Sakha pride in the genre. Quite possibly Yakutia would not have invested so intensely in revitalization efforts had olonkho simply been declared a "representative" example of ICH.

A 2006 UNESCO document explains the organization's retreat from the "Masterpiece" terminology. In light of the close connection between group identities and examples of ICH, UNESCO felt it should not "attempt to create a hierarchy among such elements, or among cultures."[10] Despite the merits of this position, my conversations with Sakha people reveal that the hierarchical nature of the award actually provided them with strong motivation to apply. Fortunately for the Sakha, since the convention was not fully ratified until 2006, olonkho was not subsumed into the Representative List until fully a year after its declaration as a Masterpiece.[11]

For olonkho's proud proponents, the lag in UNESCO's policies on whether a genre held "outstanding value" or served as "representative" made all the difference. For Yakutia, the significance of the designation lay precisely in being proclaimed a "Masterpiece" rather than being considered merely representative of the intangible cultural heritage of humanity and of the Sakha people. In fact, my dialogues with a broad spread of Sakha people revealed a unanimous perception of the Masterpiece declaration as the primary cause leading to revitalization for olonkho, a conclusion confirmed by the research of Ignatieva and her colleagues (2013). Most people who knew about the connection with UNESCO viewed the international organization as representing the whole world. For them, the Masterpiece award took on global significance.

92   CHAPTER 4

Infused with this perspective, the Masterpiece proclamation tapped into the pride running deep in Sakha consciousness—a pride in their people's artistic, linguistic, and cultural accomplishments. Although they had been marginalized for many decades, they had not lost hope that the world would recognize the inimitable value of their cultural heritage. Had the Masterpiece program been subsumed into the Representative List even one year earlier, the impetus behind subsequent revitalization activities would have been robbed of one of its primary engines—ubiquitous and heartfelt pride in UNESCO's proclamation that the Republic of Sakha (Yakutia) had a hidden treasure of comparatively outstanding value. They felt that such a masterpiece merited the use of enormous amounts of government resources for protection and preservation.

Safeguarding

UNESCO's definition of *safeguarding* conveys a wide-ranging approach to achieving sustainability, emphasizing that safeguarding measures must ensure "the viability of the intangible cultural heritage, including the identification, documentation, research, preservation, protection, promotion, enhancement, transmission, particularly through formal and non-formal education, as well as the revitalization of the various aspects of such heritage."[12] Although scholarship focused on safeguarding intangible cultural heritage has progressed over the last few decades, additional in-depth case studies will strengthen the field through providing methodological recommendations for those wishing to revive their moribund traditions.[13]

Unfortunately, the English word *safeguarding* has no clear equivalent in Russian. The closest Russian terms relate to *preservation* and *protection* rather than to the broader values of enduring creativity and resilience as expressed in the full texts of the ICH Convention:

> To be kept alive, intangible cultural heritage must be relevant to its community, continuously recreated and transmitted from one generation to another. There is a risk that certain elements of intangible cultural heritage could die out or disappear without help, but safeguarding does not mean fixing or freezing intangible cultural heritage in some pure or primordial form. Safeguarding intangible cultural heritage is about the transferring of knowledge, skills and meaning. Transmission—or communicating heritage from generation to generation—is emphasized in the Convention rather than the production of concrete manifestations such as dances, songs, musical instruments or crafts. Therefore, to a large extent, any safeguarding measure refers to strengthening and reinforcing the diverse and varied circumstances, tangible and intangible, that are necessary for the continuous evolution and interpretation of intangible cultural heritage, as well as for its transmission to future generations.[14]

This definition stresses the facets of safeguarding emphasized in this book—continuous re-creation, evolution, and transmission, not simple preservation.[15]

Without ongoing creativity within a living cultural expression, the core of the tradition's "genetic material"—including the relevant knowledge, skills, and meaning—will disappear.[16] Instead, only the more static material, usually found as concrete manifestations in the form of "distant relatives" of the original genre, remains to be transmitted.[17] True safeguarding, on the other hand, focuses on passing along a living, mutable tradition without "fossilizing, freezing or trivializing it" (Smith and Akagawa, 2009, 3).[18]

Safeguarding also affects the grassroots level by endowing a tradition with patrimonial value. This recognition transforms and ennobles the cultural expression, repurposing the tradition for a variety of objectives, including, but not limited to, the actual process of revitalization. If one of olonkho's crucial roles is to embody a Sakha identity, then the processes of documentation, promotion, competitions, and festivals become ways of "*staging heritage* and therefore *enacting* the social identities and cultural differences that it [the tradition] represents" (Arantes 2013, 40; emphasis in the original). In this way, olonkho became an arena for negotiating Sakha identity, with various groups of Sakha culture brokers vying to wrap their particular ideology in the flag of the Sakha olonkho.[19]

Threats to safeguarding

UNESCO suggests that a number of problems play a significant role in the decline of ICH transmission, thereby threatening older traditions around the world. All germane to the context of olonkho, these issues arise from "such factors as social and demographic changes that reduce intergenerational contacts, for instance from migrations and urbanisation that often remove people from their knowledgeable elders, from the imposition of formal education systems that devalue traditional knowledge and skills, or from intrusive mass media."[20] Noting additional factors that cause significant danger to the vitality of the olonkho tradition, UNESCO also mentions the "political and technological changes in twentieth-century Russia . . . [and] the very low number of practitioners, all of old age."[21]

In responding to these administrative pressures, UNESCO employs a mix of bottom-up and top-down approaches, equally promoting measures that spring from smaller, local groups and from national and even international entities (Labadi 2013, 143). The fact that the ICH program has successfully generated initiatives at the highest levels of the Yakutian government raises some interesting questions: What should be considered "top-down" in the Yakutian context? Should the actions of a relatively small cadre of legislators, scholars, performers, and activists promoting olonkho be considered a top-down approach? The answer depends on perspective. Compared to the kind of governmental control coming from the Center, Yakutian efforts feel like regional, grassroots initiatives.[22] On the other hand, this same work seems top-down relative to the majority of the Sakha

94   CHAPTER 4

population, since the initiatives come from the republic's cultural, legislative, and educational elite. At this point, the spread of olonkho revitalization all over Yakutia to villages and far-flung outposts of the republic has created a certain amount of bottom-up response, even if most of the efforts originate with artists, educators, and other members of the cultural elite.

Like any legal document, Yakutia's Action Plan undergoes additional threats when cultural and bureaucratic power brokers interpret the content according to their personal agendas. All purported as good for the Sakha people, these ambitions often prove murky in nature, some more self-serving than others, as I explore later in this chapter.

UNESCO's and Yakutia's desired outcomes compared

Considering the significant degree to which UNESCO's desired outcomes overlap with those stated by Yakutia in the legislation for olonkho, the Action Plan for revitalizing olonkho in Yakutia reflects careful preparation based on UNESCO documents. UNESCO presents the following purposes for the ICH Convention:

> (a) to *safeguard* the intangible cultural heritage;
> (b) to ensure *respect* for the intangible cultural heritage of the communities, groups and individuals concerned;
> (c) to raise *awareness* at the local, national and international levels of the importance of the intangible cultural heritage, and of ensuring mutual *appreciation* thereof;
> (d) to provide for international *cooperation* and *assistance*.[23]

What specific actions does the ICH program recommend for achieving these outcomes? As already noted, UNESCO expects "measures aimed at ensuring the viability of the intangible cultural heritage, including the identification, documentation, research, preservation, protection, promotion, enhancement, transmission through formal and non-formal education, as well as the revitalization of the various aspects of such heritage."[24] Each of these measures factors into the three primary goals of Yakutia's plan, which was signed into law in March 2007:

> (a) the preservation of the Yakut heroic epos of Olonkho as an outstanding cultural monument for transmission to future generations;
> (b) the creation of the conditions necessary for the rebirth of the oral storytelling tradition;[25]
> (c) the promulgation of Olonkho as a Masterpiece of the oral and intangible heritage of humanity. (Republic of Sakha 2007)

The clear way in which UNESCO's recommended measures correspond closely with Yakutia's goals gives testimony to careful planning on the part of the people who drew up the law. Note, however, the proportionately stronger emphasis on preservation, with just one of the three goals relating to transmission.

The March 2007 legislation also included ten tasks derived from the three goals. I have listed those ten tasks below; the square brackets indicate my observations regarding the correlation between each point and the measures outlined by UNESCO. Once again, of these ten, only half relate to transmission:

1. ascertainment and collection of epic artifacts [*identification, documentation, preservation*];
2. systematization of scientific research in the area of epic studies and the intensification of publishing activities [*research, promotion*];
3. provision for the safeguarding of materials related to epics located in the archives of the Republic [*documentation, preservation, protection*];
4. creation, on the territory of the Republic, of a single organizational-legislative model and comprehensive standard for the legal protection of the epos of Olonkho [*preservation, protection*];
5. formation of an epic *sreda* [*promotion, enhancement, transmission*];
6. support of the activities of the narrator-olonkhosuts [*protection, promotion, transmission*];
7. introduction of Olonkho into the educational curricula of learning institutions [*transmission through formal education, revitalization*];
8. establishment of a system of training children in the art of storytelling [*promotion, transmission through formal and non-formal education, revitalization*];
9. improvement in the quality of the personnel involved in the spheres of preservation, study, and promotion of traditional culture [*enhancement, research, preservation, protection, promotion*];
10. promotion and dissemination of Olonkho [*promotion, transmission, revitalization*].

This careful legislation design, featuring a high degree of overlap with UNESCO's vision, has created a fairly stable platform for olonkho revitalization activities by tying the government-approved, budgeted activities closely to items officially mandated by UNESCO policy. While each of the identified tasks plays a role in the larger whole, I propose that the sixth item, support of the activities of the olonkhosuts, highlights one of the most urgent factors. Without any currently recognized master olonkhosuts, the core of the tradition lacks highly skilled transmitters. As a result, the seventh and eighth tasks, relating to educational curricula and training children, also take on increased priority.

Without master olonkhosuts, will the current focus on children prove too little too late? Can we still hope for the transmission of improvised solo olonkho performance to the next generation? While the answers to these questions remain elusive, the first four and the ninth activities, all unrelated to transmission, enjoy

96   CHAPTER 4

strong support and steady growth through the governmental apparatus connected to the study of olonkho. Unfortunately, achieving only these objectives will still relegate olonkho to a frozen form rather than encouraging the genre to flourish as a living tradition. In addition, the tenth task seems dangerously broad, a potential category for anything remotely related to olonkho promotion and a temptation for those who wish to tap into the budgetary funding to cast their pet projects in terms of olonkho revitalization.

Ancillary programs

In addition to the three general goals and ten tasks, Yakutia's Action Plan delineated several ancillary programs. The following list represents these programs, with their respective coordinating entities noted in italics:[26]

1. "International Center for Olonkho and the scientific study of epos"—*Institute of Humanitarian Research (IGI), Yakutsk State University (YaGU)*
2. "Protection, preservation, and activities providing for the protection of epic heritage"—*Institute of Humanitarian Research (IGI), Yakutsk State University (YaGU)*
3. "Protection and rebirth of the authentic oral epic tradition in the Republic of Sakha"—*Ministry of Culture and Spiritual Development, RS(Y) [Republic of Sakha (Yakutia)], Institute of Humanitarian Research (IGI)*
4. "Olonkho and future generations" (educational goals for teaching the art of olonkho)—*Ministry of Education, RS(Y)*
5. "Theater of Olonkho and the development of modern forms of epic expression"—*Ministry of Culture and Spiritual Development, RS(Y)*

Yakutia's Action Plan strategically uses the word "authentic" in the third ancillary program, a reference that raises a number of considerations: Who decides what is authentic? What benefits does authenticity yield, and for whom? In contexts of revitalization, judgments of authenticity can determine far-reaching decisions such as who merits a stipend, who gets an invitation to sing at an international festival, or who receives recognition and compensation as the winner of a competition.[27] Debates about authenticity stretch back to the early days of ethnomusicology and folklore societies, if not beyond (Bendix 1997; Cowdery 2009; Labadi 2013). In an amusing historical note, Schippers observes the paradox that the term "had opposite meanings in the emergence of early music practice in the 1960s and 1970s ('authentic is as close to the original as we can get') and in rock music of the same period ('authentic is as far from copying existing models as possible')" (2015, 139).

One way toward uncovering the concept of authenticity in a music culture is through investigating who or what, in the minds of the recognized authorities of

THE ROLE OF UNESCO AND ICH   97

the tradition, constitutes the "others" of authenticity (Arizpe and Amescua 2013, 129). For example, those "others" for the olonkho community of practice might include memorized performances, forms outside the solo performance of olonkho, or both. In any case, judgments regarding authenticity largely reflect the social constructs of recognized experts (Bohlman 1988, 10; Cooley 2006, 73; Labadi 2013, 13), and thus represent a form of "authorised heritage discourse" (Smith and Akagawa 2009, 3).

By encouraging the "development of modern forms of epic expression" through the creation of a Theater of Olonkho, the fifth item in the Action Plan expands the funding parameters beyond simply supporting the traditional master olonkhosut model. I can only conclude that the creators of the document wished to promote the older "authentic" solo tradition while still leaving room for the birth of hybrid developments. This two-pronged approach reflects both practicality and foresight. Targeting the support of both "authentic" improvised solo performances and more contemporary forms of epic expression affords a broader base for creating the epic *sreda* needed for olonkho revitalization.

As noted in the list above, each of the ancillary programs comes under the wing of either a ministry of the Yakutian government or an educational entity, or both. Likewise, each program receives funding legislated for the benefit of olonkho revitalization. Yakutia has made a significant financial investment in the future of olonkho by thus empowering the people and organizations involved in revitalization.

Program funding and anticipated results

Russia's decision not to sign the UNESCO Convention on ICH left Yakutia unable to tap into UNESCO funding for the Action Plan. Instead, the republic legislated its own funding, designing an ambitious ten-year budget to cover these programs. By signing this provision into law rather than making it a regularly reviewed budget item, the leaders provided for stable, substantial amounts of money to go toward olonkho revitalization during the first Decade of Olonkho (2006–2015). Originally slated at more than 2.1 billion Russian rubles, or the equivalent of over \$80 million USD in 2007, most of the resources came from the republic's governmental budget.[28] Two exceptions were 47 million rubles (approximately \$1.8 million USD) from "other sources of financing" and 52.4 million rubles (approximately \$2 million USD) from "extra-budgetary sources."[29]

Such a significant investment represents a temptation for opportunists who might use the popularity and large budget of olonkho revitalization for projects that do not actually contribute significantly to the stated purpose. Researchers of ICH describe this vulnerability as inherent to the arena generally created during the "heritagization" of a tradition—political and economic forces compete for the

98   CHAPTER 4

appropriation of resources (Bendix 2009, 6; Kuutma 2013, 3) even as they negotiate for power with the structures responsible for quality control and evaluation (Arizpe and Amescua 2013, 121). The "intangible" focus of ICH actually results in a multitude of tangible and material processes (Kuutma 2013, 4), including budgets for the infrastructures to support immense, multifaceted revitalization plans.

When I asked Sidorova about the large budget, she pointed out that the ten-year amount, when divided out, actually totaled less than $8 million USD per year. She also observed, in light of the falling exchange rate, "a million rubles isn't even really [significant] money anymore. Money is losing its value, so sometimes we can't make ends meet."[30] Her point is well taken. During the period in which I researched olonkho, from January 2009 through January 2016, the strength of the ruble fell from roughly 30 to 80 against the US dollar.[31]

The relative paucity of funds also becomes apparent in light of one particularly large recurring budget item—olonkho summer festival preparations. Each year, a different region of Yakutia hosts the "Ysyakh of Olonkho," receiving budgeted funds specifically designated for the construction projects involved in preparing for thousands of attendees: an Olonkho Diėtė (House of Olonkho); a *moghol uraha* (a large, conical-shaped traditional summer dwelling, also spelled *urasa*); prepared spaces for drinking *kumys* (fermented mare's milk) and for *kunu korsor tuhulgė* (the early morning ritual of greeting the sun); a giant wooden *aal-luuk mas* (sacred tree); an *aar-bagakh sėrgė* (carved horse-tying pole); an *ytyk duogha* (a large, ornately decorated scepter, the sacred symbol of the Ysyakh of Olonkho); grandstands for the opening and closing ceremonies; a building for performing olonkho; places for eating; areas designated for sanitary and firefighting facilities; a horseracing track; stables for the horses participating in the ceremonies; and spaces and prizes for sports competitions such as wrestling (*khapsagai*), the stick-pull, footraces, various kinds of jumping competitions (*kylyy, ystanga, kuobakh*), and archery (*dalla mёndëyii*).[32]

Russia's deepening financial crisis prompted several adjustments to the budget for olonkho revitalization—not a surprising phenomenon, given the general budgetary difficulties that followed the devaluation of the ruble in late 2008.[33] A new decree outlining an interim arrangement passed into law on December 26, 2009. This legislation provided an updated three-year "first stage" plan (2009–2011), while an extension received approval by the end of 2011.[34] Another budget alteration occurred in late 2010.[35]

The difficulty of determining the wisest use of funding remains one of the biggest challenges in large budgets with many stakeholders and partners. Anthony Seeger, who held the post of secretary-general of the International Council for Traditional Music from 2001 to 2005, oversaw the evaluation of approximately ninety Masterpiece nominations. In remarking on the challenges in preparing action plans, he noted the frequent occurrence of "a gap between stated intentions and programme budgets. . . . In many cases, most of the money went to bureaucrats and scholars; rarely were funds given to the artists and tradition bearers for things they required or for their participation in the project (in some cases it was as little as 10%)" (Seeger 2009a, 123). Although the money for Yakutia's Action Plan did not come from UNESCO, but rather from the republic's own coffers, the plan still suffered from this weakness.

Such large budgets often prove difficult to sustain, and I wondered during my initial research if governmental support for olonkho revitalization would also end with the close of the first Decade of Olonkho. The answer came during the summer festival season of 2014, when the second Decade of Olonkho (2016–2025) was signed into law.[36] The two-year lead time between this decision and its implementation gave the organizers of olonkho-related revitalization projects time to plan ahead.

The ancillary programs' anticipated results, listed below, show a high level of correspondence with UNESCO's suggested ICH measures, which I have added within square brackets:

1. the gathering of epic works into databases and identification of experts in the epic tradition [*identification, documentation, research, preservation, protection*];
2. the provision of archival safety for handwritten, audio, video, and film materials related to epics by transferring them to digital formats [*preservation, protection*];
3. the protection and further development of the epic tradition on the basis of the creation of curricula and educational systems [*promotion, enhancement, transmission*];
4. the appearance of new directions in the arts as a result of the creation of the Theater of Olonkho [*enhancement, transmission, revitalization*];
5. the spread of olonkho through the publication of texts with translations, scientific publications, art albums, the creation of new works with epic plots in various arts domains, the development of the web portal *Olonkho* (www.olonkho.info), and the organization of cultural-ethnographic complexes [*identification, documentation, research, preservation, promotion, transmission, revitalization*].

The overlap between the individual items suggests that the republic should be able, by following through on its proposed plan, to achieve UNESCO's desired results. The following section evaluates Yakutia's success in achieving these five ambitious outcomes.

100   CHAPTER 4

Results of the ICH program and Yakutia's Action Plan

The first three of the five outcomes listed above are being met primarily through the efforts of a single integrated project, the Olonkho Information System. This crucial initiative, directed by Sergei Vasiliev and housed at North-Eastern Federal University (NEFU), entails collecting and digitizing olonkho materials and creating a web portal for access to them. Its various components include the establishment of physical archives, the digitization of those archives, the creation of web access for much of the digitally archived information, and the application of the material in the educational sphere. Backed by such a wealth of accessible archived resources, the educational initiative provides hope for transmitting and promoting the olonkho performance tradition.

Vasiliev reported that as of 2010, the digital and physical archives contained 320 manuscript items, including 127 full texts: "This is quite a lot of folders, and in fact the first time I looked over this material I was very surprised to see that those who began to write at the end of the 1930s—1939, 1940, 1941—before the beginning of the war, for example, wrote and wrote in a granary book, and when they ran out of room, they then continued in a *tetrad* [copy book]. When that ran out of room, they wrote on cigarette paper; when that ended, they wrote on newspaper . . . so of course these manuscripts are not in very good condition. So the task to put these into digital format is a vital one."[37] In addition to the manuscripts, the archives include items such as magnetic tape, photographs, slides, and an online library of digital resources.[38]

In speaking about the project's web portal (www.olonkho.info), Vasiliev commented: "We think of it as a window to the outside world . . . the Internet portal is an important part of this work, because it allows all the people who need it to get access to this material for their education, their work, and their various interests. Our task is to develop this portal in such a way that the informational resources are accessible."[39]

As for the educational initiative, Vasiliev explained the reasoning behind this component of the project: "There are those who do independent study, and they are of various age groups, from various nations and places, and if they show interest, they will need material that is already prepared. We also are preparing pedagogical material and describing teaching methods."[40] The wiki-based nature of the project allows for ongoing growth and self-regulation if the initial funding for the site ends. In addition, the site allows for expansion into several languages besides Sakha and Russian, including English, French, German, Korean, Japanese, Chinese, and Turkish. From Vasiliev's perspective, "UNESCO's initiatives in support of multilingualism in cyberspace for the preservation of digital heritage

Fig. 4.1. Sergei Vasiliev with the author (June 24, 2010).

have been of immeasurable importance for the preservation of world cultural heritage in all its diversity" (Vasiliev et al. 2009, 7).[41]

When I asked Elizaveta Sidorova, Elena Protodiakonova, and Anastasia Luginova their opinions on which of the initiatives in Yakutia's Action Plan best support the revitalization of olonkho, they reported that "the Olonkho Information System is the most useful thing we have right now. They make discs that are being used all over the districts—CDs and DVDs, the Internet portal—they use these things in the school programs, in kindergartens. They produce material that is ready to use!"[42]

While the Information System largely accounts for the first three of the five goals, the successful creation of the Theater of Olonkho has fulfilled the fourth initiative. Led by Andrei Borisov, Yakutia's minister of culture for twenty-four years and the recipient of Russia's "Golden Mask" award, the Theater of Olonkho has staged many productions, even performing *Kyys Dėbiliiė* (The Girl *Dėbiliiė*) in Japan in 2005 and in Shanghai, China, in 2010.[43] The project receives funding through the Ministry of Culture.[44]

As called for in Yakutia's Action Plan, Borisov's Theater of Olonkho promotes new directions in the arts. Known for his creativity as a theatrical director, Borisov enhances traditional olonkho plots with modern elements such as LED screens and other technology-based effects.[45] In 2014 the theater performed a brand-new olonkho tale for children, *Ėrbekhchėn Bėrgėn*, written and directed by Valentin Isakov and featuring Isakov himself in the role of an olonkhosut.[46] These new

102   CHAPTER 4

forms of creativity delight olonkho audiences, who enjoy seeing a fresh perspective on the tradition (Leete and Firnhaber 2004, 194).

In addition, a 2006 conference on the topic of "Olonkho in the Theatrical Arts" brought together more than fifty scholars from all over Yakutia to present papers on topics related to olonkho and its theatrical expression. The conference proceedings and presentations were gathered into a rich volume (Vinokurova and Petrova 2006) that provides an outstanding overview of the topic from the vantage point of several disciplines.

Borisov transitioned in October 2014 from minister of culture to head of the Sakha Academic Theater, but he continues to provide leadership to the Theater of Olonkho.[47] Naturally, his future artistic choices regarding the mix of new plots with more canonical tales or the involvement of olonkhosuts as scriptwriters, directors, and performers of the olonkhosut role will greatly affect the degree of ongoing innovation within this venue.

As for the fifth expected outcome, most of the areas listed in this catchall collection of ideas exhibit observable progress.[48] One aspect not yet clearly achieved calls for "new works with epic plots in various arts domains." With few exceptions, such as the children's theater just mentioned, directors recycle olonkho plots from the canon of well-known published olonkho tales, condensing and reconfiguring the tales to meet theatrical goals.

The cultural-ethnographic complexes mentioned in the fifth outcome are being built in various regions of Yakutia, many of them in connection with each year's Ysyakh of Olonkho. Hopefully these new "Houses of Olonkho" throughout the republic will provide gathering places for performances and other transmission-focused activities.

Unfortunately, the phrase "cultural-ethnographic complexes" in the fifth outcome has also provided an opportunity for a building project not directly connected to the revitalization process. In April 2010, Viacheslav Shtyrov, the president of Yakutia at the time, decreed the development of a massive complex of buildings, "Olonkholand," with the minister of culture named as coordinator of the undertaking.[49] Following an international competition to select an architectural plan for Olonkholand, the projects chosen as finalists showed a broad variety of ultramodern buildings spread over forty-seven hectares in Yakutsk near NEFU.[50] Significantly behind schedule, the project may never come to fruition, since other men now hold both the presidency of the republic and the position of minister of culture. Still, the question remains whether resuming the project would mean drawing exorbitant amounts from the budgetary funds set aside for olonkho revitalization.[51] I agree with a number of olonkho scholars who have expressed distaste for the project and see this venture as squandering funds that could be used more effectively for revitalization (Ignatieva et al. 2013, 41).

Progress in Yakutia in regard to other UNESCO concerns

Various places on the ICH site contain statements of valued outcomes in addition to the four primary purposes listed earlier. For example, UNESCO emphasizes that ICH contributes toward "*maintaining cultural diversity* in the face of growing globalization . . . helps with *intercultural dialogue*, and encourages mutual respect for other ways of life."[52] The ICH program also emphasizes strengthening *transmission* systems so that the traditions can thrive well into the future.[53] The following section compares the initial results of olonkho revitalization in Yakutia with these additional ambitions.

(1) *Maintaining cultural diversity in the face of growing globalization*: Although UNESCO's Masterpiece program carved out a space for olonkho within the larger cultural *sreda*, the traditional solo form does not enjoy enough of a presence in modern Sakha society to maintain ground in the face of globalization and cultural unification (Ignatieva et al. 2013, 3). Neither simple to perform nor conducive to holding the attention of modern audiences, traditional olonkho is losing ground to films, books, theatrical presentations, and other olonkho "descendants" that fit better with the powerful forces of globalization in Siberia.

Instead, the cultural diversity within Yakutia comes through more easily accessible artistic expressions such as traditional dress, jewelry, crafts, pop music, the use of the Sakha language, and performances on the national instrument, the *khomus*. Unlike olonkho, which lacks a supportive epic *sreda*, each of these other cultural expressions boasts valued functions within the society, a broad audience that enjoys that particular heritage, or both.

(2) *Fostering intercultural dialogue*: Yakutia's location and underfunded transportation infrastructure make gathering for face-to-face communication difficult. Without the budget resources, few people travel either to Yakutia to hear an olonkho performance or from Yakutia to promote the genre elsewhere. Only rarely do epic scholars come to Yakutia to research olonkho. Pyotr Reshetnikov reported that, other than me, he had received visitors only from Holland, Germany, and Japan.[54]

The most active level of international dialogue concerning olonkho has occurred between Yakutia and its Asian and Central Asian near neighbors. This dialogue has focused largely on translation projects, such as the translation of olonkho into Japanese by Munehisa Yamashita of the Folklore Society of Japan. Having finished just the first half (1,341 lines) of the olonkho *Non-Stumbling Nyusur Bërgë* by N. M. Tarasov, Yamashita comments both on the challenges in translating olonkho and on the aspects of olonko that most appeal to Japanese

104   CHAPTER 4

audiences: "When olonkho is decoded, the particular rhythm and melody are lost. And when the decoded text is translated, the beauty of the poetry, such as alliteration, is also lost. But olonkho is such an amazing work of art that it is still very interesting to read the Japanese translation. Through the translation the Japanese people learn a lot, for example, the richness of similes and metaphors, the captivating nature of the plots, the similarities with Japanese mythology" (2006, 48). While translations in themselves may not engender true intercultural dialogue, Yamashita helped facilitate the Theater of Olonkho's March 2005 performance of *Kyys Débiliié* in Japan by writing the subtitles. Such performances may provide extra momentum toward dialogue, especially if accompanied by structures that support cross-cultural communication.

A current initiative that offers great hope for intercultural dialogue is a new book series entitled Epic Monuments of the Peoples of the World. Initiated by Alexander Zhirkov, Speaker of the Yakutian Parliament, the series includes plans for two-way translation projects that render *Nurgun Botur* into other languages and epics from those languages into Sakha.[55] The five-year plan currently includes epics from Altai, Tuva, Bashkiria, Tatarstan, Buryatia, Khakassia, Finland, and Dagestan. As stated in the paperwork provided for the editorial commission, three desired outcomes motivate the project: (1) language development, cultural education, and the creation of a wider readership for olonkho ; (2) stronger international relations for the republic and friendship between nations; and (3) heightened interest in the work of translation in Yakutia as a unique, expressive, and independent form of verbal art.[56]

Nakhodkina lists the bulk of olonkho translations into other languages, including French, English, Russian, and Korean, as well as works in process for German, Turkic, and Japanese (2014, 275). In addition, *Èr Sogotokh* by Afanasii Uvarovskii (1800–1861) has been translated into Russian, German, and Turkish, with a fragment rendered into Altaic. Translations into the Turkic and Mongol languages, which are closely related to Sakha, allow for the preservation of the phonetic, lexical, and grammatical structures of the original text (Vasilieva 2006, 49), making them especially interesting and understandable to these "close relatives" of the Sakha people.

Ingredients needed to foster dialogue include a minimum level of revitalization, a solid base of enthusiasts who understand and promote olonkho, and people with connections to other groups willing to facilitate conversation. The Yakutian context struggles without an epic *sreda*, while within the broader Russian Federation, knowledge of olonkho is limited to specialists. The mass media, controlled by Moscow, shows little interest. As Sakha ethnomusicologist Anna Larionova reported, "When they [UNESCO] announced the olonkho as a 'Masterpiece,' there was absolutely no sign of it—complete silence—in the [Russian] mass media.

THE ROLE OF UNESCO AND ICH   105

The regional news media had it on every single channel! But in the mass media
. . . not a word."[57]

Ideally, intercultural dialogue about olonkho would begin between the majority
and minority cultures within the borders of the Russian Federation. Conferences
about olonkho and epics in general already serve to further this kind of communication, occurring several times each year and always including some measure
of international participation. At a large international forum in June 2015 titled
"Epics of the World in the Land of Olonkho," I was one of a very large contingent
of non-Yakutian guests, with performers and scholars from Moscow and various
republics of the Russian Federation (Altai, Bashkortostan, Buriatia, Kalmykia,
Karachay-Cherkessia, Khakassia, Tatarstan, and Tuva) joining participants from
Armenia, Azerbaijan, China, Germany, Japan, Kazakhstan, Kyrgyzstan, Mongolia,
South Korea, Turkey, Turkmenistan, the USA, and Uzbekistan. The representation
at this conference reflects the increasing success of Yakutia's efforts to facilitate an
international conversation on the topic of epics and olonkho, and the interaction
at these kinds of meetings helps the participants to build and maintain collegial
relationships and mutual learning. Yakutia's great strength of hospitality will also
continue to support positive relations with other cultures—for example, after experiencing the conference, the Ysyakh of Olonkho at Churapcha, and the summer
school organized for them by NEFU and the Olonkho Institute, the five college
ethnomusicology interns studying with me came away loving Yakutia and its arts.

(3) *Safeguarding ICH through bolstering transmission systems*: With the severe
attenuation of olonkho's transmission systems in the twentieth century, a great
deal of time and effort will now be needed in order to return these processes
to sustainable levels. Transmission of any kind requires several basic components: a transmitter, content, a method of delivery, and a receptor who decodes
the message. Some of the most effective transmitters for olonkho include those
people designated as master olonkhosuts, although even olonkhosuts performing memorized versions provide exposure to the tradition. In places without live
olonkhosuts, mediated forms such as recordings, television, and radio can also
serve in the popularization of olonkho.

To ensure ongoing transmission, UNESCO "encourages States to create national
systems of 'Living Human Treasures' that honour exemplary tradition-bearers
and encourage them to transmit their knowledge and skills."[58] The standards for
such nominations demand not only excellent artistry in performance but also the
ability and dedication to pass along the cultural heritage to others:

 (a) the excellence in the application of the knowledge and skills displayed;
 (b) the dedication of the person or group;

106   CHAPTER 4

(c) the ability of the person or group to further develop his knowledge and skills;

(d) the ability of the person or group to pass on the knowledge and skills to trainees.[59]

Yakutia recognized only three qualified tradition bearers in the decade following the Masterpiece proclamation, all of whom are now gone—Daria Tomskaia died in 2008, and Afanasii Solovëv (b. 1935), named as a tradition bearer in her place, died in October 2012.[60] Pyotr Reshetnikov was the last recognized master olonkhosut, and he died in January 2013, with no known replacements at the time of this writing. The paucity of officially recognized Living Human Treasures may simply reflect a lack of candidates who can meet the high standards. On the other hand, the situation might also indicate insufficient effort in identifying additional master performers. Finances should prove no obstacle—Yakutia's Action Plan budgeted a stipend of 33,000 rubles per month for each of the Living Human Treasures.[61] Even adding stipends for new master olonkhosuts would have little impact on the total olonkho revitalization budget.

As the UNESCO site explains, the funding should free the master olonkhosut to focus on dissemination and transmission of the olonkho tradition to the next generation: "Besides public recognition, the system includes measures for the provision of, for example, special grants/subsidies to designated Living Human Treasures, so that they can assume their responsibilities for the safeguarding of the intangible cultural heritage. These measures aim especially at:

1. The perpetuation and development of their knowledge and skills;
2. The transmission of their knowledge and skills to the younger generations through formal or non-formal training programmes;
3. Contributing to the documenting and recording of the intangible cultural heritage concerned (video or audio recording, publications, etc.);
4. Dissemination of their knowledge and skills;
5. Any additional duties entrusted to them.[62]

The small number of officially recognized master olonkhosuts in the first decade of olonkho revitalization and the absence of any at the moment clearly hinder olonkho's promulgation.[63] Adequately addressing the transmission aspect of Yakutia's Action Plan will necessarily involve identifying currently living masters and compensating them so that they can focus on transmission to the next generation.[64]

As demonstrated in the previous chapters of this book, Gavriil Kolesov's recorded performance of *Nurgun Botur the Swift* proved the power of mediated forms of transmission. At least one olonkhosut, Pyotr Tikhonov, who performs memorized olonkhos, traces his appreciation for the genre back to that recording.[65] Although a number of olonkhosuts drew inspiration from Kolesov, we have no evidence that his recordings ever produced a master olonkhosut capable of improvising in the style of traditional olonkho; the actual transmission of the tradition took place through long exposure to live performances.

School programs provide yet another vital link in the transmission system. When I visited in 2009, one of Reshetnikov's students at a school in Cherkëkh performed a short memorized portion of an olonkho for us. I also met and interviewed groups of children from two other schools who attended the summer festival and performed short sections of olonkhos that they had been learning. Schools without master olonkhosuts as mentors use a combination of recordings and olonkho performers to teach the art of olonkho. Students write papers about olonkho, choose an olonkho character to study, and learn short sections of olonkho to perform at competitions and festivals.

The absence of live "carriers" cannot help but negatively affect the level of success of such programs attempting to train children in the olonkho tradition. While written olonkho tales and recordings may help expand audiences, they cannot transmit a living art as effectively as the live performances of a master olonkhosut (Kirshenblatt-Gimblett 2004, 54). UNESCO's guidelines for identifying and monitoring Living Human Treasures reflect this regard for living people as the best carriers of a living tradition: "*Intangible cultural heritage*, or living heritage, consists of practices and expressions, as well as the knowledge, skills and values associated therewith, that communities and groups recognize as part of their cultural heritage. This heritage is transmitted from generation to generation, for the most part orally. It is constantly recreated in response to changes in the social and cultural environment. It provides individuals, groups and communities with a sense of identity and continuity and constitutes a guarantee of sustainable development."[66]

UNESCO overstates the case by asserting that robust transmission *guarantees* sustainable development—encouraging resilience for olonkho also requires engagement with other crucial issues such as reinforcing the epic *sreda*, allowing new expressions of olonkho to speak to the needs of twenty-first-century Sakha, and adapting to the forces of change sweeping Yakutia. Most importantly, the chances for sustainable development increase when master olonkhosuts orally *transmit* olonkho to a new generation and *re-create* expressions in response to the current social and cultural environment. These two key processes of transmission and innovation are severely compromised for olonkho in Yakutia today. Despite the robust support of the republic's governmental structures and the momentum built by a small cadre of enthusiasts through Yakutia's broad Action Plan and the UNESCO Masterpiece program, these two essential elements for revitalization require further attention.

CHAPTER 5

ELEMENTS OF RESILIENCE
Stable and Malleable

> Tradition is constituted by the interplay of innovation and sedimentation.
> —Paul Ricoeur, *Time and Narrative*

The historical chapters of this work provide a narrative frame that informs this chapter's discussion of continuity and change in olonkho performance. Measuring change for intangible cultural heritage remains a complicated process, but sociolinguists have found ways to address issues of language shift that may contribute helpful models for assessing music shift as well. Without drawing overly strict, problematic parallels between language and music (Tilley 2014, 487), sociolinguistic and other communication-based models can be modified effectively for measuring change in forms of artistic expression. In addition, these approaches highlight key factors related to resilience, thereby providing strategic insights into encouraging sustainable revitalization.[1]

Parallels in language and music safeguarding

In addition to safeguarding intangible cultural heritage, UNESCO promotes other, similar activities related to language revitalization.[2] Several parallels related to fostering vitality emerge between ICH and language.[3] First, as cultural expressions vulnerable to analogous forces, whether from outside a community or from within, both ICH and language may suffer attenuation and even extinction.[4] Second, the safeguarding programs for ICH feature many of the same initiatives employed in safeguarding languages, such as revitalization and intergenerational transmission. Regarding language death, UNESCO documents state: "this process is neither inevitable nor irreversible: well-planned and effectively implemented language policies can bolster ongoing efforts of speaker communities to maintain or revitalize their mother tongues and pass them on to younger generations."[5]

Models for measuring language and music shift

In 2003, the UNESCO Ad Hoc Expert Group on Endangered Languages published a list of nine factors for assessing the vitality of a language and determining appropriate safeguarding measures, identifying the most decisive factor as *intergenerational language transmission*:

1. Intergenerational Language Transmission
2. Absolute Number of Speakers
3. Proportion of Speakers within the Total Population
4. Trends in Existing Language Domains
5. Response to New Domains and Media
6. Materials for Language Education and Literacy
7. Governmental and Institutional Language Attitudes and Policies, Including Official Status and Use
8. Community Members' Attitudes toward Their Own Language
9. Amount and Quality of Documentation[6]

Based on these factors, UNESCO established six degrees of vitality. The six levels, arranged from "safe" to "extinct," appear as follows:

5. *Safe*: language is spoken by all generations; intergenerational transmission is uninterrupted
4. *Vulnerable*: most children speak the language, but it may be restricted to certain domains
3. *Definitely endangered*: children no longer learn the language as mother tongue in the home
2. *Severely endangered*: language is spoken by grandparents and older generations; while the parent generation may understand it, they do not speak it to children or among themselves
1. *Critically endangered*: the youngest speakers are grandparents and older, and they speak the language partially and infrequently
0. *Extinct*: there are no speakers left[7]

According to these factors, the Yakut (Sakha) language receives a designation of "vulnerable," despite Sakha's distinction as the most widely used indigenous language in Russia (Moseley 2010). This vulnerability results predominantly from stressors placed on the use of the Sakha language during the Soviet years. More recently, a general level of cultural revitalization in Yakutia has begun ameliorating this problem. For example, since the early 1990s, grassroots and governmental programs backing Sakha language use and cultural revitalization have flourished. Despite these initiatives, several hundred years of Russian language domination

110   CHAPTER 5

in Yakutia have weakened the Sakha language to a point at which much time and energy will be required to repair it.[8]

For a number of years, SIL International has served in an advisory role to UNESCO's Intergovernmental Committee for the Safeguarding of the ICH, and SIL's sociolinguistic and ethnomusicological scholarship informs the academic dialogue on language development, revitalization, and sustainability.[9] A model by SIL sociolinguists M. Paul Lewis and Gary Simons deals with issues of language shift (2010, 2014), and extended field-based research by my teaching colleagues Neil R. Coulter and Brian Schrag addresses topics relevant to safeguarding and music vitality (Coulter 2007, 2011; Schrag 2005, 2013a, 2013b, 2015b, 2016).[10]

Coulter's dissertation on music shift (2007) and an article elaborating and expanding on his original model (2011) offer a schema for the "diagnosis of shift in music preferences within a language community . . . draw[ing] from current discussion of language shift from sociolinguistics" (2007, 2).[11] Coulter posits that sociolinguistic methodologies such as that of Lewis and Simons, although potentially useful for informing music vitality research, need adaptation in order to account for music's higher vulnerability to cultural and extra-cultural forces. Regarding this greater susceptibility of the arts, he observes, "in many cases language is among the last parts of a culture to die. Other elements, such as visual art, music, dance, and oral storytelling, can be subject to extinction long before the language itself is weakened" (5).

Coulter traces the sociolinguistic foundations of his model to Joshua Fishman's (1991) Graded Intergenerational Disruption Scale (GIDS). Fishman describes eight stages of language shift, with stage 8 describing a situation very close to extinction ("people who still know the language are few and elderly") and stage 1 demonstrating the highest level of vitality ("the language can be used in higher-level education, occupations, government, and media"). The six levels between the first and final stages represent decreasing numbers of functions engaged for that particular language. In other words, language shift in the direction of extinction occurs as a society uses a language for fewer and fewer applications.[12] To reverse this process, the community must either act to bring those functions back or encourage the use of the language in additional domains.

Lewis and Simons (2010) enlarged on the GIDS model, resulting in the more nuanced "Expanded Graded Intergenerational Disruption Scale" (EGIDS). The EGIDS model for measuring language vitality increases the number of identified levels from eight to thirteen but preserves Fishman's original category numbers by adding a stage 0 and stage 9 on either end of the spectrum and dividing a few intermediate levels into *a* and *b* sections. The resultant EGIDS stages range from most viable to most threatened: 0—International; 1—National; 2—Regional; 3—Trade; 4—Educational; 5—Written; 6a—Vigorous; 6b—Threatened; 7—Shifting; 8a—Moribund; 8b—Nearly Extinct; 9—Dormant; and 10—Extinct.

Factors in adapting EGIDS to music shift

In adapting the concepts and methodology of the measurement of language shift to that of music shift, Coulter (2007) draws a connection between linguistics and ethnomusicology. Although he acknowledges the lack of a one-to-one correspondence between language death rates and music extinction, he points out that the disappearance of a language inevitably brings the death of related cultural elements. Given this observation, he outlines two reasons why models of language shift can especially inform the study of music shift. First, language serves as an expression of identity, closely connected to local history and communication modes, including music.[13] Second, Coulter sees robust intergenerational transmission as the most significant element for sustaining both music and language. While UNESCO initiatives for language emphasize the importance of intergenerational transmission within the home, the transmission of music can happen in a wider diversity of contexts, including churches, schools, and community gathering places. Music transmission also happens between adults as well as between generations (2007, 13).

Beyond live transmission methods, modern technology allows for exposure and some level of transmission through mediated formats such as radio, television, the Internet, and recordings. On November 28, 2015, a group of young people were given the opportunity to express to the Yakutian Parliament their opinions on how to encourage youth toward olonkho performance. Among the other thoughts presented, Sakhaya Lvova voiced her desire to see more examples of young olonkhosuts posted on YouTube.[14] She felt that a stronger web-based presence would support transmission by piquing the interest of the youth so that they would want to listen to young performers; this increased exposure, in turn, would inspire more youth to pursue developing their own skills in the tradition. As we have already seen, these types of media-based transmission methods, while not ideal, can help to bridge long distances, especially in spaces like Yakutia that suffer from expensive, severely limited transportation infrastructures. Even the weakest of transmission methods may prove key to keeping the genre from becoming "frozen" or dormant.

The Graded Genre Health Assessment (GGHA)

Coulter's Graded Music Shift Scale offered an eight-stage framework based on the EGIDS model but adapted specifically for evaluating music shift. Since the *Ethnologue* uses EGIDS, Coulter retained as much of that vocabulary as possible in order to facilitate productive dialogue between linguistics and ethnomusicology.[15] In one notable exception, he modified the EGIDS terminology by introducing the word "Locked" for stage 5: "the stage at which a music style is performed for tourist shows or other non-functional occasions, therefore the repertoire is not being added to, but is frozen" (2011, 73). Note that the Locked level can also

112   CHAPTER 5

exist in tandem with other levels when thriving, broad transmission happens alongside a memorized corpus of works. Coulter's critical addition of the Locked stage to the model has particular relevance for olonkho, since nearly all current performance contexts showcase memorized versions.

Schrag (2015b, 332) condensed Coulter's model and made slight modifications to reflect a move toward using broader arts-inclusive language. My own version returns the model nearly back to Coulter's original length, retains Schrag's arts-inclusive language, and replaces the designation "Shifting" with "Stressed" for my adaptation of Schrag's Graded Genre Health Assessment (GGHA) in figure 5.1.[16]

1) *International*: An international "community of practice" forms around the artistic genre. Ideally, international participation will include performance as well as consumer consumption.

2) *National or regional*: The genre's reputation grows beyond the home community. Community members may receive financial or other types of support from the national or regional level. People outside the home community learn to perform the genre, and the performance becomes iconic of the nation or region. Though not the ultimate goal of the genre's revitalization, this level of vitality can increase confidence in the home community. The genre's high profile might open doors for community development in other domains.

3) *Vigorous*: The pivotal level for artistic vitality. Oral transmission and largely traditional contexts of education are intact and functioning. People have sufficient opportunities for performance, and young people are learning by observation, participation, and appropriate educational contexts. A genre can exist comfortably at this level without needing to move higher.

4) *Threatened*: The first level that hints at downward movement, toward endangerment. Although still performed, the genre is undergoing noticeable changes: diminishing performance contexts, increased time given to more recent introductions, and more rural-urban movement.

5) *Locked*: The genre is known by more people than just the grandparent generation, but its performance is restricted to tourist shows or other contexts that are not integrated into the everyday life of the community. The performance repertoire is fixed, with no new additions. Participation and creative energy decline noticeably.

6) *Stressed*: The grandparent generation is proficient in this genre, but fewer contexts exist for passing it on to younger people. The younger people may not express interest, or older generations may presume a lack of interest from the youth. The genre is not dead or endangered at this level, and can be revitalized, but signs indicate downward movement and likely endangerment.

7) *Dormant*: Functional contexts for performance are gone, but recordings and other ethnographic descriptions exist. A community could reacquaint itself with the genre, but its rebirth would likely take on a different character from the original.

8) *Extinct*: No one in the community is capable of creating or performing in this genre. Probably no performance has occurred in the lifetime of anyone currently living. This stage occurs fairly rarely, as most genres grow into other styles or their stylistic elements are perpetuated in related styles.

Fig. 5.1. Graded Genre Health Assessment (GGHA)

ELEMENTS OF RESILIENCE   113

The GGHA contributes both a basic framework for describing vitality levels for artistic genres and commentary on considerations of shift within that spectrum. For communities already accustomed to using EGIDS to evaluate language shift, the GGHA should provide a familiar tool that engenders productive conversations between arts researchers and linguists.

Diagnostic chart for the Graded Genre Health Assessment

As a descriptive tool, the GGHA does not indicate the key factors involved in how a genre moves from one level to another. In order to expand the usefulness of the model, I have created a diagnostic chart (fig. 5.2) for assessing specific conditions that affect a genre's vitality.[17] Note that I have omitted the first two designations—*International* and *National or regional*—from the GGHA column, since these levels rise above the minimum requirements for artistic vitality.

The left column of figure 5.2 identifies the historical periods for this study of olonkho. The second and third columns highlight two key variables that directly affect the identification of the GGHA level: *transmission*, measured by the number and diversity of transmission paths and ethnolinguistic contexts; and *innovation*, revealed through evidences of creativity within the boundaries of the genre.[18] The fourth column quantifies the number of contexts for Performers, Performances, and Appreciators/Audiences (PPAs), assessing the numbers of opportunities for performance and of people enacting and listening. Each level of PPA health sum-

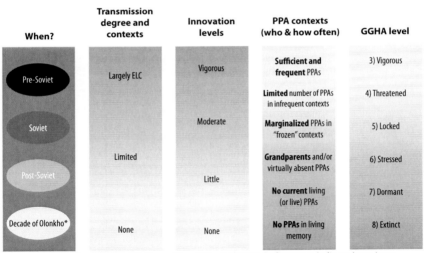

Fig. 5.2. Diagnostic chart for the GGHA

marizes a vitality level in the GGHA column. In light of the frequently strong correlation among the factors represented in the middle columns, movement from columns two to five should progress more or less horizontally, without significant peaks and valleys. In other words, the GGHA levels should largely reflect parallel realities between degrees of transmission and innovation in a genre.

Placing olonkho on the GGHA

Figure 5.3 focuses on the performance of traditional olonkho solo versions during four historical periods: the pre-Soviet period, covering roughly the first two decades of the twentieth century; the Soviet period (1920–1990); the first fifteen years of the post-Soviet period (1991–2005); and the first Decade of Olonkho (2006–2015). It reveals how solo olonkho moved from level 3, *Vigorous*, during the pre-Soviet period; through level 4, *Threatened*, during the early Soviet period; to level 6, *Stressed*, by the beginning of the post-Soviet period. Practically speaking, a tradition becomes nearly impossible to revitalize after reaching level 7, *Dormant*, since the seventh and eighth levels generally reflect situations lacking systems for the transmission of a living tradition. At the beginning of the post-Soviet period, olonkho had moved dangerously close to this state and certainly lacked a whole generation of grandparents proficient in the genre (level 6). My interviews with Sakha respondents suggest that they would have put the olonkho of the 1990s between levels 6, *Stressed*, and 7, *Dormant*, with very few performers at all.

After the Masterpiece declaration, especially during the first Decade of Olonkho, the vitality of the genre slowly began to improve. Performance opportunities for

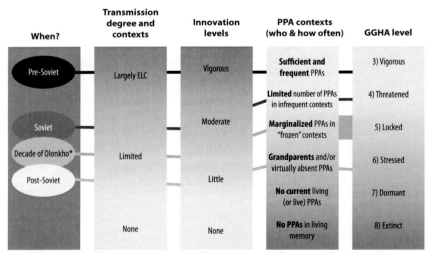

Fig. 5.3. GGHA for solo performance of olonkho

ELEMENTS OF RESILIENCE   115

olonkho increased, and more people, especially youth, performed within the tradition, although audience interest still remained low. With the vast majority of performers enacting memorized sections rather than improvising within the genre, the vitality of olonkho performance at the end of the first Decade of Olonkho had moved toward level 5, *Locked*. Only the development of master olonkhosuts in the second Decade of Olonkho (2016–2025) will give olonkho a chance to resume upward movement on the scale, no longer trapped at the *Locked* level.

Up until this point, our use of the diagnostic chart for olonkho has demonstrated how various levels of transmission and innovation relate to a given GGHA level. We have also seen how the chart allows researchers to compare a genre's vitality levels throughout various periods of history. Figure 5.4 applies this theory to another of olonkho's main enactment practices—theatrical presentations—allowing us to compare vitality levels between the two forms of olonkho.

In contrast with the bleak outlook for solo olonkho performance, olonkho theatrical versions currently register slightly under level 3 of the GGHA (fig. 5.4). This higher score relative to the solo version comes largely through the increasing numbers of theatrical productions—each staged olonkho event not only brings creativity and innovation into play but also involves a broad spectrum of people, both performers and audiences.

Since theatrical olonkho already enjoys a fairly broad audience of appreciators, continuing levels of innovation through activities such as staging a broader variety of olonkho plots or commissioning new olonkho stories written specifically for the stage may allow the genre to move in the direction of level 3, *Vigorous*. In

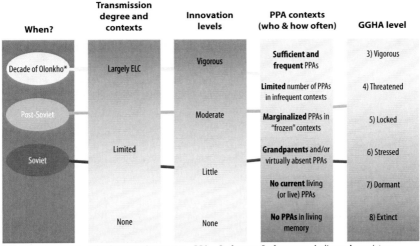

Fig. 5.4. GGHA for theatrical performance of olonkho

116   CHAPTER 5

addition, the nature of theatrical productions allows for faster and easier transmission, not requiring years of intensive exposure or the development of a broad range of expressive capabilities.

The interactions of transmission and innovation on GGHA levels

The GGHA allows for assessment of both transmission and innovation, each of which plays a crucial role in calculating olonkho's placement on the GGHA. Without some measure of dissemination, a genre's vitality narrows to two options: 7, *Dormant*, or 8, *Extinct*. The ethnolinguistic community of Sakha language speakers forms the foundational audience for the transmission of olonkho. If this community experiences moderate to vigorous transmission levels for the genre—which will happen only as the epic *sreda* grows—then the GGHA level will likely fall somewhere between levels 1 and 4. On the other hand, if *innovation* has slowed or ceased, the level could conceivably drop to level 5, *Locked*, despite strong transmission levels.

Limited transmission of the genre results in GGHA levels that are rarely higher than 5, reflecting a diminished number of performers and performances. Conversely, high levels of transmission involving groups beyond the Sakha ethnolinguistic community may encourage vigorous innovation, resulting in GGHA levels from 3, *Vigorous*, to 2, *National or regional*. Vitality might even reach level 1, *International*, though that is not necessary to create sustainability for the living tradition of a genre.[19]

Mediated performances

What about the role of recordings in transmission? Many of my respondents cited Kolesov's recording of *Nurgun Botur* as the primary olonkho performance heard during the Soviet period, and some people used this means to learn the script from memory. On the other hand, I did not find evidence that anyone learned the *improvisational* art of olonkho from this recording. The transmission of repertoire via recordings simply cannot take the place of transmission via personal interactions, especially for full-orbed performance practices such as olonkho that involve emergent aspects and other context-related facets of performance. Coulter stresses this importance of human transmission over recordings: "for communities interested in revitalizing their local musics, recordings can be useful but they do not replace the active human-to-human transmission of music knowledge" (2007, 17).

Although olonkho recordings have not played a noticeable role in the kind of transmission that leads to the development of master olonkhosuts, these resources have clearly achieved other goals. For example, olonkho recordings have expanded audience appreciation and have contributed to the growth of memorized olonkho performances. Popular olonkho performer Pyotr Tikhonov credits Kolesov's recording as helping him memorize his first short olonkho. He personally values olonkho recordings and printed versions, listing them as a key factor in the revitalization of memorized olonkho performances.

In light of these considerations, the documentation of the olonkho epic tradition through audio and video recordings remains a high priority. Fortunately, the public can now access a growing number of videos through websites and other mediated forms of communication.[20] The growth in the numbers of audio and video recordings, as well as their preservation in computer databases and on the Internet, holds great promise in making adequate resources available for Sakha people seeking to revitalize olonkho.

Mediated forms support the growth of the epic *sreda* by allowing people to see and hear olonkho in places bereft of living olonkhosuts—a description now applicable to most of the vast Republic of Sakha. Consumers can transport these mediated forms to any location via a smartphone, laptop computer, tablet, radio, or CD player, and can enjoy performances at their own convenience, rather than according to a performer's schedule. Mediated enactments allow olonkhosuts performing on television and radio to take their cues from published texts, instead of relying solely on their memories (Illarionov 2013, 6). In addition, mediated forms provide opportunity for close analysis through repeated engagement with short sections of recorded material.

Because media can have the effect of expanding audiences for olonkho, recordings from Kolesov's *Nurgun Botur* to the online modality of YouTube will continue to play a key role in olonkho revitalization. Increased numbers of high-quality recordings, accessible through the Internet and given play time on radio and television, may even serve to build up the epic *sreda* as Sakha audiences learn to appreciate their epic tradition.

In summary, achieving sustainability for olonkho requires strengthening the transmission of the tradition, and this transmission must extend beyond a memorized corpus or recordings of past olonkhosuts. Rather, people must engage with olonkhko as a living tradition and recognize innovation as one of the aesthetic values of the practice. Lord describes this type of situation as three aspects of one process: "With oral poetry we are dealing with a particular and distinctive process in which oral learning, oral composition, and oral transmission almost merge; they seem to be different facets of the same process" (2000, 5). Olonkho solo performance will achieve a sustainable future only through the restoration of this threefold integrated process of learning, creating, and transmission.

At the time of this writing, the level of vitality for olonkho hovers around level 4, *Threatened*, with traditional solo olonkho between 4.5 and 5.5 and theatrical olonkho in slightly better condition at 3.5 and growing. Given this diagnosis, what can Sakha communities do to move forward toward their goals of sustainability for the traditional version of olonkho? What strategies can they use to increase the tradition's vitality? In the next sections, I begin to explore possible answers

118   CHAPTER 5

to these questions by probing more deeply into the systems that create *resilience* in artistic cultures. I will then explore the systems that gave olonkho resilience until the twentieth century.

Resilience

Titon describes resilience as "a system's capacity to recover its integrity, identity, and continuity when subjected to forces of disturbance" (2015b, 192). The metaphor of a tree in a storm provides a vivid image. Deep roots, a sturdy trunk, and large branches will not necessarily withstand raging winds and torrential rain. Several years ago, a giant tree in our backyard crashed to the ground, upended by its roots, narrowly missing our house. For years the strong, broad trunk had given the tree an appearance of stability, but the changes in environment produced under and around the tree by the forces of wind and water revealed a lack of resilience. The tree fell, exchanging in one moment its functions of shade and beauty for firewood and heat.

Note that resilience does not simply indicate returning to a former moment— change is constant. Drawing from ecological streams of resilience theory, Lake clarifies the difference between resistance and resilience: "The capacity to weather a disturbance without loss is defined as resistance, whereas resilience is the capacity to recover from a disturbance after incurring losses, which may be considerable" (Lake 2013, 20). Resilience theory recognizes that stressors will force change in a system, even unwanted change. At the same time, resilience theory aims for *adaptation* during recovery from those stressors, resulting in an eventual state of "sufficient integrity to keep performing its core functions" (Gunderson, Allen, and Holling 2009, xiv–xvi).

Titon is breaking new ground by applying resilience theory to issues of sustainability in music cultures. He sees *adaptive management*, the application of the principles of resilience to help a system recover from the effects of undesirable change, as "the future of applied ethnomusicology" (2015b, 158). The following analysis of the ways malleable and stable aspects contributed to the resilience of olonkho during its apogee will illuminate adaptive management strategies that the Sakha people can use to enliven the epic *sreda*.[21]

Innovation: The interaction of stable and malleable in living traditions

The diagnostic chart in figure 5.2 depicts innovation as a critical factor in maintaining the vitality of a genre, even in a tradition like olonkho that values "authenticity" and a conservative stance toward canonized performance practice. In fact, the stability of this core provides a backdrop for innovation.

Philip Bohlman's insightful exploration of stability and change in oral traditions addresses the nature of an established canon: "the canonic core consists of musical and cultural, textual and contextual elements. Among the musical elements serving as the core's infrastructure are the integral units of transmission: pieces, formulae, normative settings of texts, shared musical vocabularies. The relative roles of composition, improvisation, and communal re-creation also determine what musical elements constitute the core" (1988, 30–31). For olonkho, the interactions of the core of the tradition with creative innovations will inevitably produce some variations encouraged by audience reactions. Over time, these new developments may become part of the more stable core. This process demonstrates resilience—the tradition responds to changes in the *sreda*, absorbing the needed "nutrients" such as new repertory, cultural functions, and even transmission methods, and thereby ensures ongoing growth and vitality (31–32).[22]

In further exploring the dynamics of innovation and resilience, I have found great explanatory power in Schrag's model of how the interactions between *stable* and *malleable* elements energize enduring creative traditions. Schrag's theory grew out of his work with a dance group in Cameroon, where he observed that malleable elements of the tradition interacted with stable components to create dynamism: "Artists create through plastic, malleable structures in ways that infuse new energy into the stable structures.[23] Without this [malleability], the stable structures will decay and dissipate. And without stable undergirdings, the creators in malleable forms will have no place to hang their musical hats" (2013b, 438).

Schrag's observations afford insight into the decline of olonkho performance over the last century through the loss of malleable elements such as improvisatory skills, audience responses, and the variety of spaces in which olonkhosuts and audiences meet. At the same time, this analysis suggests a practical approach for revitalizing the solo genre—by strengthening these malleable aspects of olonkho performance in ways that energize the stable elements.

Dynamism in a tradition does not result from purely unlimited innovation. Rather, the stable elements of the tradition supply a framework within which people innovate by contextualizing their use of a pool of stable elements in new and adaptable ways. Thus, the fixed elements serve as "the spring that releases innovation" (Connerton 1989, 75). This "vibrant malleable/stable engine" (Schrag 2015b, 333) has provided vitality for olonkho in the past, provoking these questions: In what ways do the interactions of stable and malleable elements provide resilience for olonkho performance? Which traditionally malleable elements have become less malleable under social and political pressures, thus stultifying the tradition's resilience?

The expressive resources of olonkho consist of a congeries of formal artistic elements. Figure 5.5 identifies six stable and malleable interactions, including the agents involved, and summarizing the resultant dynamism in the performances of master olonkhosuts during the apogee of the tradition in the pre-Soviet years.[24]

I continue my analysis of these features by more closely examining stable and malleable elements related to form (musical materials, heroic plots, poetic form), then moving toward elements connected with the epic *sreda* (performance contexts,

120 CHAPTER 5

Stable elements of solo olonkho	Locus of agency	Malleable use of elements by agent(s)	Outcomes during the apogee
Musical materials draw from both Sakha traditional vocal styles, *dėgėrėn* and *dièrėtii*, and employ *kylyhakh* ornamentation.	Olonkhosut	**Musical materials** are organized and employed by each performer in a process of re-creation.	**Dynamism:** Unique performances powerfully communicate the olonkhosut's artistic vision of the story and command rapt audiences.
Wide choice of heroic plots involves a variety of warrior heroes/heroines who overcome various challenges to defend "the tribe" and vanquish evil.	Olonkhosut	**Choice of protagonists** may vary; heroes/heroines can be impetuous, brave, brash, kind, tough, or gentle.	**Dynamism:** As a group, olonkhosuts provide audiences with many heroes/heroines to enjoy, and communicate a wide range of values.
Sakha poetical form is employed and combined with oral formulas and themes in each olonkho performance.	Olonkhosut	**Improvised re-creation of verbal text** using formulas and themes in an emergent way for each performance.	**Dynamism:** Each telling of an olonkho differs from others in length and exact text, keeping artistic communication fresh and distinctive.
Performance contexts are intimate—winter nights by the fire, hunting and fishing trips, or wherever else groups of people habitually gather.	Olonkhosut and audience	**The context** will influence how many nights the olonkhosut sings, which story is chosen from among those in the performer's repertoire, and who gathers to listen.	**Dynamism:** Performance venues flex with the availability of the audience and olonkhosut, happening whenever people gather with time to listen.
Verbal responses (short exclamations such as "eh!") during the performance.	Audience	**Timing and degree of audience reaction** show level of interest and engagement with the story.	**Dynamism:** Verbal responses influence the olonkhosut's level of enjoyment as well as the expansion (length) and depth of the performance.
Adequate compensation is given to olonkhosuts in thanks for their performance.	Audience	**Form and amount of compensation** depends on the resources available but could include food, housing, prizes, and gifts.	**Dynamism:** Olonkhosuts are able to focus much of their lives on performance, since they do not need to provide for their living in other ways.

Fig. 5.5. *Stable* and *malleable* for master olonkhosut performances (early 1900s)

audience verbal responses, and compensation for performances). In each case, I compare my initial summary chart data (fig. 5.5) with the realities at the end of the first Decade of Olonkho. Though these salient stable-malleable relationships do not form an exhaustive list, they demonstrate generally decreasing levels of malleability, weakening stability, and declining dynamism in olonkho and the epic *sreda*.

ELEMENTS OF RESILIENCE 121

Stable elements of solo olonkho	Locus of agency	Malleable use of elements by agent(s)	Outcomes during the apogee
Musical materials draw from both Sakha traditional vocal styles, *dėgėrėn* and *diėrėtii*, and employ *kylyhakh* ornamentation.	Olonkhosut	**Musical materials** are organized and employed by each performer in a process of re-creation.	**Dynamism:** Unique performances powerfully communicate the olonkhosut's artistic vision of the story and command rapt audiences.

Comparison to current level of stable/malleable vitality

Similar: Contemporary olonkhosuts demonstrate competency in their mastery of traditional Sakha musical materials (vocal styles and ornamentation) and use them in creative ways to reflect their artistic vision of the story, but musical materials alone are not enough to hold large audiences, as other, shorter genres also use these materials.

Fig. 5.6. Musical materials

MUSICAL MATERIALS Musical materials in the performances of olonkho constitute only one small part of the complex oral-verbal-dramatic-musical-community experience. As described in the first chapter, master olonkhosuts of the pre-Soviet years drew on the musical resources of the two overarching song styles, *dėgėrėn* and *diėrėtii*, and employed ornamentation (*kylyhakh*) in ways that demonstrated virtuosity and marked their unique vision of each story. These musical materials have changed only slightly—while olonkhosuts' artistic expression has likely narrowed in terms of variety, performers continue to adapt musical materials creatively to express the characteristics and actions of characters in the moment.[25] Despite the high level of degradation shown for many stable-malleable relationships in the comparison chart, competency with musical materials remains an outstanding quality of modern olonkho performances. Unfortunately, strong musical dynamism has proven insufficient for holding audiences, since Sakha people enjoy frequent exposure to shorter genres of Sakha song consisting of these same musical materials. Many Sakha singers use *kylyhakh* ornamentation and offer gripping performances of *diėrėtii* or *dėgėrėn* song styles, so competency in the malleable use of musical materials alone will not create resilience for olonkho.

HEROIC PLOTS The plots of olonkho still express both the stable and malleable aspects of epic stories that distinguish them from other genres, like the folk tales and fables common in Russian contexts and around the world. Olonkho's wide range of heroic personalities and characteristics, including both female and male protagonists, created great interest for listeners in the early twentieth century and may continue to serve as one of the driving forces behind the success of olonkho theatrical productions. Unfortunately, since many of the stories have not been

122 CHAPTER 5

Stable elements of solo olonkho	Locus of agency	Malleable use of elements by agent(s)	Outcomes during the apogee
Wide choice of heroic plots involves a variety of warrior heroes/heroines who overcome various challenges to defend "the tribe" and vanquish evil.	Olonkhosut	**Choice of protagonists** may vary; heroes/heroines can be impetuous, brave, brash, kind, tough, or gentle, and born either strong or weak.	**Dynamism:** As a group, olonkhosuts provide audiences with many heroes/heroines to enjoy, and communicate a wide range of values.
Comparison to current level of stable/malleable vitality			
Fewer plot materials, less malleability: Whereas in pre-Soviet years olonkho plots numbered in the hundreds and each olonkhosut had a repertoire that included multiple olonkhos, the contemporary pool of olonkho tales is very small, resulting in less variety for audiences.			

Fig. 5.7. Heroic plots

passed down, the pool of olonkho tales has decreased, resulting in less variety for contemporary audiences and decreased dynamism for the tradition.[26]

POETIC FORM AND ORAL-VERBAL ARTS (POETRY, ORAL FORMULAS) Widespread during the height of olonkho in the pre-Soviet years, the stable presence of textual formulas and themes in olonkho performance survives today largely in frozen form through transcribed and published olonkho tales. Without master olonkhosuts expertly crafting the stories, the art of using those formulas and themes malleably in the re-creation of texts has fallen out of practice. The resulting paucity of innovation in traditional olonkho performance appears to contribute to audience apathy for solo olonkho performances. Recognition by scholars and olonkhosuts of the desirability of innovation would encourage more olonkhosuts to improve their improvisatory skills rather than maintaining frozen versions of the stories.

Stable elements of solo olonkho	Locus of agency	Malleable use of elements by agent(s)	Outcomes during the apogee
Sakha poetical form is employed and combined with oral formulas and themes in each olonkho performance.	Olonkhosut	**Improvised re-creation of verbal text** using formulas and themes in an emergent way for each performance.	**Dynamism:** Each telling of an olonkho differs from others in length and exact text, keeping artistic communication fresh and distinctive.
Comparison to current level of stable/malleable vitality			
Decreased malleability: Although poetic form is still employed, as are formulas, the text is usually memorized, so performances are not as unique or as well adapted to audience sensibilities.			

Fig. 5.8. Poetic form and oral-verbal arts

Stable elements of solo olonkho	Locus of agency	Malleable use of elements by agent(s)	Outcomes during the apogee
Performance contexts are intimate—winter nights by the fire, hunting and fishing trips, or wherever else groups of people habitually gather.	Olonkhosut and audience	**The context** will influence how many nights the olonkhosut sings, which story is chosen from among those in the performer's repertoire, and who gathers to listen.	**Dynamism:** Performance venues flex with the availability of the audience and olonkhosut, happening whenever people gather with time to listen.

Comparison to current level of stable/malleable vitality

Decreased malleability: Intimate performance contexts are rare and not integrated into people's everyday lives. Most performances are subject to drastically shortened performance times and held in large venues where they must compete with other soundscapes and nearby events.

Fig. 5.9. Performance contexts

PERFORMANCE CONTEXTS   While the smaller, more intimate home-based venues of the early twentieth century allowed the olonkhosut to adapt his story to the audience's tastes and demographics, modern venues such as competitions and olonkho summer festivals do not afford such close proximity to audiences. On the other hand, enthusiasts who organize home-based events provide opportunities for olonkhosuts to contextualize performances for each audience. Given continued promotion, this practice of hosting smaller performances may spread to become a more commonplace occurrence.

AUDIENCE VERBAL RESPONSES   *Audience verbal responses* offer a prime example of a weakened stable-malleable relationship. Once integral to performances, verbal feedback can no longer influence the length of an olonkho in most cases, as the performers do not have the skilled flexibility required to expand their memorized material. Even if olonkhosuts could augment their performances in response to verbal encouragement from an audience, concert organizers have historically limited performance times to short excerpts. Expanded versions would not fit within these imposed restrictions, a fact that was bitterly lamented by the olonkhosuts I interviewed. This decreased malleability in the length of performance times corresponds to the withering of the dynamic relationship of feedback between the olonkho performer and the audience. While the underlying factors for this situation remain complex, the epic *sreda* has suffered over the last half century from a constricted relationship between performer and audience. Fortunately, audiences have recently begun to engage verbally during performances; their responses could conceivably reach former levels, given time.

124   CHAPTER 5

Stable elements of solo olonkho	Locus of agency	Malleable use of elements by agent(s)	Outcomes during the apogee
Verbal responses (short exclamations such as "eh!") during the performance.	Audience	**Timing and degree of audience reaction** show level of interest and engagement with the story.	**Dynamism:** Verbal responses influence the olonkhosut's level of enjoyment as well as the expansion (length) and depth of the performance.

Comparison to current level of stable/malleable vitality

Decreased malleability: Audience verbal responses virtually disappeared but are slowly reappearing as audiences become educated. Olonkhosuts no longer have the ability to change the performance in response, but the audience's verbal participation does increase their enjoyment in performance.

Fig. 5.10. Audience verbal responses

COMPENSATION   Current practices related to compensation have decreased the former levels of dynamism in traditional performance. In pre-Soviet times, olonkhosuts could rely on compensation that allowed them to travel from place to place, dedicating much of their lives, at least during the winter, to the performance of olonkho. Although the actual means of compensation remained malleable, olonkhosuts had their needs met through their hosts' provision of food, lodging, and gifts. During the Soviet period, collectivization slowly destroyed that way of life, and, like most people, olonkhosuts became employees of the state, their performances viewed as peripheral pastimes.

Stable elements of solo olonkho	Locus of agency	Malleable use of elements by agent(s)	Outcomes during the apogee
Adequate compensation is given to olonkhosuts in thanks for their performance.	Audience	**Form and amount of compensation** depends on the resources available but could include food, housing, prizes, and gifts.	**Dynamism:** Olonkhosuts are able to focus much of their lives on performance, since they do not need to provide for their living in other ways.

Comparison to current level of stable/malleable vitality

Decreased malleability: Compensation comes largely from competitions, in which large prizes are given to winners but lesser performances are not rewarded. Government stipends are currently not being given; most olonkhosuts have other jobs or small pensions.

Fig. 5.11. Compensation

After the Masterpiece proclamation, the Living Human Treasures program began awarding modest stipends to two master olonkhosuts. Now, with those masters gone, the system needs modification in order to support the currently developing olonkhosuts. Providing these performers with financial security will afford them the opportunity to devote their lives not only to honing their performance skills, but also to supporting the transmission of olonkho by passing their skills on to others.

In order to engage full-time with olonkho, performers must be able to depend on a compensation system. To neglect this source of stability means leaving a key element in the resilience of olonkho performance practice completely untapped. The vast budgetary resources available in Yakutia's Action Plan make this oversight all the more unconscionable. An initiative in 2016 by the Theater of Olonkho to provide financial compensation to a limited number of olonkho performers for their activities in transmission and performance provides hope for the future in this regard.[27]

Naturally, mere support for performers will not have a lasting effect without an improvement in the sociocultural context of appreciation for olonkho performance. Without interested audiences, even well-supported olonkhosuts may struggle to find the motivation to work on improving their skills.

Moving away from the analysis of traditional solo olonkho performance, figure 5.12 highlights some stable-malleable relationships connected to the current practice of olonkho theatrical productions. In contrast with the weakening interactions of stable and malleable elements in the solo tradition, the olonkho theatrical tradition demonstrates a dynamic resilience that is sustainable at least for the near future.

SCRIPT   The huge variety of theatrical interpretations of olonkho ranges from edgy, avant-garde modern productions like Andrei Borisov's to children's productions with simplified language and only a few actors. At the same time, the stability of script and interpretation from one performance to another allows audience members who read reviews in the newspaper to know what to expect when they buy tickets. Intrinsic to theatrical performances, the stability provided by the consistent interpretation of a script provides one of the keys to the success of this genre.

MUSICAL MATERIALS LINKED TO PHYSICAL MOVEMENT   The two domains of music and movement intertwine in olonkho theatrical performance. With musical orchestration undergirding the choreography, elements of dance often play a large role in theatrical productions.

Stable elements of theatrical olonkho	Locus of agency	Malleable use of elements by agent(s)	Outcomes
Script reflects the story of a chosen olonkho tale combined with contemporary theatrical materials, resulting in a production that is stable across performances.	Directors and actors	**Interpretation of the script** reflects the artistic vision of the directors/ actors to communicate with specific intended audiences (children, adults, urban or rural contexts).	**Dynamism:** Each production draws from both historical and modern resources, interpreted and contextualized for the interests, values, and concerns of the intended audience.
Musical materials include at least some of the Sakha traditional singing styles in order to "set the frame" of the story.	Score composers	**Musical materials** may include orchestration or synthesized sound, ranging from minimal to extensive, depending on the goals of the production and the available resources.	**Dynamism:** Music scores are made more accessible to younger and more urbanized audiences, striking a dynamic balance between tradition and modernity.
Physical movement such as blocking, gestures, elements of dance, and facial expressions are planned or choreographed for each production.	Directors, actors, and choreographers	**Physical movement** such as blocking and choreography can be adapted for smaller and larger venues and stages, if needed.	**Dynamism:** Each production uniquely suits the stage on which it is performed, the size of the audience, the abilities of the dancers, etc.
Themes of love, faithfulness, bravery, strength, and overcoming various challenges to defend "the tribe" and to vanquish evil enemies.	Scriptwriters	**The development of themes** depends on the choice of heroes/ heroines, who are impetuous, brave, brash, kind, tough, or gentle.	**Dynamism:** Productions provide audiences with many heroes/heroines to enjoy, communicating a wide range of contemporary Sakha values.
Performance times and lengths are set in advance and advertised.	Audiences	**Audiences choose** which performance suits their schedule and purchase tickets accordingly.	**Dynamism:** Productions see good attendance and robust ticket sales.
Funding for productions may come from "Decade of Olonkho" budgets and from income from ticket sales and sponsors.	Producers	**Amount of funding needed** depends on size and scope of production, from thousands of participants (at summer Ysyakh of Olonkho) to small-scale and even free events for children.	**Dynamism:** Productions can be based on either large or small budgets, allowing for a broad range of complexity and professionalism.
Expressing Sakha identity is seen as an important part of theatrical olonkho performances.	Scriptwriters, producers, directors, and actors	**Identity may be expressed** in contemporary terms, emphasizing current global concerns, mediated elements, and even international venues and intercultural relationships.	**Dynamism:** Varying expressions of Sakha identity in productions are always fresh, visionary, and evolving.

Fig. 5.12. *Stable* and *malleable* in olonkho theatrical productions (2016)

ELEMENTS OF RESILIENCE   127

Stable elements of theatrical olonkho	Locus of agency	Malleable use of elements by agent(s)	Outcomes
Script reflects the story of a chosen olonkho tale combined with contemporary theatrical materials, resulting in a production that is stable across performances.	Directors and actors	**Interpretation of the script** reflects the artistic vision of the directors/actors to communicate with specific intended audiences (children, adults, urban or rural contexts).	**Dynamism:** Each production draws from both historical and modern resources, interpreted and contextualized for the interests, values, and concerns of the intended audience.

Fig. 5.13. Script

Stable elements of theatrical olonkho	Locus of agency	Malleable use of elements by agent(s)	Outcomes
Musical materials include at least some of the Sakha traditional singing styles in order to "set the frame" of the story.	Score composers	**Musical materials** may include orchestration or synthesized sound, ranging from minimal to extensive, depending on the goals of the production and the available resources.	**Dynamism:** Music scores are made more accessible to younger and more urbanized audiences, striking a dynamic balance between tradition and modernity.
Physical movement such as blocking, gestures, elements of dance, and facial expressions are planned or choreographed for each production.	Directors, actors, and choreographers	**Physical movement** such as blocking and choreography can be adapted for smaller and larger venues and stages, if needed.	**Dynamism:** Each production uniquely suits the stage on which it is performed, the size of the audience, the abilities of the dancers, etc.

Fig. 5.14. Musical materials and physical movement

Although olonkho theatrical presentations still include traditional Sakha singing styles such as *dièrètii*, the rest of the musical material may include modern orchestration and even electronically mediated background tracks. For example, a 2015 production of *Kulan Kugas Attakh Kullustai Bèrgèn* combined traditional solo Sakha singing styles with live orchestral accompaniment, including an ensemble of Sakha traditional instruments such as the violin-like *kyryympa* and the *khomus*. As a celebration of the 115th anniversary of the birth of Sergei Zverev, singer, playwright, and founder of Sakha dance troupes, the artistic choices of this "ethno-ballet" reflected a conservative setting of an olonkho theatrical production (fig. 5.15). The orchestration employed a fusion of Sakha and Russian musical sensibilities, reflecting the collaborative nature of the production.[28]

Fig. 5.15. Ethno-ballet based on the olonkho *Kullustai Bèrgèn*. This December 14, 2015, performance took place at the Hermitage Theater, St. Petersburg, as part of an event co-sponsored by UNESCO—an International Cultural Forum—at which I spoke. Photo used by permission of www.ysia.ru and the Sergei Zverev–Kyyl Uola National Dance Theater of Yakutia, www.dancesakha.ru.

STORY THEMES   Just as in the solo-performed olonkho, theatrical productions draw from a stable and fairly broad corpus of heroic epic themes and plots, with each olonkho tale featuring a particular set of heroes and heroines. The choice of which olonkho tale to feature as a base for the theatrical script allows the writers to address a range of issues, from historical to contemporary. On the other hand, story choices may also stem from motivations other than the perceived relevance

Stable elements of theatrical olonkho	Locus of agency	Malleable use of elements by agent(s)	Outcomes
Themes of love, faithfulness, bravery, strength, and overcoming various challenges to defend "the tribe" and to vanquish evil enemies.	Scriptwriters	**The development of themes** depends on the choice of heroes/heroines, who are impetuous, brave, brash, kind, tough, or gentle.	**Dynamism:** Productions provide audiences with many heroes/heroines to enjoy, communicating a wide range of contemporary Sakha values.

Fig. 5.16. Story themes

Stable elements of theatrical olonkho	Locus of agency	Malleable use of elements by agent(s)	Outcomes
Performance times and lengths are set in advance and advertised.	Audiences	**Audiences choose** which performance suits their schedule and purchase tickets accordingly.	**Dynamism:** Productions see good attendance and robust ticket sales.

Fig. 5.17. Performance times and lengths

of certain themes or the promotion of specific olonkho characters. For example, the planners for the olonkho festival each summer look for an olonkho originating from within the region in which the event will be held. Since the event changes location from year to year, different regions receive the chance to highlight one of their own olonkhos.

PERFORMANCE TIMES AND LENGTHS   The dependability of a schedule works together with the flexibility of other choices to make theatrical presentations of olonkho highly accessible to the public. In addition, ticket prices for theatrical productions in Yakutia remain reasonably affordable for most people, compared with the relatively high prices for an opera in Moscow. In the bustling, full life of a Sakha person living in an urban center today, the convenience of knowing in advance when a theatrical performance will take place, how much it will cost, and how long the event will run creates a stable context in which people can make choices such as whether they can afford to attend, when it will be convenient, and who might be able to attend with them.

FUNDING SOURCES   A broad range of funding options from state budgets, ticket sales, sponsors, and other sources undergirds a stable financial base for theatrical production. Smaller theatrical productions require only modest budgets, fund-

Stable elements of theatrical olonkho	Locus of agency	Malleable use of elements by agent(s)	Outcomes
Funding for productions can be found in "Decade of Olonkho" budgets and from income from ticket sales and sponsors.	Producers	**Amount of funding needed** depends on size and scope of production, from thousands of participants (at summer Ysyakh of Olonkho) to small-scale and even free events for children.	**Dynamism:** Productions can be based on either large or small budgets, allowing for a broad range of complexity and professionalism.

Fig. 5.18. Funding sources

130   CHAPTER 5

able through ticket sales and volunteer, amateur talent. Productions that tap into generous Decade of Olonkho funding can engage personnel with high levels of professionalism and creativity, thereby generating greater interest among the public and broadening the epic *sreda* supporting olonkho. Depending on the available funding, producers can adjust the size and scope of performances to fit a wide range of budgets, thereby providing resilience for the theatrical tradition even through times of financial uncertainty.

AN EXPRESSION OF SAKHA IDENTITY   Producers of theatrical versions consider Sakha identity an essential backdrop to all their performances. At the same time, theatrical productions offer malleability in terms of expressing individuality, thereby providing a perfect avenue for addressing the multiple streams and layers of Sakha identities.

Theatrical settings can also connect both ancient and modern elements of Sakha identities, resonating with the particular audience the producers wish to draw. For example, Andrei Borisov usually stages his edgy Theater of Olonkho productions in the sleek, modern-looking new structure in the center of town across from the Central Post Office. These productions tap into Sakha historical roots but also express globalized twenty-first-century Sahka sensibilities. Large Ysyakh of Olonkho performances gaze largely to the past, strengthening ties to Sakha cultural roots and practices. At the same time, these festivalized theatrical performances at Ysyakh also reflect some Soviet ways of packaging and presenting culture, creating continuities not only with cultural heritage but also with modernist ideologies inherited from the Soviet period (Peers 2013, 109). From open-air festivals to simple classroom dramas, olonkho theater both draws from and expresses varied Sakha identities to produce creative depictions of olonkho tales for diverse twenty-first-century Sakha audiences.

Stable elements of theatrical olonkho	Locus of agency	Malleable use of elements by agent(s)	Outcomes
Expressing Sakha identity is seen as an important part of theatrical olonkho performances.	Scriptwriters, producers, directors, and actors	**Identity may be expressed** in contemporary terms, emphasizing current global concerns, mediated elements, and even international venues and intercultural relationships.	**Dynamism:** Varying expressions of Sakha identity in productions are always fresh, visionary, and evolving.

Fig. 5.19. Expression of Sakha identity

Dynamism in the interaction of stable and malleable elements

If the interaction of stable and malleable creates dynamism in the tradition of olonkho, then damage to the stable-malleable balance can harm the resilience of performance practice. For example, if stable elements become so strong that they cancel out the malleable elements, olonkho will lose vitality. On the other hand, without *any* stable elements, the olonkhosut lacks the framework to re-create a story within the tradition (Bauman 1975, 303). Even new plots need to reflect traditional formulas and themes in order to maintain the aesthetic standards necessary for wide acceptance by Sakha society.

Other writers have observed the phenomenon of dynamism in stable and malleable interactions, employing different terms to describe similar realities. Victor Turner, writing about the incorporation and transformation of existing patterns in rituals, states that "many transformations are, of course, within the limits of social structure and have to do with its internal adjustments and external adaptions to environmental changes" (1980, 165). Thus, if olonkho performers flex to adapt to the significant changes taking place in the entertainment tastes, worldviews, and values of the tumultuous post-Soviet cultural environment, they may enjoy renewed interest by Sakha audiences.

In a passage that resonates with the stable-malleable model as applied to tradition and innovation, Paul Ricoeur describes tradition as "not the inert transmission of some already dead deposit of material but the living transmission of an innovation always capable of being reactivated by a return to the most creative moments of poetic activity. . . . [A] tradition is constituted by the interplay of innovation and sedimentation" (1984, 68).[29] Ricoeur's description enlivens the definition of *tradition* by revealing the malleable processes that work together to produce the continuity of well-established conventions—through innovation, agents influence the sedimentation built up over time, creating an "interpretation of the past in terms of the needs of the present" (Adams 2010, 11). Connerty writes in analogous terms, commenting on Ricoeur's innovation and sedimentation model: "[T]he act of innovation presupposes a sedimented or conventional form, while the sedimented form can only be seen as conventional once it has an innovation which deviates from it. . . . The narrative paradigm is not ahistorical, but is itself a sedimented structure that could be transformed by innovation" (1990, 393). Coulter touches on similar themes regarding innovation's role in revitalization: "the goal of revitalization is surely exemplified by a community that is actively creating, developing, and changing music . . . with people playing around in that stylistic space. Although the upper levels . . . include regional, national, and international support, the focus always remains on the home community. Therefore,

132   CHAPTER 5

the crucial stage for music revitalization is Stage 3, Vigorous. This is the point at which the music's existence is very stable, and continued creation within that style is assured" (2011, 73). Despite an ongoing dearth of in-depth case studies such as Coulter's, recent research into the revitalization of moribund traditions in other contexts has revealed similar conclusions regarding the role of transmission, innovation, malleability, and stability.[30] The following case studies from Korea, Bali, and Cambodia offer hope for a feasible positive future for olonkho and its descendants.

As one example, Keith Howard explores the balance between preservation and creativity in the revitalization of the intangible cultural heritage of South Korea. In light of the uncanny parallels between Yakutia and South Korea, Howard's conclusion resonates with what may happen for olonkho: "Initially, the motivation was a fear of loss and a desire to retain a national identity, but as time passed, the system became a foundation on which to create relevance for today, with icons of the past being utilized in new creativity" (2014, 136).

Howard describes this ICH movement in South Korea as being energized by the goal of strengthening national identity and pride. Initially, the cultural expressions marked for preservation appeared in danger of calcification, with little malleability; however, infused over time with creative energy contributed especially by student movements, these same traditions have now begun to flourish: "Preservation in Korea has been a process formulated by government agencies and a broad assembly of scholars, journalists, and nationalists. It has sought to retain archetypes and in so doing may have given ammunition to those who criticize the apparent freezing of cultural production. However, and most important, preservation has created icons of performance arts and crafts. These form the basis of new creativity. . . . The two elements, preservation and creativity, go side-by-side, one validating the other, and one ensuring the maintenance of activity in the other. Preservation and creativity are, then, equally important elements in revival" (2014, 152–153). When viewed through the lens of stable and malleable, *preservation* reflects some aspects of stability, while *creativity* highlights the malleability inherent in innovation. The interaction of these two elements in the South Korean case study outlined above supplies a model for Sakha olonkho revitalization, especially with regard to the incorporation of students and other young people as a dynamic part of revitalization processes. Given Yakutia's support of youth involvement in olonkho, the small cadre of young people promoting olonkho may end up proving to be, just as in South Korea, the key to resilience and sustainability for olonkho.

Leslie Tilley's case study (2014) of the Balinese drumming tradition *kendang arja* offers a second example for consideration. Tilley observed that performers' levels of proficiency within the drumming tradition affected their willingness to improvise within that creative space, with accomplished drummers engaging more readily in improvisation. Other factors influencing levels of innovation included years of experience, dynamics of isolation and contact, the number of drumming patterns in performers' repertories, and an ideology of "weak ties" that encouraged experimentation. Tilley's insightful case study adapts linguistic theories for the purpose of better understanding how Balinese drummers learned the language of *kendang arja* well enough to exercise flexibility of style and "code-switch" between musical dialects.[31]

As a third example, Todd Saurman's work with Tampuan ethnolinguistic communities in Cambodia examines the reasons for the decline of their music and explores ways that some Tampuan people have found to work toward revitalization (2012, 97). Drawing parallels with the process of language revitalization, Saurman concludes: "the revitalization or cultivation of music consists of three essential intergenerational components: community ownership of the process, transmission of music knowledge, and active use of music as communication" (95).

Close examination of the study shows that the third element, the use of music as communication, connects directly with the presence of innovation in Tampuan communities. The need for particular kinds of communication motivated the creation of new songs, which, while retaining aspects such as Tampuan musical structures, instruments, and poetic forms, reflected innovation through new contexts of use, new forms of participation, and of course the newly created songs themselves (Saurman 2012, 101).

Note that Saurman also identifies community ownership as key to revitalization, a component likewise required by UNESCO in the Masterpiece application. In some cases, identifying the scope of that community may require reexamining the usual ethnolinguistic boundaries.[32] For the olonkho revitalization of the last decade, the primary group driving the process has been Yakutia's intellectual and cultural elite: a vast number of educators, particularly in the humanities; musicians and artists of all kinds; and those involved in government structures, especially the Ministry of Culture. These Sakha thought leaders, with positions of influence in systems related to education, legislation, and the arts, form a large community that shapes the values and priorities of the region. Through a combination of personal sacrifices in time and energy, republic-level legislation, active public relations, and educational reform, this influential group has convinced people of olonkho's importance as an essential part of Sakha culture.[33]

In summary, the levels of transmission, innovation, and resilience fueled by stable and malleable interactions will determine olonkho's chances of survival. The belief that the revitalization of a centuries-old tradition like olonkho requires the maintenance of canonical texts may dampen or even completely snuff out the innovative moments and creative bursts needed for the genre's continuation

134   CHAPTER 5

as a living tradition. Likewise, without transmission to a new generation of both the stable and malleable elements, the traditional live olonkho performance will eventually die out, perhaps retained merely as a Sakha national symbol and displayed only in locked forms for government-sponsored concerts and exhibitions. In the coming decades, the Sakha people will decide to what extent they wish to support balanced levels of innovation and provide for living transmission of olonkho performance, thus increasing the tradition's resilience in the midst of change.

CHAPTER 6

EPIC REVITALIZATION

Negotiating Identities and Other Challenges

> The nature of tradition is not to preserve intact a heritage from the
> past, but to enrich it according to present circumstances and transmit
> the result to future generations.
> —Laurent Aubert, *The Music of the Other*

Attaining the Masterpiece award greatly affected the fate of olonkho, likely turning it back from the brink of permanent disappearance. Still, the future of olonkho remains unclear, and whether to implement ongoing plans for transmission and encourage further innovation in the genre is a decision that rests primarily in the hands of the Sakha people. While they seek to create additional strategies to achieve their goals for olonkho, various historical, global, and political forces have affected olonkho and the entire epic *sreda* for more than a century. These forces will continue to exert pressure on performance practice by changing the way in which olonkho is performed and enjoyed by audiences. "Sitting under the mouth" undeniably affords a different experience now than it did a century ago. Although many of these shifts in Sakha life appeared as threads in the preceding historical narrative, the following short summary reiterates the range of sweeping and profound evidences of change.

1. During the past century, three major political regimes (tsarist, Soviet, and post-Soviet Russia) have ruled Yakutia, each leaving its own mark on olonkho performance practice.
2. Performance spaces have changed from intimate home contexts with family and close friends around a fireplace to concert stages with the attendant noise, bright lights, and limited performance times.
3. Performance seasons and times have moved from mostly long, dark winter nights to daytime performances staged at any time throughout the year.
4. Performance lengths have shrunk from multiple nights of singing to highly compressed snippets of five or ten minutes, with up to twenty minutes in unusual venues.

136   CHAPTER 6

5. Competition in entertainment types and venues has increased to include a vast array of mediated entertainment available in the cinema and on television, radio, and even YouTube.
6. Sakha language fluency has decreased, with older audiences understanding some archaic terms, but many under fifty years of age finding themselves struggling to understand high-register Sakha poetic vocabulary.[1]
7. Material compensation for performance has changed from predominantly gifts of food and lodging to modest government stipends or honorariums, or even no compensation at all.
8. The oral genre of olonkho has gained a more literary presence as the population has become highly literate.
9. Retention of tales has transferred from the memories of olonkhosuts to repositories of written texts.
10. The average age of olonkhosuts, previously middle-aged or older, has now skipped a generation as a burgeoning number of youth have embraced the tradition.
11. Transmission contexts for olonkho have moved from family performances with relatives at home to formal school lessons or special clubs for learning olonkho.
12. Worldviews have diversified from a more unified view of spiritual and physical realities to a wider array of worldviews with their underlying values and ontologies.
13. Performance formats have morphed from solo into multi-person and theatrical productions.
14. The economies undergirding the everyday lives of Sakha people initially changed from animal husbandry to collective farms, then to urbanization (Ignatieva et al. 2013, 3).[2]
15. Olonkho's value as worldview-affirming entertainment has shifted to a new primary role as an ethnic identity marker and source of pride for a post-Soviet indigenous group in neocolonial relations with the Center.

Most of the forces of change listed above have been discussed in preceding chapters, but the last element deserves further exploration, since it provides us with clues to possible future paths for olonkho.

The role of colonial and postcolonial relations in ethnic identity

When it comes to the politics surrounding cultural identity, attempts at control by a government tend to backfire, underscoring marginalization and creating pressures that eventually erupt. As a result, the revitalization of repressed genres appears ubiquitously in postcolonial contexts, where state control has served only to heighten a sense of ethnic identity (Balzer 1995; Coplan 1985, 226; Slobin 1996; Smith and Akagawa 2009).[3] The history of olonkho also reflects this reality. Precipitated by Stalin's movement toward populating his gulags with members of the Sakha intelligentsia, including poets, writers, and spiritual leaders considered proponents of olonkho, the genre began gaining recognition as an ethnic identity marker as early as the 1930s (Cruikshank and Argounova 2000, 103).

Although Communist laws would not have openly sent an olonkhosut to the gulag solely for performing an olonkho, many people were convicted for crimes of "bourgeois nationalism" (Cruikshank and Argounova 2000, 102). Such allegations usually entailed a host of accusations, ranging from "inappropriate song texts" to religious beliefs not in accordance with the "scientific-atheistic propaganda" of official Soviet policy (N. A. Alekseyev 2008, 17; Khazanov 1993, 185). Over time, artistic expressions like olonkho, marginalized by the Soviets, accrued anti-Soviet but pro-Sakha associations. These connotations haunted anyone connected with olonkho: performers, scholars, and even those who transcribed it into literary forms—all activities that the Soviets wanted to control.

American ethnomusicologist Ted Levin's extensive fieldwork in Russia and Central Asia, both during and after the Soviet period, has led him to speak about a disastrous ideological effect on the people colonized by the Soviets (1993). He remarks: "the Soviets were imperial micromanagers. No aspect of life or art was too trivial to attempt to bring into conformity with the prescriptions of Marxist-Leninist doctrine" (2002, 192). One need not even identify as a musician or performer to experience strong systems of control—some ethnographers writing about minority cultures in the Soviet Union were also imprisoned during those years (Knight 2004).

The attempt to forbid the expression of certain ideas marked Soviet rule over its territories. Rather than being satisfied with simply reforming the political and economic foundations of the North, the state sought complete ideological control, including over the content and performed expression of approved folklore genres crucial to Soviet ideology. Izaly Zemtsovsky calls the Soviet system's relationship to folklore "the pathological coupling of demagoguery and repression . . . against the texts, against folklore experts, and with the entire traditional medium as a necessary context for folklore" (2002, 178). Additionally, he comments on the battle not only against folklore carriers but also against its scholars: "The ideological criteria and censorship that were applied in the world of literature were transferred to the area of folklore as well. . . . It became just as dangerous to sing about what one wanted to sing as it was to publish" (179). How did this situation affect the Sakha during the Soviet years and beyond? Their stories give insight into their perceptions of this control as a battle against culture.

138   CHAPTER 6

As one example, when Cruikshank and Argounova asked people in Yakutia's Tatta district about their memories during the time of prohibitions against local writers, the respondents spoke in terms of having their cultural roots pulled from the ground: "All subsequent expressions of Sakha culture were forbidden on the grounds that Tatta manifested 'the worst expressions of bourgeois nationalism' so that, in the words of one older man with whom we spoke, '. . . to speak openly, they wanted to remove the roots from the ground so that no new cultural writers would emerge from this place. Those who continued to sing, to tell stories or to write them, were imprisoned or lost their jobs'" (2000, 110). Soviet measures to control intellectuals, including writers of all kinds—poets, scholars, and even olonkhosuts—intensified throughout the 1930s, then were eased during World War II, only to intensify again after the war.

While repression definitely contributed to damaging cultural identity in the Soviet Union, an even greater issue lay in the unpredictability of Soviet policies. This swinging pendulum led to a pervasive feeling of uncertainty and fear, as waves of support for national expressions of culture were followed by periods of repression when olonkho became viewed as "too nationalistic." These policy swings recurred periodically throughout Soviet rule, creating a dangerous situation for those connected to olonkho. With the resulting repression and eventual incarceration of some Sakha olonkhosuts and epic scholars such as Platon Oyunsky, Tong Suorun, Dmitrii Govorov, and Aleksei Boiarov, Sakha people who cared about olonkho naturally began to see the art form as an anti-Soviet activity. Over time, the seeds for olonkho's role as an ethnic identity marker took root deep in their national consciousness.[4] As other changes in Sakha society edged out olonkho as a widely enjoyed form of entertainment, these seeds germinated and grew, eventually transforming the reception of performances from pleasurable pastimes to marginalized and vaguely dangerous activities. Now powerfully bound to Sakha ethnic identity, olonkho became a weapon wielded in both directions by the state. On the one hand, the government might support olonkho for the purpose of controlling its performers, or in order to show the world the state's proficiency in creating a "brotherhood of nations." Alternatively, when the pendulum had swung the other way, the state would repress and imprison those who had been connected with olonkho and other expressions of culture, accusing them of raising the banner of olonkho too high.

During the period of perestroika, Soviet opposition toward indigenous art expressions slowly thawed, and a cultural revitalization movement began to develop. After the Soviet Union's collapse in 1990–1991, the state finished the process of rehabilitating the names of those persecuted and killed in the gulags.[5] This process served only to sharpen the association between these historical figures of the Sakha intelligentsia and the activities for which they had been punished—activities connected to their ethnic identity. In this way, individuals once linked with "bourgeois nationalism" became the cultural and national heroes of the Republic of Sakha (Cruikshank and Argounova 2000, 111), their lives celebrated with large monuments in the public squares and their names attached to universities and institutes. Cultural pride in these repressed heroes of Sakha history continues to be expressed everywhere in Yakutia—repeated in conversations, in the news, in history books, and in the media. Furthermore, respect for these cultural heroes extends beyond their character and achievements. In a sense, the products of their hands, heads, and hearts—olonkhos, poetry, and other writings—have become sacrosanct, elevated to the status of cultural iconicity partly because of the suffering that accompanied their creation.

The process of revitalization set in motion during the post-Soviet period initially affected cultural elements that had not completely died out—those expressions that were easily accessible to performers and audiences alike. For example, the favorite national instrument, the *khomus*, and song forms such as *toyuk* and especially *dègèrèn* saw immediate revitalization, as did the circle dance (*ohuokhai*).[6] On the other hand, olonkho proved less accessible for a number of reasons. Its practitioners, the olonkhosuts, had all but died out, and the few remaining tradition bearers lived primarily in remote locations far from the capital. Olonkho's archaic language, increasingly difficult to absorb, could not compete with other, more accessible forms of storytelling such as films and books. Lifestyles had changed; no one wanted to stay up all night for several nights in a row listening to a story they could barely understand. With the exception of Sakha folklore scholars and ethnomusicologists, few others thought about olonkho revitalization during the difficult decade following the fall of the Soviet Union. Having been almost completely forgotten, how did olonkho subsequently become a widespread symbol of Sakha ethnic pride, supported and fed by a deep well of government funding? What could possibly have turned things around so abruptly?

My conversations with Sakha people reveal a clear answer. Building on the foundation laid during the Soviet era, when olonkho gained a strong connection with Sakha identity, the key turning point came with the proclamation of the genre as a Masterpiece of the Oral and Intangible Heritage of Humanity. Their deep joy that "the world" (UNESCO) had proclaimed the superior value of this uniquely Sakha genre gave them a sense of achievement and ethnic pride, launching olonkho into the political, social, and cultural visibility that it still enjoys to this day.

Lauri Harvilahti's works (1996, 2000) explore a variety of epic traditions in which negotiations of national, ethnic, ideological, and religious values play a central role, often superseding the actual enjoyment of the epos.[7] He asserts that revitalization of an epic tradition sometimes has much more to do with the

140   CHAPTER 6

function of expressing a people's cultural identity than with actually enjoying a work's performance: "the desire to reinforce the people's self-esteem and to arouse respect for their own heritage and culture is among the main tasks of an epos . . . strengthening cultural and national identity" (1996, 45–46). Harvilahti's emphasis on function accurately describes the current role of olonkho in modern-day Yakutia.

For intangible traditions, "refunctionalization" (Arizpe and Amescua 2013, 126) or "transfer of function" (Kidula 2013, 314) often accompanies the revitalization process.[8] An article by sociologist Olga Osipova confirms that refunctionalization is happening for olonkho in modern Sakha society. Osipova researched the degree to which olonkho, as a cultural value of the people, plays a role in the formation of ethnic identity (2011, 1). She conducted her sociological fieldwork during 2009–2010 in the districts of Yakutia historically recognized as the strongest in olonkho performance.[9] The resulting data demonstrate that "the recognition by UNESCO of olonkho as a masterpiece of oral folk creativity led to an increased status for the epos as a national symbol" (4).[10] When asked how they view the heroic epos of olonkho, 83 percent of Osipova's respondents chose this answer: "Olonkho is the foundation of the national culture of the Sakha people" (5).[11] With olonkho recognized in these districts as connected to Sakha culture and identity, a full 81 percent of respondents felt that it should be protected as a *narodnoe dostoianie* (people's achievement) (5).

This research confirmed my impressions based on conversations with a broad spectrum of Sakha people. Osipova underscores a key point when she asserts that for "the majority of respondents . . . the primary problem [is] that olonkho, in and of itself, is not popular, not needed by society, regardless of the acknowledgment by people of its [intrinsic] value"[12] (2011, 7). Although olonkho is highly respected and strongly connected to Sakha identity, it garners little recognition for its musical, poetic, or narrative entertainment value. Osipova concludes that "olonkho undoubtedly is seen as a cultural treasure for the Sakha people, even though it does not enjoy popularity in mainstream society" (8).[13] Her research demonstrates that governmental programs may be effectively promoting olonkho as a vital cultural heritage of the Sakha, but these efforts fall short of creating enthusiastic audiences for olonkho performances. The epic *sreda* remains weak, leaving the most robust role for olonkho as strengthening Sakha identity rather than entertaining or communicating values and worldview.[14] Clearly, rallying around olonkho as a symbol of ethnic identity offers an easier goal than fostering appreciative audiences for "sitting under the mouth."

Revitalization in the context of national awakening frequently occurs in post-colonial contexts. While the term "colonialism" commonly connotes physical distance from the imperial power to the colonized, often requiring passage over a large body of water, a geographical definition of colonialism does not prove adequate in this case. Said points out that "Russia . . . acquired its imperial territories almost exclusively by adjacence. Unlike Britain or France, which jumped thousands of miles beyond their own borders to other continents, Russia moved to swallow whatever land or peoples stood next to its borders, which in the process kept moving farther and farther east and south" (1994, 10). While the implosion of the Soviet Union caused a temporary reversal in this pattern of land acquisition, with many countries emerging again as independent nations on the borders of Russia, Yakutia, despite its vast mineral wealth, has never pressed for separation from the Russian Federation. Still, Yakutia's several-hundred-year relationship with Russia remains one of "acquired adjacent territory," fitting Said's definition of a colonized space.

With his term "internal colonialism," Hechter (1975) makes similar claims, acknowledging the unusual nature of Russian and Soviet expansion and challenging, like Said, the limitations of viewing colonialism in relation to distance or bodies of water. These two concepts—*internal colonialism* and *colonialism through conquest of adjacent territory*—help establish the relevance of the term "colonialism" in relation to the Soviet period. Even during the periods in which Soviet authorities ostensibly supported olonkho with gestures such as naming a World War II–era tank after the *bogatyr* Nurgun Botur, staging an olonkho theatrical performance in Moscow, and receiving olonkhosuts into the Union of Soviet Writers, these "supportive" actions chiefly benefited the colonial power rather than the colonized. In essence, a portion of the creative elites were co-opted, not just in Yakutia, but over many parts of the Soviet Union (Adams 2010, 11). The Soviets' treatment of indigenous musical culture simply reflected the significant ideological tensions between national and state interests. Fanning notes the multiple effects of this ideology: "As elsewhere, folk and popular musics helped to give these nations a voice. But at the same time, centralized support for those musics—generous subsidies for folk ensembles and for the dissemination of information throughout the Soviet Union—was conceived as contributing ultimately towards the cohesion of the State itself . . . in a spirit of affirmation and meta-national pride" (2005, 513). These observations place the Soviet support structures for folk music culture directly in the realm of colonial impetus. The stated benefit focused not on the peoples from which the musics came, but on the state's broader goals, aimed at maintaining an image of a peaceful Soviet brotherhood of nations and on keeping "the regions" from revolting.

The folklorization of music traditions during the Soviet era provided just one more form of control—a surface impression of support for minority musics, undermined by the removal of these artistic expressions from their natural contexts and meanings. Perceived as "backward," these traditions underwent "refining"

142   CHAPTER 6

through a system of institutionalized music training (Merchant 2014) for display on the concert stage. Aubert, writing about folklore ensembles supported by the state, explains how these groups retained an outward appearance of tradition but subverted the essence of the production's meaning to the people, effectively stripping the result of "all substance, all metaphysical significance" (2007, 50). For example, consider Levin's conversations with famed Russian folk music revivalist Dmitrii Pokrovsky, who noted that the job of a folklore specialist at a House of Culture was to "make sure that thirty percent of the authentic folklore would be fakelore. That is, thirty percent had to be songs about the Soviet system and how great it is, about collective farms, tractors, and so on" (Levin 1996, 19). Pokrovsky went on to say, "To publish any collection of folk songs at that time, you had to have a song about Stalin at the beginning; a song about electricity, a tractor; and after that, you could have your love songs, calendar songs, or whatever. After a while, no one looked at the first few pages of those books" (20).

An extended and complex genre, olonkho proved especially difficult to squeeze into the parameters of Soviet folklorization. As we saw in the historical accounts of my respondents, Soviet efforts to folklorize olonkho resulted in truncated performances—a few in Moscow, and short olonkho excerpts of less than ten minutes in Yakutian local concerts.[15]

In her insightful article "Traditional Music in the Context of the Socio-political Development in the USSR," Kosacheva (1990) echoes this theme, describing the ways in which attitudes toward folklore reflected the colonial aspirations of Soviet powers under Stalin. She also confirms an arts policy focused on central control, maintained through systems that the government and its apparatus could manage—folk music festivals, contests, and auditions. Consequently, Kosacheva concludes, the administration "largely suppressed and belittled the improvisational character of folklore. Folklore became professionalized; professional music of oral tradition had to comply with the requirements of European-type concert performance based on numerous rehearsals. It also had to comply with rather severe constraints on performance duration" (18–19).[16] In summary, olonkho performance practice changed drastically during the Soviet period, with a growing emphasis on olonkho theatrical productions presented in concert halls rather than homes. One could now measure performance durations in minutes rather than days.

Sakha responses to neocolonial relations with the Center

In Yakutia's case, postcolonialism has extended into the twenty-first century, for the region must still deal with the effects of colonial policies. Although still part of Russia, the Republic of Sakha (Yakutia), like other Russian "autonomous republics," endures a continuing attenuation of the small measure of autonomy gained in the early 1990s. In the mid-1990s, the Russian government repealed a 1992 agreement granting control of a large percentage of the profits from local mineral assets to the republic (Bahry 2005, 137–139; Balzer and Vinokurova 1996, 107). Beginning in December 2004, the residents could no longer elect the president of Yakutia. Instead, the Yakutian legislature retained power only to ratify a leader appointed by the state. As of 2014, this position no longer even bears the title of "president," but rather is "head of the Sakha Republic."[17] In these ways and more, the Center is taking back control after a brief period of increased autonomy for the republic. As a result, the term "neocolonial"—the recalling of freedoms once given—best describes the relationship between Yakutia and Moscow (Ashcroft, Griffiths, and Tiffin 1995, 381; Moore 2001, 112).[18]

The gathering of control back to the Center focused largely on dictating policy for the republic rather than on limiting Sakha involvement in the government, and the post-Soviet years saw the Sakha capitalizing on the opportunity to increase their engagement with the legislative structures of the republic. In just five years (1990–1995), they increased their representation in the parliament from approximately 46 to 61 percent. Furthermore, "at the end of the 1990s they made up 59% of personnel in the executive branch and 63% at the city and *raion* [regional] level" (Bahry 2002, 677–678), allowing for an increased solidarity in the limited areas in which the Sakha still had a voice. These high levels of participation provided a necessary "pressure valve" for the mounting control from the Center, possibly averting an explosive situation.

Marginalized peoples often react to neocolonial relations by strongly identifying with a cherished heroic past. Within the world of olonkho, these heroes take the form of the ancestral *zashitniki plemena* (defenders of the tribe). Often observed in religious and national revivals (Boym 2001; Pistrick 2015), this nostalgic connection to a glorious past can be strongly connected to perceptions of identity (Um 2013, 3). The genre of epic narrative gives full expression to this nostalgia, providing a powerful source of constructed meaning for a people experiencing a "desire for authentic sources, generally a mythic set of heroic, purer ancestors who once controlled a greater zone than the people now possess" (Moore 2001, 118). In *Performing Nostalgia*, a study of Albanian migration songs, Pistrick asserts that "nostalgia may help in overcoming disillusions and re-establishing self-esteem. It is this distinct creative potential that distinguishes nostalgia from the static depression of pain . . . a mental source for social performance and creativity" (2015, 83). Nostalgia, as it impacts performance, can be employed as a means to integrate the glories of either our historical or our imagined past into our present sufferings and our future hopes. Um describes one element of this phenomenon as "the postcolonial desire to repossess history and the contemporary aspiration

144   CHAPTER 6

to attain cultural supremacy in a global world" (2013, 212). In all likelihood, the flourishing of a variety of epic traditions in post-Soviet Central Asia can be traced to similarly complex dynamics.

For many Sakha, the actual enjoyment of olonkho's historical form of performance seems far less significant than the fact that these tales exist and can be celebrated in a variety of forms. As long as the epic tradition endures—written in books, played on the best stages, discussed as a national treasure, studied in conferences, celebrated at festivals, and memorialized in the construction of large complexes—people remain content with these reflections of past glory. In light of Yakutia's postcolonial and neocolonial relations with the Center, the living tradition appears less necessary than the epic's role as an identity marker and nostalgic touchstone.

Although Yakutia exhibits many of the characteristics of postcolonial and neocolonial reactions to Soviet power, Sakha agency produces a number of different responses. National and minority identities often diverge in a multifarious rather than dualistic manner, especially when the colonizers have maintained power for several generations. Regarding the examination of cultural resources in postcolonial contexts, Bhabha warns against attributing "the positive aesthetic and political values we ascribe to the unity or totality of cultures, especially those who have known long and tyrannical histories of domination and misrecognition. Cultures are never unitary in themselves, nor simply dualistic in relation of Self to Other" (2006, 155–156). Yakutia exemplifies Bhabha's observation—reflections on a colonializing past range from an intense aversion to anything Soviet to a strong preference for anything pro-Russian or even pro-Stalin.[19]

While Sakha people respond to the post-Soviet state in a variety of ways, one of the most widespread reactions embraces a Sakha identity featuring olonkho as a major, iconic representation.[20] Perhaps most poignantly, olonkho may serve as a metonym, signifying the entirety of the Sakha people. For example, media and marketing sources often refer to the Republic of Sakha (Yakutia) as the "Land of Olonkho." A headline in the republic-wide newspaper *Yakutia* on June 6, 2009, heralded the presence of "Titans of Wrestling in the Land of Olonkho." The annual children's olonkho competition took the title *Deti zemli olonkho* ("Children of the Land of Olonkho"). The craft competition at the 2011 summer festival operated as *Mastera zemli olonkho* (Masters of the Land of Olonkho). The dreams of a few for a multi-million-dollar building complex called Olonkholand provide yet another example among many of the widespread use of the phrase "Land of Olonkho" to represent the republic and its people.

Discussions of Sakha reactions to postcolonial and neocolonial realities must also acknowledge both the agency of the Sakha in negotiating their relationships to current Russian state dynamics and their development of ties with other political entities internal and external to Russia. Far from powerless, marginalized victims of a monolithic Russian state, the Sakha have created a web of regional and transnational relationships that serves them well and leverages their strengths and aspirations. The acquisition of Masterpiece status for olonkho attests to their resourcefulness in the pursuit of their valued objectives. Furthermore, Sakha representatives in the legislative and cultural sectors of Yakutia frequently invoke olonkho in their public discourse as the most potent symbol of Sakha identity.

For example, in his address to the Yakutian Parliament (Il Tumen) on November 26, 2015, Egor Borisov, head of the Sakha Republic, used the ideals of olonkho as a rallying point for Sakha ethnic consciousness and values, specifically regarding how the Sakha relate to the Russian Federation and its enemies:

> Dear friends! Yesterday, in the Republic, according to tradition, the Day of Olonkho was celebrated. This is not just an ancient legend that has become a mythological and folkloric symbol of Yakutia. Olonkho is the unique cultural foundation of our multinational people, and most importantly, it integrates our whole philosophy of life—the eternal struggle between good and evil.
>
> We are obliged to always overcome various trials, barriers, and troubles in order to follow the laws of conscience and justice, emerging victorious from the most difficult situations. These important lessons are taught to us by our Yakut national epic Olonkho, recognized as one of the masterpieces of intangible heritage of humanity.[21]

The rest of Borisov's address exemplifies an officially approved, although not universally agreed-upon, statement emphasizing Yakutia's peoples as patriotic citizens of an increasingly beleaguered Russia, buffeted by terrorism, extremism, pressure from Western countries, and "sanctioning regimes." Borisov appeals to olonkho as a unifying symbol drawn from an archaic past but having impact in the present, asserting that patriotism and a unified Russian Federation are not incompatible with preserving roots: "And these are not merely sublime words, but express *the essence of how we think as a unified Russian nation*, including the Sakha people, who have preserved their roots through their ancient epic Olonkho."[22]

Others among the Sakha intelligentsia have proven highly adept at invoking olonkho and its newfound status to form relationships with other nations. From theatrical exchange performances in Asia to international bilateral translation projects for epic tales, these advocates reach out to other nations from a position of strength and pride in the strength of Sakha culture.[23] Their leveraging of the UNESCO Masterpiece program to bring international recognition and connections to the Land of Olonkho powerfully exhibits the role of intangible cultural heritage in promoting an "imagined community" (Anderson 2006).

146   CHAPTER 6

My own reception in Yakutia as a foreign olonkho researcher further demonstrates this outward-facing posture of engagement. I am one of those extralocal links viewed as contributing to Sakha transnational identity, a connection to a wider world that recognizes and respects Sakha scholarship and culture. Although the Sakha are known for their hospitality and warmth to all outsiders, I have experienced extra cordiality in my role as foreign researcher, and I have enjoyed frequent invitations to speak at regional and international conferences, probably due to my study of the favored genre of olonkho.[24] For example, in 2015 I was invited to become a member of the international editorial committee of the book series Epic Monuments of the Peoples of the World, an initiative of the Yakutian Parliament led by Alexander Zhirkov. He mentioned this project, among others, in a 2015 speech on the Day of Olonkho (November 25), noting that plans for 2016 included publication of two translations: the Altaic epos *Maadai Khara* translated into Sakha, and the olonkho *Nurgun Botur* translated into Altaic.[25] The bilateral nature of this publishing project intrigues me, since all the translations planned for the series reflect international or interregional cooperation in the context of mutual respect for epic traditions.

The twenty-first century commenced as an uncertain period for the Sakha Republic, especially in regard to the freedoms bestowed and then inexorably retaken by Moscow.[26] Stability has proven elusive for the Sakha, not only because of power struggles, but also on account of a series of Russian financial crises over the last several decades. During such liminal periods of turmoil, a return to nostalgia invokes historical and geographical attachments, thereby creating an illusion of stability and articulating desires for both present and future greatness. As Rethman remarks, nostalgia "on the one hand enables its users to appropriate and assert feelings toward their own history and, on the other hand, allows them to express their detachment from a disempowering, harsh present. . . . nostalgic practices articulate a vision that desires what cannot be had: stable histories and a stable reality" (1997, 772). Does olonkho express a "restorative nostalgia," seeking to preserve notions of truth and tradition by reproducing aspects of an imagined past in the present (Boym 2001)? Celebrating an ancient genre like olonkho affords the Sakha opportunities to come to terms with their past by connecting with their culture, history, and language in life-affirming ways. In turn, these positive experiences will aid them in grappling with the challenges of the future. A robustly revitalized olonkho, even if expressed primarily in related forms, may crucially impact the Sakha people's future in forging an identity that not only embraces their heritage but also deploys that legacy into the coming years.

This past-present-future connection in establishing Sakha identity could advance further with the revival of olonkho as a national ideal. Consider the evocative description by Ernest Renan: "A heroic past, great men, glory . . . this is the social capital upon which one bases a national idea. To have common glories in the past and to have a common will in the present; to have performed great deeds together, to wish to perform still more—these are the essential conditions for being a people" (1990, 19). This multitemporal aspect of olonkho plays a key role in undergirding the genre's revitalization: olonkho expresses the glories of the past through an invocation of cultural heroes and legends, represents a common will for good to win over evil in the present, and provides hope for a future lived in safety and security from one's enemies.

Increasingly, this sentiment of olonkho as a national ideal resounds from the podiums of Sakha cultural, religious, and governmental leaders and appears in the communications of other members of the intelligentsia.[27] In his speech on the Day of Olonkho, Zhirkov expounded at length on a number of olonkho-related projects initiated by his office. He concluded: "May our work on the conservation, perpetuation, and promotion of this rich historical and cultural heritage support the prosperity of our motherland and be a source of stability for a prosperous life!"[28] No empty slogan, Zhirkov's words reflect his tireless work to see these projects succeed. His efforts join those of the intellectuals and elites of the cultural, educational, and legislative sectors focusing an enormous amount of postcolonial energy into cultural activism.

Adams refers to a similar phenomenon in Uzbekistan, remarking, "This politics of culture must also be seen as a way that highly educated professionals, intellectuals, and artists organize their work. While some of Uzbekistan's intelligentsia actively resisted this top-down, ideology-oriented way of producing culture, the vast majority tolerated or even enjoyed such an arrangement because it provided them with opportunities to feel they were influencing the public and the future of the nation" (2010, 2).[29] In Yakutia, many among the intelligentsia consider their involvement in cultural revitalization to be a form of service—their contribution to creating a better future for Yakutia. They see their activities in relation to heritage in much the same way as Kirshenblatt-Gimblett describes the concept: "Heritage is a mode of cultural production in the present that has recourse to the past" (1998, 7). Invested in their vision of Sakha identity, they view their understanding of Sakha worldview, ideals, and values as crucial to a thriving Sakha society.

In post-Soviet Yakutia, the presence of the intelligentsia corresponds precisely with those areas in which I have observed the most energy for olonkho renewal—the cultural, educational, and legislative sectors. Adams notes a similar correspondence in Uzbekistan: "A striking feature of post-Soviet societies is the disproportionately high presence and extremely influential role of intellectual elites in positions previously held by the now demoralized and ousted old guard" (Adams 2010, 10). Because of the high value Yakutia places on education and

148   CHAPTER 6

the arts, a large cadre of well-educated and culturally adept Sakha were ready to step into positions of influence when the migration of Russians out of Yakutia began at the end of the Soviet Union.

A number of scholars employ postcolonial approaches and apply them to an analysis of the indigenous cultures in Russia's northern regions. For example, Serguei Oushakine addresses Turner's concept (1969, 103) of "liminal entities" and the ways in which people express their attachments to signifiers invoked from the past. In exploring individuals' negotiation of choices in relation to cultural symbols, Turner notes two common responses. In some cases, individuals may change the usage pattern of old symbols—the *paradigm of remake*. Alternatively, they may alter their "attitude to the old symbols; this pattern of symbolic production can be labeled the *paradigm of revival*. Both strategies, however, are aimed at keeping the old signifier/symbol intact . . . [and] both activate the individual's creative ability within the rigid symbolic frames of the previous era" (Oushakine 2000, 1007).

Remake and *revival* both play a part in olonkho's revitalization in the second decade of the twenty-first century. For example, Yakutia's enthusiastic policies toward revitalizing traditional olonkho practices constitute examples of *revival*. Likewise, multiple evidences of *remake* surface within olonkho's expansion of acceptable performance possibilities: theatrical and staged versions, strictly memorized rather than improvised material, and a yearly Ysyakh summer festival on an olonkho theme.

Epic traditions may succumb to repression and even cease to function as living epics, lost forever or relegated to a written form, like the Homeric epics. On the other hand, the malleability of epic traditions naturally predisposes them to endure the ebb and flow of societal change. This inclination may explain how the oral form of the Sakha epic survived over so many centuries. As Rene Louis observes, "[An epic tradition] passes from singer to singer and from audience to audience, to assume new forms according to the tasks and the profound tendencies of the eras which it traverses and the countries into which [it] spreads, above all in response to the sovereign imagination of the singers who adopt it as their own. Within the supple and accommodating framework of tradition these singers of epic themes, narrative schemas, and formulaic styles never stop improvising new details, new episodes, and creating countless 'variants' of the original work" (1958, 10).

Despite the natural durability of oral epic traditions, the history of olonkho and the conclusions emerging from my research demonstrate that epics can lose that resilience and become brittle through attenuations of either transmission or innovation. As proposed in the preceding chapter, strengthening the malleable aspects of a genre will support the levels of innovation needed to prevent its becoming frozen. Malleability provides the genre with the resilience necessary to withstand the winds of change, winds that might otherwise cause an epic's demise as a living tradition. In the face of inevitable change, a malleable, living epic tradition connects to the identities of its people and responds to contextual change through innovation. Faithfully transmitted to the next generation, such a dynamic tradition will enjoy a long life.

Lessons learned from the revitalization of other Asian epic traditions

UNESCO's initiatives in revitalizing other epic traditions besides olonkho afford the opportunity to compare my conclusions with the histories of similar genres. Observations and lessons learned about change in other Asian contexts may also increase our understanding of olonkho's revitalization process. To that end, I focus on two forms of epos that benefited from UNESCO's ICH program—the Kyrgyz epic trilogy *Manas*, which parallels olonkho as a Turkic-based oral tradition, and the Korean p'ansori.

Revitalization in Kyrgyz Manas

The Kyrgyz epic cycle of *Manas* features more lines of verse than any other known epic.[30] UNESCO revitalization initiatives such as festivals, competitions, conferences, and other government-funded events facilitate a transmission system based primarily on apprenticeships. Van der Heide's description of the revitalization of *Manas* in 2008 indicates the widespread presence of both innovation and transmission in the decade following the turn of the century: "the Manas is passed on through a living and lively oral tradition. . . . a core of Manas narrators called *Manaschï* . . . give recitals at festivals and Manas competitions. Manaschïs also recite at social gatherings or in schools and universities, and their recitals are broadcasted on radio and television. There are Manaschïs of all generations, all with their own version of the Manas epic, reaching audiences of all generations" (2008, 17). The fact that singers perform unique versions of the *Manas* epic indicates that the Manaschïs do not produce frozen, memorized versions of the epic's content, but rather re-create the material in a manner similar to that of Yakutia's master olonkhosuts. These skills result directly from the transmission of *Manas* by apprenticeship. With this approach, learners can "sit under the mouth" of a master and soak in the oral formulaic language needed for a unique re-creation of the *Manas* tale by each individual performer.

The UNESCO description of *Manas* at the time of its inscription into the ICH lists highlights the role of apprenticeship in transmission and underscores the genre's ongoing role in society and connection to Kyrgyz identity:[31] "The epics

150   CHAPTER 6

remain an essential component of Kyrgyz identity and continue to inspire contemporary writers, poets, and composers; even today, the traditional performances are still linked to sacred cultural spaces. Although there are fewer practitioners nowadays, master[s] . . . continue to train young apprentices and are helped by recent revitalization initiatives supported by the Kyrgyz government."[32] In addition, the revitalization of *Manas* benefits from the creation of innovative related forms, with the flourishing production of theatrical performances, movies (Reichl 2016, 331–332), and novels (Van der Heide 2008, 218).

Just as with olonkho, transcriptions of *Manas* produced by the Soviets in the twentieth century reflected the push for literacy and the development of an academy of universities and research centers. Van der Heide relates the changes as *Manas* underwent literary transcription and analysis: "The written [form of *Manas*] gained in importance over the oral, both as authoritative source for knowledge production and as forms of disseminating the tales. Scholars who worked with written texts gained prestige over learned persons who produced orally transmitted knowledge. The introduction of the scholarly view on the *Manas*, in combination with the prestige awarded to the scholars, transformed the ways people regarded the epic. Next to the image of the *Manas* as an oral epic sustained by the spiritual world arose an image of the *Manas* as a book assessed by intellectuals" (2008, 207). This intellectual image and the perceived high value for the literary forms afforded a short-lived boon for the Kyrgyz and Russian scholars who were involved in proliferating *Manas* transcriptions.

Unfortunately, government beneficence came to an end during the economic crisis of post-Soviet government, and *Manas* publications virtually ceased as well. Scholars either did not receive their paychecks at all or were paid so little that many of them were forced to gain employment in other arenas. Over time, Van der Heide reports, "funding for Manas publications slowly emerged from other sources, such as UNESCO, European, American and Kyrgyzstani NGOs, Turkish government and private organisations and private Kyrgyz businessmen. Most of this funding was given in the framework of the 1995 Manas 1,000 celebration" (2008, 209), that is, through UNESCO.

In interviews during her fieldwork in Kyrgyzstan, Van der Heide consistently found that few people actually read the available texts.[33] She noted that even Manaschïs did not read the written versions to learn the stories, although they did listen to recordings. Although the literary version was not read much, it still enjoyed perceived value at the grassroots level. The official position supported by UNESCO and sponsored by the government values and supports both the oral transmission process and the literary versions. Bohlman notes the importance of considering both forms when studying folk music: "It is virtually impossible in the twentieth century to discover folk music traditions that are purely oral or

EPIC REVITALIZATION   151

exclusively literate. . . . It becomes increasingly necessary, in fact, to expand our understanding of the range spanned by such concepts as orality and literacy, especially when electronic and other media of transmission exert a growing influence on folk music. The essential issue for the study of folk music is therefore not either oral or written, but the dynamics and direction of change inherent in the coexistence of these two aspects of tradition" (1988, 30).[34]

Oral and literary aspects also intertwine in olonkho. Scholars, authors, and translators create written versions of various olonkho tales, often beautifully illustrated and published with the glossy paper and good-quality bindings that reflect high production values. Used for educational purposes in schools and for research by scholars, these books may help to bolster the epic *sreda*, provide texts for olonkhosut performers to memorize, and preserve olonkho tales for future generations.

Revitalization in Korean p'ansori

Another epic tradition experiencing revitalization, Korean p'ansori also boasts the ongoing development of innovative related forms and plays a role in the expression of identity. A few new p'ansori-related forms appearing in the last century have tapped into a stream of arts connected to modern Korean identities. After p'ansori solidified into a canonical repertoire in the nineteenth century, the related multi-person theatrical version *ch'anngŭk* emerged, serving "as a vehicle for the introduction of new works" (Pihl 1993, 229). In a similar way, theatrical versions of olonkho provide an outlet for innovation.

A second p'ansori-related form evolved through a new trend of casting glamorous young female singers rather than experienced p'ansori singers in lead roles. *Yŏsŏng kukkŭk*, an all-female theater, or "women's national drama," became known for embracing the sentimental and sensational. This genre featured "the modern and cosmopolitan alongside the national, and in today's productions it is not unusual to hear traditional voices and instruments accompanied by synthesizers" (Killick 2003, 191). In this symbiotic relationship between ancient and modern, *yŏsŏng kukkŭk* employs mediated outlets such as the recording industry and radio in "the making of tradition in modernity" (Um 2013). Tapping into these resources not only fosters p'ansori renewal among Korean youth, but also connects the tradition to Korean diasporas through a process that Um describes as "cultural heritage conceived as the nation's desired continuity" (3).[35]

Korea's modern theatrical fusions of new and old include storylines drawn from epic tales and the use of synthesized orchestration to accompany traditional song styles, paralleling the performances of the Theater of Olonkho in Yakutia. Both Korean and Yakutian audiences enjoy enactments of their respective traditional-modern fusions—these unique blends represent high levels of innovation, yet they

152   CHAPTER 6

also maintain clear connections with older genres and traditions that tap into a sense of national identity.

The challenges affecting traditional p'ansori performance reveal even more significant implications for olonkho. In 1964, UNESCO identified p'ansori as part of Korea's cultural and historical heritage and declared the genre "Intangible Cultural Property No. Five," thereby demonstrating its high value for Korean people and for the whole world. Park explains how, in an unforeseen development, this recognition actually began to isolate p'ansori from its formerly intimate audiences, decreasing active participation such as verbal engagement and resulting in a form of passive alienation (2000, 276).[36] Furthermore, Yeonok Jang observes that government-organized performances of p'ansori tend to minimize the original function of the Korean epic tales—entertainment—in favor of using the genre to promote traditional Korean culture to national and international audiences. Used largely for symbolic purposes, p'ansori performances currently represent a strong link to Korean national heritage and identity, although they still retain some element of entertainment (2001, 118).

Just as with olonkho, new performance settings for p'ansori serve to decrease the strength of the audience's connection to the performance. In contrast with more traditional, intimate venues like parks and courtyards, modern, formal stage venues now separate performer and audience. A lack of knowledge about appropriate audience participation further weakens this connection. Increasingly silent and "polite," audiences more often respond by clapping after a performance than by shouting ch'uimsae (responsive vocal interjections) throughout. P'ansori performers, just like olonkhosuts, increasingly complain that it is "not inspiring to perform for an audience that does not respond" (Jang 2001, 105). Sometimes performers have been known to teach the audience how to shout ch'uimsae, despite the challenges in conveying a sense of appropriate timing, word choice, and tone of voice.[37] For p'ansori, Park suggests that "the process of learning starts with unlearning the sanitized manners of a polite spectator" (2000, 280).

Similar complaints by Pyotr Reshetnikov echo in my ears, and I remember how he took the time to teach me to respond verbally during his performance in 2009. In 2014, Nurguyana Illarionova told me that some Sakha audiences are once again beginning to respond verbally to olonkho tales, a practice not widely observed during the initial years of the first Decade of Olonkho.[38] My subsequent visits to Yakutia in 2015 confirmed her observation—after being lost for some time, verbal responses from the audience in olonkho performance are once again becoming a habit. The slow expansion of this level of audience response heralds a positive development for the Sakha olonkho. If schoolchildren throughout Yakutia learn these vocal responses as part of their lessons in audience etiquette, the resulting

EPIC REVITALIZATION 153

change in audience engagement will help inspire olonkhosuts to new heights of performing prowess.

Another scholar of p'ansori, Keith Howard, proposes that revitalization should include openness to new lyric themes. Even though the state's role tends to fossilize the form, "the tradition is recycled and reinvented as it seeks to embrace new lyrics about colonialism, tyranny, and oppression" (2004, 125). The tradition of olonkho would similarly benefit from new lyrics and plots reflecting the contexts and concerns of a new generation of olonkhosuts, even if those concerns involve painful topics such as dealing with a colonial past.

Park presents a poignant question with implications for olonkho and other epics on the UNESCO Representative Lists: "Will p'ansori remain forever encased as an antique reminder of the past, or will it be allowed a dialectical process—to live, perish, or change? Is the duration of preservation finite, and what follows? Incredulous of its resuscitation at any time in the future, is the government performing taxidermy on p'ansori?" (2000, 279). Park's questions implicitly emphasize the need to transmit a living tradition rather than a dead "stuffed animal"—the reference to taxidermy viscerally reminds us that fur and claws do not necessarily indicate life. In that vein, the lessons gleaned from p'ansori—the need for new texts that address relevant themes, and the importance of educating a new generation of listeners toward a more engaged, verbally responsive listening posture—exemplify the kinds of innovation and transmission needed in olonkho revitalization.

From common challenges to a hopeful future

Reports around the world from scholars studying epics such as p'ansori, *Manas*, olonkho, and other traditions show many parallel challenges in epic revitalization. For example, changes in performance arenas negatively impact audience engagement levels. What began as small, intimate, entertainment-oriented family gatherings have grown into public, government-sponsored festival events calculated to foster pride in a monolithic, often nostalgia-infused ethnic identity. Audience verbal responses, at one time an unconscious, natural part of being engrossed in the story, return only with coaching. Without these responses, "singers of tales" tend to lose energy and shorten their texts.

Written texts and translations into other languages, produced by enthusiastic folklorists, anthropologists, ethnomusicologists, and comparative literature scholars, provide crucial support for the documentation required for safeguarding epic traditions. At the same time, this growing corpus of texts preserves only the frozen corpses of the once-living epics, not necessarily supporting the living tradition.

Scholars may simply dissect the texts for their semiotic, patriotic, mythic, historic, or cosmic significance, while performers memorize and reproduce abbreviated versions for competitions, concerts, and festival audiences. Even these shortened renditions of olonkho still fulfill a number of vital functions, such as affirming enduring aspects of Sakha cultural identities, worldviews, and values. In addition, they transmit to current and future generations a wealth of linguistic resources in the stories of their legendary and historical characters.

As I watch the academic texts grow, even contributing to their numbers myself, I grieve the loss of Yakutia's master olonkhosuts and their oral art. I can only hope that somewhere in the 1.2 million square miles of Yakutian territory, a future tradition bearer lives quietly hidden from the limelight. Perhaps a little-known olonkho performer or a student studying the genre is already developing facility in creating with the formulaic language and themes, growing in proficiency until the day this talent emerges to be recognized, supported, and transmitted to others.

Members of the younger generation offer hopeful examples of innovation and transmission as they create new olonkho tales and perform them in a variety of contexts, from competitions to classrooms. Yuri Borisov, the young olonkhosut who was briefly mentioned in chapter 3, works at NEFU's Olonkho Institute.[39] Having completed a master's degree with a focus on olonkho, he now devotes considerable energy to transmission of the tradition and to innovation within

Fig. 6.1. Olonkhosut Yuri Borisov (2010). Photo by www.ysia.ru. Used by permission.

EPIC REVITALIZATION 155

Fig. 6.2. The Association of Young Olonkhosuts (Verkhoyansk, 2016). Photo by www.ysia.ru. Used by permission.

it. During the largest olonkho competition of 2015, the Ysyakh of Olonkho in Churapcha, this talented young olonkho scholar and singer won the grand prize for olonkhosuts, taking away a brand-new Russian automobile as his reward.

Thankfully, other Sakha of Borisov's generation also perform and promote olonkho, which stimulated the launch of an Association of Young Olonkhosuts (Ychchat Olongkhohut) in December 2015. At the time of its formation, one of its initiators, Galina Popova, excitedly described to me her vision for the group's prospects, and expressed gratitude for Alexander Zhirkov's promise of parliament-level support.[40] Yuri Borisov now serves as the president of this organization. In the first six months of its existence, the group held at least two collective performances of young olonkhosuts in the *balaghan* of the Olonkho Institute in Yakutsk and sent a large contingent of performers to the 2016 Ysyakh of Olonkho in Verkhoyansk (fig. 6.2).[41]

The spark of creativity in these young performers provides a ray of hope for olonkho. With encouragement, new tales, new forms, and new approaches to old tales can flourish, thereby strengthening olonkho's resilience. This resilience, in turn, will allow the tradition to flex, adapt to the contexts of the twenty-first century, and meet the needs of the shifting sociocultural environment. In this way, today's new layers of innovation for olonkho may settle like sediment to form the stable soil of a new living tradition, thereby giving life to resilient new forms of olonkho that can thrive even in the face of turbulent change.

CHAPTER 7

Ensuring Sustainability through Transmission and Innovation

> Even when people seem to be reviving things, that is, exhuming them and breathing life into them, what they get is something new.
> —Mark Slobin, "Rethinking 'Revival' of American Ethnic Music"

A wise Russian aphorism declares, "You don't have to be a prophet to predict the demise of a people deprived of their mother tongue."[1] Many Sakha people feel this way, not only about their language, but also about their arts. In the most potent way possible, these unique artistic expressions energize the self-expression and well-being of the Sakha, pushing back against decades, even centuries, of marginalization. Their arts create a space for breathing, for creating, and for celebrating the unique voices of Sakha people.[2] And although change is inevitable, many Sakha people desire to see olonkho continue in some form into the future.[3]

On foam and deep waters

Which olonkho forms will endure remains unclear. The clamor surrounding olonkho revitalization, particularly the many activities resulting from the enormous amounts of government money being poured into the process, has obscured the true state of the living, improvisatory tradition. Does this bleak prognosis leave any room for hope?

With a half century of experience in folklore, both in Yakutia and beyond, Eduard Alekseyev contributes a perspective of hopefulness through his metaphor of "foam" and "deep waters," surmising that beneath the foam of ephemeral popular and political opinion, the tradition can still endure: "folklore has this characteristic, including olonkho—it continues on because it can endure a latent form of existence. [. . .] And when the situation changes, it is born again, as if from nothing. But the fact is, it was just underground, and the deeper it goes, the better, because it is there that its true nature is preserved. But on the surface sometimes all you can see is the 'foam'—and the foam is—whoosh, blown away by the wind. For the 'foam' they may put you in prison. . . . Or they raise you up to the heavens, make you a member of the Union of Writers. I think that ten (or something like that) olonkhosuts were made members of the Union of Writers when it was urgently needed for the war effort. Or they create a 'Day of Olonkho,' or a 'last olonkhosut'—last this—last that—last, last, . . . and government stipends and so forth. This is not so much 'foam' as it is a wave, and waves always have foamy moments. But way down deep in the ocean, it is not affected by waves."[4]

Slobin compares this phenomenon of "going underground" to "silence" or "sleep" and asks, "To what extent are we watching the rise and fall of breath of a slumbering system, or are we helping to kiss a music awake from dormancy through activism and advocacy?" (2014, 670). The hope that the living tradition of the master olonkhosut might still be awakened from sleep has motivated me throughout this research. I therefore propose a few possible directions for the future of olonkho. I view these potential developments as paths, likely to diverge from one another in the near future.

Paths into the future

If the diagnostic chart (fig. 5.2) and the Graded Genre Health Assessment (fig. 5.1) prove to be robust predictors of genre viability, then *transmission* and *innovation*, the two primary components of *resilience*, will significantly influence the direction of change. With these factors in mind, I see at least three possible future paths for olonkho:

(1) *Vigorous transmission* of traditionally performed olonkho to the next generation *without innovation* in plots, related forms, or adaptations to the modern context will result in canonization of the transmitted material. The state of epic creativity will be "locked" into standardized performances, exhibitions, concerts, and festivals, with the primary purpose of supporting national concepts of ethnic identity. Not just Yakutia but the world will lose a uniquely improvisational art.

(2) *Lack of transmission* of the solo tradition along with *abundant innovation* will produce many related forms, such as theatrical settings, books, movies, and computer games, but the traditional version will eventually die out. Functional substitutes that satisfy the need for affirming Sakha ethnic identities will replace longer solo performances, crowding out the unique improvisatory art of the master olonkhosuts.

(3) *Transmission* of the traditional improvisatory art of olonkho, coupled with *abundant innovation* both within the traditional form's boundaries and in the

158   CHAPTER 7

creation of new, related forms, will allow olonkho to flourish. The many resulting forms will ensure a truly sustainable revitalization.

Since mediated and theatrical forms of olonkho are enjoying successful revitalization, olonkho will very likely continue to exist in some form or another into the distant future. For example, olonkho's performance contexts have grown from small family gatherings around the fireplace on long winter nights to lavish stage settings and festival crowds. They have even grown beyond Russia, from regional and republic-wide Yakutian contexts to the international stage of the prestigious UNESCO Masterpiece awards, and now include Japanese and Chinese audiences watching olonkho theatrical extravaganzas with subtitles. Olonkho's mediated presence has similarly grown from the lone radio voice of Gavriil Kolesov to the huge archives of audio and video recordings accessible through Sergei Vasiliev's web portal to anyone in the world with a computer and broadband Internet access.

The Sakha people, individually and collectively, hold in their hands the future paths of olonkho performance. Neglecting or actively opposing either of the two vital processes, *innovation* or *transmission*, will diminish resilience. As a result, true revitalization of the traditional form will necessarily fail, although olonkho will undoubtedly endure as a significant symbol of Sakha identity.

Already the Sakha are exploring opportunities for olonkho transmission through school programs, workshops, camps, master classes, and competitions. In addition, general education about the tradition has produced a noticeable increase in levels of knowledge about olonkho. At this point, however, olonkho lacks vigorous transmission levels for the *improvisational*, oral aspect of performance, with innovations such as new plots or related forms still few and far between. While the vast weight of history and tradition furnish adequate stability for the genre, olonkho's malleable facets need nurturing for resilience to return.

Recommendations

We can foster resilience for olonkho by addressing levels of innovation and transmission in a number of practical ways. The following thoughts combine my own ideas with those I received from others in the process of research.

One suggestion concentrates on those who perform olonkho. Given the fact that no olonkhosuts currently carry an officially recognized status of tradition bearers, concerted efforts should be made to investigate whether anyone might qualify. In the meantime, many olonkhosuts who regularly perform, albeit not yet as "masters," would benefit from outside financial support in their transmission efforts. Money is more than just a medium of exchange; it makes a value statement, bestowing status. As a result, providing stipends for tradition bearers confers prestige and may encourage others to invest time in learning the art of olonkho. Without the incentive of seeing that their efforts can provide a living, few Sakha young people will want to spend the many years required to become an olonkhosut. Millions of dollars each year already go toward olonkho revitalization projects such as books, conferences, "Houses of Olonkho," festivals, and theatrical productions. These investments, although valuable, do not benefit the living transmitters of the oral tradition, who need the opportunity to devote their lives to passing on their art. In addition to stipends, the government could reimburse money spent on transmission activities, thereby further relieving the olonkhosut's personal burden of such expenses.

An encouraging development in this regard appeared in a news article on April 17, 2016, outlining a creative solution to the need for stipends for olonkhosuts:

> Four award-winning olonkhosuts and twelve performers of the Yakut national epic have been accepted as honorary members of the High Council of the republic's Theater of Olonkho. According to the leadership of the theater, from now on each of the honorary members will be given a work plan for the year, in which time he should give master classes, meet with the public, work with youth, and perform the national epic for the public. As each olonkhosut follows through on his plan, he will receive a monetary reward.
>
> Olonkhosut and honorary member of the theater Pyotr Tikhonov remarked, "I see some positive aspects in this innovation. Although we will be doing the same job as before, now we will receive a reward for that work. And now we will look more carefully at our repertoire—for example, instead of two or three olonkhos performed all the time, each olonkhosut will add a few more. It will also result in an expansion of the audience. We will not have to confine ourselves to festivals or events held exclusively for people who are already in the sphere of olonkho. Fortunately, the audience is almost ready to listen to olonkhos that are a few hours in length. I believe we must work closely with the Theater of Olonkho, then there will be a big step forward in the promotion of the epic to the population of the republic." . . . The author of this innovative idea is the state advisor of Yakutia, Andrei Borisov[, and it] . . . has been implemented under the auspices of Yakutia's Ministry of Culture and Spiritual Development.[5]

Although the article does not say how large the stipend is, or what will happen to these performers should they become unable to perform their duties due to poor health or old age, this development represents a significant step in a positive direction for these olonkho performers. It reflects an innovation in the arena of compensation that rewards both transmission and innovation. Furthermore, this intriguing development demonstrates stable and malleable components that should lead to resilience. For example, while it relies on the stable income of the Theater of Olonkho for funding, it incentivizes the malleable creativity of the olonkho performers, encouraging them to increase their productivity and the numbers of

160   CHAPTER 7

olonkhos they can perform. In the end, just as grandchildren in Yakutia sometimes end up caring for the health of their grandparents, the theatrical "descendant" of the original solo tradition may end up being a factor contributing to the resilience, and sustainability, of the olonkho performance tradition. Certainly, the intertwining of the theatrical and solo traditions has the potential to strengthen both, just as multigenerational households can provide more robust support for each generation represented in the "family."

As a second recommendation, Yakutia could create *performance* and *learning contexts* that better reflect traditional spaces. As we saw in Ekaterina Chekhorduna's account of her childhood experiences, the home atmosphere on long winter nights contributed to the magic of olonkho a century ago—the mesmerizing flickering fire in the fireplace, the moaning wind, the dark, cold winter night beyond the frosted windows, and the late-night hours with loved ones gathered around. Attention to creating intimate performance contexts with an appropriate atmosphere would greatly contribute to a multisensory aesthetic experience. In contrast, modern olonkho performance contexts often take place under stage lights or even in broad daylight, such as during the summer Ysyakh festivals. In some cases, the nearby thumping strains of semi-Russianized festival music may easily overwhelm the fragile soundscape created by the lone olonkhosut.

Teaching and learning can also take place in more traditional settings. Yakutia could create a state-funded—or, even better, philanthropy-funded—mentorship system, allowing those who wish to study the oral art of olonkho to apprentice themselves to an olonkhosut, possibly even to one of those named as honorary members of the High Council for the Theater of Olonkho.[6] Learners might accompany their mentors in their travels. Alternatively, apprentices might train through a studio-based system, spending hours each week listening to olonkho, practicing skills, and acquiring the formulaic mastery required to improvise within the genre.[7] This system could benefit from capitalizing on twenty-first-century Sakha values—a sense of ethnic pride and an appeal to a certain degree of professionalism—by enrolling only students with the most potential and by finally endorsing only the highest-quality olonkhosuts.[8]

Yakutia already has such a system for classical musicians. The campus of the Higher School of Music outside Yakutsk provides a boarding school for musically gifted young people who come from within the republic. A select few audition for the limited spots available and study with the top classical musicians in Yakutia. The Sakha government pays for the education of the children who obtain these coveted spots, and in return, Yakutia enjoys the prestige of a cadre of students who regularly win international music competitions.[9] The artistic milieu of the Higher School of Music demonstrates the importance of a focused environment in producing top specialists.[10] Likewise, transmission of olonkho, whether achieved

ENSURING SUSTAINABILITY 161

through a studio or a nomadic model, requires the crucial ingredient of large amounts of time devoted to acquiring the art. Most importantly, this time must be spent "under the mouth"—in other words, in face-to-face contact with the master of the living oral art.

A third consideration is whether Yakutia can rebuild an epic *sreda* by educating and attracting enthusiastic audiences. Yakutia's Action Plan already includes this goal, and olonkho activists have seen some progress through projects such as theatrical presentations by the Theater of Olonkho or Ysyakh festivals showcasing olonkho. Nevertheless, appreciative audiences for traditionally performed solo olonkho remain rare. What actions might cultivate the growth of engaged audiences?

As many of my respondents indicated, one possible approach encourages increased innovation within the boundaries of the genre itself. Contemporary olonkhos, reflecting modern Sakha life, language, values, and worldviews, will conceivably draw new audiences in a way that older stories will not. Settings that reproduce the conditions of being "under the mouth" will draw audiences into the world of olonkho, increasing their focused appreciation for the stories.[11]

Final reflections

Reflecting on the unusual opportunity I have had over the last decade to observe olonkho move from marginalized to celebrated, from "forgotten" to recognized as a Masterpiece, I am both elated and humbled by the responsibilities and privileges I have been given through relationships with the people of Yakutia. They have encouraged me to join hands with them in their efforts to preserve, memorialize, and mediate the olonkho tradition (Shelemay 2008, 149) both for themselves and for others beyond the borders of the Russian Federation.[12] As I review my field journals, remembering the sleepless nights and mosquito-bitten days jouncing around the dusty, sweltering back roads of Yakutia, I appreciate anew this entry from June 16, 2009: *Maria has gotten permission for us to videotape an interview and performance of Pyotr Reshetnikov, who is considered the last living master olonkhosut. This is a privilege that I can hardly comprehend.*

Indeed, I count both the interview with Reshetnikov and the opportunity to experience his performance among the unforgettable days of my life. Most memorably, the master olonkhosut revealed something during that interview that helped me better understand my place in the story of olonkho revitalization: "The audience for olonkho is less now because they have forgotten how to listen to olonkho, as an oral creation, as a compellingly beautiful, really, creation of humanity. There used to be lots of olonkhosuts, great olonkhosuts, because there was a community of listeners. In the past . . . olonkhosuts were elevated, and if the olonkhosut was good, even great, one whose name was spread around the republic, people would make an effort to come, even from far away, to hear."[13] As I reflect on the effect of my presence that day, I am reminded that my "effort to come, even from far away, to hear" has been appreciated by Reshetnikov and other Sakha people. Even more significantly, my time with them has allowed for these reflections on the revitalization process of an astounding genre from the northern regions of Siberia.

With gratitude I recognize that although the Sakha people, especially the olonkhosuts, value my efforts within their artistic world, I find myself in their debt. I have been immeasurably enriched, forever changed by their stories of overcoming marginalization and by their commitment to the cause of olonkho revitalization. I will always be grateful for the privilege of "sitting under the mouth."

Glossary of Russian and Sakha Words

bogatyr (богатырь)—warrior hero.

dėgėrėn (дэгэрэн)—one of the two major traditional Sakha song styles, *dėgėrėn* features a strictly organized metrical rhythm and less ornamentation than the *diėrėtii* style.

diėrėtii (дьиэрэтии)—a Sakha song style characterized as unmetered, exalted, solemn, ceremonial, ornate, and drawn-out, with smoothly flowing phrases. Improvisatory in nature, *diėrėtii* is marked by abundant *kylyhakh* (ornamentation).

khomus (хомус)—Sakha jaw harp

kylyhakh (кылыһах)—a unique form of ornamentation characteristic of the *diėrėtii* style of Sakha singing. The plural in Sakha (*kylyhakhtar*), when quoted in Russian text, is normally given the Russian plural form (*kylyhakhi*).

ohuokhai (оһуохай/осуохай)—Sakha round dance, with lyrics sung in a call-and-response, improvisatory form.

olonkhosut (олонхонут/олонхосут)—a specialist in performing the tales of the olonkho epos.

perestroika (перестройка)—literally: *restructuring*—a period marked by political and economic reforms in the Soviet Union, begun under Mikhail Gorbachev's leadership in the mid-1980s.[1]

sreda (среда)—a Russian word that, like the similar French word *milieu*, does not have a precise equivalent in English. It denotes not only the physical surroundings and visible environment of a place and time, but also the broad social environment, including the attitudes and perceptions of people in relation to the object being discussed and any associated activities.

syngaakh annygar (сынаах анныгар)—a Sakha phrase meaning "sitting under the mouth" and connoting "to listen or look intently, to try to absorb everything and every single word," thereby describing the audience's experience during a live olonkho performance.[2]

---

1. For an expanded definition, see https://www.britannica.com/topic/perestroika-Soviet-government-policy.

2. This definition comes from personal correspondence with Tatiana Argounova-Low, who during her research found reference to *syngaakh annygar* in the writings of Aleksei Kulakovskii, a famous Sakha intellectual and author of the early twentieth century, describing his fascination with olonkho in his youth.

164 GLOSSARY

toyuk (тойук)—a Sakha praise song genre; the most characteristic genre within the broader category of *dièrètii* song style

tsentr (центр)—when used in contexts referring to power and political control, *Center* refers to center-periphery relations, and most specifically to Moscow as symbolizing the seat of authority for the federal government

Ysyakh (Ысыах)—a uniquely Sakha ethnic festival, celebrated out of doors in a large field during the summer solstice. The Sakha celebrate Ysyakh each year at the regional level and in smaller festivals associated with cities, towns, or even organizations. Beginning in 2007, a different region has hosted the "Ysyakh of Olonkho" each year, specifically highlighting this genre as its central theme.

Notes

INTRODUCTION: ENCOUNTERING OLONKHO

1. See the recording of this event at https://www.youtube.com/watch?v=8ee0EXY0q0g, accessed October 20, 2014. Most epics worldwide are identified by their titles and are capitalized accordingly (*Manas*, *Sunjata*, etc.); the initial lowercase *o* in "olonkho" reflects its designation as a genre rather than as a specific epic.

2. Some Sakha pronounce the word "olonkhohut," with an *h* instead of an *s* beginning the last syllable. Since the Russian alphabet does not have an *h*, the sound is often replaced by *s*. I have thus chosen to use the more widespread spelling *olonkhosut*, which should prove easier for English speakers to read and pronounce. This same phenomenon occurs with another common Sakha word, *Ysyakh* (*Yhyakh*), which might otherwise be difficult for Anglophones to decipher.

3. I am grateful to Tatiana Argounova-Low for the discovery of this phrase in the writings of Aleksei Kulakovskii (in Emelianov 1964, 80) and for providing its English translation (Cruikshank and Argounova 2000, 109).

4. Designated the Yakut Autonomous Soviet Socialist Republic from 1923 until 1992, the region became the Republic of Sakha (Yakutia) in 1992 and is commonly called Yakutia in informal conversation. Yakutsk, the capital city, was founded by Russian Cossacks in 1632, and within another century, Slavic peoples in the area had increased in influence. See http://www.yakutiatravel.com/facts-about-yakutia/history, accessed August 31, 2016.

5. For Russian census numbers for 2010 by nationality, see http://demoscope.ru/weekly/ssp/rus_nac_10.php, accessed December 5, 2016.

6. Sakha is a Turkic language with Russian and Mongolian influences. For a list of Turkic languages, see https://www.ethnologue.com/subgroups/turkic-0, accessed January 25, 2016. The widespread continued use of the appellation "Yakut" rather than "Sakha" in common speech may stem from the fact that "Yakut" declines in Russian, whereas "Sakha" does not, making adjectival forms awkward.

7. In this sense, the word "Russians" does not refer to all citizens of the Russian Federation (RF) but rather refers to those who do not identify with a minority in the RF and refer

166 NOTES TO INTRODUCTION

to themselves in common parlance as *russkii* (Russian). Hobsbawm provides additional insights into the semantic complexity of terms related to this Russian majority (1990, 50). For additional considerations regarding the general terminology surrounding ethnic identity, see Hobsbawm (1990, 64), Post (2006, 415), Pegg (2001, 7), and Stokes (1994).

8. Guinness World Records notes that "the coldest permanently inhabited place" is "the Siberian village of Oymyakon . . . , in Russia, where the temperature reached −68°C (−90°F) in 1933 (the coldest ever recorded outside Antarctica)." http://www.guinness worldrecords.com/world-records/3000/lowest-temperature-inhabited, accessed December 5, 2016. Compared with Oymyakon, a small village of fewer than eight hundred people, Yakutsk (1,000 km away) claims the status of "the coldest inhabited *city* on earth." Steeve Iuncker, "Yakutsk: The Coldest City on Earth," *Time*, http://lightbox.time.com/2013/04/10/yakutsk-the-coldest-city-on-earth/#1, accessed April 19, 2017.

9. Although the definition of "ethnomusicology" has been debated at length, Titon's compact description, "the study of people making music" (1989), prioritizes the "ethno" component over the "music" aspect and best aligns with the purposes of this research.

10. Harris (2012a).

11. My research questions became more focused in 2009 at the 40th Annual World Conference of the International Council for Traditional Music in Durban, South Africa. At that time, Anthony Seeger, who served as secretary general of the International Council for Traditional Music from 2001 to 2005 and supervised the evaluation of many of the Masterpiece awards, challenged conference attendees to conduct long-term research on the effect of the Masterpiece awards on revitalization. In his presentation, "Towards an Ecology of Musical Practice" (2009b), Seeger stressed the importance of examining the entire sociocultural ecology surrounding music, for a tradition may continue in another form even in the face of apparently diminishing diversity. This insightful perspective proved true in the case of olonkho. UNESCO's Masterpiece program is explained in more detail in chap. 3.

12. I use the following definition of "artistic genre": "a community's category of artistic communication characterized by a unique set of formal characteristics, performance practices, and social meanings" (Schrag 2013a, 267).

13. I like Schippers's commentary on the terms "maintaining" vs. "sustaining": "Etymologically, *maintaining* means holding *in* the hand, (Fr., *maintenir*), while *sustaining* implies holding a hand *under* something for support (Fr., *soustenir*). Therefore, I would argue that the term *sustaining* has the best chance at transcending any 'tradition under siege' associations, suggesting a gentler process, and leaving room for taking into account more than a single force working on a phenomenon—while it is still allowed to breathe" (2015, 137).

14. Older works that helped to gauge the process of change include a classic describing the nineteenth-century Yakutian context—Vatslav Seroshevskii's ethnography of the Sakha, written during his exile in Yakutia (1896; 2nd ed. 1993). Anthropologists, explorers, and folklorists such as Dunn and Dunn (1963), Jochelson (1933), Kirby (1980), Krueger (1962), and Tokarev and Gurvich (1964) also contributed to the literature on the Sakha cultural context. Likewise, archaeologist Okladnikov (1970) includes a comparison of olonkho with the epics of other Siberian peoples.

NOTES TO INTRODUCTION   167

15. Marjorie Balzer aptly notes: "The word 'Russia' itself is a colloquial convention in English for the multiethnic state that is formally termed the Federation of Rossiia, a state that, in recent years, has become decreasingly 'federal' by Western definitions" (2010, ix).

16. Post's definition of "nation" emphasizes historical connections to a common identity and a "real or imagined homeland" (2006, 416).

17. Anderson goes on to point out that "[a nation] is imagined as a community, because, regardless of the actual inequality and exploitation that may prevail in each, the nation is always conceived as a deep, horizontal comradeship" (2006, 7).

18. The German term *landschaft* demonstrates a broad semantic domain that overlaps significantly with that of the term *sreda*.

19. See Howard (2012, 2014) for the effect of top-down interventions on intangible cultural heritage in East Asia.

20. In their introduction to *The Oxford Handbook of Music Revival*, Juniper Hill and Caroline Bithell observe, "The most obvious limitation of the extant English language literature on music revivals is, of course, its geographical coverage" (2014, 9). Indeed, far too few English-language monographs document arts of Siberian peoples, and none focus on the Sakha. Harris (2012b) reviews a set of two DVDs by Maltsev and Howard (2008) that focuses primarily on the music of the Buriat but also documents some features of Sakha music, dance, and ritual. See also Harris (2013), a festschrift for Eduard Alekseyev focused especially on his connections to olonkho.

21. English-language works about the Sakha Republic (Yakutia) from anthropologists, sociologists, and other scholars in the last three decades include Argounova (1992), Bremmer and Taras (1993), Bychkova Jordan and Jordan-Bychkov (2001), Crate (2006), Cruikshank and Argounova (2000), Gogolev (1992a, 1992b, 1992c), Kempton (1996), Khazanov (1993), Peers (2010, 2013, 2015), Robbek (1998), Slezkine (1994), Tichotsky (2000), Vinokurova (1995a, 1995b), and Vitebsky (1987, 2005). Their works provide perspectives on the cultural, political, religious, educational, and everyday realities of life in the Sakha Republic since perestroika and the fall of the Soviet Union. Other writers, such as Batalden and Batalden (1997), Forsyth (1992), Leete (2005), Leete and Firnhaber (2004), Lincoln (1994), and Service (2009), offer invaluable background in Eurasian anthropology, history, and the demographics of various regions of Siberia. Perhaps most notably, American anthropologist Marjorie Balzer writes prolifically in English about the Sakha Republic. Her early (1991) entry in the *Encyclopedia of World Cultures* provided, at the time of its writing, one of the most concise English-language overviews of the history and culture of the Sakha. Balzer's 1993 article on religion and atheism in Yakutia notes the beginnings of a cultural revival in the early 1990s, but does not mention olonkho, which was dormant at the time. Other works cited in this book (Balzer 1995, 1999, 2005, 2006, 2010, 2011; Balzer and Vinokurova 1996) address issues related to cultural revival, especially ethnicity, federalism, nationalism, religion, and shamanism. Readers may also wish to consult the book summary in English of Sheikin's Russian-language monograph (2002, 716), which provides a comparative-historical study of the musical cultures of the people of Siberia and a scholarly perspective on how Sakha musical resources can be compared to those of other Siberian groups.

168 NOTES TO INTRODUCTION

22. In a more thorough description of the outcomes of applied ethnomusicology, Titon suggests that the discipline "[is] best regarded as music-centered intervention in a particular community" but also warns: "It is music-centered, but above all the intervention is people-centered" (2015a, 4). See also these works specifically outlining methodologies for applied ethnomusicology work: Bithell and Hill (2014), Coulter (2011), Grant (2014, 2015), Howard (2012), Lassiter (2005), Saurman (2012), Schrag (2013a, 2013b, 2015a, 2015b), Sheehy (1992), Titon (1992), and Titon and Pettan (2015b). The description of the ethnographer, practitioner, and theorist "cohabiting" in one person captures my experience well (Noyes 2016, 73).

23. In a 2015 conversation I had with Parliament Speaker Alexander Zhirkov about my role in cultural revitalization in Yakutia, he pronounced emphatically, "Finish the book!" I have greatly appreciated support from him and his staff, most notably Nurguyana Illarionova, whose attention to detail and warm friendship have greatly facilitated my participation in several events.

24. While this vision leans toward intervention, what Pettan calls "direct mediation" (2015, 34), Titon also bluntly observes: "The issue isn't whether intervention is an option; like it or not, ethnomusicologists intervene" (1992, 316). Considering mutuality and ethical responsibilities, Daniel Sheehy asks which of us as ethnomusicologists has "never gone out of his or her way to act for the benefit of an informant or a community they have studied?" (1992, 323–324).

I also appreciate the observations of Angela Impey in this regard: "Historically, there has always been something of an uncomfortable relationship between theoretical and applied fields in the human sciences, the subtext being that academia is superior to the theoretically unsophisticated and ethically problematic wanderings of applied work. To some extent this schism remains, despite recent reconsideration that applied anthropology (and by extension, ethnomusicology) be viewed as an integrated theoretical and practical field. Within this frame, the action-orientated undertakings of applied anthropology do not detract from the unity of general anthropology, but rather enrich it" (2006, 404).

25. My first exposure to the intersection of sustainability and resilience came through reading a post on Titon's blog from July 7, 2011: "in ecological thinking today, sustainability is allied more with adaptation and resiliency than with preservation." "Resilience," *Sustainable Music: A Research Blog on the Subject of Sustainability and Music*, http://sustainablemusic.blogspot.com/2011/07/resilience.html, accessed February 20, 2016. Titon explores the metaphor of ecology at length through his blog.

26. While Geertz's "thick description" (1973) provides a worthy methodology for subject-centered ethnographies, local voices should also be included as a primary resource in such work. Consider Titon's compelling observation regarding the lack of local voices in Geertz: "He is so thorough, so smart, so graceful, and so reassuring that the reader is lulled, and does not worry that Geertz's is the only authoritative voice speaking from within the inscribed account. Geertz very seldom quotes his Balinese informants, and when he does it usually appears in a footnote, well below the level of the discourse inscribed as thick description. That is, although we are given to understand that Geertz has conversed with the Balinese about cockfights, the kind of meaning he is after is presumably not something that most Balinese would be able to articulate" (2003, 175).

NOTES TO INTRODUCTION   169

27. The Russification that came with tsarist expansion into Siberia beginning in the seventeenth century strongly affected Sakha language and culture (Lincoln 1994, 52–53, 62).

28. According to the 2010 Russian census, more than 99 percent of the population of the Russian Federation speaks Russian. http://www.perepis-2010.ru/, accessed January 23, 2016.

29. I have benefited from the published collections of papers resulting from these conferences, namely from authors, editors, and compilers such as Biliukina (2006), Ivanov, Romanova, and Pakharova (2006), Larionova (2010), Mákharov (2000), Sysoliatina (2006), Vasilieva (2006), and Yamashita (2006).

30. I enjoyed presenting with and translating for three delegations of Sakha scholars who were visiting Harvard in connection with their work on Eduard Alekseyev's field recordings, housed in the Archive of World Music in the Loeb Music Library. I worked alongside Anna Larionova in 2010, Vasilii Illarionov and Sergei Vasiliev in 2013, and Nurguyana Illarionova and Alexandra Tatarinova in 2014.

31. A few of the many resources presenting historical information on the performance practice of olonkho and the lives of olonkhosuts include Emsheimer (1991), Krueger (1962; in English), Pukhov (1962), and Pukhov and Ergis (1985). When the text reflects my translations of Russian-language written resources, the original Russian has been retained in the footnotes for convenient comparison by the reader.

32. This approach of focusing on collaborator narratives accomplishes two out of three components in Rice's (1987) tripartite model: *historical construction* through the recounting of historical narrative and *individual creation/experience* through the recounting of people's personal experience as performers or audiences. For a good model of reporting various voices in the discourse of a community, see Levin's model of writing (1996, 1999, 2006). In discussing power and the politics of representation, Lassiter highlights "the gap between academically positioned and community-positioned narratives" and the question of "who has the right to represent whom and for what purposes, and . . . whose discourse will be privileged in the ethnographic text" (2005, 4).

33. Hill and Bithell use the term "revival" "as a type of shorthand to encompass a range of more nuanced processes . . . namely regeneration, renaissance, revitalization, rediscovery, reshaping, re-interpretation, re-focusing, re-assessment, re-articulation. To these we might add reclamation, recovery, rescue, recuperation, restitution, restoration, renovation, reinvention, re-implementation, reactivation, re-traditionalization, re-indigenization, re-appropriation, resumption, resurgence, recycling, reproduction, revision, and re-creation. As the ubiquitous 're' prefix suggests, what these processes share is fundamental motivation to draw upon the past and/or to intensify some aspect of the present" (2014, 5). In the same book, Slobin (2014) likewise addresses these issues.

34. Too numerous to list comprehensively, Russian-language resources describing and analyzing the Sakha cultural context and placing olonkho within the context of other legends, tales, and myths include works such as N. A. Alekseyev's (2008) volume on the ethnography and folklore of the peoples of Siberia and the volume edited by N. A. Alekseyev, N. V. Emelianov, and V. T. Petrov (1995) on the stories, legends, and myths of the Sakha. Ivanov (2007) has produced one of the newest and most comprehensive

170   NOTES TO INTRODUCTION AND CHAPTER 1

resources for Sakha culture, an 872-page full-color encyclopedia with text, charts, maps, illustrations, and photos. A 15-page section furnishes a scholarly summary of olonkho. In addition, Bragina (2005) and Kulikova (2009) provide insight into broader ethnocultural and ethnoreligious processes in Yakutia during the last several decades.

35. See "Olonkho, Yakut Heroic Epos," http://www.unesco.org/culture/ich/en/RL/olonkho-yakut-heroic-epos-00145.

1. Epic Traditions, Performers, and Audiences

1. The English term "poetry" is used for a broad range of forms and remains inordinately difficult to describe in a way that adequately addresses all contextual variations. In this regard, I resonate with Giorgio Banti and Francesco Giannattasio's conception of its placement on the continuum between speech and song: "It is thus in the frame of a virtual continuum from language to music or, better, from speaking to singing, that one has to try and identify the constitutive elements that underlie the oral and written scatter of the different 'poetic' forms and behaviors. The point here is not to assign poetry a definite position within this continuum in a Procrustean and—unavoidably—arbitrary way. Rather, it is to look into the problem of poetic formalization and the typology of poetry across cultures and time in a wider perspective, by studying them not only within the traditional limits of literature and linguistics, but also in the wider horizons of ethnomusicology and anthropology" (2006, 292; see also 293–294). Their descriptive phrase "poetically organized discourse (POD)" as a broader category than "poetry" is useful (310), but since olonkho is closer in actuality to narrative poetry, I will use that more descriptive term, rather than "POD," for discussions of olonkho.

2. Albert Lord's *Singer of Tales* (2000) describes Lord's and Milman Parry's foundational work uncovering the oral history of Homer's *Iliad* and *Odyssey*.

3. The vast literature on epics cannot be summarized adequately here. Information on the epic traditions inscribed on UNESCO's ICH lists can be found at http://www.unesco.org/culture/ich/en/lists, accessed December 5, 2016. For more detail on the epic traditions represented by authors mentioned in this book, see Beliaev 1975; Biebuyck 1976; Chadwick and Zhirmunsky 1969; Emsheimer 1991; Harvilahti 1996, 2000; Jang 2001; Johnson 1992; Levin 2006; Park 2000, 2003; Pegg 2001; Reichl 1989, 1992; Rice, Porter, and Goertzen 2000; Shoolbraid 1975; Um 2013, and Van der Heide 2008, among others. I regret that Anikin and Alieva's volume *Skazki narodov Sibiri, Srednei Azii i Kazakhstana* (1995) is currently not available in the United States. Note that Alieva's description of the many epic traditions of the Russian Federation and Eurasia (including a focus on the Caucasian epics) can be found in her article "Caucasian Epics" (1996).

4. N. V. Emelianov and E. N. Kuzmina provide an outstanding overview of the differences between olonkho and other genres of Sakha folk tales—*kėpsėėn/kėpsii* and *ustuoruia*—along with the history of how the genre names came to be used, in the introductory material of Illarionov, Diakonova, Mukhoplëva, et al. (2008).

5. Olonkho's ancient origins are widely accepted in Yakutia and likely date back to the time when the Sakha had close contact with other Turkic-Mongol peoples before migrating north. This conclusion is based on "common plots of olonkho with the plots of these

NOTES TO CHAPTER 1   171

[Turkic] peoples, as well as commonalities in linguistic constructions and vocabulary. . . . Taking into account the fact that olonkho contains echoes of connection to the ancient Turkic peoples, it is entirely possible that its origins trace back to the end of the first millennium, sometime around the 8th to 9th centuries CE." http://yakutia.com/culture/8/, accessed September 3, 2016. I agree with Titon's use of the term "culture" in the "anthropological sense as the learned inheritance that makes one people's way of thinking and doing different from another's" (2003, 172).

6. Tatiana Argounova, personal communication, February 22, 2012.

7. http://dictionary.reference.com/browse/epos, accessed January 10, 2012.

8. A downloadable PDF version of *Nurgun Botur*, translated into Russian, is available at https://books.google.com/books?id=Ix9evQ8v-H4C&p, accesssed September 6, 2016. For a short description of *Muldju Bëghë*, see www.olonkho.info or go directly to http://tinyurl.com/MuldjuBeghe, accessed February 9, 2016.

9. For short descriptions of the heroes featured in well-known olonkho tales, see http://tinyurl.com/olonkhoheroes.

10. Translated and adapted from Emelianov (2000).

11. "Той историчности, которая есть в 'Манасе' или в 'Давиде Сасунском', в якутском олонхо нет. . . . Из исторических лиц упоминается лишь имя одного Чингис-хана, и то только как образ рока. Исторический характер олонхо заключается в общем отражении быта, нравов, пережитой истории, геогргафической среды, духовной и материальной культуры этноса саха" (Sivtsev 2003, 17).

12. Kant originally coined the term "worldview" (from the German *Weltanschauung*) in *Critique of Judgement* (1790). By the nineteenth century it was in broad use in a number of languages (including in Russian as *mirovozzrenie*), encompassing aspects of ontology, epistemology, and teleology (Vidal 2008). Bakan asserts that community rituals "are special events during which individuals or communities enact, through performance, their core beliefs, values, and ideals. They often take the form of communal performances of myths, legends, epics, or sacred texts or stories that are foundational to a culture's identity. As a result, rituals reveal a great deal about the worldviews of the people who perform them, that is, about the ways in which these people conceive of their world and their place and purpose within it" (2012, 24).

13. Interview with Pyotr Reshetnikov, master olonkhosut, Cherkëkh, Yakutia, June 16, 2009; see press.uillinois.edu/books/harris/storytelling.

14. Translated from http://ysia.ru/kultura/2016-2025-gody-v-yakutii-obyavleny-ii -desyatiletiem-olonho/, accessed February 23, 2016.

15. In a description of the worldview expressed in a Yedigei epic tale from Uzbekistan, Levin recounts the words of a collaborator, OM, who noted, "We need to understand that for people who listened to this epic and who listen to it still, there's no dividing line between the natural and the supernatural. . . . For them, the demon is as real as any human." Levin continues, "No wonder the [storytellers] *baxshi* and *zhirau*, like the shaman, had ended up on the blacklist in the Soviet 'struggle with the old.' A more antimaterialist worldview would be hard to find than that represented in the epic" (1999, 188).

16. Romanova and Ignatieva note that during the 1990s, "the Ministry of Culture and Spiritual Development of the Republic of Sakha initiated a national project to revive

172   NOTES TO CHAPTER 1

traditional culture, in which the key symbols became *Khomus* (music), *Ysyakh* (ritual), *Olonkho* (epos), and *Traditional beliefs*" (2012, 50).

17. Peers notes this complexity as well: "Sakha 'shamanism' can be regarded as a 'free floating' signifier in the sense elaborated by Thomas Csordas: it has many referents within the local cultural context which can be shaped by competing interests (Lindquist 2006; Csordas 1997)" (2013, 98).

18. Buchanan points out that all constructions of identity are intrinsically pluralistic, transient, and performative (2014, 4). Warden undertakes a diachronic overview of the concept of "identity" in the ethnomusicological literature and synthesizes the following definition: "concepts about groups and individuals and one's relationship to them" (2016, 17), based on an expanded list of seven widely agreed-upon conceptualizations (16).

19. The discourses of identity involve "the delimitation of both a set of *shared* characteristics that a community considers part of itself as well as a group of *excluded* qualities to which it defines itself in opposition. . . . The problem with exclusionary collective identities is that they can *lead to the rejection of the actual diversity that exists* within the national space" (Labadi 2013, 68; my emphasis). In this vein, Bakan writes, "To a significant degree, music always provides partial answers to two fundamental questions: *Who am I?* and *Who are we?*" (2012, 11).

20. Peers's article on this topic is supported by years of fieldwork in the Sakha Republic and ongoing research and scholarship related to Sakha identity and cultural production, including her PhD thesis, "Print, Power and Personhood: Newspapers and Ethnic Identity in East Siberia" (2010).

21. Peers describes "a preoccupation with shamanism that characterizes recent discourses on culture and ethnicity" (2013, 93).

22. One group interview with olonkho experts and scholars even resulted in a vigorous argument on the subject!

23. "Но мифы олонхо ничего общего не имеют с религиозной шаманской мифологией якутов. Об этом свидетельствует сам народ, сами олонхосуты, а с другой стороны - служители культа - шаманы не признавали мифов олонхо . . . по сути художественные обобщения и гениальные символы. По моему убеждению, все это - широкие поэтические обобщения грозных сил стихии и общества, борющихся, с одной стороны, между собой, а с другой стороны - борьбы с ними богоподобного человека, противопоставляющего себя им, побеждающего, покоряющего их ради блага всего человеческого рода" (Sivtsev 2003, 18). Sivtsev eventually became part of the team translating the New Testament of the Bible into Sakha. His introduction (in Sakha) to the completed work, published by the Institute for Bible Translation in 2008, is available for download at http://ibtrussia.org/en/ebook?id=YKT, accessed February 19, 2016.

24. Interview with Eduard Alekseyev, Malden, MA, May 18, 2009; see either http://eduard.alekseyev.org/video10.html, with English subtitles, or press.uillinois.edu/books/harris/storytelling.

25. Hunt describes a similar division of song and recitation in the "historical epic" of Edige, from the Caucasus region of the Russian Federation, noting that "the action is pre-

NOTES TO CHAPTER 1   173

sented in prose, while the thoughts and feelings of the main actors are presented in verse" (2012, 15).

26. Interview with Agafia Zakharova, head of the Olonkho Department at IGI, Yakutsk, Yakutia, December 4, 2011; see press.uillinois.edu/books/harris/storytelling.

27. Eduard Alekseyev, personal communication, February 25, 2012.

28. Reshetnikov interview, 2009.

29. Ibid. Tomskaia is now deceased.

30. The second edition of Lord's *Singer of Tales*, published in 2000, retained the original text and added only an introduction and a CD of recordings. Among other languages, the book has been translated into Russian and is used by epic scholars in Russia.

31. In 1942, years before Parry and Lord's research was published, C. S. Lewis asserted that the oral technique of composition in "Primary Epics" was demonstrated through the "continual use of stock words, phrases, or even whole lines" (1961, 20).

32. See, for example, the website and journal of the leading organization for this discipline, the Center for Studies in Oral Tradition (http://oraltradition.org), which continues to build on the foundation established by Parry and Lord. The founding director, John Miles Foley, was until his death in 2012 one of the foremost American scholars of epics and oral traditions. His book *The Singer of Tales in Performance* (1995) makes connections between oral-formulaic and performance-centered theories, an approach I adopt in my work (see also Finnegan 1996, 43).

33. Lord was a professor of Slavic and comparative literature at Harvard University from 1950 to 1983.

34. The extensive English-language literature on epic traditions cannot be summarized here; the following limited list of works may prove helpful for further study: Abusch (2001—Gilgamesh), Ahmad (1963—Persian and Hindi epics), Biebuyck (1976—African epics), Bynum (1968—Serbo-Croatian epics), Chadwick and Zhirmunsky (1969—*Manas*), Clark (1900—history of European epics), de Vries (1963—the "heroic" in epics), Finnegan (1978, 1996, and 2005—various traditions), Harvilahti (1996—Latvia's *Bear Slayer* and Tibet's *Geser*; 2000—Altaic oral epic), Jansen (2001—the *Sunjata* epic), Johnson (1980—Mandekan epics), Kruks (2004—Latvian epic), Lutgendorf (1989—*Rāmacaritmānas*), Mori (1997—epic elements), Oinas (1978—African *Sunjata*, Kyrgyz *Manas*, Russian *byliny*), Pegg (2001—Mongolian epics), Shoolbraid (1975—brief description of the plots of ten epic traditions from Siberia, with more detail on Burjat-Mongol *Uliger* and the Turkic epic cycle *Manas*), Slobin's translation of Beliaev (1975—Uzbek *dastan*, Turkmen *destan*, Kazakh *jir*, and Kyrgyz *Manas*), Seydou and Biebuyck (1983—Bambara and Fulani epics), Smith (1977—the *Pabuji* epic of India), Vansina (1971—historical methodology in oral tradition), and Weeda (2005—Russian *byliny* epics). The Korean p'ansori has been thoroughly documented by Jang (2001), Killick (2003), Kim (2004), Park (2000, 2003), Pihl (1993, 1994), and Um (2013), among others. Jansen and Maier's (2004) *Epic Adventures* brings together fourteen essays on various epic traditions from four continents, including scholarship on Siberian Buriat epics (by Hamayon) and the Kyrgyz *Manas* (by Van der Heide), both of which are particularly relevant for comparative purposes in the study of

174   NOTES TO CHAPTER 1

olonkho. Other authors describing *Manas* include Reichl (1992), Thompson et al. (2006), and Van der Heide (2008), with the most current work for *Manas* and other Central Asian epics reflected in Levin, Daukeyeva, and Köchümkulova (2016). None of the resources listed above, however, contain more than cryptic descriptions of olonkho.

35. Interview with Ekaterina Chekhorduna, scholar and author of olonkho materials for children, Yakutsk, December 6, 2011; see press.uillinois.edu/books/harris/storytelling.

36. That first olonkho was *The Great-Hearted Lord Juragastai, Warrior Hero*: in Russian, Великодушный Айыы Дьурагастай богатырь [Velikodushny Aiyy Diuragastai bogatyr]; in transliterated Sakha, *Ahynygas sanaalaakh Aiyy Djuraghastai bukhatyyr.*

37. Reshetnikov interview, 2009; see http://www.press.uillinois.edu/books/harris/story telling/.

38. Throughout this work, I have privileged Sakha scholarship in regard to my representation of olonkho, seeking to present an emic analytical approach rather than relying on my own limited power of observation. Even so, the burgeoning number of Sakha and Russian books on olonkho cannot be fully documented in this work. Larionova's two books on the major Sakha singing styles of *dègèrèn* (2000) and *dièrètii* (2004) present genre-thematic classification of the artistic resources of each style and in-depth description of their musical, textual, poetic, and regional stylistic distinctives. Beyond providing a broad description of Sakha musical resources, these works describe how the two singing styles are employed in olonkho.

39. Alekseyev was a member of the first Soviet-American joint ethnomusicological expedition in 1987, joining Ted Levin in his fieldwork in Tuva, a project documented in Levin's book *Where Rivers and Mountains Sing* (2006), recently published in Russian translation. Some of Alekseyev's writing (1969, 1988) touches on the changes that occurred in Sakha folklore and musical resources during the Soviet years, offering a historical perspective from the viewpoint of an ethnomusicologist who struggled to work within the constraints of the Soviet system, ultimately stretching the boundaries of the system and eventually escaping it altogether (Larionova 2013). His other books and articles (1989a, 1989b, 1996), as well as the digitized field recordings in the holdings of Harvard's Loeb Music Library (Dordzhieva and Vick 2013), provide information on Sakha music in general and olonkho research specifically. His doctoral dissertation expanded on Grant Grigorian's (1957) initial documentation of the "unfolding mode" of the Sakha. I began learning from and collaborating with Alekseyev in 2006.

40. Alekseyev has authored more than 150 works on various facets of Sakha and other musics, including several on the musicological aspects of olonkho. For a full list of his publications, see the bibliography in Russian on his website, http://www.eduard.alekseyev .org/author4.html, or a shortened list in English at http://www.eduard.alekseyev.org/author6 .html, accessed January 18, 2012.

41. "Олонхо примечательно прежде всего как художественно неповторимое и органичное сочетание возвышенно-поэтической речи и выразительного разнохарактерного пения. Оно действительно неповторимо как музыкально-поэтическое явление, обладающее своим двуединым мелодико-стиховым языком, своей развитой и сложной и вместе с тем стройной и экономной системой средств словесной и музыкальной выразительности, особыми приёмами поэтической и мелодической

NOTES TO CHAPTER 1   **175**

импровизации, тесно связанными и гибко взаимодействующими друг с другом" (Alekseyev 1996, 44).

42. "особые навыки темброво-характеристического голосового перевоплощения" (Alekseyev 1996, 45).

43. Sakha tongue-twisters (*chabyrgakhi*) also require great speed and articulation from the teller (*chabyrgakhsut*).

44. "Несмотря на сказовое произнесение, в речитативе довольно отчётливо прослушивается определённая звуковысотность, что позволяет условно нотировать его основные контуры. Звуковысотно речитативы строятся на двух ступенях-опорах ... Расстояние между ступенями трудно уловимо на слух, но чаще всего колеблется в промежутке от полутора до двух тонов. Особенность нижней ступени такова, что она как бы постоянно подтягивается к верхней, глиссандоподобно 'въезжает' в неё (в этих случаях обычно и становятся возможными изредка встречающиеся внутрислоговые распевы)" (Alekseyev 1996, 46).

45. Tonal specificity in these transcriptions is avoided by using an "x" for a note head.

46. See "Pyotr Reshetnikov—Olonkho Performance Montage," https://vimeo.com/37039828, or press.uillinois.edu/books/harris/storytelling.

47. Kofi Agawu explores the minimalist impulse in African musical creativity and concludes, "The material resources that comprise African minimalism may be modest, but the ingenuity and creativity displayed by performer-composers are surely of the highest order—maximal rather than minimal" (2013, 53). His conclusion describes well the minimalism that can be observed in the tonal resources employed by performers in the olonkho tradition. A few modern olonkhsuts employ a wider range of tonal resources in their narratives and more demonstrative facial expressions and gestures (see Finnegan 1996 on analysis of "kinesics" and Gabysheva 2009 on the role of gestures during performance). While modern audiences seem to appreciate the additional dramatic intensity it gives, some Sakha olonkho scholars privately disparage the inauthenticity of this intensified expression, preferring a more restrained style of recitation.

48. For a clear explanation of this (in Russian, with translated Sakha examples), see Larionova (2004, 71–81).

49. The multimedia aspects included in this research exemplify the sonic textures of traditional Sakha musical expression, especially of olonkho; see press.uillinois.edu/books/harris/storytelling. For a brief overview of both the *narrative-poetry recitation* mode and the *song* style of olonkho, see "Pyotr Reshetnikov—Olonkho Performance Montage" at press.uillinois.edu/books/harris/storytelling or at http://vimeo.com/37039828. This 49-second video clip demonstrates short alternating phrases of these two modes from a performance by master olonkhosut Pyotr Reshetnikov, the recipient of a special governmental stipend for his role as a carrier of traditional improvised olonkho performance. For a more extended look at the interaction between the two modes, see a longer, 50-minute fragment of an olonkho by Reshetnikov at https://www.youtube.com/watch?v=8ee0EXY0q0g or at press.uillinois .edu/books/harris/storytelling.

50. Steven Feld's theoretical framework, combining insights from linguistics, ethnomusicology, and what he terms "acoustemology" (acoustic knowing), proposes that we explore the connections between our soundscapes and how we understand the world. He

176 NOTES TO CHAPTER 1

writes: "Acoustemology means an exploration of sonic sensibilities, specifically of ways in which sound is central to making sense, to knowing, to experiential truth" (1996, 97).

51. The Sakha plural *kylyhakhtar*, when quoted in Russian text, is normally given the Russian plural form, *kylyhakhi*.

52. "характерные для якутского эпического пения краткие акцентные призвуки—*кылыhахи*. О них стоит сказать особо. Кылысахи, выделяющиеся своим высоким и чистым тембром, подобные то острым, сверкающим ударам, то мерцающим, словно в отдалении, искрам, наслаиваются на звучание основной мелодии, зачастую рождая иллюзию раздвоения поющего голоса. Украшая и расцвечивая его, они придают якутскому пению неповторимое своеобразие" (Alekseyev 1996, 56).

53. For other notated examples of *kylyhakh*, see http://www.eduard.alekseyev.org/work20.html, accessed February 22, 2012.

54. I have used the term "mode" as a translation of the Russian term *lad*, which Mazo credits as being etymologically related to *ladit*, "to be in accord with" (1994, 37), in order to distinguish it from the alternative term "scale," which carries semantic overtones related to common-practice harmony. Alekseyev (1976), quoted from www.eduard.alekseyev.org, explains these modal distinctives in terms of "unfolding modes" in which "the distance between the neighboring tones of the tune can vary to extremely wide margins, from a whole tone interval to . . . even a tritone in its 'unfolding.' The latter, conveniently available in whole tone scales, is usually connected to an increase in emotional energy, often visible within the parameters of one song. In general, the width of the intonational step is generally related to the character of the personage being sung and the tessitura of the tune." ["раскрывающихся ладов"-расстояние между соседними (смежными) ступенями напева может варьировать в весьма широких пределах—от целотонового промежутка (расстояние в один тон) до более чем двухтонового или далее бо́льшего (тритонового) его "раскрытия". Последнее связано обычно с подъёмом эмоционального тонуса, нередко отмечаемым и в пределах одной песни. В целом, ширина интонационного шага так или иначе соотносится с характером поющего персонажа и с высотным положением напева.]

55. See also http://eduard.alekseyev.org/work26.html, accessed January 19, 2017: "Если вилюйский певец быстро и чётко излагает содержание песни (*этэн ыллыыр*—«поёт, выговаривая»), то приленский певец значительно медленнее «расходует» текст (*тардан ыллыыр*—«поёт, украшая, растягивая каждый слог»)."

56. "Стиль *дьиэрэтии ырыа* представляет собой особую технику, способ озвучивания поэтической импровизации" (Larionova 2004, 12).

57. Alekseyev notes at his site that the original publication of this article, "Toward a Typology Construction of the Musical Epos" [K postroeniiu tipologii muzykalnogo ėposa], appeared in the edited volume *Muzyka ėposa: Stati i materialy* [Music of the Epos: Article and Materials] (1989a). He further notes that significant and frustrating typesetting errors prevented the article from successfully portraying his ideas. The version at his site is thus more accurate and is the version I used to prepare this summary. See http://www.eduard.alekseyev.org/work21.html, accessed January 19, 2017.

NOTES TO CHAPTERS 1 AND 2 · 177

58. I have observed this technique used to sing the text of a Psalm from the Sakha translation of the Old Testament of the Bible.

59. "Наличествует лишь обобщённый образ остранённой и возвышенной эпической речи . . . этот принцип порождает своеобразную распевную речитацию" (from the fourth paragraph at http://www.eduard.alekseyev.org/work21.html).

60. "*Дэгэрэн ырыа* . . . основанный на строго организованной метроритмике и развитой, рельефно очерченной, структурно замкнутой индивидуализированной мелодике" (Larionova 2000, 36).

61. "Со звуковысотной точки зрения, напевы *дэгэрэн* выделяются бо́льшим ступеневым составом и более широким диапазоном, заметно превосходящим сравнительно скромные звуковысотные нормы *тойуков*" (Alekseyev 1996, 54).

62. *-tar* is the Sakha plural suffix. Svetlana Mukhoplёva (1993) summarizes the classification of Sakha ritual songs and related aspects such as spells and dances. Although it does not have any major sections dealing with olonkho, this work provides insights for understanding the broader musical contexts in which olonkho is performed.

63. "Отчётливые и разновысотные кылысахи появляются как отдельные украшающие штрихи на определённых долях в мотивах-формулах *дэгэрэн*. Иной раз они выразительно сочетаются с голосовым вибрато. Это многообразие кылысахных призвуков . . . неотъемлемых для национальной певческой культуры якутов и для искусства якутских олонхосутов специфических приёмов звукоизвлечения" (Alekseyev 1996b, 56).

64. For an article written on the neologism of a "multi-generic" genre, see Ren (2010). Ren's article goes into great depth regarding the integration of various genres into a multi-generic whole.

65. Further study of the complex relations between the musical and verbal aspects of olonkho has much to offer researchers of other epos traditions, chiefly due to the burgeoning of academic research and writing on the topic of folklore (and olonkho in particular) in Yakutia. The growing number of Russian-language musicology, folklore, and philology-related volumes written on the topic of olonkho would provide new insights for the field of epic studies if the geographical and linguistic boundaries could be overcome. I hope that the insights of my Sakha colleagues chosen for highlighting in this chapter will motivate other researchers of epics to become better acquainted with this material.

66. Alekseyev remarks that this term in Sakha, *étèn yllyyr* (этэн ыллыыр), is in Russian поёт, выговаривая. Personal communication, January 25, 2012. See http://eduard.alekseyev.org/work26.html, accessed January 19, 2017.

2. Effects of Change during the Soviet Era

1. See Suny (1997) for an outstanding overview of the implosion of the Soviet Union and what followed.

2. The time of uncertainty and turbulence at the dissolution of the Soviet Union provided a powerful motivation for a revitalization movement. Balzer elaborates on the concept

178   NOTES TO CHAPTER 2

of revitalization as a response to an uncertain future (1999, 75), although she notes that "theories stressing 'objective' material causes, charismatic leadership, widespread psychological depression, or relative deprivation rarely do such movements justice" (76).

3. For an insightful essay on music, remembrance, and the turmoil associated with exile, migration, and diaspora, see Muller (2014).

4. Anna Liesowska, "Siberia's Great New Railway Starts Operating to Yakutsk," *Siberian Times*, September 1, 2014, http://siberiantimes.com/business/casestudy/news/siberias-great-new-railway-starts-operating-to-yakutsk/, accessed January 19, 2017.

5. Interview with Boris Mikhailov, scholar and olonkho promoter, Yakutsk, December 13, 2011; see press.uillinois.edu/books/harris/storytelling.

6. If Yakutia were a country, its landmass (3,103,200 square kilometers or 1,198,152 square miles) would make it the eighth-largest nation in the world. See http://www.nations online.org/oneworld/countries_by_area.htm, accessed August 31, 2016.

7. An interactive map of the districts in Yakutia with lists of olonkhosuts according to districts and counties can be found at http://tinyurl.com/mapofolonkhosuts (from www .olonkho.info), accessed January 22, 2012.

8. *Handful*: десятки or "tens" in the original Russian. For an outstanding Russian-language analysis of the Tatta school of olonkho performance, see Orosina (2015).

9. "По данным исследователей «таттинская школа» олонхосутов начала слагаться со второй половины XVIII в. В каждом наслеге проживало по десятке олонхосутов. Сегодня нами дописьменным и архивным источникам выявлено свыше 700 олохосутов (XVII–XXI вв.) прошлого и настоящего, что свидетельствует о подлинном расцвете этой устной традиции в прошлом" (Zakharova and Protodiakonova 2010, 22).

10. Reshetnikov interview, 2009; see press.uillinois.edu/books/harris/storytelling.

11. Ibid.

12. Ibid.

13. In order to keep the conversations reported in this book from losing focus on my Sakha interlocutors, my interspersed questions have often been left out of the transcribed text. Wherever possible, those omitted sections have been noted with bracketed ellipsis points: [. . .]. On some occasions, when I was talking to a group, several people at a time would respond, interrupting and talking over one another, so that full indications of conversational omissions were not practical. In those cases, I transcribed only one person at a time, leaving out the interjections of others.

14. Mikhailov interview, 2011; see http://www.press.uillinois.edu/books/harris/story telling/.

15. Life in Bodaibo was not just a series of long evenings by the fire, singing olonkho, although if Mikhailov is correct, they must have somehow found time to perform for one another. The gold fields at Bodaibo opened in the 1860s, and by 1912, the working conditions imposed by the British and Russian shareholders (including Russian royalty) were so brutal that the workers finally rebelled with a general strike on March 13. Over the next month, they communicated their demands and assembled for demonstrations. On April 17, 1912, troops sent by the tsarist government began shooting into the gathered crowd of workers, killing hundreds of people. This event, called the "Lena Massacre," resulted in

NOTES TO CHAPTER 2   179

strikes breaking out all over Russia, which continued until the onset of World War I. The Lena Massacre was used as propaganda against the tsarist government by the communists, who eventually succeeded in overthrowing tsarist rule (Melancon 2004).

16. Tong Suorun is a pseudonym. Many Sakha artists and writers take a Sakha pseudonym and use it in tandem with, or even in place of, the "Russian" names they were given by the Russian Orthodox Church upon baptism.

17. Mikhailov interview, 2011; see http://www.press.uillinois.edu/books/harris/storytelling/.

18. Interview with Valerii Kononov, Borogontsy, Yakutia, June 19, 2009; see press.uillinois.edu/books/harris/storytelling. He and his wife, Maria Kononova, were vitally interested in my research on olonkho and spent many weeks working on the logistics of my travel around Yakutia during the summers of 2009 and 2010. They clearly fit into the category of "enthusiasts" for olonkho revitalization.

19. Eduard Alekseyev interview, 2009; see http://eduard.alekseyev.org/video10.html, with English subtitles, or press.uillinois.edu/books/harris/storytelling.

20. David Crystal (1992) writes of other dimensions of literacy, such as economic, scientific, and computer literacy.

21. For a thorough analysis of the issues related to orality and literacy, see Finnegan (2007). Beyond merely the aural and the printed, Finnegan considers factors such as "non-verbal sonic components (including music), kinesic and proxemic elements, the role of the audience—co-creators of performance but not necessarily in verbalised ways—and material and visual accoutrements: all features which may be essential for the recognized conventions of performance in any given genre, but neglected by focusing on the verbal constituents suggested by this sense of 'oral'" (147). See also Rubin (1995, 310–312) for a thorough discussion of the effects of writing on thought, memory, and orality.

22. Located in Yakutsk, the Institute of Humanitarian Research and Problems of the Minority Peoples of the North (Institut gumanitarnykh issledovanii i problem malochislennykh narodov Severa) is part of the Siberian Branch of the Russian Academy of Sciences, Sakha Republic (Yakutia). See http://igi.ysn.ru.

23. Interview with Dekabrina Vinokurova and Yuri Zhegusov, Yakutsk, December 13, 2011; see press.uillinois.edu/books/harris/storytelling.

24. Ibid.

25. Catherine Grant characterizes the decrease in diversity and vitality of musical heritage as a "'wicked problem': one with complex interdependencies, uncertainties, and conflicting stakeholder perspectives, which defies resolution more than some of the ecological metaphors arguably imply" (2015, abstract).

26. The current generation of olonkhosuts depends almost completely on the written form of olonkho, and at the time of this writing few olonkhosuts, if any, create olonkhos in the traditional oral style. Okladnikov's assertion that the content of the written versions differs from the oral will likely prove true, but the degree of change should be studied by comparing newer, written olonkhos with the older, oral ones.

27. Peers comments on the domination of atheism in communist thought: "In the Soviet Union, the 'Crossed-out God,' an absented presence that Bruno Latour (1993) identifies as

180   NOTES TO CHAPTER 2

key to the development of modernity, was a legion of crossed-out ancestors, area spirits, saints, prophets, local demons, and deities who, along with the moralities and philosophies they espoused, were designated by the Soviet authorities as both non-existent and actively malevolent" (2013, 102–103).

28. Baily, in his study of music censorship in Afghanistan, observes the following about control of musical expression: "Not only do we see (yet again) how sensitive an indicator of broader social and cultural processes music is, but how fiercely control over music is contested. One ponders the mystery of what it is about music that makes it so powerful, and how that power might be harnessed for performances of reconciliation instead of conflict" (2009, 163).

29. Given the precedent of the centralized Soviet system, with the vast majority of people working in one way or another for the government, most initiatives in post-Soviet Russia still come top-down. In fact, most people still work for the government, even in the villages, as noted by Aimar Ventsel in his research in Saidy, a "very traditional village" in Yakutia: "half of the village population are *biudzetniki*, or people working in state paid jobs in the school, village administration, kindergarten, or heating station. The other half of the population is mostly officially unemployed" (2015, 96–97).

An example of censoring less approved themes in music occurred as late as 2007, when a small group of Sakha Christians calling themselves Algys ("blessing" in Sakha, and also the name of a song genre) planned to have a festival of newly composed music (including Christian-themed *ohuokhai* and *toyuk*). They rented a large hall in Yakutsk for the event, gave out two thousand invitations, and invited participants from all over Yakutia to come and debut new songs. The leader of Algys received a phone call two days before the festival and was informed that the hall was "no longer available for the event." They concluded that the owner of the hall had been pressured into rescinding the contract. I was present as a guest and noted that their forced transfer to a small church building nearby meant there was not nearly enough room for everyone, even though local church members stayed home to give the available seats to guests.

30. Reshetnikov interview, 2009; see http://www.press.uillinois.edu/books/harris/story telling/.

31. Literally: He was an ancient person.

32. Interview with Pyotr Tikhonov, olonkho performer, Borogontsy, June 20, 2009; see press.uillinois.edu/books/harris/storytelling.

33. For specific examples of how tradition bearers dealt with the psychological aspects of this fear, see Harris (2015). A media-rich version is available at http://eduard.alekseyev.org/guests16.html, accessed January 19, 2017.

34. Benedict Anderson's term "unisonality" captures this idea that music can create a connection within an imagined community. Reciting from the Book of Common Prayer and singing a national anthem serve as additional examples of the power of a collective performance across a community of participants separated by distance and time. While the Soviets used the "echoed physical realization of the imagined community" (Anderson 2006, 149) to achieve their own goals, they also feared any unisonance outside their control.

NOTES TO CHAPTER 2   181

35. Olonkho fragments had been published as early as the late nineteenth century, but these documents described only the verbal aspects—texts and plots—without providing musical notation.

36. Marjorie Balzer describes Oyunsky as "one of the first Sakha ethnographers and collectors of epic folklore, and founder of the Institute of Languages, Literature, and History" (1995, 27 n. 18). Oyunsky's *Nurgun Botur* has been published in Russian translation (Oyunsky 1975) and in English (Oyunsky 2014).

37. Mikhailov interview, 2011; see http://www.press.uillinois.edu/books/harris/story telling/.

38. In addition to archaic terminology, olonkho occasionally incorporates words from other languages, an aspect of performance that serves to give it mystical and esoteric associations (Feld 1990, 140).

39. The letter is documented in Emelianov (1964, 80), translation by Tatiana Argounova.

40. Zakharova interview, 2011; see press.uillinois.edu/books/harris/storytelling.

41. Ibid.

42. *Nasleg* (наслег) is a Sakha word denoting a geopolitical administrative division that roughly parallels a county. Yakutia has 362 counties (*naslegs*) within 33 large districts. For the 2004 legislation that created these boundaries, see http://nvk520.narod.ru/municipal/sakha30112004-172.html, accessed February 20, 2012.

43. Zakharova interview, 2011. Note that World War II was known as the "Great Patriotic War" in Russia.

44. The acceptance of olonkhosuts into the Union of Soviet Writers of the USSR began in 1939 with olonkhosuts such as Sergei Zverev, Yegor Okhlopkov, Ekaterina Ivanova, Nikolai Stepanov, and Dmitrii Govorov. For the full list of olonkhosuts, see http://olonkho theatre.ru/olonhosuty/303-narodnye-pevtsy-i-olonhosuty-chleny-sojuza-pisatelej-sssr.html, accessed October 20, 2014.

45. Mikhailov interview, 2011; see recording of the interview at press.uillinois.edu/books/harris/storytelling, starting at :47.

46. Ibid., starting at 1:53.

47. Kulikova cites here Vdovin (2002, 47).

48. "Со стороны советского руководства утверждалась . . . идеология приобщения всех народов СССР к социалистической культуре и сплочению их в «новую историческую общность» советских людей. Это достигалось посредством ликвидации национальных районов, реорганизацию и перевод национальных меньшинств на язык советской республики, а также закрытие национальных школ" (Kulikova 2009, 98).

49. Interview with Maria Kononova, Sakha poet and project collaborator, Borogontsy, June 19, 2009; see press.uillinois.edu/books/harris/storytelling.

50. Chekhorduna interview, 2011; see press.uillinois.edu/books/harris/storytelling.

51. Reshetnikov interview, 2009; see press.uillinois.edu/books/harris/storytelling.

52. Interview with Eduard Alekseyev and Anna Larionova, Malden, MA, April 20, 2010; see press.uillinois.edu/books/harris/storytelling.

182   NOTES TO CHAPTER 2

53. The effect of Soviet censors and ideological constrictions on artists and those who wrote about them beginning in the mid-1920s has been noted by David Haas in the introduction to his translation of Asafyev's *Symphonic Etudes* (Asafyev 2008, xvii–xx).

54. Czekanowska describes the difference between destructive forms of nationalism and a healthy need for self-identity as "differentiat[ing] between the need to confirm one's self and values and the incitement of prejudice and discrimination against others" (1996, 94).

55. Alekseyev's "rules," as well as the story he recounted here, are described in more detail in the book. See Alekseyev (1988, 145).

56. Alekseyev and Larionova interview, 2010; see http://www.press.uillinois.edu/books/harris/storytelling/.

57. Brezhnev served as the general secretary of the Communist Party from 1964 until his death in 1982. His period of power in the Soviet Union was marked by brutal methods of dealing with dissent through "trumped-up charges, long prison terms, psychiatric prisons, and punishment through drugs and torture" (Josephson 2014, 169).

58. An article at www.olonkho.info tells more about R. P. Alekseyev. See http://tinyurl.com/RPAlekseyev, accessed April 19, 2017.

59. The *khomus*, the Sakha jaw harp, is the most beloved and widespread of all Sakha instruments.

60. Interview with Liubov Shelkovnikova, Gavriil Shelkovnikov, and Anna Andreyeva, Borogontsy, 2009. See this interview in Russian at http://vimeo.com/34207733 or press.uillinois.edu/books/harris/storytelling

61. Oyunsky (1997). This oral story, told in many versions, was the first olonkho transferred into literary form; Oyunsky, a noted literary and cultural hero of the Sakha people, penned the script in the Sakha language before his death in the camps in 1939. The script was later translated into Russian (Oyunsky 1975). Skrybykin translated the first section of this tale and a glossary of key terms into English in 1995, and the first full English translation of *Olonkho: Nurgun Botur the Swift* was initiated by the Institute of Foreign Philology and Regional Studies of North-Eastern Federal University in 2007 and published in 2014 (Oyunsky 2014). Although a direct transliteration of "Нюргун Боотур" would be "Niurgun Bootur," Nakhodkina and her translation team decided to use a spelling that was somewhat simplified and more likely to result in proper pronunciation by non-Russians who immediately see the word "boot" and mispronounce that syllable (Nakhodkina 2014, 278). I follow Nakhodkina's use of "Nurgun Botur" in this work.

62. A short collection of fragments from this set of recordings can be found at www.olonkho.info, with a direct link here: http://tinyurl.com/ggkolesov-nyurgunbotur, accessed January 18, 2012.

63. For a modern recording of Kolesov performing olonkho in a *balaghan* on the grounds of the Oyunsky Literature Museum in Yakutsk, see https://www.youtube.com/watch?v=jxhnkBt00xk, accessed September 12, 2016.

64. Vinokurova and Zhegusov interview, 2011; see http://www.press.uillinois.edu/books/harris/storytelling.

65. This Russian word has multiple layers of meaning. Its roots mean "self-born," alluding to the "self-taught" characteristic.

NOTES TO CHAPTERS 2 AND 3 183

66. Interview with Elena Kugdanova-Egorova, Yakutsk, June 18, 2010; see press.uillinois
.edu/books/harris/storytelling.

67. Ibid.

68. Interview with Irina Aksyonova, Yakutsk, June 8, 2009; see press.uillinois.edu/
books/harris/storytelling.

69. Interview with Dora Gerasimova and Maria Kononova, Yakutia, June 19, 2010; see
press.uillinois.edu/books/harris/storytelling.

70. Tikhonov interview, 2009; see press.uillinois.edu/books/harris/storytelling.

71. As part of the class Expressive Form Analysis offered through GIAL's Center for
Excellence in World Arts (www.gial.edu/arts), my master's-level students study this performance. See "Ysyakh" at https://www.youtube.com/user/SiberianEthnoArts/video or
press.uillinois.edu/books/harris/storytelling. Semyon Chernogradskii is visible from 14:12
to 15:35 in his role as olonkhosut. I am deeply grateful for his collaboration, which has
included providing my class with translations of the script and answering a number of
questions to help us understand this olonkho better.

72. This olonkho is also known by the title *Nepobedimy Müljü Bòghò* (The Invincible
Müljü Bòghò).

73. The Russian term *rukovoditel'*—translated here as "advisor"—can mean anything
from "secretary" to "director."

74. Chernogradskii also noted that he is able to perform three short olonkho excerpts
in Sakha, Russian, and English. Personal communication, May 25, 2014, and January 15,
2016.

75. Vinokurova and Zhegusov interview, 2011; see http://www.press.uillinois.edu/books/
harris/storytelling/.

76. A short biography of Uustarabys is available in Russian at www.olonkho.info. See
http://tinyurl.com/Ustarabys, accessed February 9, 2016.

77. Interview with Nikolai Alekseyev, olonkhosut, at his home in Mytakh, Yakutia, June
21, 2010; see press.uillinois.edu/books/harris/storytelling.

78. Chekhorduna interview, 2011.

79. Reshetnikov interview, 2009; see http://www.press.uillinois.edu/books/harris/story
telling/.

80. Vol. 4: *Kyys Dèbiliiè: A Yakut Heroic Epic* (Reshetnikova 1993; note Reshetnikova's
musicological introduction) and vol. 10: *The Mighty Èr Sogotokh: A Yakut Heroic Epic*
(Illarionov 1996; with E. Alekseyev's musicological introduction).

81. My own research is greatly indebted to those who collaborated on the publication
of those two volumes.

82. Alekseyev and Larionova interview, 2010; see http://www.press.uillinois.edu/books/
harris/storytelling/.

3. Esteem for a Masterpiece: The Quest for Recognition

1. Figures rounded to the nearest percent. See Federal State Statistics Service,
"Информационные материалы об окончательных итогах Всероссийской переписи

184   NOTES TO CHAPTER 3

населения 2010 года" [Information on the final results of the 2010 All-Russian Population Census], Всероссийская перепись населения 2010 года [2010 All-Russia Population Census], http://www.gks.ru/free_doc/new_site/perepis2010/perepis_itogi1612.htm, retrieved December 28, 2011. The site includes a helpful breakdown of various categories, which shows that out of approximately 960,000 people living in Yakutia in 2010, 466,000 identified themselves as Sakha (of those, 450,000 claimed to "speak Sakha"), and 354,000 as Russians.

2. Interview with (anonymous) Russian music teacher, Yakutsk, December 8, 2011.

3. Interview with Sakha poet and project collaborator Maria Kononova, Borogontsy, June 19, 2009; see press.uillinois.edu/books/harris/storytelling.

4. Mikhailov interview, 2011; see press.uillinois.edu/books/harris/storytelling.

5. Ibid.

6. Note that UNESCO refers to nations as "states." For the convention text, see "Text of the Convention for the Safeguarding of the Intangible Cultural Heritage," http://unesdoc.unesco.org/images/0013/001325/132540e.pdf, accessed January 17, 2017.

7. "The States Parties to the Convention for the Safeguarding of the Intangible Cultural Heritage (2003)," http://www.unesco.org/culture/ich/en/states-parties-00024, accessed December 5, 2016. (For a definition of "states parties," see http://whc.unesco.org/en/states parties/.)

8. See Republic of Sakha (2007).

9. Interview with Elizaveta Sidorova, Elena Protodiakonova, and Anastasia Luginova, the leaders of the Olonkho Association, Yakutsk, December 7, 2011; see press.uillinois.edu/books/harris/storytelling.

10. Alekseyev underscored the widespread reality of this misconception: "I think that during this time, in the understanding of the masses, there was a huge confusion of ideas regarding what a true olonkhosut was." Personal communication, April 26, 2010.

11. Sidorova, Protodiakonova, and Luginova interview, 2011; see press.uillinois.edu/books/harris/storytelling.

12. Ibid.

13. Ibid.

14. Ibid.

15. Ibid. Although olonkho is not traditionally performed with dancing, Lukina (2005) examines the semantics of fundamental movements of ritual dances, tracing their connections to olonkho.

16. Severo-Vostochny federalny universitet in Yakutsk (formerly Yakutsk State University, or YaGU) uses the name North-Eastern Federal University in English. See http://s-vfu.ru/en, accessed April 19, 2017.

17. Interview with Sergei Vasiliev, director of the Olonkho Information System at NEFU, Yakutsk, June 24, 2010. From field notes of our conversation.

18. From field notes of a conversation with Larionova in Malden, MA, April 19, 2010.

19. For example, interviews with Dmitrii Krivoshapkin, Valentina Struchkova, and Anastasia Ivanova, Berdigestyakh, Yakutia, June 20, 2010; see press.uillinois.edu/books/harris/storytelling.

NOTES TO CHAPTER 3   185

20. See the legislation at http://docs.cntd.ru/document/802096821, accessed September 12, 2016.

21. Statistics quoted here are rounded to the nearest percent.

22. This research was carried out at the beginning of government-sponsored efforts to revitalize olonkho. As a result, the 11 percent who did not observe efforts to support olonkho would now, five years later, likely answer differently, especially with the robust levels of top-down (from the government to the people) communication supporting olonkho revitalization.

23. Eventually published in Russian (Ignatieva et. al. 2013), the results of their research provide the most thorough examination of this topic to date.

24. Several years later, I noted the same phenomenon during the summer festival of 2015.

25. Vinokurova and Zhegusov interview, 2011; see press.uillinois.edu/books/harris/storytelling. Naturally, exceptions to this observation can be found, ameliorating the grim prognosis. My subsequent visits demonstrated the possibility of progress in audience appreciation, mainly through growth in the numbers of people who have studied or performed olonkho.

26. Interview with Dora Gerasimova, Sakha amateur musician, Yakutsk, June 24, 2010; see press.uillinois.edu/books/harris/storytelling. A theatrical version of the olonkho *Jėbirièljin Bėrgèn* (Дьэбириэлдьин Бэргэн) by S. G. Alekseyev-Uustarabys was performed for the opening ceremonies.

27. Ibid.

28. Ibid.

29. Reshetnikov interview, 2009; see press.uillinois.edu/books/harris/storytelling.

30. See "Ysyakh 'Olonkho' Festival Montage," http://vimeo.com/37968248, or press.uillinois.edu/books/harris/storytelling. Kirshenblatt-Gimblett calls festivals a form of "environmental performance" (1998, 59) and points out that the etymological roots of "festival" are in the term "feast" (1998, 66).

31. Historically, p'ansori has always been in a state of flux; the *kwangdae* were highly responsive to the preferences of their audiences, "adding here and deleting there, emphasizing one theme at the expense of another, all in order to shape a whole that would gain the best response from the audience of the moment and hence, financial reward. In this sense, popular audiences of the early nineteenth century were parties to the act of composition and thus had an indirect role in shaping the content and emphasis of *p'ansori* songs" (Pihl 1993, 229).

32. Chekhorduna interview, 2011; see press.uillinois.edu/books/harris/storytelling.

33. Ibid.

34. Lord asserts that written texts may directly affect the dynamic of improvisatory composition: "The oral singer thinks in terms of these formulas and formula patterns. He *must* do so in order to compose. But when writing enters, the 'must' is eliminated. The formulas and formula patterns can be broken. . . . An *oral* text will yield a predominance of clearly demonstrable formulas. . . . A *literary* text will show a predominance of non-formulaic expressions" (2000, 130).

35. Alexander Zhirkov, "Deputies of *Il Tumen* Participate in the Decade of Olonkho," speech, November 28, 2011.

36. For a performance by Yuri Borisov, see http://olonkho.info/internettv/?q=node/115, accessed December 5, 2016.

186 NOTES TO CHAPTER 3

37. See Borisov's description of his interaction with children and the success of the book's accessible language and attractive illustrations at http://yakutia.com/culture/616/, accessed February 20, 2016.

38. "Anyone Can Become a Storyteller," http://s-vfu.ru/news/detail.php?SECTION _ID=21&ELEMENT_ID=26726, accessed February 20, 2016. Although I have heard the genre mentioned only this one time, it provides another, interesting option for the future of olonkho.

39. Popov's remarks were given in the context of a forum on epic creativity in Yakutsk, December 4, 2015; her presentation was titled "On the Phenomenon of a Young Olonkhosut of the Twenty-First Century."

40. The first Sakha theater performance presented a setting of the olonkho *Udaliy dobriy molodets Bėriėt Bėrgėn* in 1906 and *Bogatyr Kulantai na rezvom kone* in 1907 (Biliukina 2006, 125).

41. For an overview of the various theatrical performances of *Nurgun Botur* over the last century, including historical pictures of performances and program posters, see http://www.kuyaar.ru/index.php?id=282, accessed September 12, 2016.

42. Schrag describes the emergence of hybridized artistic forms as "liminal enactments [that] lead to the development of new genres. If people invest enough energy into the enactment and institutionalization of liminal forms over time, new genres emerge" (2015b, 329).

43. In addition to the artist that Zhegusov mentions, Timofei Stepanov, there are several other artists whose works based on olonkho tales have become widely known, such as Vladimir Karamzin, Afanasii Munkhalov, Mikhail Nosov, Pyotr Romanov, Ėllei Sivtsev, and Valerian Vasiliev. For some well-known olonkho illustrations by these artists in the collections of the National Art Museum of the Republic of Sakha (Yakutia), see https://www.google.com/culturalinstitute/beta/exhibit/1QKize-aoQmYLQ, accessed January 19, 2017.

44. Vinokurova and Zhegusov interview, 2011; see http://www.press.uillinois.edu/books/harris/storytelling/.

45. Ibid.

46. Struchkova interview, 2010; see press.uillinois.edu/books/harris/storytelling.

47. A YouTube search on terms such as "khomus" and "ohuokhai" turns up increasing numbers of fusion examples, such as the rock band "103" playing a *khomus*–rock–nature sounds fusion featuring the talents of Olga Podluzhnaya. An interesting example of fusion can be heard in the "Sakha Round Dance," which is sung in English and accompanied by percussion. https://www.youtube.com/watch?v=JvxpWwfQC_8&feature=youtu.be, accessed August 31, 2016. It was created by Mira Maximova, and the caller is Alex Montyro.

48. Banti and Giannattasio summarize this phenomenon well: "'archaism and dialectalism' are features that characterize this register, that is, a high occurrence of older forms and words and of borrowings from other dialects. Poetic registers are indeed often more or less supradialectal, in the sense of being less bound to local varieties than ordinary language. This is particularly true when they are used for oral texts that circulate among a wider community, such as epic poems performed by traveling professionals, or poetry composed for political debate among different clans as among the Somalis, as well as for written texts addressed to a large readership" (2006, 306).

NOTES TO CHAPTER 3 187

49. Tatiana Argounova reports that in 1986, in the capital of Yakutsk, only 16 percent of Sakha schoolchildren were fluent in their native language (1992, 75).

50. Vinokurova and Zhegusov interview, 2011; see http://www.press.uillinois.edu/books/harris/storytelling/.

51. Reshetnikov interview, 2009; see http://www.press.uillinois.edu/books/harris/story telling/.

52. Interview with Vera Solovyeva, Atlanta, Georgia, March 10, 2010.

53. As further evidence of the likelihood of this connection, the reader will remember Kulakovskii's story of how "sitting under the mouth" as a child made him want to learn the Sakha language better (Cruikshank and Argounova 2000, 109).

54. Reshetnikov interview, 2009; see http://www.press.uillinois.edu/books/harris/story telling/.

55. Ibid.

56. Vinokurova and Zhegusov interview, 2011; see http://www.press.uillinois.edu/books/harris/storytelling/. When I checked in 2015 to see if Vinokurova was able to give me the name of this teacher, she said the woman wished to remain anonymous.

57. Zakharova interview, 2011; see press.uillinois.edu/books/harris/storytelling.

58. Kononov interview, 2009; see press.uillinois.edu/books/harris/storytelling.

59. Ibid.

60. For more information, see http://tinyurl.com/suntaar-olonkho-camp, accessed January 18, 2012.

61. Vasiliev interview, 2010; see http://www.press.uillinois.edu/books/harris/story telling/.

62. http://tinyurl.com/khangalas-olonkho-camp, accessed January 18, 2012.

63. Sysoliatina (2006) reports a yearly festival-competition, *Min olonkho doidutun oghotobun*, for young performers of olonkho. Cruikshank and Argounova (2000, 106) also document a children's camp near Cherkëkh.

64. Updates on this competition can be found by searching online using the title of the event: Мин олонхо дойдутун оҕотобун. The information in this section comes from the www.olonkho.info site, shortened here to https://goo.gl/B4q1wD. Accessed January 13, 2017.

65. Interview with Spiridon Shishigin, Pokrovsk, Yakutia, June 25, 2010; see press.uillinois.edu/books/harris/storytelling.

66. Kurdiarov made this comment during a discussion at an international forum on Epics of the World's Peoples in Yakutsk on June 19, 2015.

67. Mikhailov interview, 2011; see http://www.press.uillinois.edu/books/harris/story telling/.

68. Vinokurova and Zhegusov interview, 2011; see http://www.press.uillinois.edu/books/harris/storytelling/.

69. Interview with museum curator, Berdigestyakh, June 20, 2010; see http://www.press.uillinois.edu/books/harris/storytelling/.

70. Interview with olonkho teacher in Berdigestyakh, June 20, 2010. While this teacher asked that her name not be used, her observations are key, demonstrating the changes in symbolic content in Ysyakhs between Soviet times and now. The Ysyakh festivals,

188 NOTES TO CHAPTERS 3 AND 4

including those focused on olonkho, have always performed the function of "ritual" through the symbolic representations and transformative power of the events (Cooley 2006, 67). Like many kinds of ritual, Ysyakh operates on "a continuum that spans the distance between two opposing motivations for performance: efficacy (a quality of ritual) and entertainment (a quality of theater)" (Schechner 1983, 137–138). In accordance with this nature of festivals, both the Soviet and the current Ysyakhs reflect the spectrum of motivations from efficacy to entertainment. For discussions regarding motivations for performance that impact festivals and rituals, see Solomon (2014, 163) and Bakan (2012, 24), respectively.

71. The Declaration of the Second Decade of Olonkho (2016–2025) was signed into law on June 19, 2014, with plans and budgets prepared in 2015. See http://docs.cntd.ru/document/412381060, accessed December 5, 2016.

72. 2016—Verkhoyansk; 2017—Aldan; 2018—Viliui; 2019—Olëlminsk; 2020—Namsk; 2021—Amga. See http://docs.cntd.ru/document/422400877, accessed February 29, 2016. The budget has not been posted online yet, but it should be soon.

4. Examining the Role of UNESCO and Intangible Cultural Heritage

1. The limitations of ICH were discussed by Justin Hunter, Man Yang, Da Lin, and Robin Harris in a panel titled "Perceiving the Intangible: Critical Perspectives of 'Intangible Cultural Heritage' in Four Asian Contexts" at the Society for Ethnomusicology meetings in Philadelphia, Pennsylvania, November 19, 2011, http://www.indiana.edu/~semhome/2011/pdf/SEM2011%20Program%20101911.pdf, 21–22, accessed October 22, 2011.

2. "International Round Table: Intangible Cultural Heritage, Working Definitions," http://www.unesco.org/culture/ich/en/events?meeting_id=00057, accessed December 5, 2016.

3. "The World Heritage Convention," http://whc.unesco.org/en/convention/, accessed January 18, 2012. For further information on World Heritage sites, see DiGiovine (2009).

4. "What Is Intangible Cultural Heritage?," http://www.unesco.org/culture/ich/en/what-is-intangible-heritage-00003, accessed December 5, 2016.

5. Regarding the relationship between tangible and intangible, Kirshenblatt-Gimblett notes: "As for intangible heritage, it is not only embodied, but also inseparable from the material and social worlds of persons" (2004, 60).

6. "Proclamation of the Masterpieces of the Oral and Intangible Heritage of Humanity (2001–2005)," http://www.unesco.org/culture/ich/en/proclamation-of-masterpieces-00103, accessed December 5, 2016, my emphasis.

7. Ibid.

8. "Representative List of the Intangible Cultural Heritage of Humanity," http://www.unesco-bg.org/file_store/188328e.pdf, accessed December 5, 2016.

9. "Masterpiece" is the normal translation of *shedevr*, which likely came into the Russian language from the French term *chef d'oeuvre*.

10. "Masterpieces of the Oral and Intangible Heritage of Humanity: Proclamations 2001, 2003 and 2005," http://unesdoc.unesco.org/images/0014/001473/147344e.pdf, accessed January 17, 2017.

NOTES TO CHAPTER 4   189

11. "Text of the Convention," http://www.unesco.org/culture/ich/en/convention, art. 31. For the subsuming of masterpiece awards into the Representative List, see "Proclamation of the Masterpieces of the Oral and Intangible Heritage of Humanity (2001–2005)," http:// www.unesco.org/culture/ich/en/proclamation-of-masterpieces-00103, accessed January 17, 2017.

12. Ibid., art. 2.3.

13. Launched in 2009, the collaborative project that began as "Sustainable Futures" and morphed into "Sound Futures" is now one of the most wide-ranging projects related to sustainability of music traditions. Read more at the website, http://soundfutures.org, which is nearly complete at the time of this writing. This work holds special promise in developing approaches and resources for communities seeking to bolster the vitality of their artistic traditions. Note that at least some parts of Sakha society had a strong desire to revitalize olonkho while disregarding the many other genres that disappeared during the Soviet period. Revitalization focuses on a genre not for the genre's sake, but for the value that it has in the eyes of those who love it (Schippers 2015, 138). Schrag observes a growth of interest in "the precarious status of many ethnolinguistically-based artistic traditions. . . . Sometimes missing, however, is a grasp of the underlying mechanisms through which artists' activities may propel a tradition toward sustainability" (2013b, 440). In chapter 5 I explore his proposed framework for encouraging resilience and apply the principles toward a better understanding of olonkho revitalization.

14. "Safeguarding without Freezing," http://www.unesco.org/culture/ich/en/safeguarding -00012, accessed December 5, 2016.

15. Even beyond the Russian context, translation has a significant impact on a nation's understanding of key words. Titon notes that "in its 1989 Recommendation, UNESCO defined preservation and conservation exactly opposite to the common US understanding of the two terms" (2015b, 167).

16. Other authors who write about safeguarding ICH, such as Skounti (2009, 77), also employ the metaphor of transmitting genetic material.

17. In the case of olonkho, these forms might include theatrical presentations, memorized scripts, and other "distant relatives" as described in this book.

18. Kirshenblatt-Gimblett's comment in this regard summarizes well the challenges facing revitalizers of olonkho: "Change is intrinsic to culture, and measures intended to preserve, conserve, safeguard, and sustain particular cultural practices are caught between freezing the practice and addressing the inherently processual nature of culture" (2004, 58–59).

19. Culture brokers may try to add "the value of pastness, exhibition, difference, and, where possible, indigeneity" to heritage expressions (Kirshenblatt-Gimblett 1998, 150).

20. "Transmission," http://www.unesco.org/culture/ich/en/transmission-00078, accessed December 5, 2016.

21. "Masterpieces of the Oral and Intangible Heritage," http://unesdoc.unesco.org/ images/0014/001473/147344e.pdf, 83, accessed April 19, 2017.

22. Post-Soviet societies negotiating the reconstruction of their identities face a common challenge: the old "Soviet habitus" continues to affect the process of reinventing national cultures (Adams 2010, 13). In the early 1990s, when the state lost the ability to enforce

190   NOTES TO CHAPTER 4

communist values, many Soviet power structures merely underwent rebranding or some level of refashioning. Effectively, the Russian Federation retained the ability to educate, rule, and artistically train the population using many of the same ways employed during the communist era. As a result, ensuring broader community engagement at a grassroots level poses challenges for UNESCO projects.

Levin describes with great insight the way Soviet structures have permeated the post-Soviet space in Central Asia: "No amount of enthusiasm for the recovery of a vanished pre-Soviet reality has been able to stop the inertia of seventy years of Soviet rule. The innovations of Soviet culture policy continue to cast a long shadow over the cultural landscape of Central Asia, and many of these innovations have become so much a part of the landscape that one can hardly imagine Central Asian life without them. The 'traditional' practices, beliefs, and social relationships that OM and I set out to explore in fact comprise a patchwork of traditions of various provenance: Soviet traditions intermingled with Soviet transformations of pre-Soviet traditions and with reemergent pre-Soviet traditions, reconstructed and reinterpreted to serve the farrago of nationalist, socialist, capitalist, ethnic, and religious interests that have shaped, and are shaping, post-Soviet society and culture" (1999, xv).

23. "Text of the Convention," http://www.unesco.org/culture/ich/en/convention, art. 1, accessed April 19, 2017, my emphasis.

24. Ibid., art. 2.3.

25. "Conditions necessary" refers to creating an epic *sreda*—the widespread understanding of and appreciation for olonkho.

26. None of these coordinating entities were created specifically for the purpose of olonkho revitalization; all four were extant governmental and educational structures.

27. Hill and Bithell note that "the process of establishing authenticity begins with the highly selective and subjective identification of particular aspects or elements in a music-culture, followed by the decision that they should be perpetuated and the assertion of their value. These selections become ideals, models to strive towards, measures of assessment, and the criteria for establishing authenticity. . . . Conflicting assertions of authenticity amongst different parties are not uncommon" (2014, 20). For other chapters in Hill and Bithell dealing with authenticity, see Hill (2014), Merchant (2014), Shay (2014), and Walker (2014).

28. The exchange rate was approximately 26 rubles to 1 US dollar in early 2007; http://www.x-rates.com/historical/?from=USD&amount=1&date=2007-02-01, accessed January 14, 2017. By the end of 2014, the rate had more than doubled, and was more than 58 rubles to the dollar; http://www.x-rates.com/historical/?from=USD&amount=1&date=2014-12-31, accessed January 14, 2017.

29. Republic of Sakha (2007). This document provided proposed budgets, outcomes, and programs for olonkho revitalization.

30. Sidorova, Protodiakonova, and Luginova interview, 2011; see press.uillinois.edu/books/harris/storytelling.

31. For a RUB-USD conversion chart, see http://www.xe.com/currencycharts/?from=USD&to=RUB&view=10Y, accessed February 22, 2016.

32. For a Russian-language description of the budgeting and expectations for hosting the "Ysyakh of Olonkho," see the law passed on June 3, 2009, http://docs.cntd.ru/document/815000717, accessed February 17, 2016.

NOTES TO CHAPTER 4 191

33. See http://www.xe.com/currencycharts/?from=RUB&to=USD&view=10Y, accessed April 19, 2017.

34. The legislation for the "2009–2011 Plan" can be found at http://docs.cntd.ru/document/473502513, accessed February 17, 2016. For the extension, dated October 28, 2011, see http://docs.cntd.ru/document/473500412, accessed February 17, 2016.

35. The original legislation (3 N 887-III), rescinded on December 30, 2010, was replaced with legislation 874-3 N 641-IV, a copy of which is available at http://docs.cntd.ru/document/895278783, accessed February 17, 2016.

36. See http://ysia.ru/kultura/v-yakutske-otkrylas-dekada-olonho/, accessed January 19, 2017.

37. Vasiliev interview, 2010. From field notes of our conversation.

38. Larionova (2010) reported over 100 extracts and short summaries of plots and around 300 phonograph and video recordings.

39. Vasiliev interview, 2010; see http://www.press.uillinois.edu/books/harris/storytelling/.

40. Ibid.

41. "Инициативы ЮНЕСКО в обеспечении многоязычия в киберпространстве и сохранении цифрового наследия имеют неоценимое значение для сохранения мирового культурного наследия во всем его многообразии" (Vasiliev et al. 2009, 7).

42. Sidorova, Protodiakonova, and Luginova interview, 2011; see http://www.press.uillinois.edu/books/harris/storytelling/.

43. For a full repertoire list (in Russian) of the Theater of Olonkho, see http://olonkhotheatre.ru/repertuar.html, accessed October 7, 2014.

44. The full title of this governmental structure, the Ministry of Culture and Spiritual Development (Ministerstvo kulturi i dukhovnovnoi razvitiia), is sometimes translated as Ministry of Culture and Intellectual Development—see, for example, the last page of the booklet prepared for UNESCO, "Yakut Heroic Epos Olonkho—a Masterpiece of Oral and Intangible Heritage of Humanity" (Zakharova and Protodiakonova 2010).

45. See "ОБ ИСПОЛЬЗОВАНИИ ЭКРАНА" [On the use of the screen], toward the bottom of the page at http://olonkhotheatre.ru/esteika-teatra-olonxo.html, accessed January 20, 2017.

46. I learned of this olonkho when I presented with Nurguyana Illarionova at Harvard University's Loeb Music Library on September 22, 2014. Her Harvard lecture, titled "Theatrical Interpretation of the Yakut Heroic Epos (Olonkho)," provided this information about Isakov's theatrical olonkho.

47. "Andrei Borisov ukhodit s posta ministra kultury Yakutii" [Andrei Borisov leaves the post of Yakutia's minister of culture], http://news.ykt.ru/article/25181, accessed October 13, 2014.

48. As already indicated, the web portal shows great promise. Nakhodkina identifies a variety of languages into which olonkho has been translated (2014, 275). Scientific publications and texts abound, largely in Russian; I have listed many of them in the Works Cited section of this book.

49. For a copy of the decree, see http://docs.cntd.ru/document/815003396, accessed February 17, 2016.

192 NOTES TO CHAPTER 4

50. See http://news.ykt.ru/article/24453 for some of the architectural designs submitted for the competition, and http://news.ykt.ru/article/27252?qf=12165689&qs=59744251 for an interview with the winner of the design contest; both accessed January 26, 2016. The official site is http://olonkholand.ru/en/. The last article available on the web about the project as of this writing is from January 22, 2015: http://news.ykt.ru/article/28209?qf=12165686 &qs=59744251, accessed January 26, 2016.

51. Funding for the film *Welcome to Olonkholand* also drew from Yakutia's budget for revitalization. Shtyrov authorized the minister of culture to produce the presentational film at a cost of almost three million rubles (over $100,000 USD at the exchange rate of the time) for the World Expo in Shanghai, China. See the 6:21-minute film at https://www .youtube.com/watch?v=rX03qdN9uuQ. It is hosted with English commentary at http:// www.fourthworldmusic.com/?p=61. Both sites accessed February 17, 2016.

52. "What Is Intangible Cultural Heritage?," http://www.unesco.org/culture/ich/en/ what-is-intangible-heritage-00003, accessed April 19, 2017.

53. "Transmission," http://www.unesco.org/culture/ich/en/transmission-00078, accessed April 19, 2017.

54. Reshetnikov interview, 2009; see press.uillinois.edu/books/harris/storytelling.

55. I serve on the international editing council for this series, along with scholars from Kyrgystan (Beksultan Zhakiev) and Germany (Karl Reichl), as well as the rector of NEFU (Evgenia Mikhailova), the senior epic scholar at NEFU (Vasilii Illarionov), the Russian Federation's UNESCO liaison (Grigorii Ordzhonikidze), and Alexander Zhirkov, speaker of the Yakutian Parliament.

56. My translation (condensed); from the original document, dated August 1, 2014, and titled "Положение о книжной серии Национального книжного издательства «Бичик» им. С. А. Новгородова: «Эпические памятники народов мира» [Statute regarding the book series of the national publishing house "Bichik" in the name of S. A. Novgorodova: "Epic monuments of the world"]. Here is the full text in Russian, outlining the goals and tasks of the series: "- публикации переводов произведений мировой литературы на якутский язык, равно как и перевод лучших образцов якутской литературы на языки народов мира имеет непреходящую ценность для развития языка, ознакомления общественности с литературой, культурными традициями народа. Особое значение имеет выход на широкого читателя выдающихся памятников эпического наследия нашего народа. Признанных шедеврами устного и нематериального наследия человечества; - данные издания послужат инструментарием в укреплении международных связей республики и дружбы народов, культурным проводником к традициям, языкам и фольклорам разных народов; - повышение интереса к переводческой деятельности в республике, как особого, своеобразного и самостоятельного вида словесного искусства."

57. Alekseyev and Larionova interview, 2010; see press.uillinois.edu/books/harris/story telling.

58. "Transmission," http://www.unesco.org/culture/ich/en/transmission-00078, accessed April 19, 2017.

59. "Guidelines for the Establishment of National 'Living Human Treasures' Systems," http://www.unesco.org/culture/ich/doc/src/00031-EN.pdf, 8, accessed January 18, 2012.

NOTES TO CHAPTERS 4 AND 5   193

60. http://olonkhotheatre.ru/olonhosuty/135-tomskaja-darja-andreevna-chaajka.html, accessed October 7, 2014. For a biography of Afanasii Solovëv (in Russian), see http://tinyurl.com/AESolovev. For a news article noting his lifetime of achievements and marking his passing, see http://news.ykt.ru/article/6070, accessed September 12, 2016.

61. See "Decree of the President of the Sakha Republic (Yakutia) on Measures for the Preservation, Study, and Dissemination of the Yakut Heroic Epos Olonkho," 2005 (Republic of Sakha 2007). Equivalent to approximately $1,100 at the time of the initial award, this stipend provides more than what an airline pilot earned and more than twice what the average worker made in the Russian Federation. See http://www.worldsalaries.org/russia.shtml, accessed January 18, 2012.

62. "Guidelines for the Establishment of National 'Living Human Treasures' Systems," http://www.unesco.org/culture/ich/doc/src/00031-EN.pdf, 4, accessed April 19, 2017.

63. The importance of living tradition bearers cannot be underestimated. This principle is noted by many who study ICH, including Blake, who affirms that "it is only through its enactment by cultural practitioners that ICH has any current existence and by their active transmission that it can have any future existence" (2009, 65).

64. Could people qualifying for the title of master olonkhosut be identified with a little effort? Elizaveta Sidorova pointed to a committee for the "Decade of Olonkho" as the arbiters of these awards, but the exact process involved in choosing new olonkhosuts remains unclear to me.

65. Oyunsky (1997).

66. "Guidelines for the Establishment of National 'Living Human Treasures' Systems," http://www.unesco.org/culture/ich/doc/src/00031-EN.pdf, 3.

5. Elements of Resilience: Stable and Malleable

1. Feld et al. note that "linguistically motivated models for the description and analysis of music have, since the early 1980s, produced a number of intellectually productive developments toward a cognitive science of music" (2006, 322).

2. See the "Endangered Languages" program of UNESCO at http://www.unesco.org/new/en/culture/themes/endangered-languages/atlas-of-languages-in-danger/ and the electronic version of UNESCO's *Atlas of the World's Languages in Danger* (Paris, 2010), ed. Christopher Moseley, at http://unesdoc.unesco.org/images/0018/001870/187026e.pdf, both accessed January 14, 2017.

3. Catherine Grant, in applying theories of language maintenance to the problem of music endangerment (2014), proposes a nuanced, detailed tool called the Music Vitality and Endangerment Framework (MVEF), which seeks to gauge the vitality of music genres anywhere in the world based on twelve factors (see also http://www.musicendangerment.com/ and Schippers and Grant [2016]). If community decision makers have the personnel, training, and ability to measure these factors and follow Grant's model, they will get a fine-grained picture of the health of their music systems. I have chosen to employ models with fewer variables in the hope that, in addition to being workable for communities with small budgets and few trained researchers, my approach will be accessible to those with decision-making power, such as, in the Yakutian context, a member of parliament, a school

194   NOTES TO CHAPTER 5

curriculum writer, an olonkhosut, or a sociologist doing research on attitudes toward the arts.

4. A UNESCO document, "Safeguarding Endangered Languages," identifies the most significant force for language vitality as the attitudes toward the language itself. This factor could also apply to other ICH expressions. http://unesdoc.unesco.org/images/0015/001502/150220e.pdf, accessed January 18, 2012.

5. "UNESCO's Endangered Languages Programme," http://unesco.org/new/fileadmin/MULTIMEDIA/HQ/CLT/pdf/FlyerEndangeredLanguages-WebVersion.pdf, accessed January 18, 2012.

6. See p. 7 of "Language Vitality and Endangerment," http://unesdoc.unesco.org/images/0018/001836/183699E.pdf, accessed January 18, 2012.

7. "UNESCO Atlas of the World's Languages in Danger," http://www.unesco.org/new/en/culture/themes/endangered-languages/atlas-of-languages-in-danger/, accessed April 19, 2017.

8. My interviews with Pyotr Reshetnikov, 2009, and Dekabrina Vinokurova, 2011, particularly underscore this point; see press.uillinois.edu/books/harris/storytelling.

9. See http://www.sil.org/arts-ethnomusicology/stories-0 and http://www.ichngoforum.org/ngo-forum/, both accessed September 7, 2016. I have provided services to SIL as an ethnomusicology consultant and curriculum designer since 2010. For more on SIL International, a faith-based not-for-profit organization, visit https://www.sil.org/about.

10. Lewis and Simons lead the editorial team of *Ethnologue: Languages of the World*, a comprehensive reference work cataloging all of the world's known living languages. Now an online-only resource, the *Ethnologue* last appeared in print in the 17th edition (2014). The International Organization for Standardization has designated SIL International's *Ethnologue* (www.ethnologue.com) as the authority in identifying human languages (ISO 639-3 standard).

11. Mark Slobin also notes the close connection between sociolinguistics and ethnomusicology, calling them "kissing cousins in the family of academe" (1979, 1), and he affirms that sociolinguistics can provide insights into the "technical analysis" of music (1992, 3).

12. In order to clarify discussions of human agency, Errington distinguishes between two *sources* of language death: "Illegitimate language shift is the *causal* outcome of coercive forces external to a minority community and needs to be distinguished from that arising from cumulative, self-interested, knowledgeable choices by social *agents* between one language rather than another" (2003, 728). The Sakha olonkho definitely experienced a period of what Errington calls a "loss of language rights" (729), yet the extent to which that period of repression played a role in the current choices of Sakha people remains a complex question. I believe the issue of causation for language loss should be viewed as a spectrum ranging from coercive forces to community and individual agency, or as overlapping fields of factors, rather than as a binary choice.

13. Note that drawing an essentialist relationship between Sakha language and identity would overstate their complex linkage (Bucholtz and Hall 2006, 374).

14. See http://ysia.ru/glavnoe/aleksandr-zhirkov-respublika-nuzhdaetsya-v-obedinenii-molodyh-olonhosutov/ for a summary of this meeting, accessed September 2, 2016. Yuri Borisov, a talented young olonkho scholar and singer, serves as the president of a recently

NOTES TO CHAPTER 5   195

formed organization for young olonkhosuts, Ychchat Olongkhohut. See Borisov's site, http://s-vfu.ru/user/user.php?id=631017124, accessed April 19, 2017.

15. "Language Status," *Ethnologue: Languages of the World*, https://www.ethnologue.com /about/language-status, accessed April 19, 2017.

16. I posit that the use of Lewis and Simons's term "Shifting" at level 6 may cause confusion, as "shifting" should be a term describing movement in either direction along the scale rather than designating a static picture of lessened vitality. In consultation with Coulter, I changed this term, used both in EGIDS and in subsequent art-related versions, to "Stressed."

17. In creating this tool, I drew from the diagnostic decision tree developed by Lewis and Simons for identifying the stage of language vitality through a series of questions (2009, fig. 1).

18. Note the color gradation behind the levels in columns two and three, indicating that these dynamics represent a continuum rather than bounded sets.

19. The Sakha would definitely like to see olonkho reach international fame. When the movie *Avatar* first appeared, Minister of Culture Andrei Borisov accused James Cameron of plagiarizing from the olonkho *Nurgun Botur*, an allegation that reached the international press. See "Sakha Minister Says 'Avatar' Copied Local Epic," *Moscow Times*, July 12, 2012, http://www.themoscowtimes.com/news/article/sakha-minister-says-avatar-film-copied -local-epic/462049.html, which includes the article and the official video of UNESCO featuring Pyotr Reshetnikov as olonkhosut, accessed February 17, 2016. Others took a more pragmatic approach by sending Cameron an invitation to film *Avatar II* in Yakutia. Their invitation included an English translation of *Nurgun Botur* (2014) and a flash-mob video they had created. "Avatar Film Director to Receive a Video about Olonkho and a Book from People of Yakutia," May 14, 2015, http://yatoday.ru/news/culture/377-avatar-film -director-to-receive-a-video-about-olonkho-and-a-book-from-people-of-yakutia, accessed February 17, 2016.

20. A curated site for olonkho-related videos has been created by the World News (WN) Network and is available online at http://wn.com/the_olonkho,_yakut_heroic_epos, accessed December 5, 2016. It currently contains some of my own research as well as the UNESCO video, an exhibition of Timofei Stepanov's visual art on the theme of olonkho, an animated cartoon in Japanese, and several clips of Pyotr Tikhonov performing at an exhibition.

21. Titon encourages research that seeks to find keys to resilience when music systems are disturbed: "resilience recognizes that perturbation, disturbance, and flux are constant characteristics of any complex system. Resilience theory and adaptive management practice therefore attempt to identify what makes a music culture vulnerable to regime shift, and what makes one resilient, and to ameliorate the former and strengthen the latter. Resilience theory and adaptive management offer promising directions for applied ethnomusicologists working toward sustainability in music cultures" (2015b, 193). The analysis that follows is inspired by this challenge, and since this study examines a tradition that is much broader than just music, I hope the results can help to clarify differences between ecological re- silience and resilience of cultural traditions and systems.

22. Bohlman further adds that these new additions to the "canonical core" must first be "transformed by the canon's boundaries into texts and contexts appropriate to the aesthetic

196   NOTES TO CHAPTER 5

and social criteria of the community at its core. The formation and maintenance of the canon, therefore, are predicated on stability and change, both of which are ongoing and inseparable forces in the determination of the oral tradition of folk music" (1988, 32).

23. Adapting Schrag's theories to the context of this case study, I have chosen to use the term (stable and malleable) "elements" instead of "structures."

24. In developing this chart, I determined the historical apex—the period reflecting the most flourishing—for each type of olonkho performance (solo and theatrical) using data from the diagnostic chart. Theatrical olonkho is still growing toward its apogee, so the description of stable and malleable reflects contemporary realities at the date of this publication. For traditional master olonkhosuts, on the other hand, the pinnacle of flourishing was in the pre-Soviet period, so the description reflects that time frame (early 1900s).

25. Briggs affirms the agency of performers rather than the forces of the *sreda*, noting that "performers are not passive, unreflecting creatures who simply respond to the dictates of tradition or the physical and social environment. They interpret both traditions and social settings, actively transforming both in the course of their performances" (1988, 7).

26. Pukhov (1962), Reshetnikova (2005), and Emelianov (2000) have analyzed plots of olonkho stories. Emelianov outlines the plots of several epic tales, providing parallel texts in Russian and Sakha. Putilov (1997) and Trepavlov (1995; in English) discuss the social status of the epic hero and the heroic typology of the olonkho.

27. "V Iakutii trud olonkhosuta stal oplachivaemym" [The work of an olonkhosut in Yakutia begins to bring financial compensation], http://ysia.ru/kultura/teatr-olonho-obedinyaet-ispolnitelej-eposa-so-vsej-yakutii/, accessed January 25, 2017. For a more in-depth discussion of this development, see the "Recommendations" section in chap. 7.

28. For details and more pictures, see http://ysia.ru/kultura/etno-balet-po-motivam-olonho-sergeya-zvereva-s-uspehom-proshel-v-sankt-peterburge/, accessed February 8, 2016.

29. Ekaterina Romanova, a scholar at IGI specializing in mythology and ritual studies, challenged me to provide an accurate definition of tradition. Heartily concurring with my description of the sedimented nature of tradition, she applied the concept to olonkho: "some people think it should be exactly the same way it was in the nineteenth century. But it can never be that way again!" Interview, Yakutsk, December 8, 2011; see press.uillinois.edu/books/harris/storytelling.

30. A study of the transmission of traditional religious belief among the Sakha may provide some interesting parallels regarding the interaction between innovation and tradition. Marjorie Balzer, researching Siberian shamanism, analyzed practitioners of both an older and a younger generation, along with their communities, and argues that "sustainable faith has been passed on in flexible, innovative ways" (2011, 11).

31. In *Code Switching and Code Superimposition in Music*, Mark Slobin illustrates how the "citation method" used both indigenous music styles and Western orchestral elements in the creation of operas in the Soviet context. He writes, "Carried out by composers sent from Moscow to places like Tashkent and Alma-Ata, [the citation method] consisted of well-calculated code switching from European to local styles for which the linguistic notion of a quotation has been very aptly borrowed. . . . In these operas, one can hear a full orchestra play an overture with Western harmony, followed by a solo singer's entry with a purely Kazakh or Uzbek text, voice quality, and melody" (1979, 12). Widespread

NOTES TO CHAPTERS 5 AND 6 197

across the Soviet Union, including Yakutia, this compositional method is employed in the compositions of contemporary composers.

32. I use the following definition of community: "A social group of any size whose members share a story, identity, and ongoing patterns of interaction, and whose identity and social practices are constantly in flux" (Schrag 2013a, 268).

33. I find it amusing that although the Russian word *propaganda* carries negative connotations in English, in Russian it simply denotes "public relations."

6. Epic Revitalization: Negotiating Identities and Other Challenges

1. Asif Agha provides a succinct definition of "linguistic register": "A register is a linguistic *repertoire* that is associated, culture-internally, with particular social practices and with persons who engage in such practices" (2006, 24). In a later chapter of the same edited volume, Banti and Giannattasio identify the elements that distinguish poetic registers from normal high-level register: "Quite frequently, the language used for poetic texts is also characterized as a special register, beyond ordinary speech, by features such as (1) special morphology, (2) special syntax, (3) a special lexicon, as well as by (4) special stylistic features" (2006, 306).

2. See also Kirby (1980).

3. Slobin notes another example from Soviet space in Central Asia: "Take, for example, the controversy in the 1960s over the survival of the Bukharan court music (*shashmaqam*) in Central Asia. As a remnant of the 'feudal' past, the Russian authorities felt this tradition was negative and should be silenced. Yet the logic of the social order of the republics left a space for local cultural management, and the *shashmaqam* not only survived but was even enshrined as a key component of Uzbek identity in the cultural renaissance of the late Soviet period, allowing it to survive into the postcommunist period" (1996, 9). Levin has also written extensively about this genre and its adaptations and calcifications during the Soviet and post-Soviet periods (1984, 1999).

4. Eduard Alekseyev, personal communication, October 20, 2014.

5. In Russian, *reabilitatsiia* refers to clearing the names and reputations of the people in question, with official state acknowledgment that they had been repressed for political and/or ideological reasons.

6. See recordings at press.uillinois.edu/books/harris/storytelling for examples of *khomus*, *toyuk*, and *ohuokhai*.

7. Harvilahti has studied Latvia's *Bear Slayer* and Tibet's *Geser*, a cycle of epic poems from Tibet, China, Buriatia, and India (1996, 40), as well as Altaic epics (2000).

8. Jean Kidula, writing about African contexts, invokes Kwabena Nketia's notion of "transfer of function" (Nketia 1974, 245) as "an ideology and practice embraced—consciously and unconsciously—by displaced or colonized Africans to contest, accept and internalize change" (2013, 290). Kidula contends that "expression[s] of this adjustment [can be] found in the process, product and contexts of music . . . as well as in the defining and re-defining of practitioners" (314). All of these phenomena appear to be taking place in Yakutia in relation to olonkho.

198   NOTES TO CHAPTER 6

9. These were the "Amginskii, Megino-Kangalasskii, Tattinskii, Ust-Aldanskii, Gorny, Namskii, Khangalassskii, and Churapchinskii districts" (Osipova 2011, 3).

10. "Признание олонхо шедевром устного народного творчества ЮНЕСКО привело к повышению статуса эпоса как национального символа" (Osipova 2011, 4).

11. These percentages are rounded to the nearest percent. The questions and answers mentioned here, in Russian, follow: "Как вы оцениваете героический эпос олонхо?" Answers: "Олонхо - фундамент национальной культуры народа саха" (83.2%) . . . Большинство (81.1%) опрошенного населения считает, что олонхо - народное достояние, которое надо беречь и сохранять" (Osipova 2011, 5).

12. "Большинство прошенного населения главную проблему видят . . . в том, что сам олонхо не востребовано у общества, даже несмотря на осознание людьми его ценности" (Osipova 2011, 7).

13. "Олонхо, безусловно, рассматривается как культурная ценность народа саха, однако не имеет популярности в обществе" (Osipova 2011, 8).

14. Ignatieva et al. state it this way: "With the accentuation on the prestige of olonkho, the triumphal return from a passive phase of functionality to an active one (as it seemed to us then), the ancient epos received, if not a second life, then certainly at least its deserved place in the modern sociocultural processes. However, as time has demonstrated, the modern phenomenon of olonkho differs greatly from the 'classic' tradition, and no longer represents the traditional artistic creativity of the people, merely claiming the status of an archaic element of culture in the structures of mass culture. There is a widespread feeling that olonkho has generally lost its original form and deep meaning, and is now destined to be viewed as a stylized and exhibitable form of national arts, torn away from its place in everyday life. This unhappy perspective on olonkho is connected, in a large way, to the reduction and even disappearance of the folkloric *sreda*, including the audiences for epics in our modern society" (2013, 3–4).

15. Reshetnikov interview, 2009; see press.uillinois.edu/books/harris/storytelling.

16. An article by Krader (1990), although affording a somewhat contrasting picture to Kosacheva's in regard to the politicization of folklore during the Soviet period, includes a unique resource for this project—a discussion of some widely used Russian terms in the field of ethnomusicology. Her work clarifies certain concepts and theories central to the development of music research up to the fall of the Soviet Union.

17. The legislation (N 1349-3 N 253-V), passed on October 9, 2014, documents the terminology change from "president" to "head" of the Sakha Republic (Yakutia). http://docs.cntd.ru/document/423845379, accessed February 17, 2016.

18. Ashcroft, Griffiths, and Tiffin posit that neocolonial relations involve "the continuing process of imperial suppressions and exchanges throughout this diverse range of societies, in their institutions and their discursive practices" (1995, 3). Bhabha (2006) comments on the hybridity and complexity of postcolonial cultural expressions, while Battaglia (1995), Rethman (1997), Renan (1990), and Fanon (1967) explore how people in postcolonial contexts negotiate complex and layered national identities. These authors provide models for better understanding the revitalization of olonkho within the post-Soviet Yakutian context.

19. A divergence of opinions about Stalin can be found all across Russia. Reflecting a minority who still revere him, the "Truth about Stalin" website attempts to deconstruct

NOTES TO CHAPTER 6   199

Stalin's negative image and appeals to "thinking people who want to know the truth about the history of their country." http://www.greatstalin.ru/, accessed October 10, 2014.

20. A Russian-language book by Sakha sociology, folklore, and ethnology scholars describes olonkho as "associated with not only the renaissance of national self-awareness of the Sakha, but also with the growing efforts to protect and safeguard the cultural achievements of the people and their ethnic uniqueness in the epoch of globalization. In a fundamental way . . . [it is] connected to the search for ontological foundations of national existence [and] cultural and civilizational identity" (Ignatieva et al. 2013, 3).

21. See http://www.egorborisov.ru/poslanija-prezidenta/4292-vystuplenija.html, accessed February 1, 2016.

22. Ibid., my emphasis.

23. For descriptions of olonkho and other theatrical productions in China in December 2015, see http://ysia.ru/kultura/yakutiya-vezet-v-kitaj-tri-masshtabnyh-spektaklya/ and http://ysia.ru/kultura/kitajskij-teatr-s-uspehom-predstavil-premeru-spektaklya-po -yakutskomu-eposu-olonho/, accessed February 1, 2016.

24. Most often these events were held in Yakutsk, but one particularly interesting conference, cosponsored by UNESCO, took place in St. Petersburg in 2015. My presentation (Harris 2015), prepared in collaboration with Eduard Alekseyev, challenged the cultural elite not to over-control the ideology in the creative output of olonkhosuts. To my relief, our work was apparently well received, as it was mentioned positively in the press. http:// ysia.ru/kultura/v-sankt-peterburge-obsudili-rol-yakutskogo-olonhosuta-sergeya-zvereva -v-sohranenii-natsionalnogo-svoeobraziya/, accessed February 1, 2016.

25. See the whole article at http://ysia.ru/obshhestvo/aleksandr-zhirkov-olonho-ne otemlemaya-chast-mnogovekovoj-duhovnoj-kultury-yakutskogo-naroda/, accessed February 1, 2016.

26. Donna Bahry observes that when the Center needs the support of the regions, treaties are made to transfer control of resources to the Center, but once power is regained at the Center, those agreements are revoked. She observes, "With the election of 2000 Putin set out to strengthen the 'vertical flow of power,' imposing seven new federal supervisors over Russia's eighty-nine subjects, removing regional leaders from the upper house of parliament, and demanding that regional laws and constitutions conform to federal ones. Within a year a number of Yeltsin-era decrees granting regions special privileges were revoked. . . . Within two years, twenty-eight of the forty-two power-sharing treaties were renounced, and federal authorities hollowed out most of the others" (2005, 127). In the intervening decade since this was published, the trajectory of regathering power to the Center has continued.

27. Daughtry notes that the Russian intelligentsia includes "musicians, artists, academics, literary figures and critics" (2006, 254). These categories roughly parallel those seen as "intelligentsia" among the Sakha.

28. See http://ysia.ru/obshhestvo/aleksandr-zhirkov-olonho-neotemlemaya-chast-mno-govekovoj-duhovnoj-kultury-yakutskogo-naroda/, accessed February 2, 2016.

29. The case study on "spectacle nationalism" in Uzbekistan by Laura Adams (2010) is outstanding. A few more case studies of cultural activism in postcolonial contexts can be seen in the examples of Bolivia (Solomon 2014, 145), Korea (Killick 2003, 199; Um 2013, 1), and West Africa (McGuire 199, 253), and in the essays by several authors included

200   NOTES TO CHAPTER 6

in *The Oxford Handbook of Music Revival* (Bithell and Hill 2014), e.g., Bithell, Conlon, Helbig, Levine, Neveu Kringelbach, and Norton.

30. One version of the three books of *Manas* adds up to over 500,000 lines, twenty times longer than Homer's *Iliad* and *Odyssey* (Freland 2009, 104; Reichl 2016, 327). Although *Manas* has more total lines of verse, most lines are only seven or eight syllables long (Chadwick and Zhirmunsky 1969, 336), so the *Geser* and the *Mahabharata* epics can be considered longer due to the length of the total verbiage. Of course, as Van der Heide points out, any discussion of length must be understood to be relative, since "the oral nature of the epic makes it impossible to reduce the *Manas* to a certain number of lines" (2008, 17).

31. While the majority of the Kyrgyz live in Kyrgyzstan, a group of about 100,000 Kyrgyz live in Xinjiang, China (Reichl 1992, 23), and claim *Manas* as their own.

32. "Art of Akyns, Kyrgyz Epic Tellers," http://www.unesco.org/culture/ich/en/RL/00065, accessed January 18, 2012. Regarding the disappearance of master performers in many Turkic epic traditions, Reichl notes: "In 2005, the last traditional Karakalpak *jyrau*, Jumabay Bazarov, died, as did the last performer of Shor epics (in the Altai), Vladimir Yegorovich Tannagashev, in 2007. The Kyrgyz *manaschy* Jüsüp Mamy, whose justly celebrated version of *Manas* comprises about 220,000 verse lines . . . died in June 2014 at the age of 96" (2016, 329). Still, Reichl asserts that despite its decline, "the [*Manas*] tradition continues, and it is visibly appreciated by the audience" (340).

33. "There was general consensus that books contained the truth, because they are well-researched, and if you read a book, you can study the details. . . . However . . . in the two years I spent in Kyrgyzstan, I never saw anyone reading the Manas tale in any published form. The tale was not read by individuals to pass the time, and apart from the eldest son of my host family, no-one ever claimed that they did. Manas books were not used in classes in schools or at universities either" (Van der Heide 2008, 217).

34. See Naroditskaya (2002), chap. 6, for a discussion of masters, disciples, and the oral transmission of musical knowledge in the *mugham* tradition of Azerbaijan.

35. Hackyung Um (2013) provides a thorough exploration of this topic.

36. "In p'ansori, the audience's presence as a participating supporter or critic initiates an intertextual negotiation—positive or negative—between the audience's communal needs and the performers' narrative preferences" (Park 2000, 273).

37. UNESCO recognizes the effect of its preservation methods on p'ansori: "Threatened by Korea's rapid modernization, Pansori was designated a National Intangible Cultural Property in 1964. This measure spurred generous institutional support, which in turn fostered the revival of this tradition. Although Pansori remains one of the most prominent genres among traditional stage arts, it has lost much of its original spontaneous character. Ironically, this recent evolution is a direct result of the preservation process itself, for improvisation is tending to be stifled by the increasing number of written texts. Indeed, few singers nowadays can successfully improvise, and contemporary audiences are less receptive to the impromptu creativity and language of traditional Pansori." "Pansori Epic Chant," http://www.unesco.org/culture/ich/en/RL/00070, accessed January 18, 2012.

38. When I served as translator for Illarionova's presentation at Harvard University's Loeb Music Library on September 22, 2014, this conversation occurred during our preparation for the event.

NOTES TO CHAPTERS 6 AND 7   201

39. For documentation of this achievement, and pictures of Borisov, see http://yakutia
.com/culture/616/ and http://xn--e1akdgpckdhcy4ej.xn--p1ai/?p=3539. A YouTube interview with him at the event can be viewed at https://www.youtube.com/watch?v
=dRtAFDArf6w, starting at 1:15. For a CV and contact information, see http://s-vfu.ru/
user/user.php?id=631017124, accessed September 26, 2016.

40. A news article highlighting the formation of the Association of Young Olonkhosuts is
available at http://ysia.ru/glavnoe/aleksandr-zhirkov-respublika-nuzhdaetsya-v-obedinenii
-molodyh-olonhosutov/, accessed February 20, 2016.

41. The first performance was December 13, 2015; see http://s-vfu.ru/universitet/
rukovodstvo-i-struktura/instituty/niio/news_detail.php?ELEMENT_ID=43046. The second
took place March 10, 2016; see http://www.s-vfu.ru/universitet/rukovodstvo-i-struktura/
instituty/niio/news_detail.php?ELEMENT_ID=45117. Both accessed September 12, 2016.

7. Ensuring Sustainability through Transmission and Innovation

1. "Не надо быть пророком, что предсказать гибель народа, лишённого своего
родного языка."

2. In an article on arts therapy and arts-based community development, Schrag lists
the multitude of ways that artistic communications affect us: "they mark messages as
important, separate from everyday activities; they touch not only cognitive, but also
experiential and emotional ways of knowing; they are embedded in both individuals
and communities, and so touch many important aspects of a society; they aid memory
of messages; they increase the impact of messages through multiple media that often
include the whole body; they instill solidarity in performers and experiencers; they
provide socially acceptable frameworks for expressing difficult or new ideas; they inspire and move people to action; they can act as strong signs of identity; and they open
spaces for people to imagine and dream" (2015a). Sugarman notes similar realities in
her research on an Albanian singing tradition: "Ultimately, for Presparë, singing is not
an end in itself but a means to social ends" (1988, 2).

3. Levin is also optimistic about the ability of artistic traditions to adapt to change:
"Identities and communities, of course, change with time, and so do the traditional musics
that serve them. Genres, styles, and techniques constantly evolve, and while traditions can
and do really die when they no longer serve a social need, more commonly the energy of
moribund traditions is redirected and reactivated in living cultural practices" (1999, 286).

4. Alekseyev and Larionova interview, 2010; see press.uillinois.edu/books/harris/sto-
rytelling. Alekseyev expounds further on these thoughts in *Folklore in the Context of
Modern Culture*, where he describes how folklore traditions can "come back to life after
a long period of apparent extinction. . . . Any folklore tradition . . . [is comparable to a]
top—keeping upright as long as it's in motion" (1988, 235). This metaphor of a top aptly
describes the movement engendered by the intertwined dynamics of innovation and transmission, stable and malleable, oral and verbal.

5. For the Russian text, see "V Iakutii trud olonkhosuta stal oplachivaemym" [The work
of an olonkhosut in Yakutia begins to bring financial compensation], http://ysia.ru/kultura/
teatr-olonho-obedinyaet-ispolnitelej-eposa-so-vsej-yakutii/, accessed January 25, 2017.

202 NOTES TO CHAPTER 7

6. Dmitrii Pokrovsky, a well-known folklore revivalist in Russia, reminisced on how his corporate sponsors changed in their understanding of the benefits of philanthropy over time: "We have a corporate patron—a Moscow bank—that supports our performances. At first, they wanted to know each time we sang, 'What's in it for us?' They'd ask, 'How many times will you mention us during the concert? How big will our name be on the publicity posters?' Now, they're more relaxed. It's more like American corporate philanthropy. They're aware that you can't look for immediate results. It's more about image" (Levin 1996, 34–35).

7. As a music educator and ethnomusicologist, Patricia Campbell promotes the effectiveness of "participatory consciousness" as a teaching method, in which engaged listeners "find their place in a musical piece through the making of it" (2004, 92). The apprenticeship system would be a far more participatory method of learning than, for example, merely listening to performances of olonkho on an infrequent basis, or through the mediation of recordings.

8. Titon notes in a discussion of sustainability that "apprenticeship, funded by arts agencies, in which younger members of an arts community learn from respected elders, is one of the most widely praised forms of intervention" (2015b, 177).

9. I am grateful to the Republic of Sakha for providing this facility for music education, as my own family benefited greatly from it. Not only did my daughter receive her early music education at the Higher School of Music, winning her first piano competitions as a student during the late 1990s, but the musical foundation she received eventually led to a doctorate in music at a conservatory in the US and a job as a college music professor and performer. This would not have been possible without the government funding of the Higher School of Music, as we could not have afforded to pay for that level of intensive training had payment been required.

10. The effect of an intensive artistic milieu can have surprising results. When I was in close contact with the Higher School of Music in the late 1990s, my daughter's piano teacher, Valentina Larionova, told me that by the time the students were in fourth grade, half of them had developed perfect pitch.

11. Briggs reports that Kirshenblatt-Gimblett and Young coined the term "tale-world" to denote the "realm invoked by the events themselves; for our purposes, this is the world of bygone days" (1988, 281).

12. While my Sakha collaborators seem to have great faith in the ability of this publication to help popularize their epos, I often wonder if it will really achieve what they hope for. On the other hand, I realize that my Sakha colleagues are encouraged simply by knowing that the book exists in English, just like the Masterpiece award is recognized in international discourse, both marks of distinction for the epos as a metonym for the Sakha people. A study such as this becomes "justifiable in its own terms as an act of public or private (interpersonal) good" (Bendrups 2015, 89)—one of the positive outcomes of applied work in communities.

13. Reshetnikov interview, 2009; see recording of the interview at press.uillinois.edu/books/harris/storytelling, starting at 31:10.

Works Cited

Abusch, Tzvi. 2001. "The Development and Meaning of the Epic of Gilgamesh: An Interpretive Essay." *Journal of the American Oriental Society* 121 (4): 614–622.

Adams, Laura. 2010. *The Spectacular State: Culture and National Identity in Uzbekistan.* Durham, NC: Duke University Press.

Agawu, Kofi. 2013. "The Minimalist Impulse in African Musical Creativity." In *Resiliency and Distinction: Beliefs, Endurance and Creativity in the Musical Arts of Continental and Diasporic Africa; A Festschrift in Honor of Jacqueline Cogdell DjeDje,* edited by Kimasi L. Browne and Jean N. Kidula, 39–55. Richmond, CA: Music Research Institute.

Agha, Asif. 2006. "Registers of Language." In *A Companion to Linguistic Anthropology,* edited by Alessandro Duranti, 23–45. Malden, MA: Blackwell.

Ahmad, Aziz. 1963. "Epic and Counter-Epic in Medieval India." *Journal of the American Oriental Society* 83 (4): 470–476.

Aikawa-Faure, Noriko. 2009. "From the Proclamation of Masterpieces to the *Convention for the Safeguarding of Intangible Cultural Heritage.*" In *Intangible Heritage,* edited by Laurajane Smith and Natsuko Akagawa, 13–44. New York: Routledge.

Alekseyev, Eduard Ye. 1969. "Novoe v iakutskom muzikalnom folklore" [New trends in Yakut musical folklore]. In *Muzyka narodov Azii i Afriki* [Music of the peoples of Asia and Africa], compiled and edited by V. S. Vinogradov, 116–131. Moscow: Sov. kompozitor.

———. 1976. *Problemy formirovaniia lada: Na material iakutskoi narodnoi pesni* [Yakut folk song and the genesis of tonal organization]. Moscow: Muzyka.

———. 1988. *Folklor v kontekste sovremennoi kultury: Rassuzhdeniia o sudbakh narodnoi pesni* [Folklore in the context of modern culture: Thoughts on the fates of folk songs]. Moscow: Soviet Composer.

———. 1989a. "K postroeniiu tipologii muzykalnogo èposa" [Toward the construction of a typology of the musical epos]. In *Muzyka èposa: Stati i materialy* [Music of the epos: Articles and materials], compiled and edited by I. Zemtsovskii, 24–27. Ioshkar Ola, Russia: Komissiia muzykovedenii i folklora Soiuza kompozitorov RSFSR.

204 WORKS CITED

———. 1989b. "In Search of Adequate Methods for Analysis of Traditional Music: Towards a Theory of Meaningful Sound Production." Paper given at the Second Soviet-American Meeting of Ethnomusicologists, Wesleyan University, Middletown, CT.

———. 1996. "O muzykalnom voploshchenii olonkho" [On the musical embodiment of olonkho]. In *Moguchii Ėr Sogotokh: Iakutskii geroicheskii ėpos* [The Mighty Ėr Sogotokh: A Yakut heroic epic], edited by V. V. Illarionov, translated by P. E. Efremov, S. P. Oyunsky, and N. V. Emelianov, 42–72. Monuments of Folklore of the Peoples of Siberia and the Far East, vol. 10. Novosibirsk: Nauka.

Alekseyev, N. A. 2008. *Ėtnografiia i folklor narodov Sibirii* [Ethnography and folklore of the people of Siberia]. Novosibirsk: Nauka.

Alekseyev, N. A, N. V. Emelianov, and V. T. Petrov, eds. 1995. *Predaniia, legendy i mify Sakha (Iakutov)* [Stories, legends, and myths of the Sakha (Yakuts)]. Monuments of Folklore of the Peoples of Siberia and the Far East, vol. 9. Novosibirsk: Nauka.

Alieva, Alla. 1996. "Caucasian Epics: Textualist Principles in Publishing." *Oral Tradition* 11 (1): 154–162.

Anderson, Benedict R. 2006. *Imagined Communities: Reflections on the Origin and Spread of Nationalism.* Rev. ed. New York: Verso.

Anikin, Vladimir Prokopevich, and Alla Ivanovna Alieva. 1995. *Skazki narodov Sibiri, Srednei Azii i Kazakhstana* [Tales of the peoples of Siberia, Central Asia, and Kazakhstan]. Moscow: Detskaia literatura.

Arantes, Antonio A. 2013. "Beyond Tradition: Cultural Mediation in the Safeguarding of ICH." In *Anthropological Perspectives on Intangible Cultural Heritage*, edited by Lourdes Arizpe and Cristina Amescua, 39–55. SpringerBriefs in Environment, Security, Development, and Peace, vol. 6. New York: Springer.

Argounova, Tatiana. 1992. *Iakutsko-russkoe dvuiazychie* [Yakut-Russian bilingualism]. Yakutsk: Iakutskii nauchny tsentr SO RAN.

Arizpe, Lourdes, and Cristina Amescua, eds. 2013. *Anthropological Perspectives on Intangible Cultural Heritage.* SpringerBriefs in Environment, Security, Development, and Peace, vol. 6. New York: Springer.

Asafyev, Boris. 2008. *Symphonic Etudes: Portraits of Russian Operas and Ballets.* Translated by David Haas. Lanham, MD: Scarecrow Press.

Ashcroft, Bill, Gareth Griffiths, and Helen Tiffin, eds. 1995. *The Post-Colonial Studies Reader.* New York: Routledge.

Aubert, Laurent. 2007. *The Music of the Other: New Challenges for Ethnomusicology in a Global Age.* Translated by Carla Ribiero. Burlington, VT: Ashgate.

Bahry, Donna. 2002. "Ethnicity and Equality in Post-Communist Economic Transition: Evidence from Russia's Republics." *Europe-Asia Studies* 54 (5): 673–699.

———. 2005. "The New Federalism and the Paradoxes of Regional Sovereignty in Russia." *Comparative Politics* 37 (2): 127–146.

Baily, John. 2009. "Music and Censorship in Afghanistan, 1973–2003." In *Music and the Play of Power in the Middle East, North Africa and Central Asia*, edited by Laudan Nooshin, 143–163. SOAS Musicology Series. Farnham, Surrey: Ashgate.

WORKS CITED 205

Bakan, Michael B. 2012. *World Music: Traditions and Transformations*. 2nd ed. New York: McGraw-Hill.

Balzer, Marjorie Mandelstam. 1991. "Yakut." In *Encyclopedia of World Cultures*, 10 vols., 6: 404–407. Boston: G. K. Hall.

———. 1993. "Dilemmas of the Spirit: Religion and Atheism in the Yakut-Sakha Republic." In *Religious Policy in the Soviet Union*, edited by Sabrina Petra Ramet, 231–251. Cambridge: Cambridge University Press.

———. 1995. *Culture Incarnate: Native Anthropology from Russia*. Armonk, NY: M. E. Sharpe.

———. 1999. *The Tenacity of Ethnicity: A Siberian Saga in Global Perspective*. Princeton, NJ: Princeton University Press.

———. 2005. "Whose Steeple Is Higher? Religious Competition in Siberia." *Religion, State and Society* 33 (1): 57–68.

———. 2006. "The Tension between Might and Rights: Siberians and Energy Developers in Post-Socialist Binds." *Europe-Asia Studies* 58 (4): 567–588.

———. 2010. *Religion and Politics in Russia: A Reader*. Armonk, NY: M. E. Sharpe.

———. 2011. *Shamans, Spirituality, and Cultural Revitalization: Explorations in Siberia and Beyond*. New York: Palgrave Macmillan.

Balzer, Marjorie Mandelstam, and Uliana Alekseyevna Vinokurova. 1996. "Nationalism, Inter-ethnic Relations and Federalism: The Case of the Sakha Republic (Yakutia)." *Europe-Asia Studies* 48 (1): 101–120.

Banti, Giorgio, and Francesco Giannattasio. 2006. "Poetry." In *A Companion to Linguistic Anthropology*, edited by Alessandro Duranti, 290–320. Malden, MA: Blackwell.

Barthel-Boucher, Diane. 2013. *Cultural Heritage and the Challenge of Sustainability*. Walnut Creek, CA: Left Coast Press.

Batalden, Stephan, and Sandra L. Batalden. 1997. *The Newly Independent States of Eurasia: Handbook of Former Soviet Republics*. 2nd ed. Phoenix, AZ: Oryx.

Battaglia, Debbora. 1995. *Rhetorics of Self-Making*. Berkeley: University of California Press.

Bauman, Richard. 1975. "Verbal Art as Performance." *American Anthropologist* 77 (2): 290–311.

Beliaev, Viktor Mikhailovich. 1975. *Central Asian Music: Essays in the History of the Music of the Peoples of the U.S.S.R.* Edited and annotated by Mark Slobin. Translated by Mark and Greta Slobin. Middletown, CT: Wesleyan University Press.

Bendix, Regina. 1997. *In Search of Authenticity: The Formation of Folklore Studies*. Madison: University of Wisconsin Press.

———. 2009. "Heritage between Economy and Politics: An Assessment from the Perspective of Cultural Anthropology." In *Intangible Heritage*, edited by Laurajane Smith and Natsuko Akagawa, 253–269. New York: Routledge.

Bendrups, Dan. 2015. "Transcending Researcher Vulnerability through Applied Ethnomusicology." In *The Oxford Handbook of Applied Ethnomusicology*, edited by Jeff Todd Titon and Svanibor Pettan, 71–92. New York: Oxford University Press.

206 WORKS CITED

Bhabha, Homi K. 2006. "Cultural Diversity and Cultural Differences." In *The Post-Colonial Studies Reader*, edited by Bill Ashcroft, Gareth Griffiths, and Helen Tiffin, 155–157. New York: Routledge.

Biebuyck, Daniel. 1976. "The African Heroic Epic." *Journal of the Folklore Institute* 13 (1): 5–36.

Biliukina, A. A. 2006. "Olonkho i zarozhdenie iakutskogo teatra" [Olonkho and the Birth of Yakut Theater]. In *Olonkho v teatralnom iskusstve: 1 respublikanskaia nauchno-prakticheskaia konferentsiia (tezisy i materialy)* [Olonkho in the theater arts: The first republic-wide scientific-practical conference (theses and materials)], edited by U. A. Vinokurova and L. D. Petrova, 124–125. Yakutsk: Arctic State Institute of Culture and Arts.

Bithell, Caroline, and Juniper Hill, eds. 2014. *The Oxford Handbook of Music Revival*. New York: Oxford University Press.

Blake, Janet. 2009. "UNESCO's 2003 Convention on Intangible Cultural Heritage: The Implications of Community Involvement in 'Safeguarding.'" In *Intangible Heritage*, edited by Laurajane Smith and Natsuko Akagawa, 45–73. New York: Routledge.

Bohlman, Philip V. 1988. *The Study of Folk Music in the Modern World*. Bloomington: Indiana University Press.

Borisov, Yuri. 2014. *Basyrgastaah aattaah Baabe Baatyr*. Yakutsk: Bichik.

Boym, Svetlana. 2001. *The Future of Nostalgia*. New York: Basic Books.

Bragina, D. G. 2005. *Ètnicheskie i ètnokulturnye protsessy v Respublike Sakha (Yakutia): 70–90-e gg. XX v.* [Ethnic and ethnocultural processes in the Republic of Sakha (Yakutia): The 70s–90s of the Twentieth Century]. Novosibirsk: Nauka.

Bremmer, Ian, and Ray Taras, eds. 1993. *Nations and Politics in the Soviet Successor States*. Cambridge: Cambridge University Press.

Briggs, Charles L. 1988. *Competence in Performance: The Creativity of Tradition in Mexicano Verbal Art*. Philadelphia: University of Pennsylvania Press.

Bruner, Edward M. 1986. "Ethnography as Narrative." In *The Anthropology of Experience*, edited by Victor W. Turner and Edward M. Bruner, 139–155. Urbana: University of Illinois Press.

Buchanan, Donna A. 2014. "Doing Ethnomusicology 'Texas-Style': A Musical (Re)turn to Performance." In *Soundscapes from the Americas: Ethnomusicological Essays on the Power, Poetics, and Ontology of Performance*, edited by Donna A. Buchanan, 1–21. SOAS Musicology Series. Burlington, VT: Ashgate.

Bucholtz, Mary, and Kira Hall. 2006. "Language and Identity." In *A Companion to Linguistic Anthropology*, edited by Alessandro Duranti, 369–394. Malden, MA: Blackwell.

Bunkowske, Eugene. 2002. *The Cultural Onion*. St. Paul, MN: Concordia University.

Bychkova Jordan, Bella, and Terry Jordan-Bychkov. 2001. *Siberian Village: Land and Life in the Sakha Republic*. Minneapolis: University of Minnesota Press.

Bynum, David E. 1968. "Themes of the Young Hero in Serbocroatian Oral Epic Tradition." *PMLA* 83 (5): 1296–1303.

———. 1980. "Review of Oinas' *Heroic Epic and Saga*." *Western Folklore* 39 (4): 327–332.

Campbell, Patricia Shehan. 2004. *Teaching Music Globally: Experiencing Music, Expressing Culture*. New York: Oxford University Press.

WORKS CITED 207

Chadwick, Nora K., and Victor Zhirmunsky. 1969. *Oral Epics of Central Asia*. Cambridge: Cambridge University Press.

Chekhorduna, Ekaterina Petrovna. 2014. *Dėgittėr olongkhohut P. A. Chekhordun* [The olonkhosut P. A. Chekhordun]. Yakutsk: Media Holding Yakutia.

Clark, John. 1900. *A History of Epic Poetry (Post-Virgilian)*. Edinburgh: Oliver and Boyd.

Connerton, Paul. 1989. *How Societies Remember*. New York: Cambridge University Press.

Connerty, J. P. 1990. "History's Many Cunning Passages: Paul Ricoeur's *Time and Narrative*." *Poetics Today* 11 (2): 383–403.

Cooley, Timothy J. 2006. "Folk Festival as Modern Ritual in the Polish Tatra Mountains." In *Ethnomusicology: A Contemporary Reader*, edited by Jennifer C. Post, 67–83. New York: Routledge.

Coplan, David. 1985. *In Township Tonight! South Africa's Black City Music and Theatre*. London: Longman.

Coulter, Neil R. 2007. "Music Shift: Evaluating the Vitality and Viability of Music Styles among the Alamblak of Papua New Guinea." PhD diss., Kent State University.

———. 2011. "Assessing Music Shift: Adapting EGIDS for a Papua New Guinea Community." *Language Documentation and Description* 10: 61–81.

Cowdery, James. 2009. "*Kategorie* or *Wertidee*: The Early Years of the International Folk Music Council." In *Music's Intellectual History*, edited by Zdravko Blažeković and Barbara Dobbs Mackenzie, 805–811. New York: Répertoire International de Littérature Musicale.

Crate, Susan A. 2006. "*Ohuokhai*: Sakhas' Unique Integration of Social Meaning and Movement." *Journal of American Folklore* 119 (472): 161–183.

Cruikshank, Julie, and Tatiana Argounova. 2000. "Reinscribing Meaning: Memory and Indigenous Identity in the Sakha Republic, Yakutia." *Arctic Anthropology* 37 (1): 96–119.

Crystal, David. 1992. *An Encyclopedic Dictionary of Language and Languages*. Cambridge, MA: Blackwell.

Csordas, Thomas. 1997. *The Sacred Self: A Cultural Phenomenology of Religious Healing*. Berkeley: University of California Press.

Czekanowska, Anna. 1996. "Continuity and Change in Eastern and Central European Traditional Music." In *Retuning Culture: Musical Changes in Central and Eastern Europe*, edited by Mark Slobin, 92–98. Durham, NC: Duke University Press.

Danilova, A. N. 2014. *Obraz: Zhenshchiny-bogatyrki v iakutskom olonkho* [Image: Female warrior heroes in the Yakut olonkho]. Novosibirsk: Nauka.

Daughtry, J. Martin. 2006. "Russia's New Anthem and the Negotiation of National Identity." In *Ethnomusicology: A Contemporary Reader*, edited by Jennifer C. Post, 243–260. New York: Routledge.

De Vries, Jan. 1963. *Heroic Song and Heroic Legend*. London: Oxford University Press.

DiGiovine, Michael A. 2009. *The Heritage-scape: UNESCO, World Heritage, and Tourism*. Lanham, MD: Lexington Books.

Dordzhieva, Ghilyana, and Liza Vick. 2013. "Olonkho in the Eduard Alekseyev Fieldwork Collection of Harvard University." *GIALens* 7 (3). http://www.gial.edu/documents/gialens/Vol7-3/Larionova-Harris_Alekseyev.pdf. Accessed December 5, 2016.

208 WORKS CITED

Dunn, Stephen P., and Ethel Dunn. 1963. "The Transformation of Economy and Culture in the Soviet North." *Arctic Anthropology* 1 (2): 37–38.

Duranti, Alessandro, ed. 2006. *A Companion to Linguistic Anthropology*. Malden, MA: Blackwell.

Eaton, Katherine Bliss. 2002. *Enemies of the People: The Destruction of Soviet Literary, Theater, and Film Arts in the 1930s*. Evanston, IL: Northwestern University Press.

Egorova, Aelita. 2008. *Kürüng Küllêi*. Berdigestyakh: Ülê küühe.

Emelianov, Nikolai V. 1964. "Pismo A. E. Kulakovskogo E. K. Pekarskomu" [Letter from A. E. Kulakovskii to E. K. Pekarskii]. In *Kulakovskii: Sbornik dokladov k 85-letiiu o dnia rozhdeniia Alekseia Eliseevicha Kulakovskogo* [Collected papers from the 85th anniversary of Aleksei Eliseevich Kulakovskii], edited by G. Basharin, n.p. Yakutsk: Yakutskoe knizhnoe izdatelstvo.

————. 2000. *Siuzhety olonkho o zashchitnikakh plemeni* [Plots of olonkho about guardians of the tribe]. Novosibirsk: Nauka.

Emsheimer, Ernst. 1991. "On the Ideology, Function, Musical Structure and Style of Performance of Siberian Epics." In *Studia Ethnomusicologica Eurasiatica II*, translated by Robert Carroll, 151–168. Stockholm: Royal Swedish Academy of Music.

Errington, Joseph. 2003. "Getting Language Rights: The Rhetorics of Language Endangerment and Loss." *American Anthropologist* 105 (4): 723–732.

Fanning, David. 2005. "Review of Soviet Music and Society under Lenin and Stalin: The Baton and the Sickle." *Music and Letters* 86 (3): 512–513.

Fanon, Franz. 1967. *The Wretched Earth*. Harmondsworth: Penguin.

Feld, Steven. 1990. *Sound and Sentiment: Birds, Weeping, Poetics, and Song in Kaluli Expression*. Philadelphia: University of Pennsylvania Press.

————. 1996. "Waterfalls of Song: An Acoustemology of Place Resounding in Bosavi, Papua New Guinea." In *Senses of Place*, edited by Steven Feld and Keith H. Basso, 91–135. Santa Fe, NM: School of American Research Press.

Feld, Steven, Aaron A. Fox, Thomas Porcello, and David Samuels. 2006. "Vocal Anthropology: From the Music of Language to the Language of Song." In *A Companion to Linguistic Anthropology*, edited by Alessandro Duranti, 321–325. Malden, MA: Blackwell.

Fenn, John, and Jeff Todd Titon. 2003. "A Conversation with Jeff Todd Titon." *Folklore Forum* 34 (1/2): 119–131.

Finnegan, Ruth H. 1978. *A World Treasury of Oral Poetry*. Bloomington: Indiana University Press.

————. 1996. *Oral Traditions and the Verbal Arts: A Guide to Research Practices*. New York: Routledge.

————. 2005. *Communicating: The Multiple Modes of Human Interconnection*. New York: Routledge.

————. 2007. *The Oral and Beyond: Doing Things with Words in Africa*. Chicago: University of Chicago Press.

Fishman, Joshua A. 1991. *Reversing Language Shift: Theoretical and Empirical Foundations of Assistance to Threatened Languages*. Clevedon, UK: Multilingual Matters.

Foley, John Miles. 1995. *The Singer of Tales in Performance*. Bloomington: Indiana University Press.

WORKS CITED 209

Forsyth, James. 1992. *A History of the Peoples of Siberia: Russia's North Asian Colony, 1581–1990*. Cambridge: Cambridge University Press.

Freland, Francois-Xavier. 2009. *Saisir l'immatériel: Un regard sur le patrimoine vivant* [Capturing the intangible: A look at a living heritage]. Paris: UNESCO.

Frigyesi, Judit. 1993. "Preliminary Thoughts toward the Study of Music without Clear Beat: The Example of 'Flowing Rhythm' in Jewish Nusah."*Asian Music* 24 (2): 59–88.

Gabysheva, L. L. 2009. *Folklorny tekst: Semioticheskie mekhanizmy ustnoi pamiati* [The folklore text: Semiotic mechanisms of oral memory]. Novosibirsk: Nauka.

Geertz, Clifford. 1973. "Thick Description: Towards an Interpretive Theory of Culture." In *The Interpretation of Cultures: Selected Essays*, 3–30. New York: Basic Books.

Gogolev, A. I. 1992a. "Basic Stages of the Formation of the Yakut People." *Anthropology and Archeology of Eurasia* 31 (2): 63–69.

———. 1992b. "Dualism in the Traditional Beliefs of the Yakuts." *Anthropology and Archeology of Eurasia* 31 (2): 70–84.

———. 1992c. "Several Features of the Yakut Ethnoculture." *Anthropology and Archeology of Eurasia* 31 (2): 10–18.

Govorov, Dmitrii. 1938 [2010]. *Nepobedimy Müljü Böghö* [The Invincible Müljü Böghö] (Russian translation). Yakutsk: Bichik. http://iolonkho.s-vfu.ru/archive/node/5. Accessed December 5, 2016.

Grant, Catherine. 2014. *Music Endangerment: How Language Maintenance Can Help*. New York: Oxford University Press.

———. 2015. "Endangered Musical Heritage as a Wicked Problem." *International Journal of Heritage Studies* 21 (7): 629–641.

Grigorian, Grant Abramovich. 1957. "Muzykalnaia kultura Iakutskoi ASSR" [Musical culture of the Yakut ASSR]. In *Muzykalnaia kultura avtonomnykh respublik RSFSR* [Musical culture of the autonomous republics of the RSFSR], edited by G. I. Litinskii, 331–348. Moscow: Muzgiz.

Gunderson, L. H., C. R. Allen, and C. S. Holling. 2009. *Foundations of Ecological Resilience*. Washington, DC: Island Press.

Harris, Robin P. 2012a. "Sitting 'under the Mouth': Decline and Revitalization in the Sakha Epic Tradition Olonkho." PhD diss., University of Georgia Athens.

———. 2012b. "Siberia: At the Centre of the World—Music, Dance and Ritual in Sakha-Yakutia and Buryatia (2008)." Recording review. *The World of Music*, n.s., 1 (2): 157–159.

———. 2013. "Introduction to Festschrift for Eduard Alekseyev." *GIALens* 7 (3). http://www.gial.edu/documents/gialens/Vol7-3/Harris_IntroductiontoFestschrift.pdf. Accessed December 5, 2016.

———. 2015. "Psikhologicheskie aspekty raboty s nositeliami folklornikh traditsii (po materialam E. Ye. Alekseyeva)" [Psychological aspects of work with tradition bearers (based on the material of E. Ye. Alekseyev)]. Paper presented at the international scientific conference "Rol lichnosti narodnogo pevtsa v sokhranenii natsionalnogo svoeobraziia v kontekste kultur narodov mira" [The Role of the Personality of Folk Singers in the Preservation of National Distinctiveness in the Context of the Cultures of the People of the World], St. Petersburg, Russian Federation, December 14. An electronic version of the paper, with recordings, is available at http://eduard.alekseyev.org/guests16.html.

210   WORKS CITED

Harvilahti, Lauri. 1996. "Epos and National Identity: Transformations and Incarnations." *Oral Tradition* 11 (1): 37–49.

———. 2000. "Altai Oral Epic." *Oral Tradition* 15 (2): 215–229.

Hechter, Michael. 1975. *Internal Colonialism: The Celtic Fringe in British National Development.* London: Routledge and Kegan Paul.

Hiebert, Paul G. 2008. *Transforming Worldviews: An Anthropological Understanding of How People Change.* Grand Rapids, MI: Baker Academic.

Hill, Juniper. 2014. "Innovation and Cultural Activism through the Reimagined Pasts of Finnish Music Revivals." In *The Oxford Handbook of Music Revival*, edited by Caroline Bithell and Juniper Hill, 393–417. New York: Oxford University Press.

Hill, Juniper, and Caroline Bithell. 2014. "An Introduction to Music Revival as Concept, Cultural Process, and Medium of Change." In *The Oxford Handbook of Music Revival*, edited by Caroline Bithell and Juniper Hill, 3–42. New York: Oxford University Press.

Hobsbawm, E. J. 1990. *Nations and Nationalism since 1780: Programme, Myth, Reality.* 2nd ed. Cambridge: Cambridge University Press.

Howard, Keith. 2004. "Review of Voices from the Straw Mat: Toward an Ethnography of Korean Story Telling by Chan E. Park." *Bulletin of the School of Oriental and African Studies, University of London* 67 (1): 124–126.

———. 2012. *Music as Intangible Cultural Heritage: Policy, Ideology, and Practice in the Preservation of East Asian Traditions.* Burlington, VT: Ashgate.

———. 2014. "Reviving Korean Identity through Intangible Cultural Heritage." In *The Oxford Handbook of Music Revival*, edited by Caroline Bithell and Juniper Hill, 135–159. New York: Oxford University Press.

Hunt, David. 2012. *Legends of the Caucasus.* London: SAQI Books.

Hunter, Justin, Man Yang, Da Lin, and Robin Harris. 2011. "Perceiving the Intangible: Critical Perspectives of Intangible Cultural Heritage in Four Asian Contexts." Panel of four papers chaired by Ricardo Trimillos at the Society for Ethnomusicology (SEM)/ Congress on Research and Dance (CORD) 2011 Joint Annual Meeting, Philadelphia, PA, November 19.

Ignatieva, V. B., E. N. Romanova, O. V. Osipova, D. M. Vinokurova, and Yu. I. Zhegusov. 2013. *Olonkho i obshchestvo: Tezaurus sovremennykh ètnokulturnykh predstavlenii o geroicheskom èpose naroda Sakha* [Olonkho and society: Thesaurus of modern ethnocultural conceptions of the heroic epos of the Sakha]. Yakutsk: FGBUN Institute of Humanitarian Research and Problems of the Minority Peoples of the North, Siberian Branch of the Russian Academy of Sciences, Sakha Republic (Yakutia).

Illarionov, V. V., ed. 1996. *Moguchii Èr Sogotokh: Iakutskii geroicheskii èpos* [The Mighty Èr Sogotokh: A Yakut heroic epic]. Translated by P. E. Efremov, S. P. Oyunsky, and N. V. Emelianov. Monuments of Folklore of the Peoples of Siberia and the Far East, vol. 10. Novosibirsk: Nauka.

Illarionov, V. V., U. H. Diakonova, S. D. Mukhoplëva, et al. 2008. *Iakutskie narodnye skazki* [Yakut folk tales]. Monuments of Folklore of the Peoples of Siberia and the Far East, vol. 27. Novosibirsk: Nauka.

WORKS CITED   211

Illarionov, Vasilii V. 2013. "The Performance Tradition of the Sakha Heroic Epic Olonkho and Its Transformations in Modern Life." *GIALens* 7 (3). http://www.gial.edu/documents/gialens/Vol7-3/Illarionov_PerformanceTradition.pdf. Accessed December 5, 2016.

Illarionova, Nurguyana. 2014. "Theatrical Interpretation of the Yakut Heroic Epos (Olonkho)." Presentation at Harvard University's Loeb Music Library, Cambridge, MA, September 22.

Impey, Angela. 2006. "Culture, Conservation, and Community Reconstruction: Explorations in Advocacy Ethnomusicology and Participatory Action Research in Northern KwaZulu Natal." In *Ethnomusicology: A Contemporary Reader*, edited by Jennifer C. Post, 401–411. New York: Routledge.

Ivanov, V. N., ed. 2007. *Iakutiia: Istoriko-kulturny atlas* [Yakutia: Historical-cultural atlas]. Moscow: Government of the Republic of Sakha (Yakutia) and the Institute of Humanitarian Research of the Republic of Sakha.

Ivanov, V. N., E. N. Romanova, and A. E. Pakharova, eds. 2006. *Ustoichivoe razvitie stran arktiki i severnykh regionov Rossiiskoi Federatsii v kontekste obrazovaniia, nauki i kultury: Tezisy dokladov mezhdunarodnogo foruma* [Stable development of the arctic regions of the Russian Federation in the context of education, science, and culture: Theses of presentations at the international forum] (Yakutsk, July 24–25, 2006). Yakutsk: IGI RS(Y).

Jang, Yeonok. 2001. "P'ansori Performance Style: Audience Responses and Singers' Perspectives." *British Journal of Ethnomusicology* 10 (2): 99–121.

Jansen, Jan. 2001. "The Sunjata Epic: The Ultimate Version." *Research in African Literatures* 32 (1): 14–46.

Jansen, Jan, and Henk M. J. Maier, eds. 2004. *Epic Adventures: Heroic Narrative in the Oral Performance Traditions of Four Continents*. New Brunswick, NJ: Transaction.

Jochelson, Waldemar. 1933. *The Yakut*. Anthropological Papers of the American Museum of Natural History, vol. 33, pt. 2. New York: American Museum of Natural History.

Johnson, John William. 1980. "Yes, Virginia, There Is an Epic in Africa." *Research in African Literatures* 11 (3): 308–326.

———. 1992. *The Epic of Son-Jara: A West African Tradition*. Bloomington: Indiana University Press.

Josephson, Paul R. 2014. *The Conquest of the Russian Arctic*. Cambridge, MA: Harvard University Press.

Kempton, Daniel R. 1996. "The Republic of Sakha (Yakutia): The Evolution of Centre-Periphery Relations in the Russian Federation." *Europe-Asia Studies* 48 (4): 587–613.

Khazanov, Anatoly. 1993. "Yakutian Nationalism in a Search for Identities." In *After the USSR: Ethnicity, Nationalism, and Politics in the Commonwealth of Independent States*, 175–191. Madison: University of Wisconsin Press.

Kidula, Jean Ngoya. 2013. "Of Spirituals and Songs of the Spirit: Exploring the 'Transfer of Function' in the Musicking of African American and Kenyan Christians." In *Resiliency and Distinction: Beliefs, Endurance and Creativity in the Musical Arts of Continental and Diasporic Africa; A Festschrift in Honor of Jacqueline Cogdell DjeDje*, edited by Kimasi L. Browne and Jean N. Kidula, 289–319. Richmond, CA: Music Research Institute.

212 WORKS CITED

Killick, Andrew. 2003. "Road Test for a New Model: Korean Musical Narrative and Theater in Comparative Context." *Ethnomusicology* 47 (2): 180–204.

Kim, Seong-Nae. 2004. "Shamanic Epics and Narrative Construction of Identity on Cheju Island." *Asian Folklore Studies* 63 (1): 57–78.

Kirby, E. Stuart. 1980. "Communism in Yakutia: The First Decade (1918–1928)." *Slavic Studies* 25: 27–42.

Kirshenblatt-Gimblett, Barbara. 1995. "Theorizing Heritage." *Ethnomusicology* 39 (3): 367–380.

———. 1998. *Destination Culture: Tourism, Museums, and Heritage*. Los Angeles: University of California Press.

———. 2004. "Intangible Heritage as Metacultural Production." *Museum International* 56 (1–2): 52–65.

Knight, Nathaniel. 2004. "Ethnography, Russian and Soviet." In *Encyclopedia of Russian History*. http://www.encyclopedia.com/doc/1G2-3404100416.html. Accessed December 5, 2016.

Kosacheva, Rimma. 1990. "Traditional Music in the Context of the Socio-political Development in the USSR." *Yearbook for Traditional Music* 22: 17–19.

Krader, Barbara. 1990. "Recent Achievements in Soviet Ethnomusicology, with Remarks on Russian Terminology." *Yearbook for Traditional Music* 22: 1–16.

Krueger, John R. 1962. *Yakut Manual: Area Handbook, Grammar, Graded Reader and Glossary*. Uralic and Altaic Series, vol. 21. Bloomington: Indiana University Publications.

Kruks, Sergei. 2004. "The Latvian Epic *Lāčplēsis*: *Passe-partout* Ideology, Traumatic Imagination of Community." *Journal of Folklore Research* 41 (1): 1–32.

Kulakovskii, Aleksei. 1910 [1990]. *Snovidenie shamana: Stikhotvoreniia, poèmy* [The dream of the shaman: Verses and poems]. Moscow: Khudozhestvennaia literatura.

Kulikova, Anna Nikolaevna. 2009. "Sovremennye ètnokulturnye i ètnoreligioznye protsessy v Iakutii: Filosofsko-religiovedcheskii analiz" [Modern ethnocultural and ethnoreligious processes in Yakutia: A philosophical-religious analysis]. PhD diss., Amur State University.

Kuutma, Kristen. 2013. "Concepts and Contingencies in Heritage Politics." In *Anthropological Perspectives on Intangible Cultural Heritage*, edited by Lourdes Arizpe and Cristina Amescua, 1–15. SpringerBriefs in Environment, Security, Development and Peace, vol. 6. New York: Springer.

Labadi, Sophia. 2013. *UNESCO, Cultural Heritage, and Outstanding Universal Value: Value-Based Analyses of the World Heritage and Intangible Cultural Heritage Conventions*. Lanham, MD: AltaMira Press.

Lake, Philip S. 2013. "Resistance, Resilience and Restoration." *Ecological Management and Restoration* 14 (1): 20–24.

Larionova, Anna S. 2000. *Dègèrèn yrya: Pesënnaia lirika iakutov* [Dègèrèn yrya: Lyrical song of the Yakuts]. Novosibirsk: Nauka.

———. 2004. *Verbalnoe i muzykalnoe v iakutskom dièrètii yrya* [Verbal and musical in Yakut dièrètii song]. Novosibirsk: Nauka.

WORKS CITED   213

———. 2010. "A Living Epic Tradition from Siberia: The Yakut Olonkho." Translated from Russian by Robin Harris. Lecture presented at Harvard University, Cambridge, MA, April 19.

———. 2013. "Eduard Alekseyev: One of the Founders of Sakha Ethnomusicology." *GIALens* 7 (3). http://www.gial.edu/documents/gialens/Vol7-3/Larionova-Harris_Alekseyev.pdf. Accessed December 5, 2016.

Lassiter, Luke Eric. 2005. *The Chicago Guide to Collaborative Ethnography*. Chicago: University of Chicago Press.

Latour, Bruno. 1993. *We Have Never Been Modern*. Translated by Catherine Porter. Harlow, England: Pearson Education.

Lee, Richard E. 2012. *The Longue Durée and World Systems Analysis*. Albany: State University of New York.

Leete, Art. 2005. "Religious Revival as Reaction to the Hegemonization of Power in Siberia in the 1920s to 1940s." *Asian Folklore Studies* 64 (2): 233–245.

Leete, Art, and R. Paul Firnhaber, eds. 2004. *Shamanism in the Interdisciplinary Context*. Boca Raton, FL: BrownWalker Press.

Levin, Theodore. 1984. "The Music and Tradition of the Bukharan Shashmaqam in Soviet Uzbekistan." PhD diss., Princeton University.

———. 1993. "The Reterritorialization of Culture in the New Central Asian States: A Report from Uzbekistan." *Yearbook for Traditional Music* 25: 51–59.

———. 1996. "Dmitri Pokrovsky and the Russian Folk Music Revival Movement." In *Retuning Culture: Musical Changes in Central and Eastern Europe*, edited by Mark Slobin, 14–36. Durham, NC: Duke University Press.

———. 1999. *The Hundred Thousand Fools of God: Musical Travels in Central Asia (and Queens, New York)*. Bloomington: Indiana University Press.

———. 2002. "Making Marxist-Leninist Music in Uzbekistan." In *Music and Marx*, edited by Regula Qureshi, 190–203. New York: Routledge.

———. 2006. *Where Rivers and Mountains Sing: Sound, Music, and Nomadism in Tuva and Beyond*. Bloomington: Indiana University Press.

Levin, Theodore, Saida Daukeyeva, and Elmira Köchümkulova, eds. 2016. *The Music of Central Asia*. Bloomington: Indiana University Press.

Levine, Victoria Lindsay. 2014. "Declaiming Choctaw and Chickasaw Cultural Identity through Music Revival." In *The Oxford Handbook of Music Revival*, edited by Caroline Bithell and Juniper Hill, 300–322. New York: Oxford University Press.

Lewis, C. S. 1961. *A Preface to Paradise Lost*. New York: Oxford University Press.

Lewis, M. Paul, and Gary F. Simons. 2010. "Assessing Endangerment: Expanding Fishman's GIDS." *Revue roumaine de linguistique* 55 (2): 103–120.

Lewis, M. Paul, Gary F. Simons, and Charles D. Fennig, eds. 2014. *Ethnologue: Languages of the World*. 17th ed. 3 vols. Dallas, TX: SIL International.

Lincoln, W. Bruce. 1994. *The Conquest of a Continent: Siberia and the Russians*. Ithaca, NY: Cornell University Press.

Lindquist, Galina. 2006. *The Quest for the Authentic Shaman: Multiple Meanings of Shamanism on a Siberian Journey*. Uppsala: Almqvist and Wiksell International.

214 WORKS CITED

Lord, A. B. 2000. *The Singer of Tales.* 2nd ed. Cambridge, MA: Harvard University Press.

Louis, Rene. 1958. "Qu'est-ce que l'épopée vivante?" *La Table Ronde* 132: 9–17.

Lukina, A. G. 2005. *Traditsionnye tantsy Sakha: Idei, obrazy, leksika* [Traditional dances of the Sakha: Ideas, imagery, terms]. Edited by A. I. Gogolev. Novosibirsk: Nauka.

Lutgendorf, Philip. 1989. "The View from the Ghats: Traditional Exegesis of a Hindu Epic." *Journal of Asian Studies* 48 (2): 272–288.

Mákharov, E. M., ed. 2000. *Olonkho—dukhovnoe nasledie naroda sakha* [Olonkho—the cultural heritage of the Sakha people]. Yakutsk: IGI AN RS (Ya).

Maltsev, Misha, and Keith Howard. 2008. *Siberia—At the Centre of the World: Music, Dance, and Ritual in Sakha-Yakutia and Buryatia.* DVD set, SOASIS DVD6 and SOASIS DVD7. London: SOAS, University of London, and AHRC Research Centre for Cross-Cultural Music and Dance Performance.

Mazo, Margarita. 1994. "Wedding Laments in North Russian Villages." In *Music-Cultures in Contact: Convergences and Collisions*, edited by Margaret J. Kartomi and Stephen Blum, 21–39. Basel: Gordon and Breach.

———. 1996. "Change as Confirmation of Continuity as Experienced by Russian Molokans." In *Retuning Culture: Musical Changes in Central and Eastern Europe*, edited by Mark Slobin, 254–275. Durham, NC: Duke University Press.

McGuire, James. 1999. "Butchering Heroism? *Sunjata* and the Negotiation of Postcolonial Mande Identity in Diabaté's *Le Boucher de Kouta.*" In *In Search of Sunjata: The Mande Oral Epic as History, Literature and Performance*, edited by Ralph A. Austen, 253–273. Bloomington: Indiana University Press.

Melancon, Michael. 2004. "Lena Goldfields Massacre." *Encyclopedia of Russian History.* http://www.encyclopedia.com/doc/1G2-3404100745.html. Accessed December 5, 2016.

Merchant, Tanya. 2014. "Revived Musical Practices within Uzbekistan's Evolving National Project." In *The Oxford Handbook of Music Revival*, edited by Caroline Bithell and Juniper Hill, 252–276. New York: Oxford University Press.

Moore, David Chioni. 2001. "Is the Post- in Postcolonial the Post- in Post-Soviet? Toward a Global Postcolonial Critique." *PMLA* 116 (1): 111–128.

Mori, Masaki. 1997. *Epic Grandeur: Toward a Comparative Poetics of World Epic.* Albany: State University of New York Press.

Moseley, Christopher, ed. 2010. *Atlas of the World's Languages in Danger.* 3rd ed. Paris: UNESCO. http://www.unesco.org/culture/languages-atlas/en/atlasmap.html. Accessed January 17, 2017.

Mukhoplëva, S. D. 1993. *Iakutskoe obriadovye pesni (sistema zhanrov)* [Yakut ceremonial songs: A system of genres]. Novosibirsk: Nauka.

Muller, Carol Ann. 2014. "Musical Remembrance, Exile, and the Remaking of South African Jazz (1960–1979)." In *The Oxford Handbook of Music Revival*, edited by Caroline Bithell and Juniper Hill, 644–665. New York: Oxford University Press.

Nakhodkina, Alina. 2014. "Problems of (Un)translatability in the Yakut Epic Text Olonkho." *Journal of Siberian Federal University* 2 (7): 273–286.

Naroditskaya, Inna. 2002. *Song from the Land of Fire: Continuity and Change in Azerbaijanian Mugham.* New York: Routledge.

WORKS CITED 215

Nas, Peter J. M. 2002. "Masterpieces of Oral and Intangible Culture: Reflections on the UNESCO World Heritage List." *Current Anthropology* 43 (1): 139–148.

Naugle, David K. 2002. *Worldview: The History of a Concept*. Grand Rapids, MI: Eerdmans.

Nekliudov, S. Iu. and Iu. I. Sheikin. 1993. *Kyys Dėbiliiė: Iakutskii geroicheskii ėpos* [*Kyys Dėbiliiė*: A Yakut heroic epic]. Monuments of Folklore of the Peoples of Siberia and the Far East, vol. 4. Novosibirsk: Nauka.

Nketia, J. H. Kwabena. 1974. *The Music of Africa*. New York: W. W. Norton.

Noyes, Dorothy. 2016. "Humble Theory." In *Grand Theory in Folkloristics*, edited by Lee Haring, 71–77. Bloomington: Indiana University Press.

Oinas, Felix J. 1978. *Heroic Epic and Saga: An Introduction to the World's Great Folk Epics*. Bloomington: Indiana University Press.

Okladnikov, A. P. 1970. "The Yakut Epos (*Olonkho*) and Its Connections with the South." In *Yakutia before Its Incorporation into the Russian State*, edited by Henry N. Michael, 263–286. Anthropology of the North: Translations from Russian Sources, no. 8. Montreal: McGill-Queen's University Press. Original Russian version "Iakutskii ėpos (olonkho) i ego sviaz s iugom," in *Iakutiia do prisoedineniia k russkomu gosudarstvu*, 257–277. Moscow: Izd-vo Akademii nauk SSSR, 1955.

Orosina, Nadezhda Anatolevna. 2015. "Tattinskaia lokalnaia traditsiia Iakutskogo ėposa olonkho: Formy bytovaniia, osnovnye obrazy i motivy" [The Tatta local tradition of the Yakut epos olonkho: Cultural forms, principal examples, and motifs]. PhD diss., Yakut Folklore Department, Institute of Humanitarian Research and Problems of the Minority Peoples of the North (IGI), Siberian Branch of the Russian Academy of Sciences, Sakha Republic (Yakutia).

Osipova, Olga Valerevna. 2011. "Geroicheskii ėpos kak ėlement ėtnicheskoi identifikatsii sakha: Otsenka v obshchestvennom mnenii" [Heroic epos as an element of ethnic identification of the Sakha: An appraisal of societal opinions]. *Arktika i Sever* 4. http://narfu.ru/upload/iblock/3e8/09.pdf. Accessed December 14, 2011.

Oushakine, Serguei. 2000. "In the State of Post-Soviet Aphasia: Symbolic Development in Contemporary Russia." *Europe-Asia Studies* 52 (6): 991–1016.

Oyunsky, P. A. 1975. *Nurgun Botur Stremitelny: Iakutskii geroicheskii ėpos—olonkho* [Nurgun Botur the Swift: The Yakut heroic epos of olonkho]. Translated into Russian by Vladimir Derzhavin. Illustrated by Ė. Sivtsev, V. Karamzin, and I. Koriakin. Yakutsk: Yakutskoe knizhnoe izdatelstvo.

———. 1997. *Nurgun Botur Stremitelny: Iakutskii geroicheskii ėpos—olonkho* [Nurgun Botur the Swift: The Yakut heroic epos of olonkho]. Performed by Gavriil Kolesov. Recorded in 1962 by Leningradskaia studiia gramzapisi. Remastered in 1997 by Studiia Poligram [KYDYK].

Oyunsky, Platon A. 2014. *Olonkho: Nurgun Botur the Swift*. English translation supervised by Alina Nakhodkina. Edited by Vasily Ivanov and Svetlana Yegorova-Johnstone. Kent, UK: Renaissance Books.

Park, Chan E. 2000. "'Authentic Audience' in P'ansori, a Korean Storytelling Tradition." *Journal of American Folklore* 113 (449): 270–287.

216   WORKS CITED

————. 2003. *Voices from the Straw Mat: Toward an Ethnography of Korean Story Singing*. Honolulu: University of Hawai'i Press.

Peers, Eleanor. 2010. "Print, Power and Personhood: Newspapers and Ethnic Identity in East Siberia." PhD thesis, University of Cambridge.

————. 2013. "Sacred Missions and National Identities: Modernist Teleology and Personhood in Siberian Religious Revivalism (The Case of Ysyakh Summer Festival)." *Interstitio: East European Review of Historical and Cultural Anthropology* 5 (1–2): 92–111.

————. 2015. "Music and Modernity in North Siberia: How Do Pop Stars Get On with Area Spirits?" Paper given at the Social Anthropology Seminar, Aberdeen University, Scotland, December 10.

Pegg, Carole. 2001. *Mongolian Music, Dance, and Oral Narrative: Performing Diverse Identities*. Seattle: University of Washington Press.

Pettan, Svanibor. 2015. "Applied Ethnomusicology in the Global Arena." In *The Oxford Handbook of Applied Ethnomusicology*, edited by Jeff Todd Titon and Svanibor Pettan, 29–53. New York: Oxford University Press.

Pihl, Marshall R. 1993. "What Is *P'ansori?*" *Chicago Review* 39 (3/4): 227–230.

————. 1994. *The Korean Singer of Tales*. Cambridge, MA: Harvard University Press.

Pistrick, Eckehard. 2015. *Performing Nostalgia: Migration Culture and Creativity in South Albania*. SOAS Musicology Series. Burlington, VT: Ashgate.

Post, Jennifer C, ed. 2006. *Ethnomusicology: A Contemporary Reader*. New York: Routledge.

Pukhov, I. V. 1962. *Iakutskii geroicheskii èpos olonkho: Osnovnye obrazy* [The Yakut heroic epos of olonkho: Quintessential images]. Moscow: Izd-vo Akademii nauk SSSR.

Pukhov, I. V., and G. U. Ergis. 1985. *Stroptivy Kulun Kullustuur* [Obstinate Kulun Kullustuur]. Edited by A. A. Petrosyan. Èpos narodov SSSR [Epics of the peoples of the USSR]. Novosibirsk: Nauka.

Putilov, B. N. 1997. *Èpicheskoe skazitelstvo: Tipologiia i ètnicheskaia spetsifika* [Epic storytelling: Typology and ethnic particularities]. Moscow: Izdatelstvo Vostochnaia literatura.

Rapport, Evan. 2016. "Prosodic Rhythm in Jewish Sacred Music: Examples from the Persian-Speaking World." *Asian Music* 47 (1): 64–102

Reichl, Karl. 1989. "Formulaic Diction in Kazakh Epic Poetry." *Oral Tradition* 4 (3): 360–381.

————. 1992. *Turkic Oral Epic Poetry: Traditions, Forms, Poetic Structure*. New York: Garland Reference Library of the Humanities.

————. 2016. "Oral Epics into the Twenty- First Century: The Case of the Kyrgyz Epic *Manas*." *Journal of American Folklore* 129 (513): 327–344.

Ren, Guo-wei. 2010. "Text, Genre and Multi-Genre." *Studies in Literature and Language* 1 (7): 82–88.

Renan, Ernest. 1990. "What Is a Nation?" Translated and annotated by Martin Thom. In *Narration and Nation*, edited by Homi K. Bhabha, 8–22. New York: Routledge.

Republic of Sakha. 2007. Law of the Republic of Sakha (Yakutia) on the State Program for the Preservation, Study, and Propagation of the Yakut Heroic Epos Olonkho for 2007–2015. Law No. 436-3 N 887-111 (in Russian), passed March 15. http://old.lawru.info/legal2/se2/pravo2055/index.htm; http://laws-2007.narod.ru/doc407/index.htm. Accessed September 12, 2016.

WORKS CITED 217

Reshetnikova, Aisa P. 1993. "Muzyka iakutskikh olonkho" [The music of the Yakut olonkho]. In *Kyys Débiliiė: Iakutskii geroicheskii ėpos* [*Kyys Débiliiė*: A Yakut heroic epic], edited by S. Iu. Nekliudov and Iu. I. Sheikin, 26–69. Monuments of Folklore of the Peoples of Siberia and the Far East, vol. 4. Novosibirsk: Nauka.

———. 2005. *Fond siuzhetnykh motivov i muzyka olonkho v ėtnograficheskom kontekste* [Collection of plot motifs and music of olonkho in ethnographic context]. Yakutsk: Bichik.

Rethman, Petra. 1997. "*Chto delat*? Ethnography in the Post-Soviet Cultural Context." *American Anthropologist* 99 (4): 770–774.

Rice, Timothy. 1987. "Toward the Remodeling of Ethnomusicology." *Ethnomusicology* 31 (3): 469–488.

———. 2003. "Time, Place, and Metaphor in Musical Experience and Ethnography." *Ethnomusicology* 47 (2): 151–179.

Rice, Timothy, James Porter, and Chris Goertzen, eds. 2000. "Russia." In *Garland Encyclopedia of World Music*, vol. 8: *Europe*, 785–820. New York: Routledge.

Ricoeur, Paul. 1984. *Time and Narrative*. Vol. 1. Translated by Kathleen McLaughlin and David Pellauer. Chicago: University of Chicago Press. Originally published as *Temps et récit* (Paris: Ed. du Seuil, 1983).

Robbek, Vasili. 1998. "Language Situation in the Sakha Republic (Yakutia)." In *Bicultural Education in the North: Ways of Preserving and Enhancing Indigenous Peoples' Languages and Traditional Knowledge*, edited by Erich Kasten, 113–122. Münster: Waxmann Verlag.

Romanova, Ekaterina Nazarovna, and Vanda Borisovna Ignatieva. 2012. "The Yakut [Sakha] National Festival Ysyakh in Transition: Historical Myth, Ethnocultural Image, and Contemporary Festival Narrative." *Anthropology and Archeology of Eurasia* 50 (4): 42–55.

Rubin, David C. 1995. *Memory in Oral Traditions*. New York: Oxford University Press.

Said, Edward W. 1994. *Culture and Imperialism*. New York: Knopf.

Saurman, Todd W. 2012. "Singing for Survival in the Highlands of Cambodia: Tampuan Revitalization of Music as Cultural Reflexivity." In *Music and Minorities in Ethnomusicology: Challenges and Discourses from Three Continents*, edited by Ursula Hemetek, 95–103. Vienna: Institut für Volksmusikforschung und Ethnomusikologie.

Schechner, Richard. 1983. *Performative Circumstances, from the Avant Garde to Ramlila*. Calcutta: Seagull Books.

Schiffman, Harold. 2002. "Language Policies in the Former Soviet Union." Class handout. http://ccat.sas.upenn.edu/~haroldfs/540/handouts/ussr/soviet2.html. Accessed December 5, 2016.

Schippers, Huib. 2015. "Applied Ethnomusicology and Intangible Cultural Heritage: Understanding 'Ecosystems of Music' as a Tool for Sustainability." In *The Oxford Handbook of Applied Ethnomusicology*, edited by Jeff Todd Titon and Svanibor Pettan, 134–156. New York: Oxford University Press.

Schippers, Huib, and Catherine Grant, eds. 2016. *Sustainable Futures for Music Cultures: An Ecological Perspective*. New York: Oxford University Press.

Schrag, Brian. 2005. "How Bamiléké Music-Makers Create Culture in Cameroon." PhD diss., University of California, Los Angeles.

218   WORKS CITED

———. 2013a. *Creating Local Arts Together: A Manual to Help Communities Reach Their Kingdom Goals*. James Krabill, general editor. Pasadena, CA: William Carey Library.

———. 2013b. "How Artists Create Enduring Traditions." In *Resiliency and Distinction: Beliefs, Endurance and Creativity in the Musical Arts of Continental and Diasporic Africa; A Festschrift in Honor of Jacqueline Cogdell DjeDje*, edited by Kimasi L. Browne and Jean N. Kidula, 415–444. Richmond, CA: MRI Press.

———. 2015a. "A Triple Insider's Take on Arts Therapy, Arts-Based Community Development, and Huntington's Disease." *Voices: A World Forum for Music Therapy* 15 (3). https://voices.no/index.php/voices/article/view/822. Accessed December 5, 2016.

———. 2015b. "Motivations and Methods for Encouraging Artists in Longer Traditions." In *The Oxford Handbook of Applied Ethnomusicology*, edited by Jeff Todd Titon and Svanibor Pettan, 317–347. New York: Oxford University Press.

———. 2016. "Music in the Newer Churches." In *The Wiley-Blackwell Companion to World Christianity*, edited by Lamin Sanneh and Michael McClymond, 359–367. Hoboken, NJ: Wiley Blackwell.

Seeger, Anthony. 2009a. "Lessons Learned from the ICTM (NGO) Evaluation of the Masterpieces of the Oral and Intangible Heritage, 2001–2005." In *Intangible Heritage*, edited by Laurajane Smith and Natsuko Akagawa, 112–128. London: Routledge.

———. 2009b. "Towards an Ecology of Musical Practice." Paper presented at the 40th Annual World Conference of the International Council for Traditional Music, Durban, South Africa July 1–8.

Seroshevskii, Vatslav Leonidovich. 1896. *Iakuty: Opyt ètnograficheskogo issledovaniia* [The Yakuts: An experiment in ethnographic research]. 2nd ed., Moscow: Rossiiskaia politicheskaia èntsiklopediia (ROSSPEN), 1993.

Service, Robert. 2009. *A History of Modern Russia: From Tsarism to the Twenty-First Century*. 3rd ed. Cambridge, MA: Harvard University Press.

Seydou, Christiane, and Brunhilde Biebuyck. 1983. "A Few Reflections on Narrative Structures of Epic Texts: A Case Example of Bambara and Fulani Epics." *Research in African Literatures* 14 (3): 312–331.

Shay, Anthony. 2014. "Reviving the Reluctant Art of Iranian Dance in Iran and in the American Diaspora." In *The Oxford Handbook of Music Revival*, edited by Caroline Bithell and Juniper Hill, 618–643. New York: Oxford University Press.

Sheehy, Daniel. 1992. "A Few Notions about Philosophy and Strategy in Applied Ethnomusicology." *Ethnomusicology* 36 (3): 323–336.

Sheikin, Yuri. 2002. *Istoriia muzykalnoi kultury narodov Sibiri: Sravnitelno-istoricheskoe issledovanie* [History of the musical cultures of the people of Siberia: A comparative-historical study]. Moscow: Vostochnaia literatura.

Shelemay, Kay Kaufman. 2008. "The Ethnomusicologist, Ethnographic Method, and the Transmission of Tradition." In *Shadows in the Field: New Perspectives for Fieldwork in Ethnomusicology*, edited by Gregory F. Barz and Timothy J. Cooley, 2nd ed., 141–156. New York: Oxford University Press.

———. 2013. "When Ethnography Meets History: Longitudinal Research in Ethnomusicology." Paper presented at the 42nd World Conference of the International Council for Traditional Music, Shanghai, China, July 11–17.

WORKS CITED 219

Shoolbraid, G. M. H. 1975. *The Oral Epic of Siberia and Central Asia.* Bloomington: Indiana University Press for the Research Center for the Language Sciences.

Sivtsev, D. K. [Suorun Omolloon], ed. 2003. *Èpos olonkho i epicheskaia poèziia Sakha (Iakutov): Sbornik proizvedenii v perevode na russkii iazyk* [The olonkho epic and the epic poetry of the Sakha (Yakuts): Book of works in Russian translation]. Yakutsk: Institute of Humanitarian Research, Sakha Republic (Yakutia), Academy of Sciences.

Skounti, Ahmed. 2009. "The Authentic Illusion: Humanity's Intangible Cultural Heritage, the Moroccan Experience." In *Intangible Heritage*, edited by Laurajane Smith and Natsuko Akagawa, 74–92. New York: Routledge.

Skrybykin R. 1995. "Translation of Njurgun Botur the Impetuous by P. A. Oiuunuskay into English: The First Song." In *Vestnik Respublikanskogo kolledzha*, edited by I. I. Shamaev, 2–113. Yakutsk: MGP Polygrafizdat Iakutskogo nauchnogo tsentra.

Slezkine, Yuri. 1994. *Arctic Mirrors: Russia and the Small Peoples of the North.* Ithaca, NY: Cornell University Press.

Slobin, Mark. 1979. *Code Switching and Code Superimposition in Music.* Working Papers in Sociolinguistics, no. 63. Austin, TX: Southwest Educational Development Laboratory.

———. 1983. "Rethinking 'Revival' of American Ethnic Music." *New York Folklore* 9 (3–4): 37–44.

———. 1992. "Micromusics of the West: A Comparative Approach." *Ethnomusicology* 36 (1): 1–87.

———, ed. 1996. *Retuning Culture: Musical Changes in Central and Eastern Europe.* Durham, NC: Duke University Press.

———. 2014. "Re-flections." In *The Oxford Handbook of Music Revival*, edited by Caroline Bithell and Juniper Hill, 666–671. New York: Oxford University Press.

Smith, John D. 1977. "The Singer or the Song? A Reassessment of Lord's 'Oral Theory.'" *Man*, n.s., 12 (1): 141–153.

Smith, Laurajane, and Natsuko Akagawa, eds. 2009. *Intangible Heritage.* New York: Routledge.

Smith, Linda Thuiwai. 2012. *Decolonizing Methodologies: Research and Indigenous Peoples.* New York: Zed Books.

Solomon, Thomas. 2014. "Performing Indigeneity: Poetics and Politics of Music Festivals in Highland Bolivia." In *Soundscapes from the Americas: Ethnomusicological Essays on the Power, Poetics, and Ontology of Performance*, edited by Donna A. Buchanan, 143–163. SOAS Musicology Series. Burlington, VT: Ashgate.

Stokes, Martin, ed. 1994. *Ethnicity, Identity and Music: The Musical Construction of Place.* Oxford: Oxford University Press.

Stravinsky, Igor. 2003. *Poetics of Music in the Form of Six Lessons.* Cambridge, MA: Harvard University Press.

Sugarman, Jane C. 1988. "Making *Muabet*: The Social Basis of Singing among Prespa Albanian Men." *Selected Reports in Ethnomusicology* 7: 1–42.

Summit, Jeffrey A. 2015. "Advocacy and the Ethnomusicologist: Assessing Capacity, Developing Initiatives, Setting Limits, and Making Sustainable Contributions." In *The Oxford Handbook of Applied Ethnomusicology*, edited by Jeff Todd Titon and Svanibor Pettan, 199–228. New York: Oxford University Press.

220   WORKS CITED

Suny, Ronald Grigor. 1997. *The Soviet Experiment: Russia, the USSR, and the Successor States*. New York: Oxford University Press.

Sysoliatina, Z. G. 2006. "Preemstvennost traditsii: Respublikanskii detskii festival iunikh ispolnitelei olonkho" [The advantages/priority of tradition: The republic-wide festival of young performers of olonkho]. In *Olonkho v teatralnom iskusstve: 1 respublikanskaia nauchno-prakticheskaia konferentsiia (tezisy i materialy)* [Olonkho in the theater arts: The first republic-wide scientific-practical conference (theses and materials)], edited by U. A. Vinokurova and L. D. Petrova, 179–186. Yakutsk: Arctic State Institute of Culture and Arts.

Thompson, Karen, Peter Schofield, Nicola Palmer, and Gulnara Bakieva. 2006. "Kyrgyzstan's Manas Epos Millennium Celebrations: Post-colonial Resurgence of Turkic Culture and the Marketing of Cultural Tourism." In *Festivals, Tourism and Social Change: Remaking Worlds*, edited by David Picard and Mike Robinson, 172–190. Buffalo, NY: Channel View Publications.

Tichotsky, John. 2000. *Russia's Diamond Colony: The Republic of Sakha*. Amsterdam: Harwood Academic.

Tilley, Leslie. 2014. "Dialect, Diffusion, and Balinese Drumming: Using Sociolinguistic Models for the Analysis of Regional Variation in *Kendang Arja*." *Ethnomusicology* 58 (3): 481–505.

Titon, Jeff Todd. 1989. "Ethnomusicology as the Study of People Making Music." Paper delivered at the annual conference of the Society for Ethnomusicology, Northeast Chapter, Hartford, CT, April 22.

———. 1992. "Music, the Public Interest, and the Practice of Ethnomusicology." *Ethnomusicology* 36 (3): 315–322.

———. 2003. "Textual Analysis or Thick Description?" In *The Cultural Study of Music*, edited by Martin Clayton, Trevor Hebert, and Richard Middleton, 171–180. New York: Routledge.

———. 2015a. "Applied Ethnomusicology: A Descriptive and Historical Account." In *The Oxford Handbook of Applied Ethnomusicology*, edited by Jeff Todd Titon and Svanibor Pettan, 4–29. New York: Oxford University Press.

———. 2015b. "Sustainability, Resilience, and Adaptive Management for Applied Ethnomusicology." In *The Oxford Handbook of Applied Ethnomusicology*, edited by Jeff Todd Titon and Svanibor Pettan, 157–195. New York: Oxford University Press.

Titon, Jeff Todd, and Svanibor Pettan. 2015a. "Introduction to the Chapters." In *The Oxford Handbook of Applied Ethnomusicology*, edited by Jeff Todd Titon and Svanibor Pettan, 53–67. New York: Oxford University Press.

———, eds. 2015b. *The Oxford Handbook of Applied Ethnomusicology*. New York: Oxford University Press.

Tokarev, S. A., and I. S. Gurvich. 1964. "The Yakuts." In *The Peoples of Siberia*, edited by M. B. Levin and L. P. Potapov, 243–304. Chicago: University of Chicago Press.

Tomskaia, E. I. 2006. "Teoriia i praktika olonkho v teatralnom iskusstve" [Theory and Practice of Olonkho in the Theater Arts." In *Olonkho v teatralnom iskusstve: 1 respublikanskaia nauchno-prakticheskaia konferentsiia: (tezisy i materialy)* [Olonkho in the theater arts: The first republic-wide scientific-practical conference (theses and materials)], edited by Y. A. Vinokurova and L. D. Petrova, 102–104. Yakutsk: Arctic State Institute of Culture and Art.

Trepavlov, Vadim V. 1995. "The Social Status of the Yakut Epic Hero." *Asian Folklore Studies* 54 (1): 35–48.

Turner, Victor. 1969. *The Ritual Process: Structure and Anti-Structure.* New York: Aldine DeGruyter.

———. 1980. "Social Dramas and Stories about Them." *Critical Inquiry* 7 (1): 141–168.

Um, Hackyung. 2013. *Korean Musical Drama: P'ansori and the Making of Tradition in Modernity.* Burlington, VT: Ashgate.

UNESCO. 2003. "Text of the Convention for the Safeguarding of the Intangible Cultural Heritage." http://unesdoc.unesco.org/images/0013/001325/132540e.pdf. Accessed January 17, 2017.

———. 2005. "Proclamation of the Masterpieces of the Oral and Intangible Heritage of Humanity (2001–2005)." http://www.unesco.org/culture/ich/en/proclamation-of -masterpieces-00103. Accessed January 17, 2017.

———. 2006. *Masterpieces of the Oral and Intangible Heritage of Humanity: Proclamations 2001, 2003 and 2005.* http://unesdoc.unesco.org/images/0014/001473/147344e .pdf. Accessed January 17, 2017.

Van der Heide, Nienke. 2008. *Spirited Performance: The Manas Epic and Society in Kyrgyzstan.* Amsterdam: Rozenburg.

Vansina, Jan. 1971. *Oral Tradition: A Study in Historical Methodology.* London: Routledge and Kegan Paul.

Vasiliev, S. E., A. N. Zhirkov, V. V. Illarionov, and S. D. Mukhoplëva. 2009. "Épicheskoe nasledie v kiberprostranstve: Nauchno-obrazovatelnaia informatsionnaia sistema 'Olonkho'" [Epic heritage in cyberspace: The scientific-educational informational system "Olonkho"]. Unpublished paper from Yakutsk State University, State Senate (Il Tumen) of the RS(Y), and IGI RS(Y).

Vasilieva, Y. I. 2006. "O perevode iakutskogo olonkho na drugie iazyki" [On translations of the Yakut olonkho into other languages]. In *Ustoichivoe razvitie stran arktiki i severnykh regionov Rossiiskoi Federatsii v kontekste obrazovaniia, nauki i kultury: Tezisy dokladov mezhdunarodnogo foruma* [Stable development of the Arctic regions of the Russian Federation in the context of education, science, and culture: Theses of presentations at the international forum] (Yakutsk, July 24–25, 2006), edited by V. N. Ivanov, E. N. Romanova, and A. E. Pakharova, 48–49. Yakutsk: IGI RS(Y).

Vdovin, A. I. 2002. "Evoliutsiia natsionalnoi politiki SSSR, 1917–1941 gg." [The evolution of nationalities policy in the USSR, 1917–1941]. *Moscow University Herald*, series 8: Istoriia, no. 3: 3–54.

Ventsel, Aimar. 2015. "Research Report: Interdisciplinary Fieldwork in Saidy, Republic of Sakha-Iakutiia, July–August 2014." *Sibirica* 14 (2): 95–100.

Vidal, Clément. 2008. "Wat is een wereldbeeld?" [What Is a worldview?]. In *Nieuwheid denken: De wetenschappen en het creatieve aspect van de werkelijkheid,* edited by Hubert Van Belle and Jan Van der Veken, 71–85. Leuven: Acco.

Vinokurova, Dekabrina M. 2007. "Uroven osvedomlennosti selchan i gorozhan ob olonkho: Na primer g. Iakutska i s. Berdigestiakh" [Level of familiarity with olonkho for town

222 WORKS CITED

and city-dwellers: Examples from the city of Yakutsk and the town of Berdigestyakh]. In *Problemy rodnogo iazyka v usloviiakh globalizatsii i integratsii sovremennogo obshchestva* [Mother tongue issues in the contexts of the globalization and integration of modern society], edited by P. A. Sleptsov, 109–115. Yakutsk: GU ROHPO Ministerstvo nauki i proftekhobrazovaniia.

Vinokurova, U. A., and L. D. Petrova, eds. 2006. *Olonkho v teatralnom iskusstve: 1 respublikanskaia nauchno-prakticheskaia konferentsiia: (tezisy i materialy)* [Olonkho in the theater arts: The first republic-wide scientific-practical conference (theses and materials)]. Yakutsk: Arctic State Institute of Culture and Art.

Vinokurova, Uliana A. 1995a. "The Peoples of the Sakha Republic (Yakutia): Reviving the Value of Living in Harmony with Nature." *Surviving Together* 13 (2): 43–46.

———. 1995b. "The Ethnopolitical Situation in the Republic of Sakha (Yakutia)." *Anthropology and Archeology of Eurasia* 34 (1): 60–78.

Vitebsky, Piers. 1987. "Yakut." In *The Nationalities Question in the Soviet Union*, edited by Graham Smith, 304–319. London: Longman.

———. 2005. *The Reindeer People: Living with Animals and Spirits in Siberia*. Boston: Houghton Mifflin.

Walker, Margaret E. 2014. "National Purity and Postcolonial Hybridity in India's *Kathak* Dance Revival." In *The Oxford Handbook of Music Revival*, edited by Caroline Bithell and Juniper Hill, 205–227. New York: Oxford University Press.

Warden, Nolan. 2016. "Ethnomusicology's 'Identity' Problem: The History and Definitions of a Troubled Term in Music Research." *El oído pensante* 4 (2): 1–21. http://ppct.caicyt .gov.ar/index.php/oidopensante/article/view/9403/8390. Accessed December 5, 2016.

Weeda, Ed. 2005. "Rulers, Russia and the Eighteenth-Century Epic." *Slavonic and East European Review* 83 (2): 175–207.

Yamashita, Munehisa. 2006. "Problemy perevoda olonkho na iaponskii iazyk" [The problems of translating olonkho into Japanese]. In *Ustoichivoe razvitie stran arktiki i severnykh regionov Rossiiskoi Federatsii v kontekste obrazovaniia, nauki i kultury: Tezisy dokladov mezhdunarodnogo foruma* [Stable development of the arctic regions of the Russian Federation in the context of education, science, and culture: Theses of presentations at the international forum] (Yakutsk, July 24–25, 2006), edited by V. N. Ivanov, E. N. Romanova, and A. E. Pakharova, 48. Yakutsk: IGI RS(Y).

Zakharova, Agafia, and Elena Protodiakonova. 2010. *The Yakut Heroic Epos Olonkho*. Yakutsk.

Zemtsovsky, Izaly. 2002. "Musicological Memoirs on Marxism." In *Music and Marx*, edited by Regula Qureshi, 167–189. New York: Routledge.

Interviews

* Aksyonova, Irina. Yakutsk, June 8, 2009.

* Alekseyev, Eduard. Malden, MA, May 18, 2009.

---

* Recordings of these interviews are available at http://www.press.uillinois.edu/books/harris/story telling/.

WORKS CITED   223

* Alekseyev, Eduard, and Anna Larionova. Malden, MA, April 20, 2010.
* Alekseyev, Nikolai. Mytakh, Yakutia, June 21, 2010.
* Chekhorduna, Ekaterina. Yakutsk, December 6, 2011.
* Gerasimova, Dora. Yakutsk, June 24, 2010.
* Gerasimova, Dora, and Maria Kononova. Yakutia, June 19, 2010.
* Ivanova, Anastasia. Berdigestyakh, Yakutia, June 20, 2010.
* Kononov, Valerii. Borogontsy, Yakutia, June 19, 2009.
* Kononova, Maria. Borogontsy, June 19, 2009.
* Krivoshapkin, Dmitrii. Berdigestyakh, Yakutia, June 20, 2010.
* Kugdanova-Egorova, Elena. Yakutsk, June 18, 2010.
* Mikhailov, Boris. Yakutsk, December 13, 2011.
* Reshetnikov, Pyotr. Cherkëkh, Yakutia, June 16, 2009.
* Romanova, Ekaterina. Yakutsk, December 8, 2011.
* Shelkovnikova, Liubov, Gavriil Shelkovnikov, and Anna Andreyeva. Borogontsy, 2009.
* Shishigin, Spiridon. Pokrovsk, Yakutia, June 25, 2010.
* Sidorova, Elizaveta, Elena Protodiakonova, and Anastasia Luginova. Yakutsk, December 7, 2011.
Solovyeva, Vera. Atlanta, Georgia, March 10, 2010.
* Struchkova, Valentina. Berdigestyakh, Yakutia, June 20, 2010.
* Tikhonov, Pyotr. Borogontsy, June 20, 2009.
Vasiliev, Sergei. Yakutsk, June 24, 2010.
* Vinokurova, Dekabrina, and Yuri Zhegusov. Yakutsk, December 13, 2011.
* Zakharova, Agafia. Yakutsk, Yakutia, December 4, 2011.

Index

Page numbers in *italics* refer to illustrations.

aal-luuk mas (sacred/holy tree), 14, 98
abaasy (evil spirits), 15–18, 30, *31*, 42, 72. See also *aiyy* (good spirits)
Action Plan, Yakutia's, 71, 94–102, 106, 125, 161
aiyy (good spirits), 15–16, 28, 42. See also *abaasy* (evil spirits)
Akagawa, Natsuko, 93, 97, 137
Aksyonova, Irina, 57
Alekseyev, Eduard, 23, *51*, 167n20, 174n40; on folklore, 156–157, 201n4; Harvard presentation on, 169n30, 174n39; on olonkho and beliefs, 18; on olonkho characteristics, 23–31; on Soviets and folklore, 52, 174n39, 184n10, 199n24; on unfolding mode, 28, 174n39, 176n54
Alekseyev, N. A., 137, 169n34
Alekseyev, Nikolai, 60–62
Alekseyev, Roman Petrovich, 53–56, 182n58
Alekseyev, Semyon Gregorevich (Uustarabys), 60–61, 183n76, 185n26
Alekseyeva, Akulina Romanovna, 53–54
Alënushka, 82–83, 107
algys (blessing song), 51, 80
Algys (Christian arts group), 180
Andreyeva, Anna, 54–56
applied ethnomusicology, 5–6, 118, 168n2, 168n24
Archy Diètè (House of Purification), 34
Argounova-Low, Tatiana: on children's camp, 187n63; on Kulakovskii, 45, 163n2, 165n3, 187n53; on Sakha history, 34; on Sakha

language, 53, 187n49; on Soviet oppression, 44–45, 51, 137–139
Association of Olonkho, 68
Association of Young Olonkhosuts (Ychchat Olongkhohut), 155, 194–195n14, 201n40
atheism, 16, 41–42, 137, 167n21, 179n27
audience: changing, 36–38, 127, 130–131, 135; children and, 73–76, 82, 101–102, 123, 127; Chinese, 158; cultivating, 87, 120–130, 153, 159, 161; and declining interest in olonkho, 60, 72–73, 78, 140, 198n14; emergence and, 22–23, 119, 123, 179n21, 200n36; Japanese, 103–104, 158; knowledge level of, 51, 80–81, 82, 84, 136; *Manas* and, 149, 200n32; media and, 56–57, 103, 107, 117; p'ansori and, 152, 185n31, 200nn36–37; and PPAs, 113–116; pre-Soviet, 11, 36–37, 40, 74, 161–162; verbal responses by, 24, 74–75, 123, *124*, 152–153. *See also* emergence; oral formulaic theory; *sreda* (milieu); "under the mouth" (*syngaakh annygar*)
authenticity, 76–77, 96–97, 118, 142–143, 175n47

balaghan (yurt), 35–38, 59, 155, 182n63
Balzer, Marjorie Mandelstam: on identity, 16–17, 137; on Oyunsky, 181n36; on revitalization, 167n21, 177–178n2; on Russia, 40, 143, 167n15; on shamanism, 16–17, 167n21, 196n30
belief, 2, 13, 15–18; worldview and, 42, 137, 171n12, 196n30. *See also* Christianity; religion; shamanism; worldview
Berdigestyakh, 7, 57, 60–61, 71, 87–88

226   INDEX

Bodaibo, 37, 178n15
bogatyr. *See* hero (*bogatyr*)
Bohlman, Philip, 76, 97, 118–119, 150–151, 195–196n22
Boiarov, Aleksei, 138
Borisov, Andrei: *Avatar* and, 195n19; as Theater of Olonkho director, 76–77, 101–102, 125, 130, 159
Borisov, Egor, 145
Borisov, Yuri: at NEFU Olonkho Institute, 154, 194–195n14; performance by, *154*, 185n36, 201n39; with youth, 75–76, 155, 186n37, 194–195n14
Borogontsy, 7, 54, *55*, *58*, 59, 78
Brezhnev, Leonid, 52, 182n57
Buriat: epics from, 173n34, 197n7; music from, 167n20
Burnashev, Innokentii Ivanovich. *See* Tong Suorun
bylina (Russian epic tale), 30

Campbell, Patricia, 202n7
canon, 87, 102, 118–119, 133, 157; in p'ansori, 151
carriers, 11, 63, 71, 107, 137. *See also* tradition bearers
Center, 4, 164; legislation issues, 65–66, 93, 199n26; and periphery, relations between, 63, 68, 104, 136, 142–148. *See also* colonial relations; Russian Federation
Center for Studies in Oral Tradition, 173n32
Central Asia, 11, 26–27, 34, 103, 144. *See also* Levin, Theodore: fieldwork in Central Asia by; *Manas* trilogy
chabyrgakh (tongue-twister), 30, 56, 175n43
Chekhorduna, Ekaterina, 48–50, 62, 74–75, 160, 174n35
Cherkëkh: children's camp near, 187n63; museum in, 1–2, *36*; olonkho transmission in preschool in, 82–83, 107; as Reshetnikov's home, 1, 82
Chernogradskii, Semyon, 58–59, 183n71, 183n74
children. *See* youth and olonkho
Christianity: identity and, 16–17; marginalization of, 16, 42, 180n29; olonkho and, 17–18. *See also* belief; religion
Churapcha, 7, 105, 155
collective performance. *See* theatrical olonkho

colonial relations, 136–142, 153; and internal colonialism, 141; neo-, 142–149, 198n18; post-, 136–142, 148, 198n18, 199–200n29
Communism, 41. *See also* Soviet period
compensation. *See* funding: of tradition bearers; stipends
competitions: limitations in, 123, 154; of *Manas*, 149; revitalization and, 59, 93, 96, *124*, 158; Soviet, 42, 47; youth, 82, 85, 107, 144, 154–155. *See also* Masterpiece designation
Convention for the Safeguarding of the Intangible Cultural Heritage. *See* ICH Convention
Cooley, Timothy, 97, 188n70
Coulter, Neil, 110–112, 116, 131–132, 168n22, 195n16
Crate, Susan, 141, 167n21
Cruikshank, Julie, 34, 44–45, 51, 137–139, 187n53

dance (choreography), 110, 119, 167n20, 177n62, 184n15; in theatrical olonkho, 125–128. See also *ohuokhai*; Zverev, Sergei
Danilova, Elizaveta, 59
Daughtry, Martin, 51, 199n27
Day of Olonkho (November 25), 16, 70, 145–147, 157
Decade of Olonkho (First/Second), 88–89, 97–99, 114–115, 120
dègèrèn, 27, 29–31, 120–121, 163, 174n38
descendants of olonkho (derivative forms), 76–80, 103, 160, 186n42
Diachkovskii, Aleksandr, 80
diagnostic chart for GGHA, 113–116, 118, 157, 195n17, 196n24
dièrètii, 27–30, 120–121, 163–164, 174n38
dynamism, 119–134. *See also* stable and malleable elements

EGIDS (Expanded Intergenerational Disruption Scale), 110–111, 113, 195n16
Egorova, Aelita, 75
Emelianov, Nikolai V., 1, 165n3, 169n34, 170n4, 196n26
emergence, 22–23, 32, 116, *120*, 122. *See also* oral formulaic theory
endangered cultural expressions, 108–112. *See also* language
Epic Monuments of the Peoples of the World, 104, 146, 192n56

Epic of Gilgamesh, 11, 173n34
epics, 173n34; cycles, 13–14, 149, 197n7; in Siberia, 11, 67, 166n14, 173n34; tales, 13, 171n15; traditions, 11, 13, 22, 151. *See also* Epic Monuments of the Peoples of the World; Monuments of Folklore of the Peoples of Siberia and the Far East
epos, 13. *See also* epics
Èr Sogotokh: musicological analysis of, 23–31; notation of excerpts from, *25*, *28*, *31*; as olonkho tale, 14; translations of, 104, 183n80
ethno-ballet, 127, *128*
ethnography: internal timelines in, 4, 33; local voices in, 7, 169n32; multi-temporal, 4; research language for, 7; of Sakha/Siberian context, 166n14, 169n34, 181n36; subject-centered, 5, 168n26
ethnolinguistic community, *113*, *114*, *115*, 116
ethnomusicology, 166n9; applied, 5–6, 118, 168n2, 168n24; linguistics and, 111–113, 175–176n50, 194n9, 194n11
Evenki, 20
Expanded Graded Intergenerational Disruption Scale (EGIDS), 110–111, 113, 195n16

Feld, Steven, 181n38, 193n1
festivalization, 77–78, 93, 130, 185n30, 187–188n70; cultural identity and, 16–17, 144, 153, 157; revitalization and, 148–149, 159–161; Soviet control and, 42, 142. *See also* Ysyakh (summer festival)
Fishman, Joshua, 110
Foley, John Miles, 173n32
folklore: in performance, 76, 142; Soviet control and, 53, 137, 142, 174n39, 198n16; vitality of, 88, 139, 156–157, 198n14, 202n6
Folklore Society of Japan, 103
folklore studies (folkloristics), 41, 45–47, 153, 169–170n34, 177n65. *See also* Monuments of Folklore of the Peoples of Siberia and the Far East
folklorization, 53, 77–78, 141–142
folk songs, 43, 55, 142
folk tale, 121, 170n4
funding: genre vitality and, *112*; of *Manas*, 149–150; of olonkho, 66, 88, 96–102, 160, 192n51; of theatrical olonkho, 97, 129–130, 159; of tradition bearers, 19–20,

106, 124–125, 157–159, 202n8. *See also* stipends
fusion, 80

Geertz, Clifford, 168n26
gender: of characters, 14, 30, 49, 101, 121; of performers, 19–20, 151;
genre, 166n12; evolution of, 186n42, 188–189n13, 200n37, 201n3; multigeneric, 30–32, 177n64; Sakha examples of, 27–30, 51, 170n4, 174n38. *See also* Graded Genre Health Assessment (GGHA)
Gerasimova, Dora, 58, 72–73, 183n69, 185n26
GGHA. *See* Graded Genre Health Assessment
GIDS, 110
Gilgamesh epic, 11, 173n34
Gorny district, 56, 60–61, 198n9
Govorov, Dmitrii, 59, 138, 181n44
Graded Genre Health Assessment (GGHA), 111–116, 157. *See also* diagnostic chart for GGHA
Graded Intergenerational Disruption Scale, 110
Graded Music Shift Scale, 111. *See also* Graded Genre Health Assessment (GGHA)
Grant, Catherine, 89, 168n22, 179n25, 193n3
Great Patriotic War. *See* World War II
gulags, 2, 44, 137–138, 182n61

Haas, David, 182n53
Harris, Robin P. (author), *51*, *85*, *101*; connection to Yakutia, 2–3, 161–162; revitalization and, 5–6, 168n23; works by, 3, 7, 167n20, 199n24
Harris, William (Bill), 6, 12, *85*
Harvard University, 7, 173n33, 174n39, 191n46, 200n38
Harvilahti, Lauri, 139–140, 170, 173, 197n7
heritagization, 6, 8, 97. *See also* identity: heritage and
hero (*bogatyr*): as characters in olonkhos, 13–14, 120–122, 128–129, 171n9; in collective performance, 46; in epic cycles, traditions, and tales, 11, 13–14, 196n26; nostalgia and, 143, 147; pedagogy and, 88; songs of, 29; worldview and, 17, 51–52. *See also* names *of specific heroes*
Hiebert, Paul, 15
Higher School of Music, 160, 202nn9–10
Homeric epics, 11, 21, 148, 170n2, 200n30

228 INDEX

House of Olonkho (Olonkho Diėtė), 66, 98
Howard, Keith, 132, 153, 167nn19–20, 168n22
human rights, 7, 65–66, 194n12

ICH Convention: description of, 65–66,
184nn6–7, 188n2, 189n11, 190n23; key
terms of, 89–93; in Korea, 149; in Kyrgyzstan, 149; limitations of, 188n1; and Sakha
application, 66–71; and Yakutia's Action
Plan, 94–102. *See also* Intangible Cultural
Heritage (ICH)
ICTM (International Council of Traditional
Music), 98–99, 166n11
identity, 44, 165–166n7, 172nn18–19, 197n32,
201n2; heritage and, 90, 93, 107, 132,
149–153 (*see also* heritagization; Intangible
Cultural Heritage [ICH]); olonkho and, 130,
153, 157; religious, 16–18, 172n21; resilience and, 118; Sakha, 4, 136–149, 151–152,
172n20 (*see also* Sakha language). *See also*
nationalism; revitalization: identity and
IGI. *See* Institute of Humanitarian Research
and Problems of the Minority Peoples of the
North (IGI); *see also* Institute of Languages
and Cultures
Ignatieva, Vanda Borisovna: on censorship,
7, 41, 46–47; on commercialization of
olonkho, 77–78, 102–103; on dynamics
of change, 91, 136, 171–172n16, 198n14,
199n20
Illarionov, Vasilii Vasilievich, 59, 117, 169n30,
183n80, 192n55
Illarionova, Nurguyana, 152, 168n13, 169n30,
191n46, 200n38
Impey, Angela, 168n24
improvisation: in *kedang arja*, 132–133; stable
and malleable elements and, 119–122
innovation, 113–122, 131–134, 149–153,
157–161, 201n4
Institute of Humanitarian Research and Problems of the Minority Peoples of the North
(IGI): description of, 179n22; and research
on olonkho, 39, 45, 67, 71–72, 96
Institute of Languages and Cultures, 41
Intangible Cultural Heritage (ICH): descriptions of, 66, 98, 188n2, 188nn4–5; and
funding, 66, 97–98; in Korea, 132, 200n37;
parallels with language vitality, 108, 194n4;
transmission and, 93, 105, 189n16, 194n6;

UNESCO lists, 170n3. *See also* ICH Convention
intelligentsia (thought leaders), 44, 133,
137–138, 145–147, 199n27
intercultural dialogue, 103–105, 145–146
International Council for Traditional Music
(ICTM), 98–99, 166n11
Ivanov, Vasilii Nikolaevich, 67, 169n29,
169n34
iye-olonkhosut. See master olonkhosut (*iye-
olonkhosut*)

Japan: and animated olonkho cartoon, 195n20;
audiences in, 158; Kabuki theater in, 74;
language in, 100, 103–104; olonkho performance in, 101
jaw harp. See *khomus* (jaw harp)

kendang arja drumming tradition, 132–133
khomus (jaw harp): decline of, 55; recordings
of, 197n6; revitalization of, 86, 103, 127,
139, 186n47; as symbol of Sakha culture,
171–172n16, 182n59
Kidula, Jean Ngoya, 140, 197n8
Kirshenblatt-Gimblett, Barbara: on change, 64,
189n18; on festivals, 185n30; on heritage,
90, 147, 188n5; "tale-world" term by,
202n11
Kolesov, Gavriil Gavriilovich, 56–59, 79, 84,
106–107, 116–117
Kononov, Valerii, 38–39, 84, *85*, 179n18
Kononova, Maria, 48–49, 58, 64–65, *85*,
179n18
korenizatsiia (nativization), 41
Kudiarov, Anatolii, 86
Kugdanova-Egorova, Elena, 57
Kulakovskii, Aleksei, 1, 33, 45, 73, 163n2
Kulikova, Anna, 48, 65, 169–170n34,
181nn47–48
kylyhakh (ornamentation), 27–31, 120–121,
163, 176n53
kyryympa (Sakha stringed instrument), 127

Land of Olonkho, as metonym for Yakutia,
144–145; *Deti zemli olonkho* (Children
of the Land of Olonkho), 144; "Epics of
the World in the Land of Olonkho," 105;
Mastera zemli olonkho (Masters of the Land
of Olonkho), 144

INDEX   229

language: endangered, 193–194nn2–7; and *Ethnologue*, 194n10; shift in, 108–113, 133, 156, 194n12, 195n16; and speech-song continuum, 30–31, 170n1. *See also* oral formulaic theory; Russian language; Sakha language

Larionova, Anna, *51*; on Eduard Alekseyev, 174n39; Harvard visit by, 169nn29–30; on olonkho characteristics, 13–14, 18–19, 23, 26–30, 174n38; on olonkho dissemination, 43, 50, 56, 191n38; on UNESCO, 62, 71, 104

Lassiter, Luke Eric, 168n22, 169n32

Lena River, 29, 34

Lenin, Vladimir, 17, 39, 41, 52, 137

Levin, Theodore, 169n32; fieldwork by, 7, 174n39; fieldwork in Central Asia by, 27, 173n34, 174n39, 189–190n22, 197n3; on revitalization, 201n3, 202n6; on Soviet control, 137, 142, 171n15, 189–190n22

Lewis, M. Paul, 110, 194n10, 194nn16–17

liminality, 76, 146, 148, 186n42

linguistics, 5, 110–111, 170n1, 175–176n50, 194n11

literacy, 179n20; epic traditions and, 148, 150–151, 153–154, 200n37; orality and 39–40, 74–76, 136, 179n21, 185n34; written olonkho and, 44, 137, 144, 179n26, 182n61

Litinskii, Genrikh, 76

Living Human Treasures, 105–107, 125, 192n59, 193n62. *See also* tradition bearers

Lord, Albert, 20–22, 39, 86, 117, 185n34. *See also* Homeric epics

Luginova, Anastasia, 66, 101, 184n9, 184n11, 190n30

Lvova, Sakhaya, 111

malleable. *See* stable and malleable elements

Manas trilogy: description of, 13–14, 165n1, 173–174n34, 200n30; performers (*manaschi/manaschy*) of, 149–150, 200n32; revitalization of, 149–150, 200n33

marginalization, 136, 156, 162; of olonkho and olonkhosuts, 41–44, 52, 62–63. *See also* Christianity: marginalization of; intelligentsia (thought leaders); Sakha language: Soviet marginalization of

Marxism, 17, 137

master olonkhosut (*iye-olonkhosut*), 1–2, 19–20, 50, 76, 81; compensation for, 97, 106, 125 (*see also* funding: of tradition bearers; stipends); decline of, 12, 82, 95, 106–107, 125; transmission by, 105, 107, 115–116, 157–161; *See also* olonkhosut; *and specific master olonkhosuts*

Masterpiece designation, 52, 62–71, 145, 188n9; effects of, on olonkho, 77, 89–92, 114–115, 135, 139–140; ICTM and, 98–99, 166n11. *See also* Action Plan, Yakutia's; ICH Convention; Representative List of the Intangible Cultural Heritage of Humanity; UNESCO

Mazo, Margarita, 52, 176n54

media, 117, 127, 158; comics, 77; films, 77, 136, 195n20; Internet, 99–101, 111, 117, 158, 191n48; radio, 39, 111, 116–117, 136; recordings, 56–59, 106, 111, 116–117; television, 39, 93, 104–106, 111, 117, 136; YouTube, 111, 117, 136. *See also* audience: media and; transmission: mediated

Mikhailov, Boris: on post-Soviet context, 65, 86; on pre-Soviet context, 34, 37–39; on Soviet context, 44, 47–48

Ministry of Culture and Spiritual Development, 96, 101, 159, 171n16, 191n44

modernism, 17, 42, 130

Mongolia, 11, 26–27, 67, 105, 165n6

Monuments of Folklore of the Peoples of Siberia and the Far East, 62–63, 67

Moscow, performances in, 50, 52, 76, 141–142. *See also* Center

Mukhoplëva, S. D., 170n4, 177n62

multidisciplinary research, 5

multi-performer olonkho. *See* theatrical olonkho

music. *See* olonkho (solo/traditional): music materials (songs)

music shift, 108–113

Naara Suokh (Pyotr Ammosovich Okhlopkov), 45

Nakhodkina, Alina, 19, 104, 182n61, 191n48

Naroditskaya, Inna, 200n34

nasleg (county), 46, 181n42

nation, 4–5, 145, 167nn16–17

nationalism: "bourgeois," 44, 51, 137–139; identity and, 17, 182n54, 199n20, 199–200n29

NEFU. *See* North-Eastern Federal University (NEFU)

230 INDEX

neocolonial relations, 142–149, 198n18. *See
also* colonial relations
Nikolaev, Mikhail Efimovich, 68–70
Nikolaeva, N. N., *25, 28, 31*
North-Eastern Federal University (NEFU),
70, 100, 105, 182n61, 184n16; Olonkho
Institute, 75, 105, 154–155
nostalgia, 5, 143–146, 153
notation, *26*; of excerpts from *Ėr Sogotokh*, *25,
28, 31*
Nurgun Botur: Kolesov recording of, 56, 59,
106, 116–117; as olonkho tale, 14; Oyunsky
and, 42, 44, 181n36; and related forms,
61, 76–77, 195n19; as tank name, 47, 141;
theatrical performance of, 50, 186n41; translations of, 104, 146, 171n8, 181n36, 182n61
nusah, Jewish, 29

Ochirov, Vitalii, 80
ohuokhai, 3, 30, 163; decline of, 56, 58;
examples of, 180n29, 186n47, 197n6; revitalization of, 41, 139
Okhlopkov, Pyotr Ammosovich (Naara Suokh),
45
olonkho (solo/traditional): as combination of
narrative and song, 18, 23–24, 45, 170n1,
172n25; defined, 18–19, 30–32, 165n1;
historicity of, 14–15; music materials
(songs), 23–24, 26–32, 121; narrative mode
(recitative), 18, 24–25, 30–32, 56, 175n49;
translations of, 100, 104, 153–154, 191n48;
use of other languages in, 181n38. *See also*
descendants of olonkho (derivative forms)
Olonkho Diėtė (House of Olonkho), 66, 98
Olonkho Information System, 100–101
Olonkho Institute, NEFU, 75, 105, 154–155
Olonkholand, 78, 102, 144, 191nn50–51
olonkhosut (olonkho performer), 1, 18–20,
165n2; PPAs, 113–116. *See also* Association
of Young Olonkhosuts (Ychchat Olongkhohut); master olonkhosut (*iye-olonkhosut*);
and specific olonkhosuts
olonkho tales: *Ala Tuigun*, 54; *Basyrgastaah
aattaah Baabe Baatyr*, 75; *Bogatyr Kulantai
na rezvom kone*, 186n40; *Ėrbekhchėn Bėrgėn*,
101; *Jėbiriėljin Bėrgėn*, 72, 185n26; *Kullustai Bėrgėn*, 127, *128*; *Kürüng Küllėi*, 75;
Kyys Dėbiliiė, 14, 101, 104, 183n80; *Müljü
(Muldju) Bòghò (Bėghë)*, 14, 58–59, 171n8,
183n72; *Non-Stumbling Nyusur Bėrgė*, 103;

Tuiaaryma Kuo, 14, 46, 76; *Udaliy dobriy
molodets Bėriėt Bėrgėn*, 186n40. See also *Ėr
Sogotokh*; *Nurgun Botur*
oral formulaic theory, 20–22, 117, 149, 185n34.
See also emergence
orality. *See* literacy: orality and; transmission:
oral; performers
ornamentation (*kylyhakh*), 27–31, 120–121,
163, 176n53
Orosina, Nadezhda Anatolevna, 178n8
Osipova, Olga, 140, 197–198nn9–13
Oyunsky, Platon Alekseyevich (Sleptsov), 42,
44, 138, 181n36, 182n61

p'ansori, 13, 74, 151–153, 185n31, 200nn36–37
Parry, Milman, 20–22, 170n2, 173nn31–32
Peers, Eleanor, 167n21; on identity, 16–17,
172n20; on Sakha fusion, 80; on shamanism, 172n17, 172n21; on Soviet ideologies,
41–42, 130, 179–180n27
Pegg, Carole, 165–166n7, 170n3, 173n34
perestroika (restructuring), 64–65, 138, 163,
167n21
performance contexts, 112–116, 123, 158–160
performers: epic, 19–20; *Manas*, 149–150,
200n32; master, 200n32, 200n34. *See
also* master olonkhosut (*iye-olonkhosut*);
olonkhosut
Performers, Performances, and Apprecia-
tors/Audiences (PPAs), 113–116. *See also*
Graded Genre Health Assessment (GGHA)
Pettan, Svanibor, 66, 168n22, 168n24
poetry: in olonkho, 13, 23, 29–30, 122; and poetically organized discourse (POD), 170n1;
registers in, 136, 186n48, 197n1; and Sakha
poetic devices, 18–19, 23–24, 30, 103–104;
in translation, 104. *See also* Lord, Albert;
olonkho (solo/traditional): narrative mode
(recitative); oral formulaic theory
Pokrovsky, Dmitrii, 142, 202n6
pop music, 80, 103, 186n47
Popova, Galina, 76, 155
Post, Jennifer, 165–166n7
postcolonial relations, 136–142, 148, 198n18,
199–200n29. *See also* colonial relations
post-Soviet dynamics: cultural revitalization,
33, 63–65, 139, 198n18; olonkho vitality,
114–115; relations with Center, 142–149,
180n29, 189–190n22, 197n3, 198n18. *See
also* colonial relations

PPAs (Performers, Performances, and Appreciators/Audiences), 113–116. *See also* Graded Genre Health Assessment (GGHA)
pre-Soviet period, 189–190n22; olonkho performance in, 11, 18, 34–39, 74; olonkho vitality in, 114–115, 119–125, 196n24
Protodiakonova, Elena, 35, 66, 101, 178n9
Pukhov, I. V., 82, 169n31, 196n26

recitative. *See* olonkho (solo/traditional): narrative mode (recitative)
recordings. *See under* media
refunctionalization, 140
register. *See under* poetry
Reichl, Karl, 19, 150, 173–174n34, 192n55, 200n32
religion, 34, 65, 41, 167n21. *See also* belief; Christianity; shamanism
remake and revival, 148. *See also* refunctionalization; revitalization; revival
Representative List of the Intangible Cultural Heritage of Humanity, 91–92, 188n8, 189n11. *See also* Masterpiece designation
Republic of Sakha (Yakutia), 3, 34–35, 64, 88, 167n21; name of, 39, 63, 165n4. *See also* Land of Olonkho
Reshetnikov, Pyotr Egorovich, 1–2, 12, 106, 161–162; on audience apathy, 73; on beliefs, 15–16, 42; as olonkhosut, 24, 62, 80–82, 175n49, 195n19; on pre-Soviet olonkho, 35–37; published olonkhos by, 22–23; on Soviets and olonkho, 50; and transmission, 82–83, 107
Reshetnikova, Aisa P., 183n80, 196n26
resilience, 118–119, 131–134, 148–149, 157–160, 195n21; olonkho and, 107, 121, 125, 130, 155. *See also* sustainability
revitalization: Balzer on, 167n21, 177–178n2; competitions and, 59, 93, 96, *124*, 158; festivalization and, 148–149, 159–161; Harris's (author's) involvement in, 5–6, 168n23; identity and, 139–140, 147; of *khomus*, 86, 103, 127, 139, 186n47; lessons about, from other epics, 149–155, 200n33; Levin on, 201n3, 202n6; of *ohuokhai*, 41, 139; post-Soviet dynamics and, 33, 63–65, 139, 198n18; recommendations for, of olonkho, 157–161; revival and, 3, 148, 169n33; of Sakha language, 41, 45, 64–65, 74; Slobin on, 156–157,

169n33, 197n3; transmission and, 90–96, 103, 119, 133–134, 153; UNESCO and, 89–111; youth and, 82–88, *112*, 133, 136; Ysyakh (summer festival) and, 73, 79, 148, 171–172n16
revival, 3, 169n33. *See also* remake and revival; revitalization
Revolution, Russian, 37–41, 53
Rice, Timothy, 4–5, 7, 50, 169n32
Ricoeur, Paul, 108, 131
ritual, 167n20, 171–172n16, 177n62, 184n15, 187–188n70
Romanova, Ekaterina Nazarovna, 47, 77, 171n16, 196n29
RS(Y). *See* Republic of Sakha (Yakutia)
Russian Federation: demographics of, 165–166n7, 169n28, 193n61; relationship of, to UNESCO, 66, 68, 193n55; Yakutia and, 3–4, 35, 141, 145. *See also* Center
Russian language: as research language, 7, 169n28, 169n31, 169n34, 177n65; Sakha and, 58, 169n27; transliteration of, xi–xii. *See also* Sakha language
Russian Revolution, 37–41, 53

safeguarding, 64–66, 89–94, 105–110, 153, 189n16
Sakha, 3, 34, 165–166nn5–7. *See also* Republic of Sakha (Yakutia)
Sakha Kėskil, 43–44
Sakha language, 3, 165n6; archaic, in olonkho, 23, 44–45, 80–81, 136, 139; children and, 75–76, 80–81, 125; decline of, 40, 77, 88, 136, 169n27; identity and, 103, 156, 194n13; revitalization of, 41, 45, 64–65, 74; Soviet marginalization of, 44, 48, 52–53, 58, 88; transliteration of, xi–xii; vitality of, 80–81, 187n49
Sakha Republic. *See* Republic of Sakha (Yakutia)
Saurman, Todd, 133, 168n22
Schippers, Huib, 96, 188–189n13, 193n3
Schrag, Brian: on applied ethnomusicology, 6, 168n22, 188–189n13; concept definitions by, 166n12, 197n32, 201n2; on liminality, 76, 186n42; on music vitality, 110, 112; on stable and malleable elements, 119, 188–189n13, 196n23
Seeger, Anthony, 98–99, 166n11
Semyon, Yrya, 49

232   INDEX

Severo-Vostochny Federalny Universitet (SVFU). *See* North-Eastern Federal University (NEFU)
shamanism, 17–18, 44, 172n17, 172n21, 196n30. *See also* belief
shamans, 18, 49, 53, 171n15
Sheehy, Daniel, 168n22, 168n24
Sheikin, Yuri, 167
Shelemay, Kay, 4–5, 161
Shelkovnikov, Gavriil, 182n60
Shelkovnikova, Liubov, 54–55
Shtyrov, Viacheslav, 71, 102, 192n51
Siberia, 2–5, 34, 166n8, 167n21, 169–170n34
Sidorova, Elizaveta, 66–70, 98, 101, 193n64
SIL, 110, 194nn9–10
Simons, Gary, 110, 194n10, 194nn16–17
Sivtsev, Dmitrii. *See* Suoron Omolloon
Sleptsov, Platon Alekseyevich. *See* Oyunsky, Platon Alekseyevich
Slobin, Mark, 16, 173n34, 194n11, 196n31; on revitalization, 156–157, 169n33, 197n3; on Soviet control, 42, 137, 197n3
Smeets, Rieks, 66–67
Smith, Laurajane, 93, 97, 137
sociolinguistics. *See* linguistics
Sokolov, Aleksandr, 69–70
Solovëv, Afanasii, *12*, 106, 193n60
Solovyeva, Vera, 81
Solovyov, Zhargal, 81
song (*yrya*). *See* olonkho (solo/traditional): music materials (songs)
Soviet period: control in, 16, 42, 137–138, 141–142; habitus of, 189n22; olonkho during, 39–63, 114–116, 135–136. *See also* Alekseyev, Eduard: on Soviets and folklore; Brezhnev, Leonid; folklore: Soviet control and; Levin, Theodore: on Soviet control; *perestroika* (restructuring); Sakha language: Soviet marginalization of
Soviet Union, 33, 39, 177–178nn1–2
spirits. See *abaasy* (evil spirits); *aiyy* (good spirits)
sreda (milieu), 4–5, 76, 135–136, 163, 167n18; and appreciative audiences, 60, 72, 74–75, 84, 123; cultivation of, 97, 107, 116–120, 130; literacy and, 40, 136, 151; media and, 57, 117, 136; relative to broader culture, 103–104, 198n14; Yakutia's Plan of Action for, 95, 161

stable and malleable elements, 118–134, 155, 159, 201n4
state, 4. *See also* Center; Russian Federation
Stepanov, Timofei, 77, 186n43
Stepanova, Maria, 57
stipends, 96, 136, 157–159, 175n49, 193n61. *See also* funding: of tradition bearers
St. Petersburg, 7, 128, 199n24
Struchkova, Valentina, 79
Sunjata, 13, 74, 165n1, 173n34
Suoron Omolloon (Dmitrii Sivtsev), 14, 17, 34, 80–81, 172n23
sustainability, 117–118, 156–161, 168n25, 188–189n13, 195n21. *See also* innovation; resilience; safeguarding; transmission
Suzukei, Valentina, 26–27
syngaakh annygar. See "under the mouth" (*syngaakh annygar*)

Tarasov, N. M., 103
Tatarinova, Alexandra, 169n30
Tatarstan, 68, 104–5
Tatta district, 35–36, 44, 138, 178n8; school of olonkho performance in, 35, 178n8
Theater of Olonkho: Action Plan and, 96–97, 99, 101, 161; A. Borisov and, 101–102, 130; innovation and, 101–102, 151, 191n45; olonkhosuts and, 125, 159–160, 191n46, 196n27; travel by, 101, 104; website of, 191n43
theatrical olonkho: as collective performance, 45–46, 136, 155, 180n34; history of, 46, 50, 76–77, 141–142, 186nn40–41; overseas, 145, 158, 199n23; research on, 102; stable and malleable components of, 125–130; vitality of, 115–117, 148, 151, 157–159, 161; at Ysyakh of Olonkho, 58–59, 72–73, 77–78, 161, 185n26. *See also* competitions; dance; descendants of olonkho (derivative forms)
Tikhonov, Pyotr: and Kolesov recordings, 58, 106–107, 116–117; on olonkho performance, 42–43, 159, 195n20
timbre, 23–24, 26–27, 49, 74
Titon, Jeff Todd: on applied ethnomusicology, 5, 168n22, 168n24, 202n8; concept definitions by, 166n9, 170–171n5, 189n15; on Geertz, 168n26; on resilience, 6, 118, 168n25, 195n21, 202n8

Tomskaia, Daria, 20, 106
Tong Suorun (Innokentii Ivanovich Burnashev), 37–39, 42–43, 138, 179n16
tongue-twister (*chabyrgakh*), 30, 56, 175n43
toyuk, 28–29, 67, 164, 180n29, 197n6. See also *diėrėtii*
tradition bearers, 7, 106, 154; funding of, 19–20, 106, 124–125, 157–159, 202n8. *See also* carriers; Living Human Treasures
transmission, 131–132, 157–161; apprenticeships and, 149; Y. Borisov and, 154; children and, 58, 95; elements of, 117–119; families and, 61, 136; funding for, 106, 125; Graded Genre Health Assessment and, 112–115; language and, 80, 109–111; literary, 39, 150; mediated, 78, 111, 116–118; oral, 13, 34, 117, 150–151, 200n34; revitalization and, 90–96, 103, 119, 133–134, 153; schools and, 82–83, 99, 107, 136; tradition bearers and, 105–107, 115–116, 125, 157–161, 193n63. *See also* innovation
Tuva, 26–27, 85, 104–105, 174n39

"under the mouth" (*syngaakh annygar*), 1, 11, 163; applied to *Manas*, 149; Kulakovskii and, 45, 163n2, 187n53; in transmission, 161
UNESCO, 62–63, 65–71, 89–111, 140, 149–153. *See also* ICH Convention; Masterpiece designation
unfolding modes, 28, 174n39, 176n54
Union of Soviet Writers, 47–48, 53, 141, 157, 181n44
Ürüng Aiyy Toion (High God), 15–17
USSR (Union of Soviet Socialist Republics), 33, 39, 177–178nn1–2
Uustarabys (Semyon Gregorevich Alekseyev), 60–61, 183n76, 185n26
Uvarovskii, Afanasii, 104

values, 14, 139, 182n54; ICH and, 92, 107; marginalized, 51, 63; olonkho and, 15–18, *120*, *126*, 140, 145; Sakha contemporary, 73, 75, 131, 154, 160–161. *See also* belief; worldview
Van der Heide, Nienke, 149–151, 200n30, 200n33
Vasiliev, Sergei, 70–71, 84, 100–101, 169n30

Verkhoyansk, 155, 188n72
Viliui (Ysyakh venue), 188n72
Viliui River, 29
Viliuisk region, 37
Vinokurova, Dekabrina: on alternate forms of olonkho, 56–57, 77–78; on language/literacy and olonkho, 75, 80, 87; research by, on olonkho reception, 39–40, 60, 71–72, 83–84, 86–87
vitality: factors in, 93, 108–134; language and, 80–81, 194n4, 194n6, 194nn16–17
Vitebsky, Piers, 167

worldview: defined, 15, 171n12; marginalized, 41, 51, 53, 63, 171n15; olonkho and, 15–18; Sakha contemporary, 75, 87, 131, 136, 161. *See also* belief; values
World War II, 40–48, 52, 86, 138, 141

Yakut, 3, 165n6. *See also* Sakha
Yakut ASSR (Autonomous Soviet Socialist Republic), 39. *See also* Republic of Sakha (Yakutia)
Yakutia. *See* Republic of Sakha (Yakutia)
Yakutia's Action Plan, 71, 94–102, 106, 125, 161
Yakutsk, 2–3, 165n4, 166n8
Yakutsk State University (YaGU). *See* North-Eastern Federal University (NEFU)
Ychchat Olongkhohut (Association of Young Olonkhosuts), 155, 194–195n14, 201n40
Yeltsin, Boris Nikolaevich, 65, 199n26
youth and olonkho: fusions, 80; innovation, 75–76, 101–102, 154–155; revitalization, 82–88, *112*, 133, 136; transmission (*see also* transmission), 106, 108, 154, 159, 202n8; YouTube, 111. *See also* Association of Young Olonkhosuts (Ychchat Olongkhohut); audience: children; competitions: youth; Sakha language: children and
yrya (song). *See* olonkho (solo/traditional): music materials (songs)
Ysyakh (summer festival), 98, 164, 165n2; funding for, 98, 102, *129*, 190n32; revitalization and, 73, 79, 148, 171–172n16, 187–188n70 (*see also* revitalization); during Soviet period, 47–48, 53–54. *See also* festivalization

Ysyakh of Olonkho: Berdigestyakh (2010), 7, 57, 60–61, 87–88; Borogontsy (2009), 7, *58*, 59; Churapcha (2015), 7, 105, 155; other venues (2016–2020), 188n72; recordings of, 183n71, 185n30; Verkhoyansk (2016), 155. *See also* festivalization

ytyk duogha (scepter), 98

Zakharova, Agafia, 35, 45–46, 67, 83–84

Zemtsovsky, Izaly, 137

Zhegusov, Yuri, 39–40, 72, 77–78, 80

Zhirkov, Alexander, 75, 104, 146–147, 155, 168n23

Zhirkov, Mark, 76

Zverev, Sergei, 181n44, 199n24; dance ensemble, 70, 127, *128*, 196n28

ROBIN P. HARRIS is an assistant professor at the Graduate Institute of Applied Linguistics and serves as the director of GIAL's Center for Excellence in World Arts.

FOLKLORE STUDIES IN A MULTICULTURAL WORLD

The Amazing Crawfish Boat
　John Laudun
　(University Press of Mississippi)
Building New Banjos for an Old-Time World
　Richard Jones-Bamman
　(University of Illinois Press)
City of Neighborhoods: Memory, Folklore, and Ethnic Place in Boston
　Anthony Bak Buccitelli
　(University of Wisconsin Press)
Daisy Turner's Kin: An African American Family Saga
　Jane C. Beck
　(University of Illinois Press)
If You Don't Laugh You'll Cry: The Occupational Humor of White Wisconsin Prison Workers
　Claire Schmidt
　(University of Wisconsin Press)
Improvised Adolescence: Somali Bantu Teenage Refugees in America
　Sandra Grady
　(University of Wisconsin Press)
The Jumbies' Playing Ground: Old World Influence on Afro-Creole Masquerades in the Eastern Caribbean
　Robert Wyndham Nicholls
　(University Press of Mississippi)
The Last Laugh: Folk Humor, Celebrity Culture, and Mass-Mediated Disasters in the Digital Age
　Trevor J. Blank
　(University of Wisconsin Press)
The Painted Screens of Baltimore: An Urban Folk Art Revealed
　Elaine Eff
　(University Press of Mississippi)
Recasting Folk in the Himalayas: Indian Music, Media, and Social Mobility
　Stefan Fiol
　(University of Illinois Press)
Squeeze This! A Cultural History of the Accordion in American
　Marion Jacobson
　(University of Illinois Press)
Stable Views: Stories and Voices from the Thoroughbred Racetrack
　Ellen E. McHale
　(University Press of Mississippi)

Storytelling in Siberia: The Olonkho Epic in a Changing World
Robin P. Harris
(University of Illinois Press)
Ukrainian Otherlands: Diaspora, Homeland, and Folk Imagination in the Twentieth Century
Natalia Khanenko-Friesen
(University Press of Mississippi)
A Vulgar Art: A New Approach to Stand-Up Comedy
Ian Brodie
(University Press of Mississippi)

The University of Illinois Press
is a founding member of the
Association of American University Presses.

Composed in 10/13 Times New Roman
by Lisa Connery
at the University of Illinois Press
Cover designed by Jennifer S. Fisher
Cover illustration: Semën Chernogradskiy at the Third Ysyakh
of Olonkho in Borogontsy (2009). Photo by William Harris.

University of Illinois Press
1325 South Oak Street
Champaign, IL 61820-6903
www.press.uillinois.edu